Grammar Sense 3

SECOND EDITION

SERIES DIRECTOR
and AUTHOR
Susan Kesner Bland

OXFORD
UNIVERSITY PRESS

OXFORD
UNIVERSITY PRESS

198 Madison Avenue
New York, NY 10016 USA

Great Clarendon Street, Oxford, OX2 6DP, United Kingdom

Oxford University Press is a department of the University of Oxford.
It furthers the University's objective of excellence in research, scholarship,
and education by publishing worldwide. Oxford is a registered trade
mark of Oxford University Press in the UK and in certain other countries

General Manager, American ELT: Laura Pearson
Publisher: Stephanie Karras
Associate Publishing Manager: Sharon Sargent
Managing Editor: Alex Ragan
Director, ADP: Susan Sanguily
Executive Design Manager: Maj-Britt Hagsted
Electronic Production Manager: Julie Armstrong
Senior Designer: Yin Ling Wong
Image Manager: Trisha Masterson

Publishing and Editorial Management: hyphen S.A.

ISBN: 978 0 19 448916 4 Student Book 3 with Online Practice pack
ISBN: 978 0 19 448906 5 Student Book 3 as pack component
ISBN: 978 0 19 448928 7 Online Practice as pack component

Printed in China

This book is printed on paper from certified and well-managed sources

ACKNOWLEDGEMENTS

*Although every effort has been made to trace and contact copyright holders before
publication, this has not been possible in some cases. We apologize for any apparent
infringement of copyright and if notified, the publisher will be pleased to rectify any
errors or omissions at the earliest opportunity.*

*The authors and publisher are grateful to those who have given permission to
reproduce the following extracts and adaptations of copyright material:* pp. 4–5.
"You Snooze, You Win at Today's Workplace." This article first appeared
in *The Christian Science Monitor* on June 17, 1999, and is reproduced and
adapted with permission. © 1999 The Christian Science Publishing
Society. All rights reserved; pp. 28–29. Adapted from: *A Night To Remember*
by Walter Lord, © 1955, 1976 by Walter Lord. Reprinted by permission of
Henry Holt and Company, LLC.; pp. 78–79. "The Questions That Stump The
Scientists." Adapted from *Newsweek*, January 19, 1998 © 1998 Newsweek,
Inc. All rights reserved. Reprinted by permission; pp. 168–169. "The Really
Early Birds: A new theory explains how the first feathered creatures to fly
may have gotten off the ground," by Thomas Hayden. From Newsweek,
May 17, 1999 © 1999 Newsweek, Inc. All rights reserved. Reprinted by
permission; pp. 192–193. From ESSENTIALS OF PSYCHOLOGY, 5/E 5th
Edition by RATHUS. © 1997. Reprinted with permission of Wadsworth,
a division of Thomson Learning: www.thomsonrights.com. Fax 800
730-2215; pp. 230–231. From *Don't Sweat the Small Stuff ... and It's All Small
Stuff*, by Richard Carlson, Ph.D. Copyright © 1997, Richard Carlson,
Ph.D. Reprinted by permission of Hyperion; pp. 256–257. Pages 336–339
[adapted] from *Food: Your Miracle Medicine* by Jean Carper. Copyright © 1993
by Jean Carper. Reprinted by permission of HarperCollins Publishers, Inc;
pp. 302–303. "The new face of a role model." Copyright 1999, *USA Today*.
Reprinted with permission; pp. 352–353. "Ifs: Destiny and the Archduke's
Chauffeur" by Hans Koning. Copyright © 1988 by *Harper's Magazine*.
All rights reserved. Reproduced from the May 1998 issue by special
permission; pp. 372–373. "Career Currents," by Margaret Steen, Infoworld.
com, July 19, 1999, vol. 21, issue 28. Reprinted by permission; p. 387
"Work and Family Pressures Undercutting Widespread Job Statisfaction,
'Work Trends' Survey Finds," adapted from U.S. Newswire, 3/18/99.
Copyright 1999, All rights reserved.

Illustrations by: Thanos Tsilis (hyphen): 14, 37, 55, 73, 111, 133, 179, 290,
292; Alexandros Tzimeros / SmartMagna (hyphen): 11, 12, 22, 42, 44, 57,
84, 91, 108, 129, 135, 175, 224, 231, 256, 285, 334, 337, 349, 357.

*We would also like to thank the following for permission to reproduce the following
photographs:* Devation - Edwin Verbruggen / www.shutterstock.com,
Andreas Gradin / shutterstock.com, homydesign / www.shutterstock.com,
marekuliasz / www.shutterstock.com, Travel Ink / Getty Images, Cover l to
r and interior; Marcin Krygier / iStockphoto, Front matter and back cover
(laptop); Freitag / Corbis, pg. 4; GoGo Images Corporation / Alamy, pg. 8;
Rune Hellestad / Corbis, pg. 23; Tanya Constantine / Blend Images / Corbis,
pg. 25; Ralph White / Corbis, pg. 28; Deborah Feingold / Corbis, pg. 50;
David Matthew Walters / Gerald Celente, pg. 51; Corel / OUPpicturebank,
pg. 78; Paul Fleet / OUPpicturebank, pg. 99; Geray Sweeney / Corbis,
pg. 102; Photodisc / OUPpicturebank, pg. 119; Anthony West / Corbis,
pg. 122; New York Times Co. / Contributor / Getty, pg. 126;
Phase4Photography / Shutterstock, pg. 146; AF Archive / Alamy, pg. 150;
Tom & Dee Ann McCarthy / Corbis, pg. 157 (outdoor event); Serge Kozak
/ Corbis, pg. 157 (people throwing papers); Sally A. Morgan / Ecoscene
/ Corbis, pg. 168; Jonathan Blair / Corbis, pg. 172; Chris Howes / Wild
Places Photography / Alamy, pg. 177; Corbis / OUPpicturebank, pg. 192
(happiness); UpperCut / OUPpicturebank, pg. 192 (anger); Chris Carroll /
Corbis, pg. 192 (surprise); Eugene Duran / Corbis, pg. 192 (fear); Charles
O'Rear / Corbis, pg. 196; galvezrc / Demotix / Corbis, pg. 204; Anna Clopet
/ Corbis, pg. 209; Comstock / OUPpicturebank, pg. 212; JGI / Tom Grill
/ Blend Images / Corbis, pg. 220; Photodisc / OUPpicturebank, pg. 241;
Corbis/OUPpicturebank, pg. 251; Blaine Harrington III / Corbis, pg. 260;
Glowimages / Corbis, pg. 273 (spatula); StudioSource / Alamy, pg. 273 (crib);
Bill Ross / Corbis, pg. 273 (iris); Bialy / Dorota i Bogdan / the food passionates
/ Corbis, pg. 273 (octopus); Ned Therrien / Visuals Unlimited / Corbis,
pg. 273 (elm); Ingram / OUPpicturebank, pg. 273 (calculator); Photodisc
/ OUPpicturebank, pg. 273 (pineapple); OUP / OUPpicturebank, pg. 273
(screwdriver); Ambrophoto / Shutterstock, pg. 280; Jonathan Larsen /
Diadem Images / Alamy, pg. 302; Anthony J. Causi / Icon SMI / Corbis,
pg. 321; Bettmann / Corbis, pg. 352; Corbis / Corbis, pg. 353 (van gogh);
Sandro Vannini / Corbis, pg. 353 (Cleopatra); Renphoto / iStockphoto,
pg. 372; Photodisc / OUPpicturebank, pg. 389; Steve Prezant / Corbis,
pg. 392; Asia Images RF / OUPpicturebank, pg. 398; Kevin Peterson /
OUPpicturebank, pg. 405 (woman); Kevin Peterson / OUPpicturebank,
pg. 405 (man); Kevin Peterson / OUPpicturebank, pg. 406 (older
woman); Naho Yoshizawa / Aflo / Corbis, pg. 406 (man); Kevin Peterson /
OUPpicturebank, pg. 406 (woman).

Reviewers

We would like to acknowledge the following individuals for their input during the development of the series:

Marcia Adato, Delaware Technical and Community College, DE

Donette Artenie, Georgetown University, DC

Alexander Astor, Hostos Community College/CUNY, Bronx, NY

Nathalie Bailey, Lehman College, CUNY, NY

Jamie Beaton, Boston University, MA

Michael Berman, Montgomery College, MD

Linda Best, Kean University, NJ

Marcel Bolintiam, Kings Colleges, Los Angeles, CA

Houda Bouslama, Virtual University Tunis, Tunis, Tunisia

Nancy Boyer, Golden West College, Huntington Beach, CA

Glenda Bro, Mount San Antonio Community College, CA

Shannonine Caruana, Kean University, NJ

Sharon Cavusgil, Georgia State University, GA

Robin Rosen Chang, Kean University, NJ

Jorge Cordon, Colegio Internacional Montessori, Guatemala

Magali Duignan, Augusta State University, GA

Anne Ediger, Hunter College, CUNY, NY

Begoña Escourdio, Colegio Miraflores, Naucalpan, Mexico

Marcella Farina, University of Central Florida, FL

Carol Fox, Oakton Community College, Niles, IL

Glenn S. Gardner, Glendale Community College, Glendale, CA

Ruth Griffith, Kean University, NJ

Evalyn Hansen, Rogue Community College, Medford, OR

Liz Hardy, Rogue Community College, Medford, OR

Habiba Hassina, Virtual University Tunis, Tunis, Tunisia

Virginia Heringer, Pasadena City College, CA

Rocia Hernandez, Mexico City, Mexico

Kieran Hilu, Virginia Tech, VA

Rosemary Hiruma, California State University, Long Beach, CA

Linda Holden, College of Lake County, Grayslake, IL

Elke Holtz, Escuela Sierra Nevada Interlomas, Mexico City, Mexico

Kate de Jong, University of California, San Diego, CA

Gail Kellersberger, University of Houston-Downtown, ELI, Houston, TX

Pamela Kennedy, Holyoke Community College, MA

Elis Lee, Glendale Community College, Glendale, CA

Patricia Lowy, State University of New York-New Paltz, NY

Jean McConochie, Pace University, NY

Karen McRobie, Golden Gate University, CA

Hafid Mekaoui, Al Akhawayn University, Ifrane, Morocco

Elizabeth Neblett, Union County College, NJ

Patricia Palermo, Kean University, NJ

Maria E. Palma, Colegio Lationamericano Bilingue, Chihuahua, Mexico

Mary Peacock, Richland College, Dallas, TX

Dian Perkins, Wheeling High School, IL

Nancy Herzfeld-Pipkin, Grossmont College, El Cajon, CA

Kent Richmond, California State University, Long Beach, CA

Ellen Rosen, Fullerton College, CA

Jessica Saigh, University of Missouri-St. Louis, St. Louis, MO

Boutheina Lassadi-Sayadi, The Faculty of Humanities and Social Sciences of Tunis, Tunis, Tunisia

Anne-Marie Schlender, Austin Community College-Rio Grande, Austin, TX

Shira Seaman, Global English Academy, NY

Katharine Sherak, San Francisco State University, CA

Maxine Steinhaus, New York University, NY

Andrea Stewart, Houston Community College-Gulfton, Houston, TX

Nancy Storer, University of Denver, CO

Veronica Struck, Sussex Community College, Newton, NJ

Frank Tang, New York University, NY

Claude Taylor, Baruch College, NY

Marshall Thomas, California State University, Long Beach, CA

Christine Tierney, Houston Community College, Houston, TX

Anthea Tillyer, Hunter College, CUNY, NY

Julie Un, Massasoit Community College, MA

Marvaette Washington, Houston Community College, Houston, TX

Cheryl Wecksler, California State University, San Marcos, CA

Teresa Wise, Associated Colleges of the South, GA

Contents

Introduction viii

    Tour of a Chapter ix

    Grammar Sense Online Practice xv

PART 1: The Present, Past and Future

    CHAPTER 1: The Present 3

    A. GRAMMAR IN DISCOURSE: You Snooze, You Win at
    Today's Workplace 4

    B. FORM : The Simple Present and the Present Continuous 6

    C. MEANING AND USE 1: Contrasting the Simple Present and the
    Present Continuous 12

    D. MEANING AND USE 2: Verbs with Stative Meanings vs. Verbs with
    Active Meanings 17

    WRITING: Write a Profile For a Social Networking Site 24

    CHAPTER 2: The Past 27

    A. GRAMMAR IN DISCOURSE: A Night to Remember 28

    B. FORM: The Simple Past, the Past Continuous, and Time Clauses 30

    C. MEANING AND USE 1: Contrasting the Simple Past and the
    Past Continuous 35

    D. MEANING AND USE 2: The Simple Past and the Past Continuous in
    Time Clauses 41

    WRITING: Write an Essay About a Memorable Experience From
    Your Childhood 47

    CHAPTER 3: Future Forms 49

    A. GRAMMAR IN DISCOURSE: Trend Forecasters Predict Future 50

    B. FORM: The Future Continuous and Review of Future Forms 52

    C. MEANING AND USE 1: Contrasting *Will* and the Future Continuous . . 58

    D. MEANING AND USE 2: Contrasting *Be Going To*, the Present
    Continuous as Future, and the Simple Present as Future 61

    E. MEANING AND USE 3: Contrasting *Will*, the Future Continuous,
    and *Be Going To* 65

    WRITING: Write a Blog Post About Life in the Future 72

    Part 1 Test 75

PART 2: Connecting The Present, Past, and Distant Past

    CHAPTER 4: The Present Perfect 77

    A. GRAMMAR IN DISCOURSE: The Questions That Stump the Scientists . 78

    B. FORM: The Present Perfect 80

    C. MEANING AND USE 1: Indefinite Past Time 85

    D. MEANING AND USE 2: Recent Past Time and Continuing Time
    up to Now 88

    E. MEANING AND USE 3: Contrasting the Present Perfect and the
    Simple Past 93

WRITING: Write a Newspaper Article 98

CHAPTER 5: The Present Perfect Continuous 101
A. GRAMMAR IN DISCOURSE: Aging — New Answers to
Old Questions 102
B. FORM: The Present Perfect Continuous 104
C. MEANING AND USE 1: Focus on Continuing or Recent
Past Activities 109
D. MEANING AND USE 2: Contrasting the Present Perfect Continuous
and the Present Perfect 113
WRITING: Write a Letter to the Editor 118

CHAPTER 6: The Past Perfect and the Past Perfect Continuous . . 121
A. GRAMMAR IN DISCOURSE: Wild Thing 122
B. FORM: The Past Perfect and the Past Perfect Continuous 124
C. MEANING AND USE 1: The Past Perfect 130
D. MEANING AND USE 2: The Past Perfect Continuous 135
WRITING: Write a Biographical Essay About a Famous
Person's Career 140
Part 2 Test 143

PART 3: Modals
CHAPTER 7: Modals of Possibility 145
A. GRAMMAR IN DISCOURSE: Going to the Dogs 146
B. FORM: Modals of Present and Future Possibility 148
C. MEANING AND USE 1: Modals of Present Possibility 153
D. MEANING AND USE 2: Modals of Future Possibility 160
WRITING: Write an Article For Your School's Online Newspaper 165

CHAPTER 8: Past Modals 167
A. GRAMMAR IN DISCOURSE: The Really Early Birds 168
B. FORM: Past Modals 170
C. MEANING AND USE 1: Modals of Past Possibility 176
D. MEANING AND USE 2: Other Functions of Past Modals 180
WRITING: Write a Review of a Movie, TV Show, or Short Story 186
Part 3 Test. 189

PART 4: The Passive, Gerunds, and Infinitives
CHAPTER 9: Passive Sentences (Part 1) 191
A. GRAMMAR IN DISCOURSE: The Expression of Emotions 192
B. FORM: The Present and Past Passive 194
C. MEANING AND USE 1: Changing Focus from Active to Passive 198
D. MEANING AND USE 2: Reasons for Using the Passive 202
WRITING: Write an Email Informing Your Professor About Your
Lab Project For a Science Course. 208

CHAPTER 10: Passive Sentences (Part 2) 211

A. GRAMMAR IN DISCOURSE: Should Parents Be Punished for Their
Children's Crimes? 212

B. FORM: The Future, Present Perfect, and Modal Passive 214

C. MEANING AND USE 1: The Role of the Agent 218

D. MEANING AND USE 2: The Passive in Academic and Public Discourse 221
WRITING: Write a Letter to the Rditor About How Education Could
Be Improved in Your Country 226

CHAPTER 11: Contrasting Gerunds and Infinitives 229

A. GRAMMAR IN DISCOURSE: Become a Less Aggressive Driver 230

B. FORM 1: Gerunds and Infinitives 232

C. MEANING AND USE 1: Verbs Used with Gerunds and Infinitives 238

D. FORM 2: More About Gerunds and Infinitives 243

E. MEANING AND USE 2: Interpreting Gerunds and Infinitives 247
WRITING: Write a Persuasive Essay About Ways to Reduce Stress ... 250
Part 4 Test... 253

PART 5: Modifying Nouns

CHAPTER 12: Indefinite and Definite Articles; Review of Nouns . 255

A. GRAMMAR IN DISCOURSE: Chicken Soup, Always Chicken Soup 256

B. FORM: Indefinite and Definite Articles; Review of Nouns 258

C. MEANING AND USE 1: The Indefinite Article 262

D. MEANING AND USE 2: The Definite Article 265

E. MEANING AND USE 3: Article Use with Generic Nouns 271
WRITING: Write a Pamphlet About Healthy Eating 276

CHAPTER 13: Relative Clauses with Subject Relative Pronouns .. 279

A. GRAMMAR IN DISCOURSE: Office Outfits That Work 280

B. FORM: Relative Clauses with Subject Relative Pronouns 282

C. MEANING AND USE 1: Identifying Nouns with Restrictive
Relative Clauses 288

D. MEANING AND USE 2: Adding Extra Information with
Nonrestrictive Relative Clauses 294
WRITING: Write a "For and Against" Essay........................ 298

CHAPTER 14: Relative Clauses with Object Relative Pronouns ... 301

A. GRAMMAR IN DISCOURSE: The Face of a New Role Model 302

B. FORM 1: Relative Clauses with Object Relative Pronouns 304

C. MEANING AND USE 1: Identifying Nouns and Adding
Extra Information 309

D. FORM 2: Object Relative Pronouns with Prepositions 313

E. MEANING AND USE 2: Reducing Relative Clauses 317

WRITING: Write a Report About on Women's Sports
in Your Country 322
Part 5 Test.. 325

PART 6: Conditionals

**CHAPTER 15: Real Conditionals, Unreal Conditionals,
and Wishes** 327
A. GRAMMAR IN DISCOURSE: Reflections on Life 328
B. FORM: Real Conditionals, Unreal Conditionals, and Wishes 330
C. MEANING AND USE 1: Real Conditionals 335
D. MEANING AND USE 2: Unreal Conditionals 340
E. MEANING AND USE 3: Wishes.................................... 344
WRITING: Write a Public Service Annoncement 348

CHAPTER 16: Past Unreal Conditionals and Past Wishes 351
A. GRAMMAR IN DISCOURSE: The Ifs of History 352
B. FORM: Past Unreal Conditionals and Past Wishes 354
C. MEANING AND USE 1: Past Unreal Conditionals 359
D. MEANING AND USE 2: Past Wishes 363
WRITING: Write an Email Expressing Regret About Not Meeting
a Deadline 366
Part 6 Test.. 369

PART 7: Noun Clauses and Reported Speech

CHAPTER 17: Noun Clauses 71
A. GRAMMAR IN DISCOURSE: Career Currents 372
B. FORM: Noun Clauses 374
C. MEANING AND USE 1: *Wh-* and *If/Whether* Clauses 379
D. MEANING AND USE 2: *That* Clauses 384
WRITING: Write a Frequently Asked Questions Page For
a Travel Website 388

CHAPTER 18: Reported Speech 391
A. GRAMMAR IN DISCOURSE: Doctor-Patient Relationship in
Critical Condition 392
B. FORM: Reported Speech 394
C. MEANING AND USE: Reported Speech 399
WRITING: Write a Complaint 407
Part 7 Test 410

Appendices A–1

Glossary of Grammar Terms G–1

Index I–1

A Sensible Solution to Learning Grammar

Grammar Sense Second Edition gives learners a true understanding of how grammar is used in authentic contexts.

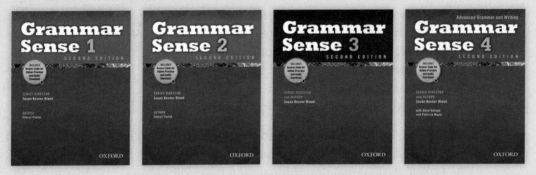

With Grammar Sense Online Practice

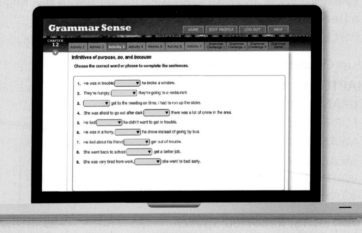

- **Student Solutions:** a **focus on Critical Thinking** for improved application of grammatical knowledge.

- **Writing Solutions:** a **Writing section in every chapter** encourages students to see the relevance of grammar in their writing.

- **Technology Solutions:** *Grammar Sense Online Practice* provides additional practice in an easy-to-use **online workbook**.

- **Assessment Solutions:** the Part Tests at the end of every section and the Grammar Sense Test Generators allow **ongoing assessment**.

Each chapter in *Grammar Sense Second Edition* **follows** this format.

The Grammar in Discourse section introduces the target grammar in its natural context via high-interest readings.

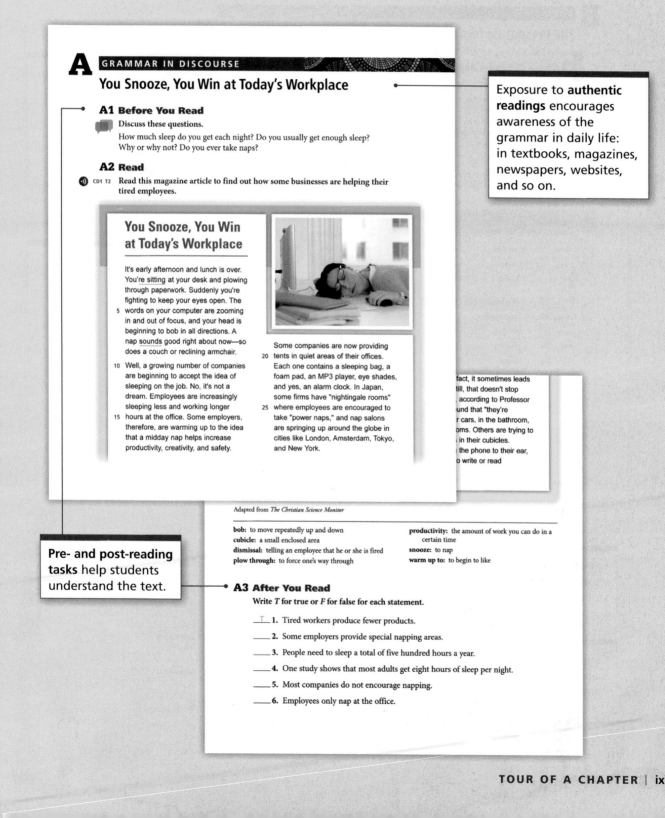

A GRAMMAR IN DISCOURSE

You Snooze, You Win at Today's Workplace

A1 Before You Read

Discuss these questions.

How much sleep do you get each night? Do you usually get enough sleep? Why or why not? Do you ever take naps?

A2 Read

CD1 T2 Read this magazine article to find out how some businesses are helping their tired employees.

You Snooze, You Win at Today's Workplace

It's early afternoon and lunch is over. You're sitting at your desk and plowing through paperwork. Suddenly you're fighting to keep your eyes open. The

5 words on your computer are zooming in and out of focus, and your head is beginning to bob in all directions. A nap sounds good right about now—so does a couch or reclining armchair.

10 Well, a growing number of companies are beginning to accept the idea of sleeping on the job. No, it's not a dream. Employees are increasingly sleeping less and working longer

15 hours at the office. Some employers, therefore, are warming up to the idea that a midday nap helps increase productivity, creativity, and safety.

Some companies are now providing

20 tents in quiet areas of their offices. Each one contains a sleeping bag, a foam pad, an MP3 player, eye shades, and yes, an alarm clock. In Japan, some firms have "nightingale rooms"

25 where employees are encouraged to take "power naps," and nap salons are springing up around the globe in cities like London, Amsterdam, Tokyo, and New York.

fact, it sometimes leads
till, that doesn't stop
, according to Professor
und that "they're
r cars, in the bathroom,
oms. Others are trying to
in their cubicles.
the phone to their ear,
o write or read

Adapted from *The Christian Science Monitor*

bob: to move repeatedly up and down
cubicle: a small enclosed area
dismissal: telling an employee that he or she is fired
plow through: to force one's way through

productivity: the amount of work you can do in a certain time
snooze: to nap
warm up to: to begin to like

A3 After You Read

Write *T* for true or *F* for false for each statement.

___T___ **1.** Tired workers produce fewer products.

_____ **2.** Some employers provide special napping areas.

_____ **3.** People need to sleep a total of five hundred hours a year.

_____ **4.** One study shows that most adults get eight hours of sleep per night.

_____ **5.** Most companies do not encourage napping.

_____ **6.** Employees only nap at the office.

Exposure to **authentic readings** encourages awareness of the grammar in daily life: in textbooks, magazines, newspapers, websites, and so on.

Pre- and post-reading **tasks** help students understand the text.

The Form section(s) provides clear presentation of the target grammar, detailed notes, and thorough practice exercises.

B FORM

The Present Perfect

Think Critically About Form

A. Look back at the article on page 78 and complete the tasks below.

1. **IDENTIFY** Two examples of the present perfect are underlined. Find seven more examples.
2. **ANALYZE** What are the two different forms of *have* in these examples? When is each one used?
3. **CATEGORIZE** Sort your examples into regular and irregular verbs. How do you know the difference?

B. Discuss your answers with the class and read the Form charts to check them.

Think Critically About Form encourages students to use their critical thinking abilities to use English outside of class and to continue learning on their own.

ONLINE PRACTICE

AFFIRMATIVE STATEMENTS		
SUBJECT + *HAVE*	PAST PARTICIPLE	
You**'ve**	studied	physics.
He**'s**	done	research.
They**'ve**	found	the answers.

NEGATIVE STATEMENTS		
SUBJECT	*HAVE* + NOT	PAST PARTICIPLE	
You	haven't	studied	physics.
He	hasn't	done	research.
They	haven't	found	the answers.

YES/NO QUESTIONS		
HAVE	SUBJECT	PAST PARTICIPLE	
Have	you	studied	physics?
Has	he	done	research?
Have	they	found	the answers?

SHORT ANSWERS					
AFFIRMATIVE			NEGATIVE		
	I	have.		I	haven't.
Yes,	he	has.	No,	he	hasn't.
	they	have.		they	haven't.

Clear and detailed **Form Charts** are easy to navigate.

Form notes **offer clear and concise explanations** students can understand.

- The past participle of regular verbs is the same as the simple past form (verb + *-ed*). See Appendices 4 and 5 for spelling and pronunciation rules for verbs ending in *-ed*.
- Irregular verbs have special past participle forms. See Appendix 6 for irregular verbs and their past participles.
- See Appendix 14 for contractions with *have*.

Common error tips help students avoid mistakes.

Do not confuse the contraction of *is* with the contraction of *has* in the present perfect.
He's **doing** research. = He is **doing** research. (He's currently doing research.)
He's **done** research. = He has **done** research. (He did research at some time in the past.)
Do not repeat *have/has* when present perfect verb phrases are connected by *and* or *or*.
He **has washed** his face and **brushed** his teeth.

The Meaning and Use section(s) offers clear and comprehensive explanations of how the target structure is used, and exercises to practice using it appropriately.

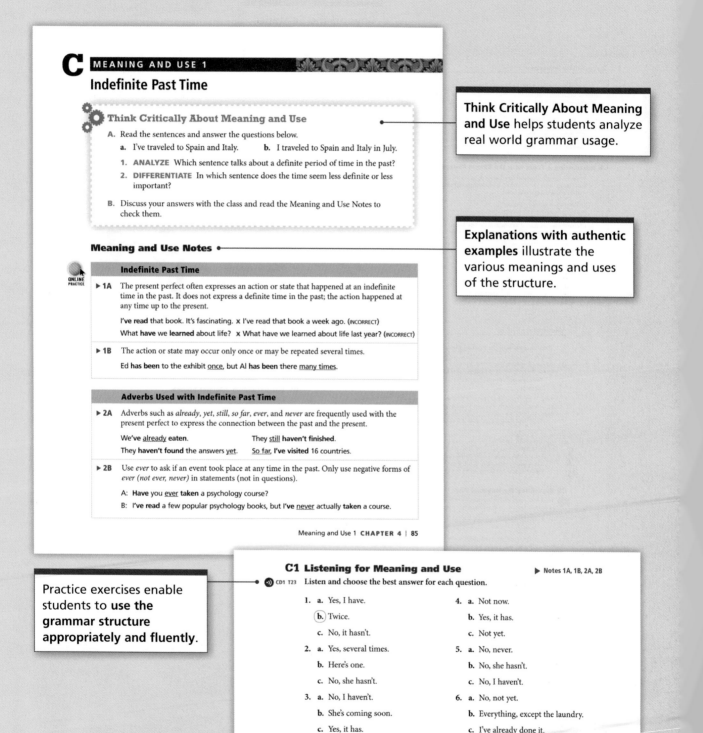

C MEANING AND USE 1

Indefinite Past Time

Think Critically About Meaning and Use

A. Read the sentences and answer the questions below.

    a. I've traveled to Spain and Italy.   **b.** I traveled to Spain and Italy in July.

    1. ANALYZE Which sentence talks about a definite period of time in the past?

    2. DIFFERENTIATE In which sentence does the time seem less definite or less important?

B. Discuss your answers with the class and read the Meaning and Use Notes to check them.

> **Think Critically About Meaning and Use** helps students analyze real world grammar usage.

Meaning and Use Notes

ONLINE PRACTICE

Indefinite Past Time

▶ **1A** The present perfect often expresses an action or state that happened at an indefinite time in the past. It does not express a definite time in the past; the action happened at any time up to the present.

    I've read that book. It's fascinating. **x** I've read that book a week ago. (INCORRECT)
    What **have** we **learned** about life? **x** What have we learned about life last year? (INCORRECT)

▶ **1B** The action or state may occur only once or may be repeated several times.

    Ed **has been** to the exhibit <u>once</u>, but Al **has been** there <u>many times</u>.

Adverbs Used with Indefinite Past Time

▶ **2A** Adverbs such as *already, yet, still, so far, ever,* and *never* are frequently used with the present perfect to express the connection between the past and the present.

    We've <u>already</u> **eaten.**   They <u>still</u> **haven't finished.**
    They **haven't found** the answers <u>yet</u>.   <u>So far</u>, **I've visited** 16 countries.

▶ **2B** Use *ever* to ask if an event took place at any time in the past. Only use negative forms of *ever (not ever, never)* in statements (not in questions).

    A: **Have** you <u>ever</u> **taken** a psychology course?
    B: **I've read** a few popular psychology books, but **I've** <u>never</u> actually **taken** a course.

Meaning and Use 1 **CHAPTER 4** | 85

> **Explanations with authentic examples** illustrate the various meanings and uses of the structure.

C1 Listening for Meaning and Use

▶ Notes 1A, 1B, 2A, 2B

🔊 CD1 T23 Listen and choose the best answer for each question.

1. **a.** Yes, I have.
    b. Twice.
    c. No, it hasn't.

2. **a.** Yes, several times.
    b. Here's one.
    c. No, she hasn't.

3. **a.** No, I haven't.
    b. She's coming soon.
    c. Yes, it has.

4. **a.** Not now.
    b. Yes, it has.
    c. Not yet.

5. **a.** No, never.
    b. No, she hasn't.
    c. No, I haven't.

6. **a.** No, not yet.
    b. Everything, except the laundry.
    c. I've already done it.

> **Practice exercises** enable students to **use the grammar structure appropriately and fluently.**

Special sections appear throughout the chapters with clear explanations, authentic examples, and follow-up exercises.

Beyond the Sentence demonstrates how structures function differently in extended discourses.

Beyond the Sentence

Introducing a Topic with the Simple Present

The simple present is often used in the first sentence of a paragraph to express a general statement about a topic. The sentences that follow offer more specific details and may be in the simple present or other tenses. For example:

Many people **suffer** from a condition called insomnia. In fact, insomnia **is becoming** the most common sleep disorder in the United States. People with insomnia **are** unable to fall asleep easily, and they **wake up** many times during the night. As a result, they always **feel** tired during the day. Their constant fatigue **can affect** their work and all aspects of their lives.

C6 Introducing a Topic with the Simple Present

A. Write five or six general statements about people in the country or city you are living in. Write about children, adults, college students, teenagers, men, women, senior citizens, and so on.

College students don't get enough sleep.
In the United States, not many people retire before they're 60.

B. Choose one of your general statements as the topic sentence of a paragraph. Write a paragraph that explains the statement in more detail.

College students don't get enough sleep. They often stay up very late. Then they sleep for only four or five hours and drag themselves to morning classes...

Informally Speaking clarifies the differences between written and spoken language.

Informally Speaking

Omitting Auxiliaries and *You*

CD1 T4 Look at the cartoon and listen to the conversation. How is each underlined form in the cartoon different from what you hear?

Simple Present Questions In informal speech, *do* is often omitted from *Yes/No* questions with *you*. *You* is omitted only if the question is easy to understand without it.

Standard Form	What You Might Hear
Do you take the subway to work?	"You take the subway to work?"
Do you want some help?	"(You) want some help?"

Present Continuous Questions In informal speech, *are* is often omitted from *Yes/No* questions with *you*. *You* may also be omitted.

Standard Form	What You Might Hear
Are you having a good time?	"(You) having a good time?"
Are you feeling OK?	"(You) feeling OK?"

B5 Understanding Informal Speech

CD1 T5 Listen to the advertisements and write the standard form of the words you hear.

1. _Are you feeling_ tired in the morning?
2. _____ a vacation?
3. _____ car problems again?
4. _____ it yourself?
5. _____ any old clothes in your closets?
6. _____ to shop late?
7. _____ too hard?
8. _____ a house sitter?

Vocabulary Notes

Habitual Past with *Used To* and *Would*

Used To *Used to* is a special simple past tense verb. *Used to* suggests a comparison between the past and the present. It suggests that a repeated action or state was true in the past, but is not true now, even if the present is not mentioned.

We **used to** go skating a lot. Now we go skiing.
We **didn't use to** play cards.

Used To* and *Would In affirmative statements, *would* can sometimes replace *used to* without changing the meaning. *Would* generally combines only with verbs that express actions.

When I was young, we **would** go skating a lot.
✗ We **would** live in China. (INCORRECT)

In a description about the past, *used to* can appear once or twice at the beginning of a paragraph, but *would* is used to provide the details in the rest of the story.

In the 1980s, I **used to** work for a big company that was far from my home. Every morning I **would** get up at 6:00 A.M. to get ready for work. I **would** leave the house by 7:00 A.M. Sometimes I **would** carpool with a neighbor...

C5 Describing the Habitual Past

Work with a partner. Put these sentences in order to form a meaningful paragraph. Discuss the use of the simple past, *used to*, and *would*.

___ That all changed a few summers ago after we finished college and got our first jobs.

___ In the mornings, my twin brother and I would get up early and go for hikes in the woods.

_1_ My family and I used to spend all our summers at a cottage on a lake.

___ We didn't have a TV at the cottage, so we would spend our evenings talking and reading.

___ We miss the lake and all the wonderful times we used to have there.

___ Our cottage there was like our home away from home, and we loved our life there.

___ In the afternoons, we'd meet our friends and go swimming at the lake.

___ Every June we would leave our apartment in New York City and head for the lake.

Vocabulary Notes highlight the connection between the key vocabulary and grammatical structures.

The Writing section guides students through the process of applying grammatical knowledge to compositions.

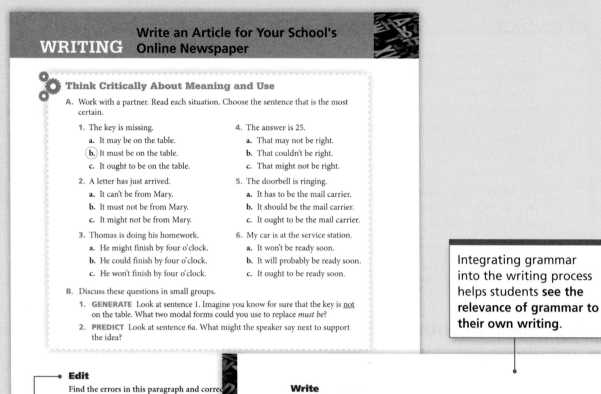

WRITING Write an Article for Your School's Online Newspaper

Think Critically About Meaning and Use

A. Work with a partner. Read each situation. Choose the sentence that is the most certain.

1. The key is missing.
   a. It may be on the table.
   b. It must be on the table.
   c. It ought to be on the table.

2. A letter has just arrived.
   a. It can't be from Mary.
   b. It must not be from Mary.
   c. It might not be from Mary.

3. Thomas is doing his homework.
   a. He might finish by four o'clock.
   b. He could finish by four o'clock.
   c. He won't finish by four o'clock.

4. The answer is 25.
   a. That may not be right.
   b. That couldn't be right.
   c. That might not be right.

5. The doorbell is ringing.
   a. It has to be the mail carrier.
   b. It should be the mail carrier.
   c. It ought to be the mail carrier.

6. My car is at the service station.
   a. It won't be ready soon.
   b. It will probably be ready soon.
   c. It ought to be ready soon.

B. Discuss these questions in small groups.

1. **GENERATE** Look at sentence 1. Imagine you know for sure that the key is <u>not</u> on the table. What two modal forms could you use to replace *must be*?

2. **PREDICT** Look at sentence 6a. What might the speaker say next to support the idea?

> Integrating grammar into the writing process helps students **see the relevance of grammar to their own writing**.

Edit

Find the errors in this paragraph and corre...

A migraine is a severe headache that can...
sufferers often experience symptoms such as...
vision. However, there are other symptoms th...
coming. You maybe sensitive to light, sound,...
The good news is that treatment must often...

> Editing exercises focus students on **identifying and correcting problems** in sentence structure and usage.

Write

Imagine that you are the health editor of your school's online newspaper. Write an article discussing ways that students might stay fit while they are studying at your school. Use modals and phrasal modals of present and future possibility.

1. **BRAINSTORM** Think about all the problems that students face and the solutions that you might include. Use these categories to help you organize your ideas into three or four paragraphs.
   • **Problems:** Why might students find it difficult to stay fit while they are studying (e.g., sitting for too many hours, study/sleep habits, food)?
   • **Solutions/Advice:** What are some of the things that students might do to stay fit (e.g., exercise, eat properly, get enough sleep)?
   • **Conclusion:** What may happen if they don't follow your advice? What benefits might they experience if they follow your suggestions?

2. **WRITE A FIRST DRAFT** Before you write your first draft, read the checklist below and look at the examples on pages 146–147. Write your draft using modals of possibility.

3. **EDIT** Read your work and check it against the checklist below. Circle grammar, spelling, and punctuation errors.

DO I ...	YES
give my article a title?	☐
organize my ideas into paragraphs?	☐
use a variety of modals of possibility to speculate about the problems students may be facing now and the solutions they might consider in the near future?	☐
use adverbs such as *maybe*, *perhaps*, and *probably* to soften my ideas?	☐

4. **PEER REVIEW** Work with a partner to help you decide how to fix your errors and improve the content. Use the checklist above.

> Collaborating with classmates in **peer review** helps students improve their own grammar skills.

Assessment

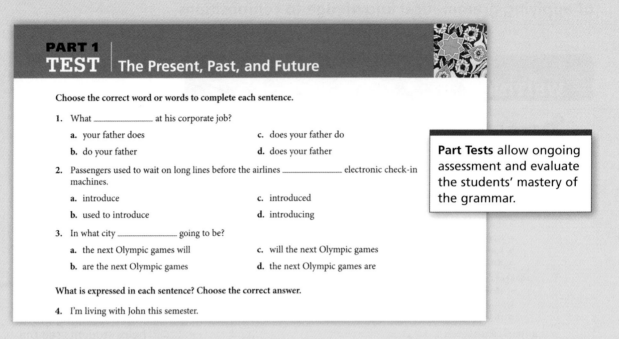

PART 1

TEST | The Present, Past, and Future

Choose the correct word or words to complete each sentence.

1. What _____ at his corporate job?
   a. your father does
   b. do your father
   c. does your father do
   d. does your father

2. Passengers used to wait on long lines before the airlines _____ electronic check-in machines.
   a. introduce
   b. used to introduce
   c. introduced
   d. introducing

3. In what city _____ going to be?
   a. the next Olympic games will
   b. are the next Olympic games
   c. will the next Olympic games
   d. the next Olympic games are

What is expressed in each sentence? Choose the correct answer.

4. I'm living with John this semester.

> **Part Tests** allow ongoing assessment and evaluate the students' mastery of the grammar.

Teacher's Resources

Teacher's Book

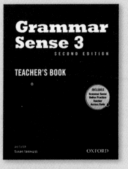

- Creative techniques for presenting the grammar, along with troubleshooting tips, and suggestions for additional activities

- Answer key and audio scripts

- Includes a *Grammar Sense Online Practice* Teacher Access Code

Class Audio

- Audio CDs feature exercises for discriminating form, understanding meaning and use, and interpreting non-standard forms

Test Generator CD-ROM

- Over 3,000 items available!

- Test-generating software allows you to customize tests for all levels of Grammar Sense

- Includes a bank of ready-made tests

Oxford **Teachers' Club**

Grammar Sense Teachers' Club site contains additional teaching resources at www.oup.com/elt/teacher/grammarsense

ONLINE PRACTICE

Grammar Sense Online Practice is an online program with all new content. It correlates with the *Grammar Sense* student books and provides additional practice.

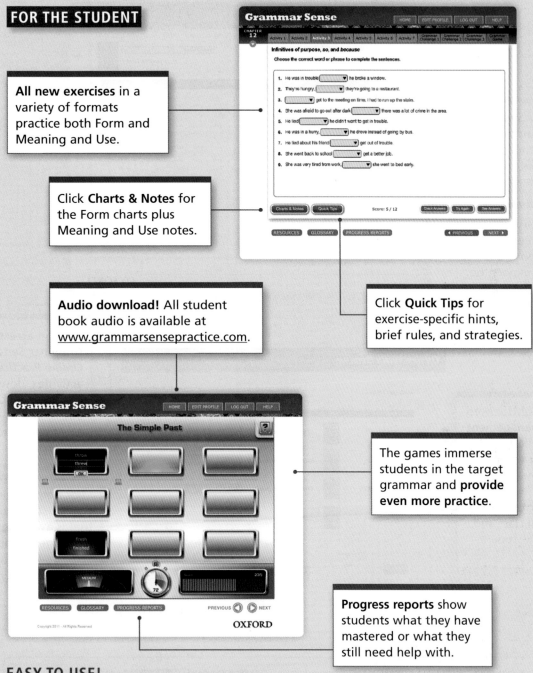

All new exercises in a variety of formats practice both Form and Meaning and Use.

Click **Charts & Notes** for the Form charts plus Meaning and Use notes.

Audio download! All student book audio is available at www.grammarsensepractice.com.

Click **Quick Tips** for exercise-specific hints, brief rules, and strategies.

The games immerse students in the target grammar and **provide even more practice**.

Progress reports show students what they have mastered or what they still need help with.

EASY TO USE!

Use the access code printed on the inside back cover of this book to register at www.grammarsensepractice.com. See the last page of the book for registration instructions.

Flexible enough for use in the classroom or easily assigned as homework.

Grammar Sense Online Practice **automatically grades** student exercises and tracks progress.

The easy-to-use online management system allows you to **review, print, or export** the reports you need.

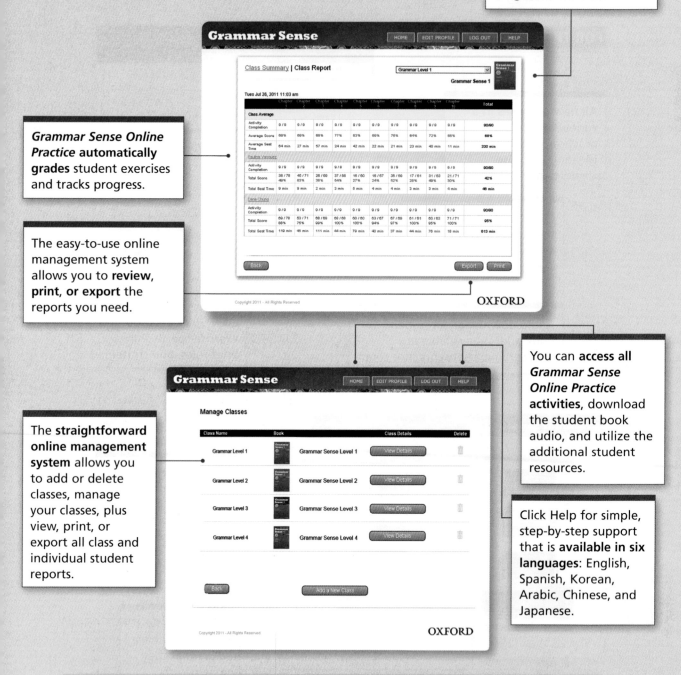

The **straightforward online management system** allows you to add or delete classes, manage your classes, plus view, print, or export all class and individual student reports.

You can **access all** *Grammar Sense Online Practice* **activities,** download the student book audio, and utilize the additional student resources.

Click Help for simple, step-by-step support that is **available in six languages**: English, Spanish, Korean, Arabic, Chinese, and Japanese.

FOR ADDITIONAL SUPPORT

Email our customer support team at grammarsensesupport@oup.com and you will receive a response within 24 hours.

FOR ADMINISTRATOR CODES

Please contact your sales representative for an Administrator Access Code. A Teacher Access Code comes with every Teacher's Book.

PART

1

The Present, Past, and Future

CHAPTER

1

The Present

A. **GRAMMAR IN DISCOURSE: You Snooze, You Win at Today's Workplace** **4**

B. **FORM: The Simple Present and the Present Continuous** **6**

The Simple Present
I usually **work** on weekends.

The Present Continuous
I'm **working** right now.

Informally Speaking: Omitting Auxiliaries and *You*

C. **MEANING AND USE 1: Contrasting the Simple Present and the Present Continuous** **12**

Using the Simple Present

Using the Present Continuous

Permanent Situations vs. Temporary Situations

Expressing Complaints vs. Expressing Facts

Beyond the Sentence: Introducing a Topic with the Simple Present

D. **MEANING AND USE 2: Verbs with Stative Meanings vs. Verbs with Active Meanings** **17**

States and Conditions

Distinguishing Verbs with Stative and Active Meanings

Expressing Physical Sensations

Using *Be* + Adjective for Behavior

Informally Speaking: Expressing Emotions in the Continuous

WRITING: Write a Profile for a Social Networking Site **24**

You Snooze, You Win at Today's Workplace

A1 Before You Read

Discuss these questions.

How much sleep do you get each night? Do you usually get enough sleep? Why or why not? Do you ever take naps?

A2 Read

CD1 T2   Read this magazine article to find out how some businesses are helping their tired employees.

You Snooze, You Win at Today's Workplace

It's early afternoon and lunch is over. You're sitting at your desk and plowing through paperwork. Suddenly you're fighting to keep your eyes open. The
5   words on your computer are zooming in and out of focus, and your head is beginning to bob in all directions. A nap sounds good right about now—so does a couch or reclining armchair.

10   Well, a growing number of companies are beginning to accept the idea of sleeping on the job. No, it's not a dream. Employees are increasingly sleeping less and working longer
15   hours at the office. Some employers, therefore, are warming up to the idea that a midday nap helps increase productivity, creativity, and safety.

Some companies are now providing
20   tents in quiet areas of their offices. Each one contains a sleeping bag, a foam pad, an MP3 player, eye shades, and yes, an alarm clock. In Japan, some firms have "nightingale rooms"
25   where employees are encouraged to take "power naps," and nap salons are springing up around the globe in cities like London, Amsterdam, Tokyo, and New York.

30 Professor William Anthony, author of *The Art of Napping*, predicts that people will see the benefits of napping more and more, especially because the workplace is getting more competitive

35 and the workforce is aging.

It's no secret that most people are not getting enough sleep. The average adult needs about 500 more hours of sleep per year, based on the

40 assumption that eight hours of sleep per night is normal. Two out of three people get less than eight hours of sleep a night during the work week, according to a recent study by a well-

45 known sleep foundation. Forty percent say they're so tired that it interferes with their daily activities.

Professor Anthony rarely misses a nap. He says that companies should permit

50 napping during breaks. "Workers are sleepy, and when they're sleepy on the job, they're not productive."

Nevertheless, at most companies, napping on the job is not yet

55 acceptable. In fact, it sometimes leads to dismissal. Still, that doesn't stop some nappers, according to Professor Anthony. He found that "they're napping in their cars, in the bathroom,

60 or in vacant rooms. Others are trying to hide their naps in their cubicles. They're putting the phone to their ear, or pretending to write or read something."

Adapted from *The Christian Science Monitor*

---

bob: to move repeatedly up and down
cubicle: a small enclosed area
dismissal: telling an employee that he or she is fired
plow through: to force one's way through

productivity: the amount of work you can do in a certain time
snooze: to nap
warm up to: to begin to like

A3 After You Read

Write *T* for true or *F* for false for each statement.

__T__ **1.** Tired workers produce fewer products.

_____ **2.** Some employers provide special napping areas.

_____ **3.** People need to sleep a total of five hundred hours a year.

_____ **4.** One study shows that most adults get eight hours of sleep per night.

_____ **5.** Most companies do not encourage napping.

_____ **6.** Employees only nap at the office.

B | FORM

The Simple Present and the Present Continuous

Think Critically About Form

A. Look back at the article on page 4 and complete the tasks below.

1. **IDENTIFY** Look at the underlined verb forms. Draw one line under six more simple present verb forms. Draw two lines under six more present continuous verb forms.

2. **COMPARE AND CONTRAST** Find a negative statement in the simple present and the present continuous. Describe the differences between them.

3. **GENERATE** Change the following sentences to *Yes/No* questions. What changes do you have to make?
   a. The average adult sleeps six hours a night.
   b. Americans are sleeping less.

B. Discuss your answers with the class and read the Form charts to check them.

▶ The Simple Present

ONLINE
PRACTICE

AFFIRMATIVE STATEMENTS			
SUBJECT		**VERB OR VERB + -S/-ES**	
I		**work**	
She	usually	**works**	on weekends.
They		**work**	

NEGATIVE STATEMENTS			
SUBJECT	**DO/DOES + NOT**	**VERB**	
I	**don't**		
She	**doesn't**	**sleep**	enough.
They	**don't**		

▶ The Present Continuous

AFFIRMATIVE STATEMENTS		
SUBJECT + *BE*	**VERB + *ING***	
I**'m**		
She**'s**	**working**	right now.
They**'re**		

NEGATIVE STATEMENTS		
SUBJECT + *BE* + *NOT*	**VERB + *ING***	
I**'m not**		
She**'s not** / She **isn't**	sleeping	well.
They**'re not** / They **aren't**		

▶ The Simple Present

YES/NO QUESTIONS			
DO/DOES	SUBJECT	VERB	
Do	you		
Does	she	**work**	on weekends?
Do	they		

SHORT ANSWERS				
AFFIRMATIVE		NEGATIVE		
	I **do**.			I **don't**.
Yes,	she **does**.	**No,**		she **doesn't**.
	they **do**.			they **don't**.

INFORMATION QUESTIONS				
WH-WORD	*DO/DOES*	SUBJECT	VERB	
Why	**do**	you	**work**	late?
Where	**does**	she	**live**?	
What	**do**	they	**think**?	

WH-WORD			VERB + -S/-ES	
Who			**works**	late?
What			**happens**	now?

▶ The Present Continuous

YES/NO QUESTIONS			
BE	SUBJECT	VERB + *ING*	
Are	you		
Is	she	**working**	now?
Are	they		

SHORT ANSWERS				
AFFIRMATIVE		NEGATIVE		
	I **am**.			I**'m not**.
Yes,	she **is**.	**No,**		she**'s not**. / she **isn't**.
	they **are**.			they**'re not**. / they **aren't**.

INFORMATION QUESTIONS				
WH-WORD	*BE*	SUBJECT	VERB + *ING*	
Why	**are**	you	**working**	late?
Where	**is**	she	**living**?	
What	**are**	they	**thinking**?	

WH-WORD	*IS*		VERB + -S/-ES	
Who			**working**	late?
What	**is**		**happening**?	

The Simple Present

- Affirmative statements can use *do* or *does*, but only for emphasis.

  You're wrong. I **do** like her.

- See Appendices 1 and 2 for spelling and pronunciation rules for verbs ending in -*s* and -*es*.

- See Appendix 14 for contractions with *do*.

(Continued on page 8)

The Present Continuous

- To combine present continuous sentences with *and*, use the subject and *am/is/are* only once.

    You**'re sitting** at your desk and **going** through paperwork.

- *Is not /are not* can be used instead of the contracted form for emphasis in negative short answers.

    No, he **is not**.   No, they **are not**.

- Stative verbs (verbs that do not express actions) are not usually used with the present continuous. The simple present is used instead.

    I **own** a house.

    x I'm owning a house. (INCORRECT)

- See Appendix 3 for spelling rules for verbs ending in *-ing*.

- See Appendix 14 for contractions with *be*.

B1 Listening for Form

CD1 T3   Lee is a student who is living away from home. Listen to the questions that his family asks him over the phone. Choose the best response for each question.

1. **a.** Yes, I am.
   b. Yes, I do.
   c. Yes, it is.

2. **a.** Yes, I do.
   b. Yes, they are.
   c. Yes, I am.

3. **a.** Yes, I have.
   b. Yes, I do.
   c. Yes, I am.

4. **a.** Yes, she is.
   b. Yes, we are.
   c. Yes, they are.

5. **a.** Yes, I do.
   b. Yes, I am.
   c. Yes, I have.

6. **a.** No, it doesn't.
   b. No, I don't.
   c. No, they don't.

7. **a.** Yes, he does.
   b. No, he's not.
   c. Yes, he is.

8. **a.** No, it doesn't.
   b. Yes, it is.
   c. Yes, there are.

B2 Working on Verb Forms

Complete the verb chart. Add *-s/-es* and *-ing* where necessary and make spelling changes.

	BASE FORM	SIMPLE PRESENT	PRESENT CONTINUOUS
1.	sleep	sleep/sleeps	sleeping
2.	open		
3.	fix		
4.	stop		
5.	wake		
6.	say		
7.	rest		
8.	dry		

B3 Working on Present Continuous Statements and Questions

Complete these conversations with the words in parentheses and the present continuous. Use contractions when possible.

Conversation 1: A child walks into the house on a rainy day.

Parent: Please take off your boots.

Child: __I'm not wearing boots.__ (I/not/wear/boots) _____
 　　　　　　　　　1　　　　　　　　　　　　　　　　　　　　　　　2
(I/wear/shoes) Do I need to take them off, too?

Conversation 2: Amy sees Sam at the vending machine.

Amy: _____ (you/buy/a soda?)
 　　　　　　　1

Sam: No, _____ (I/not/get/anything)
 　　　　　　　　　2

Amy: _____ (what/you/do?)
 　　　　　　　3

Sam: _____ (I/try/to get back/my money)
 　　　　　　4

Conversation 3: Ann is taking everything out of the desk drawer.

Bill: _____ (what/you/do?)
 　　　　　　1

Ann: _____ (I/look for/a pencil)
 　　　　　　　2

Bill: _____ (why/you/make/such a mess?)
 　　　　　　3

There are pencils in the kitchen.

B4 Working on Simple Present Statements and Questions

 A. Work with a partner. The statements below are false. Make each one true by changing it to a negative statement. Then write a true statement using the word in parentheses instead of the underlined word.

1. Water freezes at 0° <u>Fahrenheit</u>. (centigrade)

   Water doesn't freeze at 0° Fahrenheit. It freezes at 0° centigrade.

2. Earth revolves around the <u>moon</u>. (sun)

   _____

3. Palm trees grow in <u>cold</u> climates. (warm)

   _____

4. Bees live in <u>ponds</u>. (hives)

   _____

5. The sun rises in the <u>north</u>. (east)

   _____

6. Penguins live in <u>the desert</u>. (the Antarctic)

   _____

7. Flowers bloom in the <u>winter</u>. (summer)

   _____

8. Spiders have <u>six</u> legs. (eight)

   _____

 B. Make up a question related to each fact above. Then take turns asking and answering the questions with your partner.

A: What temperature does water freeze at?
B: Water freezes at 0° centigrade.

OR

A: Does water freeze at 0° Fahrenheit?
B: No, it doesn't. It freezes at 0° centigrade.

Informally Speaking

Omitting Auxiliaries and *You*

CD1 T4 Look at the cartoon and listen to the conversation. How is each underlined form in the cartoon different from what you hear?

Simple Present Questions In informal speech, *do* is often omitted from *Yes/No* questions with *you*. *You* is omitted only if the question is easy to understand without it.

Standard Form	What You Might Hear
Do you take the subway to work?	"You take the subway to work?"
Do you want some help?	"(You) want some help?"

Present Continuous Questions In informal speech, *are* is often omitted from *Yes/No* questions with *you*. *You* may also be omitted.

Standard Form	What You Might Hear
Are you having a good time?	"(You) having a good time?"
Are you feeling OK?	"(You) feeling OK?"

B5 Understanding Informal Speech

CD1 T5 Listen to the advertisements and write the standard form of the words you hear.

1. _Are you feeling_ tired in the morning?

2. _____ a vacation?

3. _____ car problems again?

4. _____ it yourself?

5. _____ any old clothes in your closets?

6. _____ to shop late?

7. _____ too hard?

8. _____ a house sitter?

Contrasting the Simple Present and the Present Continuous

Think Critically About Meaning and Use

A. Look at the pictures and answer the questions below.

> **I work at the university. What do you do?**
>
> **I work at Ace Computers. I'm a sales manager.**
>
> A
>
> **What are you doing?**
>
> **I'm looking for my earring. It fell off.**
>
> B

1. **ANALYZE** In which picture is the conversation about something that is in progress at the moment (happening now)?
2. **ANALYZE** In which picture is the conversation about a repeated action or routine?

B. Discuss your answers with the class and read the Meaning and Use Notes to check them.

Meaning and Use Notes

ONLINE PRACTICE

Using the Simple Present	
▶ **1A**	The simple present is used to talk about repeated activities, such as habits, routines, or scheduled events. Adverbs of frequency and time expressions (such as *usually* and *every hour*) often occur with the simple present.

Routines: I <u>usually</u> **drink** two cups of coffee in the morning.

Schedules: The bus **comes** <u>every hour</u>.

▶ **1B**	The simple present can also describe factual information, such as general truths or definitions.

General Truths: Some babies **don't sleep** at night.

Definitions: A recliner **is** a comfortable chair that **leans** back.

Using the Present Continuous

▶ **2A**   In contrast to the simple present, the present continuous is used for activities in progress at the exact moment of speaking. Adverbs and time expressions such as *now*, *right now*, and *at this moment* often occur with the present continuous.

Activities in Progress at This Exact Moment

I'm **drinking** a cup of coffee right now.   It's 3:00 A.M.! Why **isn't** the baby **sleeping**?

▶ **2B**   The present continuous can also express the extended present—an activity in progress over a period of time that includes the present, such as *this week* and *these days*. The activity may be ongoing or may stop and start repeatedly during the time. The extended present is often used to express changing situations.

Activities in Progress over a Period of Time (Extended Present)

I'm **drinking** a lot of coffee this week.   The baby **is sleeping** better these days.

Changing Situations

The bus **is coming** later and later this semester.

Permanent Situations vs. Temporary Situations

▶ **3**   Sometimes the simple present and present continuous are close in meaning, but not exactly the same. If a situation is permanent or habitual, choose the simple present. If a situation is new or temporary, choose the present continuous.

Simple Present **(Permanent or Habitual)**	**Present Continuous** **(New or Temporary)**
We **live** on Eddy Street. We moved there ten years ago.	We**'re living** on Eddy Street. We just moved in.
I **stay** here every summer.	I'm **staying** here for the summer.

Expressing Complaints vs. Expressing Facts

▶ **4**   Present continuous sentences with adverbs of frequency that mean "all of the time" (such as *always*, *constantly*, *continually*, and *forever*) often express complaints. Sentences in the simple present are more neutral or factual—they do not generally express complaints.

Simple Present **(Neutral Attitude)**	**Present Continuous** **(Expressing Complaints)**
They always **call** me early Sunday morning.	They **are** always **calling** me early Sunday morning. I hate when they wake me up.
My brother constantly **plays** computer games.	My brother **is** constantly **playing** computer games. He needs to study more.

C1 Listening for Meaning and Use

▶ Notes 1A, 1B, 2A, 2B

🔊 CD1 T6 Listen and choose the best answer for each question.

1. **a.** I'm relaxing.
   b. I read books.
   c. Listen to music.

2. **a.** Two kids.
   b. Yes, I do.
   c. No, it's true.

3. **a.** I'm resting.
   b. Working at night.
   c. I'm a sales associate.

4. **a.** Yes, she does.
   b. I know.
   c. He leaves.

5. **a.** No, just in the morning.
   b. Because I like it.
   c. Yes, I am.

6. **a.** I mean it.
   b. A short period of sleep.
   c. Yes, he's mean.

7. **a.** Yes, he does.
   b. No, he isn't.
   c. To Jonah.

8. **a.** Yes, it's hard.
   b. Because of my work.
   c. Yes, I am.

C2 Contrasting Activities in Progress with Routine Activities

▶ Notes 1A, 2A

A. Work in small groups. Use the present continuous to discuss what is going on in the picture. What are the people doing? What is happening?

B. Work on your own. Use the present continuous to describe what you are doing right now. Then use the simple present to write sentences that describe your daily routines at work, school, and home.

ACTIVITIES IN PROGRESS AT THE MOMENT	DAILY ROUTINES
I'm sitting in class.	I take the bus every morning at 7:00.
I'm listening to the English teacher.	I go to English class on Mondays and Wednesdays.

C3 Describing Activities in the Extended Present   ▶ Note 2B

Write five sentences describing activities that you are involved in. Use the present continuous and *this year*, *these days*, or *this semester*. Then discuss your answers in small groups. Were any of your answers the same?

I'm learning to ski this year. I'm also running a lot.

C4 Contrasting Permanent and Temporary Situations   ▶ Note 3

Work in small groups. Match each sentence on the left with the sentence on the right that provides the best context. Discuss your choices.

__c__ 1. Tomek lives on Dryden Road.

__f__ 2. Peter is living on Dryden Road.

__e__ 3. Alex wears a tie to school.

__a__ 4. Matt is wearing a tie to school.

__b__ 5. Luis works at the bank.

__d__ 6. Andrew is working at the bank.

a. He usually wears jeans and a T-shirt.

b. He has worked there since 1990.

c. He has lived there for a long time.

d. He started the job a few days ago.

e. He's a very formal dresser.

f. He just moved there a few weeks ago.

C5 Expressing Complaints

▶ Note 4

Work in small groups. Complain about the behavior of people you know, politicians, or other famous people. Use *always*, *constantly*, *continually*, and *forever* with the present continuous.

My brother is always watching sports on TV.
My neighbor is constantly playing loud music.
The governor is continually losing his temper in public.
She is forever talking on the phone.

Beyond the Sentence

Introducing a Topic with the Simple Present

The simple present is often used in the first sentence of a paragraph to express a general statement about a topic. The sentences that follow offer more specific details and may be in the simple present or other tenses. For example:

> Many people **suffer** from a condition called insomnia. In fact, insomnia **is becoming** the most common sleep disorder in the United States. People with insomnia **are** unable to fall asleep easily, and they **wake up** many times during the night. As a result, they always **feel** tired during the day. Their constant fatigue **can affect** their work and all aspects of their lives.

C6 Introducing a Topic with the Simple Present

A. Write five or six general statements about people in the country or city you are living in. Write about children, adults, college students, teenagers, men, women, senior citizens, and so on.

College students don't get enough sleep.
In the United States, not many people retire before they're 60.

B. Choose one of your general statements as the topic sentence of a paragraph. Write a paragraph that explains the statement in more detail.

College students don't get enough sleep. They often stay up very late. Then they sleep for only four or five hours and drag themselves to morning classes…

D MEANING AND USE 2

Verbs with Stative Meanings vs. Verbs with Active Meanings

⚙ Think Critically About Meaning and Use

A. Read the sentences and answer the questions below.

   a. I have a new computer at work.
   b. I usually use it quite a bit.
   c. It's more powerful than my co-workers' computers.
   d. I do research on my computer.
   e. I feel good about my job.

   1. CATEGORIZE Which sentences express actions?

   2. CATEGORIZE Which sentences express states or conditions?

B. Discuss your answers with the class and read the Meaning and Use Notes to check them.

Meaning and Use Notes

ONLINE PRACTICE

States and Conditions

▶ **1**   Stative verbs do not express actions. They express states and conditions. They commonly occur in the simple present.

My roommate's name **is** Peter. He**'s** tall and **has** brown hair. He **likes** sports cars and loud music.

Below are some common stative verbs.   *No +ing*

Descriptions and Measurements
- be, appear, look, seem, look like, resemble
- sound, sound like
- cost, measure, weigh

Possession and Relationships
- have, possess, own
- belong, owe, depend on
- consist of, contain, include

Knowledge and Beliefs
- believe, guess, hope, feel (= think), know, think, doubt
- remember, forget, recognize, notice
- mean, understand, realize, suppose
- agree, disagree

Emotions and Attitudes
- dislike, fear, hate, like, love, despise
- care, mind
- need, prefer, want, desire, appreciate

Senses and Sensations
- hear, see, smell, taste
- ache, burn, feel, hurt, itch, sting

(Continued on page 18)

Distinguishing Verbs with Stative and Active Meanings

▶ **2A** Some verbs with stative meanings also have active meanings and can express activities in the present continuous.

Simple Present (Stative)	Present Continuous (Active)
I **think** this pie is delicious. (belief)	We're **thinking** about moving. (mental activity)
It **weighs** a lot. (measurement)	I'm **weighing** it on the scale. (physical activity)

▶ **2B** When *have* means "possess" it expresses a state and can be used in the simple present, but not in the present continuous. When *have* means "experience," "eat," or "drink," it has an active meaning and can be used in the continuous.

Simple Present (Stative)	Present Continuous (Active)
Peter **has** two cars.	**Are** you **having** any problems? (experience)
We **have** a computer at home.	I'm **having** dinner with Sue. (eating)

▶ **2C** Sense verbs with stative meanings express involuntary (uncontrolled) states in the simple present. In the present continuous, *smell* and *taste* have active meanings that express voluntary actions.

Simple Present (Stative)	Present Continuous (Active)
This soup **tastes** great.	I'm **tasting** the soup to see if it's too hot.
I **smell** something awful.	I'm **smelling** each flower to find my favorite.

Expressing Physical Sensations

▶ **3** Verbs that express physical sensations can occur in the simple present or the present continuous without changing the meaning.

Simple Present (Stative)	Present Continuous (Active)
My stomach **hurts** and I **feel** sick.	My stomach **is hurting** and I'm **feeling** sick.

Using *Be* + Adjective for Behavior

▶ **4** Adjectives such as *good, bad, rude,* and *foolish* describe behavior. To express typical behavior, use these adjectives with the simple present of *be*. If the behavior is temporary or not typical, however, use them with the present continuous of *be*.

Simple Present (Typical Behavior)	Present Continuous (Not Typical Behavior)
My kids **are good**. They always behave well in restaurants.	My kids **are being good** today! They usually don't behave well in restaurants.

D1 Listening for Meaning and Use ▶ Note 1

CD1 T7 Listen to each situation. Is the speaker talking about a state or condition or about an activity? Check (✓) the correct column.

	STATE OR CONDITION	ACTIVITY
1.	✓	
2.		
3.		
4.		
5.		
6.		

D2 Making Critical Remarks with Stative Verbs ▶ Note 1

Work with a partner. You are in a bad mood. Respond to your friend's comments and questions with a critical remark. Use the words in the box. Then switch roles.

VERBS		ADJECTIVES	
be	look	awful	loud
cost	seem	cheap	small
feel	smell	crowded	strong
like	sound	expensive	terrible

1. **Your Friend:** Let's go into this store. There's a big sale.

   You: *I don't want to. It looks crowded.*

2. I think I'll buy some of this cologne. I really like it.

3. I like this shirt. The fabric is nice.

4. I love these shoes. How do they look on me?

5. Listen to this song. Doesn't it sound great?

6. I need a new tennis racket. This one looks like a good buy.

D3 Choosing the Simple Present or the Present Continuous

▶ Notes 1, 2A–2C

Work with a partner. Complete these conversations with the words in parentheses and the simple present or the present continuous. Use contractions when possible. Then practice the conversations.

Conversation 1

A: What course ___are you taking___ (you/take) with Professor Hale?
  1

B: Psychology 101.

A: ___Is it___ (it/be) a good course?
  2

B: Well, that ___depend on___ (depend on) my mood.
  3

  I ___guess___ (guess) it ___is___ (be) OK, but
  4   5

  I ___am having___ (have) trouble with our latest assignment.
  6

Conversation 2

A: Excuse me. I ___hope___ (hope) I ___am not interrupting___ (not/interrupt), 打斷
  1   2

  but I ___need___ (need) some help with my car.
  3

B: What ___seems___ (seem) to be the problem?
  4

A: I ___smell___ (smell) something bad. Maybe it's the engine.
  5

Conversation 3

A: How often ___do you dream___ (you/dream)? I ___am not dreaming___
  1   2

  (not/dream) very often at all these days.

B: That's not true. Everyone ___has___ (have) dreams every night.
  3

  You probably ___do not remember___ (not/remember) most of your dreams.
  4

Conversation 4

A: What ___are you doing___ (you/do)?
  1

B: I ___am smelling___ (smell) the milk. I ___think___ (think)
  2   3

  it's spoiled.

A: Well, how ___does it smell___ (it/smell)?
  4

B: It ___seems___ (seem) fine.
  5

D4 Describing Physical Sensations

▶ Note 3

Work with a partner. Use the simple present or the present continuous with these verbs to describe your symptoms for each of the problems below.

feel   hurt   ache   tingle   itch   burn

1. You have a sore throat.

   A: *What's wrong?*
   B: *My throat feels sore.* OR *My throat is feeling sore.*

2. You have a headache.

3. You have something in your eye.

4. You have a sprained ankle.

5. You have a stomachache.

6. You have a rash on your arm.

D5 Describing Behavior

▶ Note 4

A. Work in small groups. Build as many meaningful sentences as possible. Use an item from each column. Punctuate your sentences correctly. Discuss why some combinations are not appropriate.

The birds are quiet. The birds are being quiet.

the birds the flowers the children	are are being	quiet sick rude purple

B. Imagine you have heard these comments at work. Explain the use of *is* or *is being* by giving more details about each situation.

1. Walter is being so polite.

   He is usually very rude. OR
   He often insults people.

2. Marta is very helpful.

3. The company is being generous.

4. The employees are being so quiet.

5. Mr. Johnson is unfair.

6. My boss is being difficult.

7. My neighbor is being unfriendly.

Informally Speaking

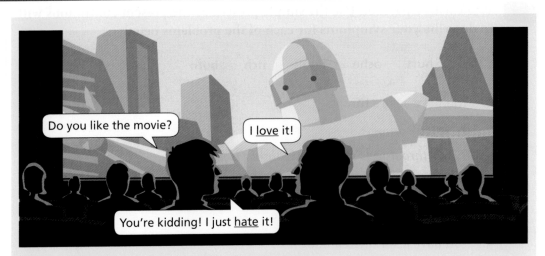

Expressing Emotions in the Continuous

CD1 T8 Look at the cartoon and listen to the conversation. How is each underlined form in the cartoon different from what you hear?

In informal speech, some verbs may be used in the continuous form but keep their stative meaning. This is especially common with verbs of emotion such as *love, hate,* and *like.* Using the continuous shows a more intense or emotional situation. Adverbs such as *just* or *really* and special emphatic intonation are often used as well.

Standard Form	What You Might Hear
I **love** this novel.	"I'm just loving this novel!"
I **hate** this movie.	"I'm really hating this movie!"
I **like** it here.	"I'm really liking it here!"

D6 Understanding Informal Speech

CD1 T9 Listen and write the standard form of the words you hear.

1. <u>I like</u> my apartment more and more each day!

2. _____ this new television show!

3. _____ the beautiful weather!

4. _____ this trip!

5. _____ this movie!

6. _____ my new job.

D7 Writing Descriptions

Follow these steps to write a summary about a favorite character in a book, movie, or TV show.

1. In small groups, brainstorm a list of three or four of your favorite books, movies, or TV shows. Discuss your favorite character in each and explain why you like him or her.

2. Choose one character that you have discussed. Write a description in the simple present about this person. Tell what happens to him or her, how the person looks, feels, and so on, using verbs with stative meaning where appropriate.

   The "Wizard of Oz" tells the story of Dorothy. She is a young girl and she lives on a farm in Kansas. After a big storm, she lands in Oz. Dorothy feels frightened at first, but soon after...

The Wizard of Oz

Think Critically About Meaning and Use

A. Read each sentence and answer the questions that follow with one of these choices: *Yes, No, Probably, Probably not,* or *It's not clear.*

1. I'm writing a book.

   a. Is the speaker finished with the book yet? _No._

   b. Did the speaker start writing the book a few days ago? _____

   c. Is the speaker writing at the moment of speaking? _____

2. The bus is stopping.

   a. Is the bus speeding up? _____

   b. Is the driver's foot on the brake? _____

   c. Are the passengers getting off the bus? _____

3. My sister works at the Computing Center.

   a. Is she working right now? _____

   b. Did she get the job yesterday? _____

   c. Does she work full-time? _____

4. I'm sleeping much better this week.

   a. Is the speaker sleeping right now? _____

   b. Did the speaker sleep well last week? _____

   c. Will the speaker sleep well next week? _____

5. I'm taking a French course right now.

   a. Is the speaker in the French class right now? _____

   b. Has the course begun? _____

   c. Is the course over? _____

6. I watch the news during breakfast.

   a. Is the speaker watching the news? _____

   b. Is the speaker eating breakfast? _____

   c. Will the speaker watch the news during breakfast tomorrow?

   _____

B. Discuss these questions in small groups.

1. **COMPARE AND CONTRAST** What is the difference in meaning between sentence 1 and the statement "I write books"?

2. **PREDICT** Look at sentences 1, 3, and 5. What do you think the speakers will say next? (Use the simple present and present continuous in your answers.)

Edit

Find the errors in these paragraphs and correct them.

It's mid-afternoon at a busy law firm. The telephones ~~is~~ *are* ringing, voice mail piles up, and faxes are arriving. But what many of the lawyers are doing? They take naps at their desks! As more and more busy professionals works from morning until night, many are sleep in their offices for

just 15 or 20 minutes during the afternoon. And they are not embarrassed about it at all. It becomes a new trend, according to a recent survey on napping.

Some people sleeps in their chairs, while some are preferring the floor or couches. Everyone agrees that a little nap help them get through their very long workday. Meanwhile, many experts are asking "What means this new trend?" It's simple, according to the most experienced nappers. They are do what people in other cultures and climates do every day. And they are pleased that napping finally gets more common in the workplace.

Write

Imagine that you are a new student at a college or university. Update your profile page on a social networking site. Use the simple present and present continuous.

1. **BRAINSTORM** Think about all the things you can say about your new life. Use these categories to help you organize your ideas into paragraphs.
   - **Self and School:** who you are; where you're going to school; what courses you're taking; how you feel about your new situation
   - **Living Situation:** where you are living; your roommates, if any; how you like it
   - **Routines, Free-Time:** study habits; typical weekday; free-time activities

2. **WRITE A FIRST DRAFT** Before you write your first draft, read the checklist below and look at the sentences you wrote for tasks C2 (part B) and C3 on page 15. Write your draft using the simple present and present continuous.

3. **EDIT** Read your work and check it against the checklist below. Circle grammar, spelling, and punctuation errors.

DO I...	YES
organize my ideas into paragraphs?	☐
use the simple present for facts, habits, schedules, and routines?	☐
use the present continuous for activities in progress now and in the extended present?	☐
use stative verbs in the simple present to describe states and conditions?	☐
use contractions to make my writing sound more friendly and natural?	☐

4. **PEER REVIEW** Work with a partner to help you decide how to fix your errors and improve the content. Use the checklist above.

5. **REWRITE YOUR DRAFT** Using the comments from your partner, write a final draft.

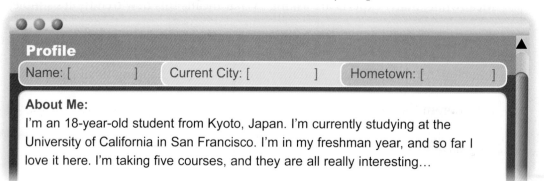

Profile

Name: [   ]   Current City: [   ]   Hometown: [   ]

About Me:
I'm an 18-year-old student from Kyoto, Japan. I'm currently studying at the University of California in San Francisco. I'm in my freshman year, and so far I love it here. I'm taking five courses, and they are all really interesting…

C H A P T E R

2

The Past

A. **GRAMMAR IN DISCOURSE: A Night to Remember** 28

B. **FORM: The Simple Past, the Past Continuous, and
Time Clauses** 30

The Simple Past
They **traveled** by ship.

The Past Continuous

They **were traveling** by ship.

The Simple Past and The Past Continuous in Time Clauses

Before the noise **interrupted** them, they **were playing** cards.

C. **MEANING AND USE 1: Contrasting the Simple Past
and the Past Continuous** 35

The Simple Past for Completed Past Situations

The Past Continuous for In-Progress Past Situations

Completed vs. In-Progress Past Situations

The Past Continuous for Background Information

Vocabulary Notes: Habitual Past with _Used To_ and _Would_

Beyond the Sentence: Using the Simple Past in Discourse

D. **MEANING AND USE 2: The Simple Past and the Past
Continuous in Time Clauses** 41

Sequential Events

Interrupted Events

Simultaneous Events

**WRITING: Write an Essay About a
Memorable Experience** 47

A GRAMMAR IN DISCOURSE

A Night to Remember

A1 Before You Read

Discuss these questions.

What are some important news events from your lifetime? Do you remember where you were when they occurred? What were you doing at that particular time?

A2 Read

CD1 T10 **Read this book excerpt to find out what was happening when the *Titanic* hit an iceberg.**

A NIGHT TO REMEMBER

It was April 14, 1912, the fifth night of the *Titanic*'s first trip. At almost 11:40 P.M., Frederick Fleet and Reginald Lee, two of the ship's "lookouts," were on duty.
5   They were watching for icebergs when Fleet suddenly saw something directly ahead. At first it was small, but every second it grew larger and closer. Quickly, Fleet banged the bell three times to warn
10   of danger ahead. He also lifted the phone and rang the bridge.

"What did you see?" asked a calm voice at the other end.

"Iceberg right ahead," replied Fleet.
15   "Thank you," said the voice calmly.

At this moment George Thomas Rowe, one of the ship's officers, was standing watch. Suddenly, he felt a curious motion break the steady rhythm of the
20   engines. He glanced forward—and stared again. He thought he saw a ship before he realized it was an iceberg. The next instant it was gone.

Meanwhile, down below in the first
25   class dining room, four other members of the *Titanic*'s crew were sitting around one of the tables. They were doing what off-duty stewards often did—they were gossiping about the passengers. Then,
30   while they were talking, a grinding vibration seemed to come from deep inside the ship. It was not much, but it was enough to break their conversation and rattle the silver that was on the
35   breakfast tables for the next morning.

In the kitchen, Chief Night Baker Walter Belford was making rolls for the following day. When the jolt came, it impressed Belford strongly. Perhaps this
40   was because a pan of fresh rolls clattered off the top of the oven and scattered about the floor.

Most of the *Titanic*'s passengers were in bed when the strange vibration
45 occurred. But a few were still up. As usual, they were in the first class smoking room. Around one table, some men were enjoying a final cigar. At another table, the ship's younger passengers were enjoying a lively
50 game of bridge. While they were playing and laughing, they suddenly felt that grinding vibration. Some people ran out onto the deck. When they got there, they saw the iceberg. It was scraping the side of
55 the ship. In another moment it faded into the darkness. The excitement, too, soon disappeared. The group went back inside, and the bridge game continued.

Down in Boiler Room No. 6, Fireman
60 Fred Barrett was talking to an assistant engineer when the warning bell rang. A quick shout of warning—an ear-splitting crash—and the whole side of the ship seemed to collapse. The sea rushed in and
65 swirled around the pipes and valves. Before the watertight door slammed down, the two men leaped through the doorway into Boiler Room No. 5. Unfortunately, they found things almost
70 as bad there...

Adapted from *A Night to Remember*

---

clatter: to make a series of knocking noises
grinding: rubbing together harshly
jolt: a sudden forceful shake
stand watch: to be on duty on a ship

steward: a man who helps passengers and serves meals
vibration: a shaking movement

A3 After You Read

Choose the answer that best completes each sentence.

1. Crew members were watching for ____.

   a. seagulls   **b.** rain   **c.** icebergs

2. The dining room stewards were ____.

   a. cleaning up   **b.** sleeping   **c.** talking

3. The baker was making ____.

   a. pies   **b.** rolls   **c.** cakes

4. ____ of the passengers were in bed.

   a. All   **b.** Most   **c.** None

5. Some of the passengers ____.

   a. saw the iceberg   **b.** warned the captain   **c.** were worried

6. Water poured into ____ first.

   a. the kitchen   **b.** the boiler rooms   **c.** the captain's quarters

FORM

The Simple Past, the Past Continuous, and Time Clauses

Think Critically About Form

A. Look back at the book excerpt on page 28 and complete the tasks below.

1. **IDENTIFY** Two examples of the simple past are underlined. Find three regular and three irregular simple past verb forms.

2. **RECOGNIZE** An example of the past continuous is circled. Find six more examples. Sort your examples into singular and plural.

3. **ANALYZE** Find examples of clauses beginning with *when*, *while*, and *before*. Do these clauses come before or after the main clause they are connected to?

B. Discuss your answers with the class and read the Form charts to check them.

▶ **The Simple Past**

ONLINE
PRACTICE

AFFIRMATIVE STATEMENTS		
SUBJECT	VERB + -*D*/-*ED* OR IRREGULAR FORM	
I	**worked**	that night.
He	**felt**	scared.
They	**traveled**	by ship.

NEGATIVE STATEMENTS			
SUBJECT	*DID* + *NOT*	VERB	
I		**work**	that night.
He	**didn't**	**feel**	scared.
They		**travel**	by ship.

▶ **The Past Continuous**

AFFIRMATIVE STATEMENTS			
SUBJECT	*WAS/WERE*	VERB + -*ING*	
I	**was**	**working**	that night.
He	**was**	**feeling**	scared.
They	**were**	**traveling**	by ship.

NEGATIVE STATEMENTS			
SUBJECT	*WAS/WERE* + *NOT*	VERB + -*ING*	
I	**wasn't**	**working**	that night.
He	**wasn't**	**feeling**	scared.
They	**weren't**	**traveling**	by ship.

▶ The Simple Past

YES/NO QUESTIONS			
DID	**SUBJECT**	**VERB**	
Did	you	**work**	that night?
	he	**feel**	scared?
	they	**travel**	by ship?

SHORT ANSWERS						
AFFIRMATIVE			**NEGATIVE**			
Yes,	I	**did.**	**No,**	I	**didn't.**	
	he			he		
	they			they		

INFORMATION QUESTIONS				
WH-WORD	**DID**	**SUBJECT**	**VERB**	
When		you	**work**	there?
Why	**did**	he	**feel**	scared?
Where		they	**travel**	to?

WH-WORD		**VERB + -D/-ED OR IRREGULAR FORM**	
Who		**worked**	late?
What		**happened?**	

▶ The Past Continuous

YES/NO QUESTIONS			
WAS/WERE	**SUBJECT**	**VERB + -ING**	
Were	you	**working**	that night?
Was	he	**feeling**	scared?
Were	they	**traveling**	by ship?

SHORT ANSWERS						
AFFIRMATIVE			**NEGATIVE**			
Yes,	I	**was.**	**No,**	I	**wasn't.**	
	he	**was.**		he	**wasn't.**	
	they	**were.**		they	**weren't.**	

INFORMATION QUESTIONS				
WH-WORD	**WAS/WERE**	**SUBJECT**	**VERB + -ING**	
When	**were**	you	**working**	there?
Why	**was**	he	**feeling**	scared?
Where	**were**	they	**traveling**	to?

WH-WORD	**WAS**	**VERB + -ING**	
Who		**working**	late?
What	**was**	**happening?**	

The Simple Past
- See Appendices 4 and 5 for spelling and pronunciation rules for verbs ending in *-ed*.
- See Appendix 6 for irregular verbs and their simple past forms and Appendix 14 for contractions with *did*.

The Past Continuous
- Stative verbs are not usually used in the past continuous. Use the simple past instead.

  I **owned** a house.   x I was owning a house. (INCORRECT)
- See Appendix 3 for spelling rules for verbs ending in *-ing* and Appendix 14 for contractions with *was/were*.

(Continued on page 32)

▶ The Simple Past and The Past Continuous in Time Clauses

⎯⎯⎯ TIME CLAUSE ⎯⎯⎯	⎯⎯⎯ MAIN CLAUSE ⎯⎯⎯
<u>While</u> the crew **was working**,	the passengers **were sleeping**.
<u>Before</u> the noise **interrupted** them,	they **were playing** cards.

⎯⎯⎯ MAIN CLAUSE ⎯⎯⎯	⎯⎯⎯ TIME CLAUSE ⎯⎯⎯
The passengers **were sleeping**	<u>while</u> the crew was **working**.
Water **flooded** the ship	<u>after</u> it **struck** the iceberg.

- Time clauses begin with time words such as *while, when, before,* or *after.* They are dependent clauses and cannot stand alone as complete sentences. They must be attached to independent main clauses to complete their meaning.
- A time clause can come before or after the main clause. The meaning is the same. If the time clause comes first, it is followed by a comma.

B1 Listening for Form

CD1 T11   **Listen to this news report and write the verb forms you hear.**

Where ___*were*___ you when the lights _____ out this morning? That's
        1   2

the question everyone is asking today. Early this morning, a construction crew

_____ on 33rd Street while people across the city _____ to work. At
     3   4

8:29 A.M., a simple mistake by the construction crew _____ a blackout that
                                                 5

_____ power to almost a million people.
     6

The blackout _____ airports to send incoming flights elsewhere. But
                7

according to one report, a jet liner _____ just when the power in the control
                                  8

tower _____. After the jet _____ contact with the tower, the pilot
        9   10

_____ the plane himself with no problems.
     11

The mayor _____ a state of emergency. Fortunately, no major accidents
               12

or injuries _____, and the power _____ after six hours and twenty minutes,
          13   14

at 2:49 this afternoon.

B2 Building Simple Past and Past Continuous Sentences

Build as many meaningful sentences as possible. Use an item from each column, or from the second and third columns only. Punctuate your sentences correctly.

When did you buy a computer?

		paid cash
when did		studying this morning
what did	who	buy a computer
what were	what	happened last night
did	you	do when the bell rang
		go online yesterday

B3 Identifying Dependent and Independent Clauses

Check (✓) the examples that can stand alone as full sentences. Correct the punctuation of those sentences.

  ✓   **1.** ~~he~~ He was standing on the deck of the Titanic.

_____ **2.** while the stewards were talking

_____ **3.** something vibrated inside the ship

_____ **4.** before midnight

_____ **5.** the iceberg hit the ship

_____ **6.** some passengers were getting ready for bed

_____ **7.** after the incident

_____ **8.** a group was still playing bridge

_____ **9.** while others were wandering about

_____ **10.** after the men escaped

B4 Combining Sentences with Time Clauses

Work with a partner. Combine the sentences with the time word in parentheses to form as many sentences with time clauses as possible.

1. I went home. I finished my work. (when)

    When I went home, I finished my work. OR *I finished my work when I went home.*
    When I finished my work, I went home. OR *I went home when I finished my work.*

2. He was reading. He was listening to music. (while)

3. He went to law school. He studied hard. (after)

4. She fell asleep. The doorbell rang. (before)

5. The fire started. We were sleeping. (when)

6. The TV show started. They went to bed. (before)

7. The phone was ringing. They were cooking dinner. (while)

8. The package arrived. She called the post office. (before)

B5 Asking and Answering Questions with Time Clauses

Work with a partner. Take turns asking and answering the questions.

1. What were you doing…
    before this class started?
    when the teacher walked in?
    when the class ended yesterday?
    while you were eating breakfast?

    A: What were you doing before this class started?

    B: I was talking to my friends.

2. Where were you living…
    when you were a child?
    while you were in high school?
    before you came to this town/city?

3. What were you thinking about…
    when you went to sleep last night?
    when you woke up this morning?
    while you were coming to class?
    before you walked in the door?

MEANING AND USE 1

Contrasting the Simple Past and the Past Continuous

Think Critically About Meaning and Use

A. Read the sentences and answer the questions below.

1a. The warning bell rang.
1b. The warning bell was ringing.

2a. The bakers cleaned up.
2b. The bakers were cleaning up.

ANALYZE Which sentences describe a completed event? an unfinished event?

B. Discuss your answers with the class and read the Meaning and Use Notes to check them.

Meaning and Use Notes

ONLINE
PRACTICE

The Simple Past for Completed Past Situations

▶ **1** The simple past describes an action or state that started and finished at a definite time in the past. The action or state can last for a short or long period of time, occur in the recent or distant past, and happen once or repeatedly.

Short Period of Time	**Long Period of Time**
The rain **lasted** for 30 seconds.	The rain **lasted** for many days.

Recent Past	**Distant Past**
She **was** very sick last week.	She **was** very sick last year.

Happened Once	**Happened Repeatedly**
She **arrived** late (last) week.	She always **arrived** late. *She was never on time.*
↑ time	routine

The Past Continuous for In-Progress Past Situations

▶ **2A** The past continuous expresses an activity in progress at an exact moment in the past. The activity began before the specific point in time and might also have continued after that time.

Activities in Progress at an Exact Moment

He **was getting ready** for bed at 11:40 P.M. He still wasn't ready ten minutes later.

(Continued on page 36)

▶ **2B**   The past continuous may also express an activity in progress over an extended period of time in the past. The activity may have been ongoing or may have stopped and started repeatedly.

Activities in Progress over an Extended Period of Time

They **were working** on the project for two years.

Completed vs. In-Progress Past Situations

▶ **3A**   The past continuous and the simple past can be similar in meaning, but not exactly the same. To describe a situation as completed, choose the simple past. To describe the same situation in progress, choose the past continuous.

Simple Past (Completed)	**Past Continuous (In Progress)**
I **lived** on Eddy Street in 1986.	I **was living** on Eddy Street while I was in school.

▶ **3B**   The simple past implies the completion of an event. The past continuous often emphasizes the activity or process. The past continuous activity may or may not have been completed.

Simple Present (Stative)	**Present Continuous (Active)**
He **wrote** a letter in the library and **mailed** it on his way home. (He finished the letter.)	He **was writing** a letter in the library when the lights went out. (We don't know if he finished the letter.)

The Past Continuous for Background Information

▶ **4**   The past continuous often appears at the beginning of a narrative to describe background activities. It can express several background activities happening at the same time as the main event. The main event is in the simple past.

It **was raining** hard outside. I **was sleeping** and my roommate **was taking** a shower. At exactly 7:00 A.M., there <u>was</u> a huge clap of thunder. I <u>jumped up</u> as the house <u>shook</u> violently…

C1 Listening for Meaning and Use

▶ Notes 3A, 3B

CD1 T12 Listen to descriptions of these activities. Check (✓) whether the activity is completed at the end of the description or may continue after the end of the description.

	ACTIVITY	COMPLETED	MAY CONTINUE
1.	writing a book		✓
2.	eating dinner		
3.	painting his kitchen		
4.	baking a cake		
5.	writing a letter		

C2 Describing Activities in Progress in the Past

▶ Notes 2A, 2B

Look at the picture and describe the different activities that were happening yesterday afternoon at the public library. Use the past continuous.

Many people were waiting in line at the reference desk.
One man was chasing his child around the book carts.

C3 Contrasting In-Progress and Completed Past Situations

▶ Notes 3A, 3B

Read this interview by a dorm advisor who is investigating a false fire alarm in a college dorm. Choose the simple past or past continuous forms that best complete the conversation.

Advisor: What ((did you notice) / were you noticing) last night?
₁

Student: It was after dinner and I was in the student lounge. Four male students

(played / were playing) a game at a table. Three others
₂

(studied / were studying) together on the couches. A female student
₃

(read / was reading) a newspaper in the corner. I (did / was doing) a
₄ ₅

crossword puzzle. At eight o'clock, I (heard / was hearing) two of my friends
₆

in the hall. They (told / were telling) jokes, so I (went / was going) into the
₇ ₈

hall to talk to them. On the way back to my seat, I (stopped / was stopping)
₉

to talk to the guys at the table. Suddenly we (heard / were hearing) the fire
₁₀

alarm go off. We all (jumped / were jumping) up and (ran / were running)
₁₁ ₁₂

out of the lounge. We (didn't smell / weren't smelling) smoke and we
₁₃

(didn't see / weren't seeing) anything suspicious, but just to be safe we
₁₄

(went / were going) down the emergency stairs and (got / were getting) out
₁₅ ₁₆

of the building as fast as we could.

C4 Describing Background Activities

▶ Note 4

A. Write two past continuous sentences that describe activities that were happening at the same time as each of the simple past events.

1. My phone rang at 7:00 A.M.

   I was sleeping. My roommate was taking a shower.

2. We watched the evening news at 6:30.

3. Lightning struck a huge tree in our yard this afternoon.

4. I stopped at the supermarket on my way home from work.

5. My computer crashed last night.

6. The fire alarm rang during class.

B. Write a paragraph about an item in part A. Begin with background information in the past continuous. Then use the simple past to describe the main event.

At 7:00 A.M., I was sleeping and my roommate was taking a shower. Suddenly, the phone rang. I jumped out of bed, picked up the phone, and said sleepily, "Hello?...

Vocabulary Notes

Habitual Past with *Used To* and *Would*

Used To *Used to* is a special simple past tense verb. *Used to* suggests a comparison between the past and the present. It suggests that a repeated action or state was true in the past, but is not true now, even if the present is not mentioned.

> We **used to go** skating a lot. Now we go skiing.

> We **didn't use to play** cards.

Used To **and** ***Would*** In affirmative statements, *would* can sometimes replace *used to* without changing the meaning. *Would* generally combines only with verbs that express actions.

> When I was young, we **would go** skating a lot.

> **x** We would live in China. (INCORRECT)

In a description about the past, *used to* can appear once or twice at the beginning of a paragraph, but *would* is used to provide the details in the rest of the story.

> In the 1980s, I **used to** work for a big company that was far from my home. Every morning I <u>would</u> get up at 6:00 A.M. to get ready for work. I <u>would</u> leave the house by 7:00 A.M. Sometimes I <u>would</u> carpool with a neighbor…

C5 Describing the Habitual Past

Work with a partner. Put these sentences in order to form a meaningful paragraph. Discuss the use of the simple past, *used to*, and *would*.

_____ That all changed a few summers ago after we finished college and got our first jobs.

_____ In the mornings, my twin brother and I would get up early and go for hikes in the woods.

__1__ My family and I used to spend all our summers at a cottage on a lake.

_____ We didn't have a TV at the cottage, so we would spend our evenings talking and reading.

_____ We miss the lake and all the wonderful times we used to have there.

_____ Our cottage there was like our home away from home, and we loved our life there.

_____ In the afternoons, we'd meet our friends and go swimming at the lake.

_____ Every June we would leave our apartment in New York City and head for the lake.

Beyond the Sentence

Using the Simple Past in Discourse

Simple Present Introductions to Descriptions of the Past General statements in the simple present can often introduce simple past descriptions. The simple past gives specific details about the simple present statement.

Voice mail systems **are** often frustrating. Last week, I <u>tried</u> to call an airline company. First, I <u>listened</u> to a menu with six different choices. Then I...

Time Expressions with the Simple Past In a simple past description, a time expression such as *last weekend* often appears in the description, but not in every sentence. Each sentence relates to this time until a new expression appears. Often a change of time expression (for example, *now*) signals a change in tense.

I **called** Jill <u>last weekend</u>, and she **was** sick with the flu. She **sounded** terrible so we **didn't talk** very long. I **spoke** to her again <u>this morning</u>, and she **was** much better. She**'s** back at work <u>now</u>, and everything **seems** fine.

C6 Using the Simple Past in Discourse

A. Read each simple present introductory statement. Then write a sentence in the simple past that adds a detail. Tell when the particular experience happened.

1. You can't depend on the weather. <u>Last year, we ran into terrible fog</u>

   <u>during our trip through Austria.</u>

2. I still remember my childhood. _____

   _____

3. I don't like long lines. _____

   _____

B. Write a short paragraph. Choose one of the items in part A. Pay attention to your use of time expressions for keeping or changing sentences.

You can't depend on the weather. Last year, we ran into terrible fog during our trip through Austria. It was our first time in the Austrian countryside, and we barely saw anything as we rode from town to town. The whole countryside was under a dense fog. We were very disappointed so we...

MEANING AND USE 2

The Simple Past and the Past Continuous in Time Clauses

Think Critically About Meaning and Use

A. Read the sentences and answer the questions below.

a. They were talking about the passengers when they suddenly felt the vibration.
b. Some people were sleeping while others were playing cards.
c. When the bell rang, he yelled to his assistant.

1. **ANALYZE** Which sentence shows that one completed event happened after another completed event?   C
2. **ANALYZE** Which sentence shows that one event interrupted another event?
3. **ANALYZE** Which sentence shows that two events were happening at the same time?

B. Discuss your answers with the class and read the Meaning and Use Notes to check them.

Sequential   ●——————●——→   *Simultaneous*   ⁓⁓⁓⁓⁓⁓——→

Interrupted   ⁓⁓⁓⁓↓——→

Meaning and Use Notes

ONLINE PRACTICE

Sequential Events

▶ **1A**   Past time clauses describe the time relationship of two past events and show the order of those events. Sentences with two simple past clauses can show that one completed event happened after the other. *Before*, *after*, or *when* introduces the time clause.

Simple Past (1st Event)	Simple Past (2nd Event)
I wrote the letter	**before I heard the news.**
After I heard the news,	I wrote the letter.
When I heard the news,	I wrote the letter.

▶ **1B**   Sometimes a sentence with a when or after time clause expresses a cause-and-effect relationship. The first event causes the second event.

Cause (1st Event)	Effect (2nd Event)
When the power went out,	the room got completely dark.
After the power went out,	the room got completely dark.

(Continued on page 42)

Interrupted Events

▶ **2A** Sentences with one simple past and one past continuous clause typically show that a simple past event interrupted a past continuous event.

He **was studying** for exams when the lights **went out**.

OR

Before the lights **went out**, he **was studying** for exams.

▶ **2B** Both *while* and *when* introduce a past continuous clause that means "during the time."

Past Continuous (1st Event)	Simple Past (2nd Event)
While I was dancing,	I lost my necklace.
When I was dancing,	I lost my necklace.

▶ **2C** *When* can also introduce a simple past clause that means "at the time," but *while* cannot.

Past Continuous (1st Event)	Simple Past (2nd Event)
I was dancing	**when I lost my necklace.**
x I was dancing	while I lost my necklace. (INCORRECT)

Simultaneous Events

▶ **3** Sentences with two past continuous clauses typically show that two activities were happening at the same time. Both *while* and *when* can introduce the time clause.

Past Continuous	Past Continuous
They were laughing	**while they were playing cards.**
They were laughing	**when they were playing cards.**

D1 Listening for Meaning and Use

▶ Notes 1A, 1B, 2A, 2B

⏩ CD1 T13 Listen to the two events in each statement and choose the event that happened or started first.

1. **a.** I went home.

   b. I opened the mail.

2. **a.** I played tennis.

   b. I took a shower.

3. **a.** The phone rang.

   b. I was fixing the bathroom sink.

4. **a.** She came home.

   b. It started to rain.

5. **a.** I was waiting for John.

   b. I saw Erica.

6. **a.** The water ran out.

   b. I opened the drain.

7. **a.** I called the operator.

   b. She connected me with Bogotá.

8. **a.** I shouted.

   b. She turned around.

D2 Using Past Time Clauses

▶ Notes 1A, 1B, 2A–C, 3

Work in groups. Read this account of the Johnstown Flood of 1889. Make notes about what happened. Then make up as many sentences as you can with *while, when, before,* and *after* time clauses. Include sequential, interrupted, and simultaneous events in your sentences.

Before the water crashed into Johnstown, the train engineer tried to warn people.

It was May 31, 1889. It was raining, and the waters of a nearby lake were rising. The South Fork Dam was sagging. A few minutes after 3:00 P.M. that day, the dam collapsed and a 40-foot wall of water headed toward Johnstown, 14 miles away. A train engineer outside of the town tried to warn people that the flood was coming. He sped down the track and blew his train whistle loudly. This time, he didn't toot the whistle three times in his usual friendly way. Instead, he made the whistle wail in a way that survivors remembered years later.

The water crashed into Johnstown at a very high speed. Some people called it a tidal wave. The flood destroyed everything in its path. It wiped out villages, bridges, and freight trains. Many people had no time to leave their homes. They ran to the upper floors of their houses and they climbed onto their roofs. The force of the water lifted some houses and knocked them into each other. Other people were luckier. They were able to escape to the hills right above Johnstown.

After the tragedy, people from around the world donated 4 million dollars to help Johnstown, and more than 200 photographers came to record the story. It was the first big international news event. Johnstown survived two more major floods in 1936 and 1977.

D3 Relating Events with *Before* and *After*

▶ Notes 1A, 1B, 2A

A. Describe the changes in each pair of pictures. Use *before* and *after*.

Situation 1: Her grades came in the mail.

Before her grades came in the mail, she was worried. After her grades came in the mail…

Situation 2: He tripped and fell.

Situation 3: Their parents came home.

B. Write a short story about one of the pairs of pictures. Use time clauses in your story to describe what happened before and after.

Elena was standing at the window, waiting for the mail. Her exam grades were late…

D4 Understanding Cause and Effect

▶ Note 1B

Work with a partner. Read each pair of sentences and label the cause and the effect. Then combine the sentences, using *when* or *after* to express the cause. Discuss why more than one answer is possible in some sentences.

1. a. The roads became icy. ___effect___ *What happened?*

    b. The temperature dropped below freezing. ___cause___ *Reason why?*

     When the temperature dropped below freezing, the roads became icy.

2. a. They had to call for help. ___effect___

    b. They ran out of gas. ___cause___

    After they ran out of gas, they had to call for help.

3. a. The lightning struck. ___cause___

    b. The lights went out. ___effect___

    After the lightning struck, the light went out.

4. a. They painted their house bright pink. ___cause___

    b. The neighbors refused to talk to them. ___effect___

    After they painted their house bright pink, the neighbors refused to talk to them.

5. a. He went on a strict diet. ___effect___

    b. His best suit didn't fit anymore. ___cause___

    When his best suit didn't fit anymore, he went on a strict diet.

6. a. Her arm started to itch. ___effect___

    b. A mosquito bit her. ___cause___

    Her arm started to itch after a mosquito bit her.

7. a. The doorbell rang. ___cause___

    b. He answered the door. ___effect___

    When the doorbell rang, he answered the door.

8. a. She found the lost jewelry. ___cause___

    b. She got a reward. ___effect___

    When she found the lost jewelry, she got a reward.

D5 Talking About Interrupted Activities ▶ Notes 2A–2C

A. Complete this email message by writing sentences with *when* and *while* time clauses about the events in parentheses. Use the simple past or the past continuous.

From: tsmith@email.com
To: miguel@email.com
Subject: A Very Bad Day

Hi Miguel!

You wouldn't believe what a terrible day I had! _While I was trying to sleep,_
1
the cat jumped on my chest (I try to sleep / the cat jumps on my chest).

So I got up to let him go out, but _I tripped on a shoe when was going_ (I go down the stairs /
2
I trip on a shoe). By this time, I was fully awake even though it was just 5:15 in the morning. So I

decided to make breakfast. Would you believe that _I spilled ... while I was making coffee._
3
(I make coffee / I spill the whole can of coffee on the floor)? I tried to calm down, eat my breakfast,

and get ready for school. But _the phone was ringing when was taking_ (I take a shower / the
4
phone rings). So I got out of the shower to answer it, but _I slipped on the wet floor when_
5
(I stepped out of the shower / I slip on the wet floor). I finally answered the phone, and it was an old friend

who drives me crazy! He asked to come and visit me. I told him he couldn't come. _He got mad_
and hanged up when was trying (I try to explain / he gets mad and hangs up).
6

Well, I got to school all right. The most important thing that I had to do today was to write a paper for

my economics class. Well, guess what? _the computer system went down when was writing_ (I write the paper
7
/ the computer system goes down). I had to go to class without my paper. Then _When I was riding_
the ... it got stuck (I ride the elevator to class / it gets stuck). I was 45 minutes late, so I
8
missed most of my class. Fortunately, my professor has a sense of humor.

Thanks for reading all of this nonsense! How was your day?

B. Work with a partner. Can you remember a day when something unexpected happened? Take turns telling each other what happened. Use time clauses and the simple past or the past continuous.

Think Critically About Meaning and Use

A. Read each sentence and the statement that follows. Write *T* if the statement is true, *F* if it is false, or *?* if you do not have enough information to decide.

1. Before the storm arrived, the weather stations were warning us about it.

   ___F___ The storm began before the weather stations warned us.

2. The children were building a snowman while it was snowing.

   _____ They finished the snowman.

3. He wrote a book about the *Titanic*.

   _____ He completed the book.

4. We lost our power when a tree came down.

   _____ A tree came down after we lost our power.

5. He was listening to the news while she was sleeping.

   _____ She fell asleep before the news started.

B. Discuss these questions in small groups.

1. **COMPARE AND CONTRAST** What happens to the meaning of sentence 2 if we change *were building* to *built*?

2. **GENERATE** How could you expand sentence 3 to make it more informative? (Make 3 different sentences using *while*, *before*, and *when*.)

Edit

Some of these sentences have errors. Find the errors and correct them.

1. While he was taking a shower, ~~when~~ someone called.

2. After he fell asleep, he was reading a book.

3. Were you having your own car in college?

4. He didn't go to class yesterday.

5. Oh, no! I was dropping my earring. I can't find it.

6. I dialed again, after I heard the dial tone.

Write

Write a narrative essay about a memorable experience from your childhood. Use the simple past, the past continuous, and the habitual past with *used to* and *would*.

1. **BRAINSTORM** Think about all the things you might want to include when writing about the experience. Use these categories to help you organize your ideas into paragraphs.

   - **What your life was like around the time of the experience:** how old you were; things you used to do or think; places and/or people that were important to you
   - **The memorable experience:** background activities that were happening when the experience began; the series of events that made up the memorable experience
   - **Why the experience was important to you:** what you learned; how it affected you

2. **WRITE A FIRST DRAFT** Before you write your first draft, read the checklist below and look at the examples in tasks C3, C4, and C5 on pages 38–39.

3. **EDIT** Read your work and check it against the checklist below. Circle grammar, spelling, and punctuation errors.

DO I ...	YES
organize my ideas into paragraphs?	☐
use *used to* and *would* to talk about the habitual past?	☐
use the past continuous for background activities and activities in progress?	☐
use the simple past for main events and completed states and situations?	☐
use past time expressions and past time clauses?	☐

4. **PEER REVIEW** Work with a partner to help you decide how to fix your errors and improve the content. Use the checklist above.

5. **REWRITE YOUR DRAFT** Using the comments from your partner, write a final draft.

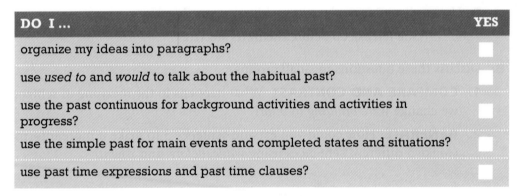

One of my most memorable experiences of my childhood happened when I was ten. At the time, I was a very lonely child. I used to come straight home from school, and after dinner, I'd go to my room and spend the evening by myself...

CHAPTER

3

Future Forms

A. **GRAMMAR IN DISCOURSE: Trend Forecasters Predict Future** **50**

B. **FORM: The Future Continuous and Review of Future Forms** **52**

The Future Continuous
They **will be coming** later.

The Future With *Be Going To*
It's **going to** rain tonight.

The Future With *Will*
I'll **finish** this soon.

The Present Continuous As Future
She's **leaving** in a few minutes.

The Simple Present As Future
The store **opens** at ten tomorrow.

C. **MEANING AND USE 1: Contrasting *Will* and the Future Continuous** **58**

Future Activities in Progress

Promises and Requests vs. Plans and Expectations

D. **MEANING AND USE 2: Contrasting *Be Going To*, the Present Continuous as Future, and the Simple Present as Future** **61**

Expressing Plans or Intentions   **Making Predictions**

Expressing Scheduled Events

E. **MEANING AND USE 3: Contrasting *Will*, the Future Continuous, and *Be Going To*** **65**

Predictions and Expectations with Similar Meanings

More Certain and Less Certain Predictions

Quick Decisions vs. Advance Plans

Ordering Events with Future Time Clauses

Beyond the Sentence: Repeating Future Forms in Discourse

WRITING: Write a Blog Post About Life in the Future **72**

PART 1 TEST: The Present, Past, and Future **75**

Trend Forecasters Predict Future

A1 Before You Read

Discuss these questions.

Do you think people can predict the future? Make some predictions that you think will come true in the next ten or twenty years.

A2 Read

CD1 T14 Read this newspaper article to find out what two experts predict for the future.

Trend Forecasters Predict Future

Want to know what the future holds for us? Ask a trend forecaster. Businesses pay them millions of dollars for help in predicting what products people <u>are going to</u>
5 <u>buy</u>. Here are a few predictions made by two well-known trend forecasters, Faith Popcorn and Gerald Celente.

According to Faith Popcorn:
• "Knowledge chips" planted in our brains <u>will</u>
10 <u>enable</u> us to speak French instantly, repair the TV, learn golf, or whatever.
• We will become more sensitive to issues related to food and consumer products. Vegan-friendly retailing is going to increase
15 dramatically, and most of us <u>will be buying</u> products like cruelty-free, animal-friendly vegan shoes and accessories or clothing and home furnishings made from eco-friendly fibers grown without pesticides and other chemicals.
20 • To make sure our foods are safe, we'll all own one of the "newly reliable portable food testers."

Faith Popcorn

According to Gerald Celente:
• Health, fitness, and nutrition are going to be key. People are going to do more to take care of
25 themselves.
• People will spend more on chemical-free food as their fear of contaminated meat, vegetables, and fish increases.
• Shopping malls will no longer exist.

30 • Technology will make it possible for people to test load a virtual washing machine or refrigerator in a virtual appliance department.

• Food, oil, and energy prices will continue to skyrocket, so more people will see the

35 importance of becoming self-sufficient. Many homeowners will be growing their own food, equipping their homes with solar, hydro, and wind technologies, and generating their own energy.

40 • We're also going to see a revolution in energy. It may be as big as the discovery of fire or the invention of the wheel. Advances in physics will lead to exciting new forms of energy.

Gerald Celente

---

contaminated: unclean; unfit for use

key: very important

reliable: dependable

self-sufficient: needing no outside help to satisfy one's basic needs

skyrocket: (prices) rise dramatically

trend: a current style or fashion; what people generally seem to be doing

vegan: not eating or using animal-derived products

A3 After You Read

Choose the products and trends that will become more popular according to the trend forecasters.

1. chemical-free foods

2. electric cars

3. robot housekeepers

4. vegan shoes

5. videophones

6. eco-friendly fibers

7. energy-independent homes

8. safe cities

9. new kinds of energy

10. larger and larger malls

11. do-it-yourself surgery

12. portable food-testers

B FORM

The Future Continuous and Review of Future Forms

Think Critically About Form

A. Look back at the article on page 50 and complete the tasks below.

1. **IDENTIFY** Examples of three different future forms are underlined. Find all the other examples of these future forms and sort them into categories:
   am/is/are + going to + verb
   will + verb
   will be + verb + *-ing*

2. **GENERATE** Do you know any other tenses that can be used to express the future?

B. Discuss your answers with the class and read the Form charts to check them.

▶ The Future Continuous

ONLINE PRACTICE

AFFIRMATIVE STATEMENTS

SUBJECT	WILL	BE	VERB + -ING	
I				
She	**will**	**be**	**coming**	later.
They				

NEGATIVE STATEMENTS

SUBJECT	WILL	NOT	BE	VERB + -ING	
I					
She	**will**	**not**	**be**	**coming**	later.
They					

YES/NO QUESTIONS

WILL	SUBJECT	BE	VERB + -ING	
	you			
Will	she	**be**	**coming**	later?
	they			

SHORT ANSWERS

YES	SUBJECT	WILL		NO	SUBJECT	WON'T
	I				I	
Yes,	she	**will.**		**No,**	she	**won't.**
	they				they	

INFORMATION QUESTIONS

WH- WORD	WILL	SUBJECT	BE	VERB + -ING	
When	will	you	be	**coming**?	
Where		they		**working**	tomorrow?

WH- WORD	WILL		BE	VERB + -ING	
Who	will		be	**coming**	later?
What				**happening**	year?

- The future continuous has the same form with every subject.
- The future continuous has two auxiliary verbs: *will* and *be*. Only *will* forms contractions.
- Verbs with stative meanings are not usually used with the future continuous.

   x I'll be knowing the answer later. (INCORRECT)

- See Appendix 3 for spelling rules for verbs ending in *-ing*.
- See Appendix 14 for contractions with *will*.

▶ Review of Future Forms

THE FUTURE WITH *BE GOING TO*
AM/IS/ARE + GOING TO + VERB
It**'s going to rain** tonight.
It**'s not going to rain** tonight.
Is it **going to rain** tonight?
Yes, it **is**. / **No**, it **isn't**.
When is it **going to rain**?

THE FUTURE WITH *WILL*
WILL + VERB
I**'ll finish** this soon.
I **won't finish** this soon.
Will you **finish** this soon?
Yes, I **will**. / **No**, I **won't**.
When will you **finish**?

THE PRESENT CONTINUOUS AS FUTURE
AM/IS/ARE + VERB + -ING
She**'s leaving** in a few minutes.
She**'s not leaving** in a few minutes.
Is she **leaving** in a few minutes?
Yes, she **is**. / **No**, she **isn't**.
When are you **leaving**?

THE SIMPLE PRESENT AS FUTURE
SIMPLE PRESENT VERB FORM
The store **opens** at ten tomorrow.
The store **doesn't open** until ten tomorrow.
Does the store **open** at ten tomorrow?
Yes, it **does**. / **No**, it **doesn't**.
What time **does** the store **open** tomorrow?

(Continued on page 54)

- All future forms can occur in the main clause of sentences with future time clauses.
- Future time clauses begin with a time word such as *when*, *before*, or *after*.
- In most sentences expressing future time, the time clause uses the simple present. Only the main clause uses a future form.

> <u>After</u> you **get** home, I'm **leaving** for work.
>
> I'll probably **leave** for work <u>when</u> you **get** home.

B1 Listening for Form

CD1 T15   Listen to each situation. Choose the future form that you hear.

1. a. I call
    b. I'll call *(circled)*
    c. I'll be calling
    d. I'm calling

2. a. It won't be raining
    b. It won't rain
    c. It's not going to rain
    d. It's not raining

3. a. The movie starts
    b. The movie will start
    c. The movie will be starting
    d. The movie is starting

4. a. We'll cruise
    b. We're cruising
    c. We'll be cruising
    d. We're going to cruise

5. a. We'll be leaving
    b. We're going to leave
    c. We're leaving
    d. We'll leave

6. a. They're sending
    b. They'll send
    c. They'll be sending
    d. They're going to send

7. a. John will arrive
    b. John will be arriving
    c. John is going to arrive
    d. John is arriving

8. a. Do you go skiing
    b. Are you going to go skiing
    c. Will you be going skiing
    d. Are you going skiing

B2 Working on the Future Continuous

Write five sentences that tell why Abdul can't go out with his friends this week. Use Abdul's calendar to explain what he will be doing.

Abdul will be studying for a history exam. He'll also be...

Monday	Friday
meet with professor Parker after dinner	
Tuesday	**Saturday**
history exam *English paper due*	
Wednesday	**Sunday**
prepare speech for debate class	
Thursday	Notes
clean apartment for Mom's visit	

B3 Building Sentences Using Future Forms

Build as many meaningful sentences as possible. Use an item from each column, or from the first and third columns only. Use contractions when possible and punctuate your sentences correctly.

I'll (I will) leave tomorrow.

I who her family	is going to will will be am	leaving soon leave tomorrow

B4 Asking *When* Questions About the Future

Work with a partner. Take turns asking and answering questions with *when*. Use the phrases below and *be going to*, the present continuous as future, or the future continuous. Use future time words in your answers.

1. take a vacation

   A: *When are you going to take / are you taking / will you be taking a vacation?*
   B: *This summer.*

2. get a medical checkup

3. take the day off

4. clean your apartment

5. finish your work

6. go out to dinner

7. do your laundry

8. shop for groceries

B5 Working on the Simple Present as Future

A. Read this fall semester schedule from an American university. Use the simple present as future and the verbs *begin*, *start*, *last*, and *end* to make as many sentences as possible about the schedule.

Classes start on September 1.

University Fall Semester Schedule

September 1	First day of classes
October 12–15	Fall vacation
November 22–25	Thanksgiving break
December 6	Last day of classes
December 13–20	Final exams

B. Work with a partner. Write a current school schedule like the one in part A. Take turns saying simple present sentences to talk about the future events on your schedule.

B6 Working on Future Time Clauses

Work with a partner. Combine the sentences with the time word in parentheses to form as many sentences with future time clauses as possible. Use the simple present in the time clause and *will* or *be going to* in the main clause. Are any combinations illogical?

1. He takes a shower.
   He gets out of bed. (after)

   After he gets out of bed, he'll take a shower.
   After he gets out of bed, he's going to take a shower.
   He'll take a shower after he gets out of bed.
   He's going to take a shower after he gets out of bed.

   ILLOGICAL:
   After he takes a shower, he'll get out of bed.
   After he takes a shower, he's going to get out of bed.

2. I go shopping.
   I call you. (before)

3. The mail arrives.
   I eat breakfast. (after)

4. He falls asleep.
   He reads the newspaper. (when)

5. He sets the table.
   He cooks dinner. (before)

6. I go home.
   I clean my house. (when)

Contrasting *Will* and the Future Continuous

> ## Think Critically About Meaning and Use
>
> **A.** Read the sentences and answer the questions below.
>
> **1a.** Don't worry. I'll pick up the kids after work.
> **1b.** I'll be picking up the kids after work. Then I'll be going straight home.
> **2a.** Don't call Bob at six. He'll probably be eating dinner then.
> **2b.** Don't call Bob at six. He'll probably eat dinner then.
>
> 1. **ANALYZE** Compare 1a and 1b. Which one describes a plan? Which one expresses a promise?
>
> 2. **ANALYZE** Compare 2a and 2b. Which one refers to an activity in progress? Which one refers to the beginning of an activity?
>
> **B.** Discuss your answers with the class and read the Meaning and Use Notes to check them.

Meaning and Use Notes

ONLINE PRACTICE

	Future Activities in Progress

▶ **1**   The future continuous expresses an activity in progress at a specific time in the future. Like all other continuous forms, the future continuous makes you think of a situation as ongoing.

At this time tomorrow, **I'll be leaving** for Hawaii.

I'll be staying in Hawaii for three weeks.

	Promises and Requests vs. Plans and Expectations

▶ **2A**   Especially in the first person, *will* and the future continuous express different meanings. A sentence with *will* can be used to make a promise. However, the same sentence in the future continuous typically expresses a plan or expectation.

Future with *Will* (a Promise)	Future Continuous (a Plan or Expectation)
I'll finish this tomorrow.	**I'll be finishing** this tomorrow.

> **▶ 2B** A question with *will* can be used to make a request. However, the same question in the future continuous asks about a plan or expectation. This question may lead to a request in a more indirect and polite way.

Future with *Will* **(a Request)**	**Future Continuous** **(a Question About a Plan)**
A: **Will** you **stop** at the post office tomorrow to send this package?	A: **Will** you **be stopping** at the post office tomorrow?
B: Sure.	B: Yes, I will.
	A: Could you send this package?

C1 Listening for Meaning and Use

▶ Notes 1, 2A, 2B

CD1 T16 Listen to each situation. Choose the sentence that most appropriately follows what you hear.

1. **a.** So hurry up. She'll be coming at 8:00.

   b. So hurry up. She'll come at 8:00.

2. **a.** Will you open it for me?

   b. Will you be opening it for me?

3. **a.** I won't be baking a cake today.

   b. I won't bake a cake.

4. **a.** I'll email it to you by 9:00 A.M. tomorrow.

   b. I'll be emailing it to you by 9:00 A.M. tomorrow.

5. **a.** We'll be getting back to you as soon as possible.

   b. We'll get back to you as soon as possible.

6. **a.** Will you be getting some more from the supply room?

   b. Will you get some more from the supply room, please?

7. **a.** Will you go past the bus stop?

   b. Will you be going past the bus stop?

8. **a.** … she'll be getting married.

   b. … she'll get married.

C2 Expressing Promises, Plans, and Expectations ▶ Notes 1, 2A, 2B

 Work with a partner. For each situation, finish writing the conversation using the future with *will* or the future continuous. Then act out your conversations.

1. **Student A:** You are the parent. You are going away for the weekend. You are nervous about leaving your teenage son or daughter alone. Discuss your concerns with him or her.

   Student B: You are the teenager. Reassure your parent.

   Parent: I hope you'll be home by 11:00.

   Teenager: I promise I won't break any rules. Anyway, I won't be going out much. I'll be studying for my exams tonight.

   Parent: When will you be... ?

2. **Student A:** You are the employee. You need to leave early because of a family problem. Make promises about your work.

   Student B: You are the boss. Your employee has a family problem and needs to leave work early. You are concerned about your employee's problem, but the project needs to get done.

   Employee: Could I leave early today? I need to help my mother.

   Boss: Will you be able to finish your work?

   Employee: I promise I'll...

C3 Using Direct and Indirect Requests ▶ Note 2B

A. Work with a partner. Write a conversation for each situation. Use *will* to make a direct request.

1. You want to borrow your friend's math notes.

   A: Will you please lend me your math notes?

   B: Sure. No problem.

2. You want your friend to drive you to school.

3. You would like to use your brother's car.

4. Your friend is going to buy concert tickets and you would like one, too.

B. Work with the same partner. Write another conversation for each situation in part A. Use the future continuous to make an indirect request that asks about a plan. Then respond to the indirect request.

A: Will you be using your math notes this afternoon?

B: No. Do you want to borrow them?

A: Yes, I do. Thanks.

D

Contrasting *Be Going To,* the Present Continuous as Future, and the Simple Present as Future

Think Critically About Meaning and Use

A. Read the sentences and answer the questions below.

   a. <u>I'm going to exercise during my lunch hour every day</u>.
   b. <u>Classes start on September 1</u>.
   c. I'm tired. <u>I'm not working tonight</u>.

Think about the meanings of the underlined sentences in each context.

  1. EVALUATE Which two sentences describe a plan that may or may not actually happen?

  2. EVALUATE Which sentence describes a scheduled event that is unlikely to change?

B. Discuss your answers with the class and read the Meaning and Use Notes to check them.

Meaning and Use Notes

ONLINE PRACTICE

Expressing Plans or Intentions

▶ **1A**   Both *be going to* and the present continuous as future are used to talk about a planned event or future intention. A future time expression is stated or implied with the present continuous.

Future with *Be Going To*

He**'s not going to take** any classes this summer. He**'s going to work** full-time.

Present Continuous as Future

He**'s not taking** any classes this summer. He**'s working** full-time.

(Continued on page 62)

▶ **1B** The meanings of *be going to* and the present continuous as future are sometimes similar, but not exactly the same. With *be going to*, the speaker may not have an exact plan. With the present continuous as future, the plan is often more definite.

Future with *Be Going To* *could change your mind*

I'm **going to leave** my job (someday). I'm just so unhappy.

Present Continuous as Future *probably not change your mind*

I'm **leaving** my job (next week). I've been unhappy for too long.

Expressing Scheduled Events

▶ **2A** The simple present as future is used for scheduled events that usually cannot be changed. It is common in more formal contexts.

Simple Present as Future

Printed Program: The conference **starts** on Tuesday evening and **ends** on Saturday afternoon.

Trip Itinerary: The flight **leaves** Chicago at 10:02 and **arrives** in Palm Beach at 12:36.

Announcement: Our new branch office **opens** this Monday at the Cedar Mall.

▶ **2B** When talking about scheduled events, the simple present, the present continuous, or *be going to* can express the same meaning. However, the simple present as future is more likely to imply that the schedule is beyond the control of the speaker.

Present Continuous as Future and Future with *Be Going To*

Student: I'm **leaving** at midnight. That's my plan.

I'm **going to leave** at midnight. That's my plan.

Simple Present as Future

Soldier: I **leave** at midnight. Those are my orders.

Making Predictions

▶ **3** Use *be going to* to make predictions. Do not use the present continuous or the simple present as future to make predictions.

Future with *Be Going To*

They'**re going to win** tonight. Everyone thinks so.

x They're winning tonight. (INCORRECT)   x They win tonight. (INCORRECT)

It'**s going to rain** later.

x It rains later. (INCORRECT)   x It is raining later. (INCORRECT)

D1 Listening for Meaning and Use

▶ Notes 1A, 1B, 2A, 2B, 3

CD1 T17 Listen to each pair of sentences. Do they have approximately the same meaning or different meanings? Check (✓) the correct column.

	SAME	DIFFERENT
1.		✓
2.		
3.		
4.		
5.		
6.		

D2 Expressing Plans, Scheduled Events, and Predictions

▶ Notes 1A, 2A, 2B, 3

A. Build as many logical sentences as possible. Use an item from each column. Punctuate your sentences correctly. Which sentences are plans or scheduled events? Which sentences can only be predictions?

We're having a meeting tomorrow.

| we're having
we're going to have
we have | a meeting
a storm
an exam
an election
a sale | tomorrow |

B. Choose the nouns below that can appropriately begin the sentence. Which nouns would make the sentence illogical? Discuss each of your choices.

_____ begins tomorrow.

An explosion	My new job
It	School
A snowstorm	Winter vacation

D3 Discussing Plans and Scheduled Events ▶ Notes 1A, 1B, 2A, 2B

 A. Work with a partner. Look at the European trip itinerary below and follow the instructions. When you are finished, switch roles for the Latin American trip itinerary.

Student A: You are the travel agent. Call your client and read the trip itinerary. Use the simple present as future to describe the itinerary.

Student B: You are the client. Take notes and ask questions.

Travel Agent: You leave New York at 7:00 P.M. on July 5.

Client: What airline do I take?

Travel Agent: French Airways.

European Trip Itinerary

July 5	Leave New York, Kennedy Airport (French Airways, Flight 139 at 7:00 P.M.)
July 6	Arrive Paris, Charles de Gaulle Airport 8:00 A.M. (Flight time: 7 hours)
July 6–11	Paris
July 11	Leave Paris, Charles de Gaulle Airport (Air Britain, Flight 267 at 11:00 A.M.) Arrive London Heathrow Airport 11:00 A.M. (Flight time: 1 hour, 15 minutes)
July 11–14	London
July 15–22	Car trip through Scotland
July 23	Return to London
July 24	Leave London Heathrow Airport (French Airways, Flight 278 at 12:00 P.M.)
July 25	Arrive New York, Kennedy Airport 3:00 P.M. (Flight time: 8 hours)

Latin American Trip Itinerary

August 19	Leave Los Angeles, LA International Airport (Skyway Airlines, Flight 299 at 7:20 A.M.) Arrive Mexico City International Airport 1:00 P.M.
August 19–21	Mexico City
August 22	Leave Mexico City International Airport (MexJet, Flight 137 at 7:04 A.M.) Arrive Buenos Aires, Ezeiza Airport, 8:16 A.M.
August 22–26	Buenos Aires
August 26	Leave Buenos Aires, Jorge Newbery Airport (Southern Air, Flight 201 at 11:15 A.M.) Arrive São Paolo, Guarulhos International Airport, 9:50 P.M.
August 26–31	São Paolo
September 1	Drive to Rio de Janeiro
September 1–7	Rio de Janeiro
September 8	Leave Rio de Janeiro, Galeão International Airport (Skyway Airlines, Flight 122 at 1:30 A.M.) Arrive Los Angeles, LA International Airport 2:10 P.M.

B. Send an email message to a friend who lives in one of the places you will be visiting in part A. Describe your itinerary and find out if your friend can meet you.

⊠

From: Isabela

To: Luiza

Hi Luiza,
I'm hoping that we can meet for dinner during my trip to Latin America next month. I leave Los Angeles on August 19, and I'll be in Mexico City from August 19-21. Then I fly to Buenos Aires for a few days. I arrive in São Paulo on August 26, and I'll be staying for six days. Are you going to be in town during that time?
Isabela

Contrasting *Will*, the Future Continuous, and *Be Going To*

Think Critically About Meaning and Use

A. Read the sentences and complete the tasks below. *I think / Maybe*

1a. Don't be disappointed about the canceled ski trip. It'll snow soon.

1b. Wear your hat. It's probably going to snow.

2a. Hanna: Can someone open that window for me?
Shelley: I'll do it. *quick decision*

2b. Kevin: What's your decision about the job?
Laura: I'm going to do it. *plan*

1. **IDENTIFY** Underline the future verb forms in the sentences.

2. **ANALYZE** Which pair contrasts a quick decision with a plan thought about in advance?

3. **ANALYZE** Which pair expresses predictions that may or may not happen?

B. Discuss your answers with the class and read the Meaning and Use Notes to check them.

Meaning and Use Notes

ONLINE
PRACTICE

Predictions and Expectations with Similar Meanings
▶ **1A** *Will*, *be going to*, and the future continuous can be used to make predictions or state expectations with similar meaning. With predictions the speaker is less certain that an event will occur. With expectations, the speaker is more certain.

Predictions	**Expectations**
It **will warm up** tomorrow.	The bank **will close** early tomorrow.
It **will be warming up** tomorrow.	The bank **will be closing** early tomorrow.
It **is going to warm up** tomorrow.	The bank **is going to close** early tomorrow.

(Continued on page 66)

▶ 1B *Will* and the future continuous are frequently used in more formal contexts than *be going to*. Information in a more formal context is usually restated with *be going to* in conversation.

Future with *Will* and Future Continuous (More Formal)

Sign: The bank **will close** at 1:00 P.M. today.

Weather Report: It **will be warming up** tomorrow.

Future with *Be Going To* (Less Formal)

Speaker: The bank **is going to close** at 1:00 P.M. today.

Speaker: It**'s going to warm up** tomorrow.

More Certain and Less Certain Predictions

▶ 2 With predictions, the meanings of *will* and *be going to* are sometimes similar, but not exactly the same. Use *be going to* when an event is fairly certain to happen very soon because there is evidence for it. Do not use *will* in this situation.

Future with Be *Going to* (More Certain Events)

They**'re going to win tonight**. They're the best team.

Look at the clouds. It**'s going to rain**.

Future with *Will* (Less Certain Events)

They**'ll win** tonight if they can keep the ball.

x Look at the clouds. It will rain. (INCORRECT)

Quick Decisions vs. Advance Plans

▶ 3 Especially in first person, *will* and *be going to* express different meanings. A sentence with *will* can express a quick decision or offer. However, the same sentence with *be going to* expresses a plan thought about in advance.

Future with *Will* (a Quick Decision)

A: Does anyone want to help me?

B: I**'ll help**. What can I do first?

Future with *Be Going To* (an Advance Plan)

A: What are your plans for the weekend?

B: I**'m going to help** my sister move tomorrow.

Ordering Events with Future Time Clauses

▶ **4** Future time clauses show the order of two future events. The specific order of events usually depends on the choice of the time word, not on the choice of future form. *Before, after, until, as soon as* (= right after), *by the time* (= before), and *when* introduce the time clause.

First Event	Second Event
I'm going to buy the novel	**before I get on the plane**.
After I buy the novel,	I'll get on the plane.
I'll be reading the novel	**until the plane lands**.
As soon as I get off the plane,	I'll get my bags.
I'll be in the baggage area	**by the time you get to the airport**.

> In sentences with *when*, the choice between using *will* or the future continuous can affect the order of events because the future continuous activity is in progress and the *will* activity is not.
>
> | First Event | Second Event | |
> |---|---|---|
> | **I'll be making** dinner | **when** you get home. | (I'll start dinner, and then you'll get home.) |
> | **When** you get home, | **I'll make** dinner. | (You'll get home, and then I'll start dinner.) |

E1 Listening for Meaning and Use

▶ Notes 1A, 1B, 2, 3

CD1 T18 Listen to each situation. Choose the sentence that most appropriately follows what you hear.

1. **(a.)** That glass is going to fall.
   b. That glass will fall.

2. **a.** An agent is going to be with you shortly.
   b. An agent will be with you shortly.

3. **a.** I'm going to get it.
   b. I'll get it.

4. **a.** I'm going to read.
   b. I'll read.

5. **a.** I'll do it.
   b. I'm going to do it.

6. **a.** It will rain.
   b. It's going to rain.

7. **a.** Sure. I'll get it for you.
   b. Sure. I'll be getting it for you.

8. **a.** I'll work in an art museum.
   b. I'm going to work in an art museum.

E2 Restating Formal Announcements

▶ Notes 1A, 1B

Work with a partner. Decide in what context you might hear or see each sentence. Then use *be going to* to state each one in a less formal way.

1. The weather will be cool tomorrow with a chance of rain.

    Context: radio weather forecast

    Restatement: It's going to be cool tomorrow with a chance of rain.

2. Flight 276 will be arriving at Gate 12.

3. On April 1, the fare will increase to $1.75.

4. Classes will resume on January 22.

5. Tonight we will begin with a short poem.

E3 Restating Predictions

▶ Note 2

Work with a partner. Restate these predictions with *will*, if possible. Discuss why *will* would be inappropriate in some contexts.

1. I think that genetic engineering is going to become more widespread.

    I think that genetic engineering will become more widespread.

2. That car is speeding and the road is icy. The driver is going to lose control.

3. Computers are probably going to cost much less in a few years.

4. There are two seconds left in the hockey game. The buzzer is going to sound.

5. In a few years, "smart refrigerators" are going to tell owners when they need milk.

6. The patient's condition is improving. He's going to be fine.

E4 Making Quick Decisions and Stating Plans

▶ Note 3

A. Work in small groups. Brainstorm a list of what needs to be done for each situation. Then go around the group and have members volunteer for specific tasks using *will*.

1. Your kitchen is a mess. Your group has 15 minutes to clean it up before some important guests arrive.

    Benito: I'll clean the sink.

    Danilo: I'll sweep the floor.

    Mei: I'll…

2. Your group is going to have a potluck dinner tomorrow night.

3. Your group is going to have a garage sale to raise money for charity.

4. Your group will be going camping next weekend.

B. Use your list for a chain summary of each situation in part A. First, restate your quick decision using *going to*. Then, restate the other volunteers' jobs with *be going to*.

Benito: *I'm going to clean the sink.*

Danilo: *Benito is going to clean the sink, and I'm going to sweep the floor.*

Mei: *Benito is going to clean the sink, Danilo is going to sweep the floor, and I'm going to...*

E5 Understanding the Order of Future Events ▶ Note 4

A. Read these predictions. For each one, choose the situation that will happen or start first.

1. People will have more time after they open their home offices.

    a. People will have more time.

    (b.) They'll open their home offices.

2. We'll be doing all the housework until we get a robot.

    a. We'll be doing all the housework.

    b. We'll get a robot.

3. By the time our children are adults, most homeowners will be generating their own energy.

    a. Our children will become adults.

    b. Most howeowners will be generating their own energy.

4. We'll all own portable food testers as soon as they become easier to use.

    a. We'll all own portable food testers.

    b. They'll become easier to use.

5. We won't use electric cars until gas gets too expensive.

    a. We'll use electric cars.

    b. Gas will get too expensive.

6. We'll all buy videophones as soon as the prices go down.

    a. We'll all buy videophones.

    b. The prices will go down.

B. Which predictions in part A do you think are likely to happen? Which ones are unlikely? Why? Discuss your opinions with your classmates.

E6 Verbs Expressing the Future

▶ Notes 1A, 1B, 2, 3

Work in small groups. Read each example and the sentences that follow. Choose the sentence that is closest in meaning to the example. Discuss your answers.

1. Yes, Jeanne, I'll pick up the children later. Don't worry.

   a. I'm about to pick up the children.

   (b.) I'm willing to pick up the children.

2. Watch out! That ladder is going to fall.

   a. The ladder will fall.

   b. The ladder is about to fall.

3. I'm going to visit my aunt this week. Would you like to come?

   a. I intend to visit my aunt this week.

   b. I promise to visit my aunt this week.

4. I'm meeting Susan at six.

   a. I'm willing to meet Susan at six.

   b. I plan to meet Susan at six.

5. I'll do it when I get home. You have my word.

   a. I promise to do it when I get home.

   b. I expect to do it when I get home.

6. **A:** No one volunteered to help me.

   B: I'll help.

   a. I'm willing to help.

   b. I'm about to help.

7. I won't clean up tonight. It's your turn.

   a. I don't expect to clean up tonight.

   b. I refuse to clean up tonight.

8. She's going to get the job. The boss was very impressed.

   a. I expect her to get the job.

   b. She intends to get the job.

9. He's starting graduate school in the fall.

   a. He plans to start graduate school.

   b. He's willing to start graduate school.

10. I'm going to China when I have enough money.

    a. I intend to go to China.

    b. I'm willing to go to China.

Beyond the Sentence

Repeating Future Forms in Discourse

In a paragraph or conversation, *be going to* or the future continuous often introduces the topic. The sentences that follow usually use the shorter forms *will* or the present continuous as future to supply more details.

I'**m going to visit** my aunt this afternoon. First, I'**ll stop** at the bakery for her favorite cookies. Then I'**ll pick up** my sister, and we'**ll get** on the interstate…

We'**re going to cook** a really nice dinner tonight. I'**m making** soup and a new pasta recipe. Kedra **is making** a salad, and Andrea **is baking** a cake.

Notice how several future forms can be used, but *will* is the most simple and the most common one to repeat as the paragraph progresses.

On Sunday, we'**re going to celebrate** my aunt's 40th birthday. We'**ll be taking** her out to her favorite restaurant where two of her friends **are joining** us. We'**ll order** her favorite meal and then, for dessert, we'**ll have** a cake with 40 candles. It'**ll be** fun to spend the afternoon with her.

E7 Repeating Future Forms in Discourse

Write a paragraph about something you are going to do in the next month, for example, take a trip or visit a friend. Be specific and explain exactly what you are going to do. Begin your paragraph with *be going to* or the future continuous, but use shorter future forms or other verbs to supply the details.

I'm going to visit my sister and her family in two weeks. I'll stop there on my way to a conference in San Francisco. We'll probably go out to dinner. We also intend to…

Think Critically About Meaning and Use

A. Choose the best response to complete each conversation.

1. **A:** The milk spilled.
   B: I'll be getting a sponge. / I'll get a sponge.

2. **A:** Why can't you come to our house this weekend?
   B: I'll work. / I'll be working.

3. **A:** Why did you leave the door open?
   B: I'm going to carry in the packages. / I'll carry in the packages.

4. **A:** The doorbell is ringing.
   B: I'll answer it. / I'll be answering it.

5. **A:** I'm ready to take your order.
   B: I'll have a bowl of soup. / I have a bowl of soup.

6. **A:** Why did you turn on the oven?
   B: I'm making a cake later. / I'll make a cake later.

7. **A:** What are your plans for dinner?
   B: I'm going to cook pasta. / I'll cook pasta.

8. **A:** What does your work schedule say about next week?
   B: I'll work Monday and Thursday. / I work Monday and Thursday.

9. **A:** You'll have some free time in an hour.
   B: Maybe I'll do my homework. / Maybe I'll be doing my homework.

10. **A:** Who volunteered before to pick up the pizza for tonight's dinner?
    B: I did. I'll get it. / I did. I'm going to get it.

B. Discuss these questions in small groups.

1. **ANALYZE** Underline the verb forms in conversations 3 and 6. What do A's questions have in common? What do B's answers have in common?

2. **EVALUATE** Look at conversations 1, 3, and 6. In which one(s) does B use a future form to explain why something happened in the past? In which does B make a sudden decision to do something in the near future about something that happened in the recent past?

Edit

Find the errors in these paragraphs and correct them. There may be more than one way to correct an error.

One of the most exciting advances in medicine in the next few years is ~~gonna~~ ^{going} ~~be~~ ^{to be} the widespread use of robots in the operating room. Experts predict that "robot assistants" are never replacing surgeons. Nevertheless, there is no doubt that robots going to revolutionize surgery.

In just a few years, robots become the standard in certain types of heart surgery, eye surgery, hip surgery, and brain surgery. Why this is going to happen? The answer is simple. No surgeon will ever be able to keep his or her hand as steady as the hand of a robot. No surgeon is ever being able to greatly magnify a microscopic blood vessel with his or her own eyes. These are simple and routine tasks for medical robots.

Some patients are still worried, however. In the words of one patient before hip surgery, "How do I know the robot doesn't go crazy? Maybe it drills a hole in my head instead of my hip!"

Surgeons are quick to reassure their patients. "That's impossible," says one optimistic surgeon. "I promise that isn't happening. Robots are medical assistants. They'll work when I am going to give them a command, and they'll stop when I will say so. I be right there the whole time."

Write

Imagine you write for a trend forecaster's blog. The New Year is approaching and you've been thinking about the future, fifty years from now. Write a blog post about your predictions. *Use be going to, will, the future continuous, and future time clauses.*

1. **BRAINSTORM** Choose two areas (e.g., homes, education), and think about the changes that will occur. Use these categories to help you organize your ideas into paragraphs.
   - **Introduction:** What overall prediction can you make about life 50 years from now?
   - **Changes for the better:** What improvements will there be? What effect will these improvements have on the way we live? (Devote one paragraph to each area.)
   - **Challenges:** What old/new challenges will we be facing?
   - **Conclusion:** How optimistic are you about the future?

2. **WRITE A FIRST DRAFT** Before you write your first draft, read the checklist below and look at the predictions on pages 50–51 and 69. Write your draft using *be going to, will,* the future continuous, and future time clauses.

3. **EDIT** Read your work and check it against the checklist below. Circle grammar, spelling and punctuation errors.

DO I ...	YES
organize my ideas into paragraphs?	☐
use *be going to* and *will* for predictions and expectations?	☐
use the future continuous for expectations and future activities in progress?	☐
use future time clauses to show the order of future events?	☐
use expressions like *I think*, *maybe*, and *probably* to show that I am speculating?	☐

4. **PEER REVIEW** Work with a partner to help you decide how to fix your errors and improve the content. Use the checklist above.

5. **REWRITE YOUR DRAFT** Using the comments from your partner, write a final draft.

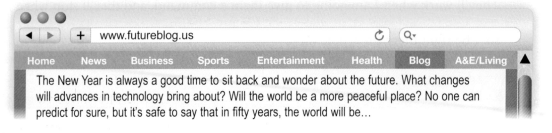

www.futureblog.us

Home | News | Business | Sports | Entertainment | Health | Blog | A&E/Living

The New Year is always a good time to sit back and wonder about the future. What changes will advances in technology bring about? Will the world be a more peaceful place? No one can predict for sure, but it's safe to say that in fifty years, the world will be…

Choose the correct word or words to complete each sentence.

1. What _____ at his corporate job?

   a. your father does

   b. do your father

   c. does your father do

   d. does your father

2. Passengers used to wait on long lines before the airlines _____ electronic check-in machines.

   a. introduce

   b. used to introduce

   c. introduced

   d. introducing

3. In what city _____ going to be?

   a. the next Olympic games will

   b. are the next Olympic games

   c. will the next Olympic games

   d. the next Olympic games are

What is expressed in each sentence? Choose the correct answer.

4. I'm living with John this semester.

   a. temporary situation

   b. habit

   c. general truth

   d. definition

5. My neighbors are always arguing. I can't sleep at night.

   a. schedule

   b. activity in progress

   c. definition

   d. complaint

6. When I ate the salad, I had an allergic reaction.

   a. interrupted event

   b. activity in progress

   c. cause and effect

   d. background info

7. My roommate was studying while I was reading.

   a. interrupted event

   b. simultaneous events

   c. habitual past

   d. sequential events

Choose the correct response to complete each conversation.

8. **A:** What time will you arrive tomorrow?

   B: _____

   a. I'm not sure. Probably late tonight.

   b. Yes, I'll be there by 10:00 A.M.

   c. The train arrives in Boston at 9:55 A.M.

   d. I will be arriving on Flight 472.

9. **A:** Where's Tanya?

   B: Look over there. _____

   a. Will you see her?

   c. Yes, she certainly is.

   b. She walks towards us.

   d. She's crossing the street.

10. **A:** Before I paid the bill, I complained to the manager.

    B: _____

    a. What did you complain about?

    c. Why did you pay first?

    b. Who did you complain to?

    d. What was he saying?

Change each statement into a question.

11. Her phone rang at 7:00.

    When _____

12. They watched the news last night.

    What _____

13. He lost 20 pounds on that diet.

    How many _____

Complete each sentence with the simple present form of the verb in parentheses. Use contractions when possible.

14. What _____ (usually/they/do) on Saturday night?

15. _____ (I/no/drink) coffee or tea because caffeine makes me jumpy.

16. _____ (you/feel) tired this morning?

17. Who _____ (know) Magda's new phone number? I need to call her.

Match the response to the statement or question below.

a. Sorry, I can't. I have to work.

d. I know. I'll work harder next semester.

b. No. If you need it, feel free to take it.

e. No, but I'll be reading it all weekend. I can't put it down!

c. Will you return this book for me? I'd really appreciate it.

f. I'll be studying for the college entrance exams.

_____ 18. Will you be using your car tomorrow?

_____ 19. If you're free, will you take me to the airport tomorrow?

_____ 20. What are your plans for the summer?

The Present Perfect

A. **GRAMMAR IN DISCOURSE: The Questions That Stump
    the Scientists** **78**

B. **FORM: The Present Perfect** **80**
    He's **done** research.

    Informally Speaking: Omitting *Have* and *You*

C. **MEANING AND USE 1: Indefinite Past Time** **85**

    Indefinite Past Time

    Adverbs Used with Indefinite Past Time

D. **MEANING AND USE 2: Recent Past Time and
    Continuing Time up to Now** **88**

    Recent Past Time

    Continuing Time up to Now

    Vocabulary Notes: Adverbs That Express Recent Past Time

E. **MEANING AND USE 3: Contrasting the Present
    Perfect and the Simple Past** **93**

    Continuing Time up to Now vs. Completed Actions

    Indefinite Past Time vs. Definite Past Time

    Just, Already*, and *Yet

    **Beyond the Sentence: Introducing Topics with the
    Present Perfect**

    WRITING: Write a Newspaper Article **98**

The Questions That Stump the Scientists

A1 Before You Read

Discuss these questions.

Can you name some important scientific discoveries that happened recently? Why are they important? Do you think there are some questions that scientists will never be able to answer? What are they?

A2 Read

CD1 T19 Read this magazine article to find out what problems scientists still hope to solve.

The Questions That Stump The Scientists

We've come to "the end of science," writer John Horgan declared recently, saying that scientists have already made all the really
5   important discoveries. With future jobs on their minds, worried young scientists quickly responded with lists of what they don't know. After all, somewhere between the big
10   unanswerable problems, like the meaning of life and the very specialized subjects of most doctoral theses, there must be some questions that are both important and
15   answerable. An informal survey of a variety of young scientists produced some topics that might be worthwhile to look at:

Memory: How does the human brain
20   store knowledge? The brain is a physical organ, so does this mean that memory has a physical part too? We haven't discovered it yet, but if we do, the results will be earthshaking.
25   Consider some possibilities: Will we be able to find certain memories in the brain, change them, or move them from person to person? And now ask yourself this question: How many new
30   technologies and terrifying possibilities from science fiction can you imagine?

Missing Matter: Physicists <u>have estimated</u> the total amount of material in the universe, but they've
35 observed only about 10 percent of it. Why can't they see the rest? For decades, they <u>have believed</u> that much of it is made up of an invisible substance known as dark matter.
40 Experts say they are close to proving its existence and solving the mystery of its composition, but the moment of truth still hasn't arrived.

Are We Alone? It's a simple yes or
45 no question. According to statistics, it's very likely that life has evolved elsewhere in the universe. However, we're still waiting for the first bit of convincing evidence of life
50 somewhere else.

Have we reached the end of scientific discovery? "No way," says one young scientist from the University of British Columbia.
55 Like most scientists, he cheerfully concludes that we've only just begun to make important discoveries. What do you think?

Adapted from *Newsweek*

---

doctoral theses: book-length papers written by university students to get advanced university degrees
matter: material that makes up the universe

physical: related to the body, not spiritual or mental
store: to collect and keep for later use
stump: to make someone unable to answer

A3 After You Read

Write *T* for true or *F* for false. Change the false statements to true ones.

_F_ **1.** John Horgan thinks we are just beginning to make important discoveries.

   John Horgan thinks that we've come to the end of science.

_____ **2.** Young scientists think there are still many questions to study.

_____ **3.** Scientists know everything about the human brain.

_____ **4.** Scientists can move memories from one person to another person.

_____ **5.** Physicists are able to observe the whole universe.

_____ **6.** Scientists think there is probably life elsewhere in the universe.

B FORM

The Present Perfect

Think Critically About Form

A. Look back at the article on page 78 and complete the tasks below.

1. **IDENTIFY** Two examples of the present perfect are underlined. Find seven more examples.
2. **ANALYZE** What are the two different forms of *have* in these examples? When is each one used?
3. **CATEGORIZE** Sort your examples into regular and irregular verbs. How do you know the difference?

B. Discuss your answers with the class and read the Form charts to check them.

ONLINE
PRACTICE

AFFIRMATIVE STATEMENTS		
SUBJECT + *HAVE*	PAST PARTICIPLE	
You**'ve**	**studied**	physics.
He**'s**	**done**	research.
They**'ve**	**found**	the answers.

NEGATIVE STATEMENTS			
SUBJECT	*HAVE* + *NOT*	PAST PARTICIPLE	
You	**haven't**	**studied**	physics.
He	**hasn't**	**done**	research.
They	**haven't**	**found**	the answers.

YES/NO QUESTIONS			
HAVE	SUBJECT	PAST PARTICIPLE	
Have	you	**studied**	physics?
Has	he	**done**	research?
Have	they	**found**	the answers?

SHORT ANSWERS					
AFFIRMATIVE			NEGATIVE		
Yes,	I	**have.**	**No,**	I	**haven't.**
	he	**has.**		he	**hasn't.**
	they	**have.**		they	**haven't.**

How much money have you spent?
How many times/have you been to Brazil?
How often

INFORMATION QUESTIONS				
WH- WORD	*HAVE*	SUBJECT	PAST PARTICIPLE	
Where	**has**	he	**studied**?	
How long	**have**	they	**done**	research?

WH- WORD + *HAVE*			PAST PARTICIPLE	
Who's			**studied**	the problem?
What's			**happened**	lately?

- The past participle of regular verbs is the same as the simple past form (verb + *-ed*). See Appendices 4 and 5 for spelling and pronunciation rules for verbs ending in *-ed*.
- Irregular verbs have special past participle forms. See Appendix 6 for irregular verbs and their past participles.
- See Appendix 14 for contractions with *have*.

Do not confuse the contraction of *is* with the contraction of *has* in the present perfect.

He's **doing** research. = He **is doing** research. (He's currently doing research.)

He's **done** research. = He **has done** research. (He did research at some time in the past.)

Do not repeat *have/has* when present perfect verb phrases are connected by *and* or *or*.

He **has washed** his face and **brushed** his teeth.

B1 Listening for Form

CD1 T20   **Listen to the sentences and choose the one that you hear.**

1. He's one of the racers. / He's won the race.

2. They called their senator. / They've called their senator.

3. Who's reading the book over there? / Who's read the book over there?

4. Where's the team playing this week? / Where's the team played this week?

5. She's worrying about her father. / She's worried about her father.

6. Who's going fishing? / Who's gone fishing?

7. You bought all of the equipment already. / You've bought all of the equipment already.

8. We looked up his telephone number. / We've looked up his telephone number.

B2 Identifying Past Participles

Choose the ten verb forms below each sentence that can correctly complete it.

1. I haven't _____ it.

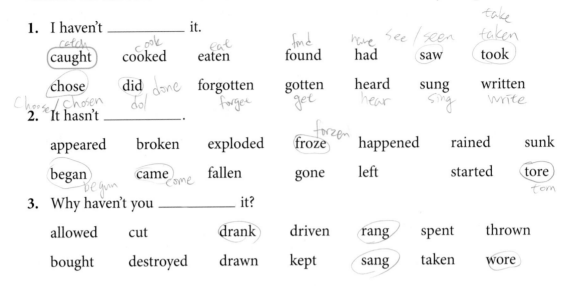

~~caught~~   cooked   eaten   found   had   saw   took

chose   did   forgotten   gotten   heard   sung   written

2. It hasn't _____.

appeared   broken   exploded   froze   happened   rained   sunk

began   came   fallen   gone   left   started   tore

3. Why haven't you _____ it?

allowed   cut   drank   driven   rang   spent   thrown

bought   destroyed   drawn   kept   sang   taken   wore

B3 Building Present Perfect Sentences

Build as many meaningful sentences as possible. Use an item from each column. Punctuate your sentences correctly.

I have arrived early.

I she it have	have hasn't you	arrived early snowed a lot melted quickly been sick forgotten your umbrella bought herself anything

B4 Completing Conversations with the Present Perfect

Complete these conversations with the words in parentheses and the present perfect. Use contractions when possible. Then practice the conversations with a partner.

Conversation 1

A: _Have you eaten_ (you/eat) in the new cafeteria yet?
        1

B: No, but I _____ (hear) that it's very good and very fast. It seems that
             2

the dean finally _____ (begin) to understand that most students
             3

don't have time for long lunch breaks.

Conversation 2

A: How long _____ (Tom/be) married?
             1

B: He _____ (be) married for only a year, but he and his wife
        2

_____ (know) each other since they were in college.
        3

Conversation 3

A: I _____ (not/send) my parents any email for a week. They probably
      1

think that something terrible _____ (happen) to me.
             2

B: I'm surprised that they _____ (not/call) or _____
             3   4

(write) you.

Conversation 4

A: We had a long list of things to do. What _____ (we/do) so far?
             1

B: Well, we _____ (make) a lot of progress. So far, I
        2

_____ (do) the laundry, you _____ (sweep) the
      3   4

kitchen, and Eric _____ (buy) the groceries. But we still
             5

_____ (not/take) the clothes to the cleaners.
      6

Informally Speaking

Omitting *Have* and *You*

CD1 T21 Look at the cartoon and listen to the conversation. How is the underlined form in the cartoon different from what you hear?

Have you seen any good movies lately?

Yes, as a matter of fact. Last night I saw that new Japanese movie.

In very informal speech, *have* and *has* are often omitted from questions. The subject *you* may also be omitted if it is clear from the context.

Standard Form	What You Might Hear
Has she **been** here already?	"She been here already?"
Have you **talked** to your brother lately?	"(You) talked to your brother lately?"

B5 Understanding Informal Speech

CD1 T22 Listen and write the standard form of the words you hear.

1. _Have you heard_ any good jokes lately?

2. _____ your vacation yet?

3. _____ to the beach yet this summer?

4. _____ at that new restaurant yet?

5. _____ yet?

6. _____ my keys?

7. _____ any programming?

8. _____ you lately?

Indefinite Past Time

Think Critically About Meaning and Use

A. Read the sentences and answer the questions below.

   a. I've traveled to Spain and Italy.   **b.** I traveled to Spain and Italy in July.

   1. ANALYZE Which sentence talks about a definite period of time in the past?

   2. DIFFERENTIATE In which sentence does the time seem less definite or less important?

B. Discuss your answers with the class and read the Meaning and Use Notes to check them.

Meaning and Use Notes

ONLINE PRACTICE

	Indefinite Past Time
▶ **1A**	The present perfect often expresses an action or state that happened at an indefinite time in the past. It does not express a definite time in the past; the action happened at any time up to the present.

I**'ve read** that book. It's fascinating. **x** I've read that book ~~a week ago~~. (INCORRECT)

What **have** we **learned** about life? **x** What have we learned about life last year? (INCORRECT)

▶ **1B**	The action or state may occur only once or may be repeated several times.

Ed **has been** to the exhibit <u>once</u>, but Al **has been** there <u>many times</u>.

	Adverbs Used with Indefinite Past Time
▶ **2A**	Adverbs such as *already*, *yet*, *still*, *so far*, *ever*, and *never* are frequently used with the present perfect to express the connection between the past and the present.

We**'ve** <u>already</u> **eaten.** *already*   They <u>still</u> **haven't finished.**

They **haven't found** the answers <u>yet</u>.   <u>So far</u>, I**'ve visited** 16 countries.

will do in future

▶ **2B**	Use *ever* to ask if an event took place at any time in the past. Only use negative forms of *ever* (*not ever*, *never*) in statements (not in questions).

A: **Have** you <u>ever</u> **taken** a psychology course?

B: I**'ve read** a few popular psychology books, but I**'ve** <u>never</u> actually **taken** a course.
(I haven't ever)

C1 Listening for Meaning and Use

🔊 CD1 T23 Listen and choose the best answer for each question.

1. a. Yes, I have.
    b. Twice. *(circled)*
    c. No, it hasn't.

2. a. Yes, several times.
    b. Here's one.
    c. No, she hasn't.

3. a. No, I haven't.
    b. She's coming soon.
    c. Yes, it has.

4. a. Not now.
    b. Yes, it has.
    c. Not yet.

5. a. No, never.
    b. No, she hasn't.
    c. No, I haven't.

6. a. No, not yet.
    b. Everything, except the laundry.
    c. I've already done it.

C2 Talking About Life Experiences with *Ever*

▶ Note 2B

A. Work with a partner. Take turns asking and answering questions about your life experiences. Make questions with the expressions below and the present perfect with *ever*. Respond with a present perfect short answer and *Have you*?

1. have a flat tire

    A: *Have you ever had a flat tire?*
    B: *Yes, I have. Have you?* OR *No, I haven't. Have you?*

2. missed a flight

    Have you ever fallen in love?

3. lose your wallet

4. run out of gas

    Has your teacher ever given you lots of HW?

5. tell a lie

6. meet a famous person

7. see a comet

8. ride a motorcycle

B. Follow these steps to ask your classmates about their life experiences.

1. Make up five questions with *Have you ever* to ask your classmates.

2. Move around the classroom and ask different classmates the questions. Return to your seat and tell the class what you have learned.

    I'm going to tell you about Paula. She has flown an airplane and…

C3 Making Up Reminders with Indefinite Past Time ▶ Notes 1A, 2A

A. List three or four things you need to do to prepare for each of these situations.

1. You are going to go to the supermarket.

check the refrigerator, make a shopping list,…

2. You have your first job interview tomorrow.

3. You have just picked out a used car to buy.

4. You are going to the park for a picnic.

B. Work with a partner. Exchange lists and take turns. Use your partner's lists to make up reminders. Ask about what has been done for each situation. Use the present perfect and adverbs where appropriate.

Have you checked the refrigerator yet?
Have you packed the picnic lunch already?

C. Take turns asking and answering the questions on your lists. Reply using short answers.

A: Have you checked the refrigerator yet?
B: Yes, I have. OR No, I haven't. I'll do it tomorrow.

C4 Writing About Accomplishments and Progress ▶ Notes 1A, 1B, 2A

A. Choose an activity that you have already started planning (for example, a family reunion). Write sentences about your progress using the suggested adverbs and the present perfect. Then tell a partner about your progress.

1. Name three things that you've accomplished. Use *so far* or *already* in each sentence.

So far, I've made a list of the guests. OR
I've already made a list of the guests.

2. Name three things you still need to do. Use *still* or *yet*.

I still haven't invited the guests. OR
I haven't invited the guests yet.

B. Write a paragraph using your ideas from part A.

I am planning a family reunion for my grandmother's 80th birthday. So far, I have made a list of the guests, but I haven't invited them yet. I still haven't bought the invitations…

D | MEANING AND USE 2

Recent Past Time and Continuing Time up to Now

⚙ Think Critically About Meaning and Use

A. Read the sentences and answer the questions below.

a. I've worked for a publishing company. ~worked~ *important*
b. I've (recently) worked for a publishing company.
c. I've worked for a publishing company (for) two years.

1. **EVALUATE** Which sentence suggests that the speaker is still working for the publishing company? *c*

2. **EVALUATE** Which sentences suggest that the speaker doesn't work for the company anymore? *a + b*

3. **EVALUATE** Which sentence refers to the recent past? *b*
   recently past not now

B. Discuss your answers with the class and read the Meaning and Use Notes to check them.

Meaning and Use Notes

ONLINE PRACTICE

Recent Past Time

▶ **1** The present perfect often describes recent past actions and experiences, especially when their results are important in the present. Adverbs like *lately*, *recently*, and *just* emphasize this meaning of recent past time. (See the Vocabulary Notes on page 91 for more information about these adverbs.)

Conversations

A: Where**'s** your sister **been** lately?
   I **haven't seen** her.

B: She **hasn't been** home very much
   recently. She's busy looking for a job.

Announcements

Flight 602 from Miami **has landed** at Gate 4.

News Broadcasts

We've just learned that the mayor **has resigned**.
soon before now

Telephone Recordings

The number you **have dialed**
   is busy.

Conclusions

(The doorbell is ringing.)
   I think the guests
   have (just) **arrived**.

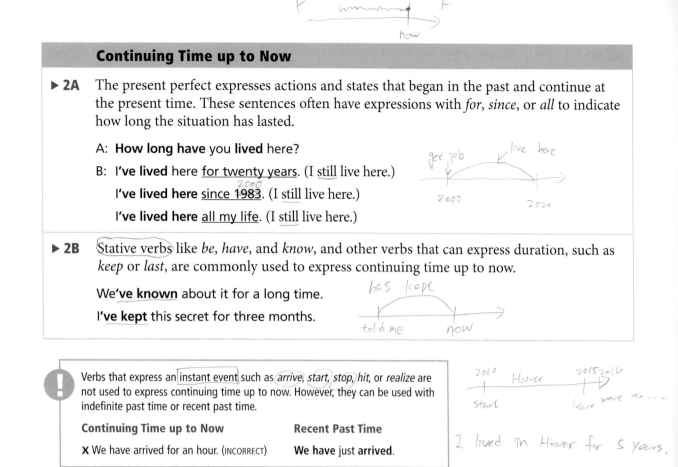

Continuing Time up to Now

▶ **2A** The present perfect expresses actions and states that began in the past and continue at the present time. These sentences often have expressions with *for*, *since*, or *all* to indicate how long the situation has lasted.

   A: **How long have** you **lived** here?

   B: **I've lived** here <u>for twenty years</u>. (I <u>still</u> live here.)

      I've lived here <u>since 1983</u>. (I <u>still</u> live here.)

      I've lived here <u>all my life</u>. (I <u>still</u> live here.)

▶ **2B** Stative verbs like *be*, *have*, and *know*, and other verbs that can express duration, such as *keep* or *last*, are commonly used to express continuing time up to now.

   We**'ve known** about it for a long time.

   I**'ve kept** this secret for three months.

! Verbs that express an instant event such as *arrive*, *start*, *stop*, *hit*, or *realize* are not used to express continuing time up to now. However, they can be used with indefinite past time or recent past time.

Continuing Time up to Now	**Recent Past Time**
X We have arrived for an hour. (INCORRECT)	We have just arrived.

D1 Listening for Meaning and Use

▶ Notes 1, 2A

CD1 T24   A. Listen to each sentence. Does the sentence express recent past time or continuing time up to now? Check (✓) the correct column.

	RECENT PAST TIME	CONTINUING TIME UP TO NOW
1.	✓	
2.		
3.		
4.		
5.		
6.		

(Continued on page 90)

CD1 T25 **B.** Listen to each situation and the question that follows it. Choose the correct answer to the question.

1. **a.** 10:00 A.M.
   b. 1:00 P.M.
   c. 11:00 A.M.
   d. 4:00 P.M.

2. **a.** All day.
   b. Since 5:00 P.M.
   c. This morning.
   d. For four hours.

3. **a.** 1:00 P.M.
   b. 3:30 P.M.
   c. 3:00 P.M.
   d. 2:00 P.M.

4. **a.** Since midnight.
   b. For three hours.
   c. For nine hours.
   d. For fifteen hours.

D2 Talking About Continuing Time up to Now ▶ Notes 2A, 2B

Work in groups of three. Switch roles for each phrase. When you are finished, think of two more phrases to ask about.

Student A: Ask a question using *how long* and a phrase below.

Students B and C: Answer using *for, all,* or *since.*

1. be in this room

   A: *How long have you been in this room?*
   B: *I've been in this room for ten minutes.*
   C: *I've been in this room all morning.*

2. know how to speak English

3. have your driver's license

4. own this book

5. be a student

6. live in your apartment / house / dorm

7. know the students in this class

8. own your car / bicycle

9. know how to use a computer

10. be in this city

She has just gotten married.
Recently, she has gotten pregnant.
She has losted weight lately.

She has just taken another apple.
Recently, she has learned how to walk.
Lately, she has stolen many apples.

He has just gotten the diploma.
He has submited his paper recently.
He has earned all credits lately.

He has just charred the food.
Recently, he has bought the steak.
Lately, he has learned how to cook.

He has just bought the food.
He has taken his salary recently.
He has driven to market lately.

Alphabet Sounds & Relative Vowels

Listen. Mark the column for the word that is different. The word that is different has a relative vowel sound.

	X	Y	Z	
1.		✓		1. add
2.		✓		2. this
3.			✓	3. less
4.			✓	4. bed
5.			✓	5. till
6.		✓		6. pin
7.	✓			7. chess
8.	`		✓	8. bit

Clear Speech, 4th edition. Gilbert, J. Cambridge University Press. Unit 2 p. 13 Act. J

Contrasting the Present Perfect and the Simple Past

Think Critically About Meaning and Use

A. Read the sentences and answer the questions below.

1a. I've worked in Los Angeles for three years. I love my job.
1b. I worked in Los Angeles for three years. I loved my job.
2a. When did you see the movie *Titanic*?
2b. Have you seen the movie *Titanic*? *focus on ACTION*

1. **ANALYZE** Compare 1a and 1b. In which sentence does the speaker still work in Los Angeles? How do you know?

2. **ANALYZE** Compare 2a and 2b. Which sentence asks about the time of a past event? Which sentence does not ask about the time of a past event?

B. Discuss your answers with the class and read the Meaning and Use Notes to check them.

Meaning and Use Notes

ONLINE PRACTICE

Continuing Time up to Now vs. Completed Actions

▶ **1** The present perfect can express situations that continue at the present time, but the simple past can only express situations that are completed. The simple past can be used to talk about historical events, whereas the present perfect cannot.

Present Perfect	**Simple Past**
She's **been** slender all her life. (She is still alive and still slender.)	She **was** slender all her life. (She is no longer alive.)
I've **worked** there for ten years. (I still work there.)	I **worked** there for ten years. (I don't work there anymore.)
x Alexander Graham Bell has invented the telephone. (INCORRECT)	Alexander Graham Bell **invented** the telephone over 100 years ago.

(Continued on page 94)

P _____ met know I _____ now

for , since , all my life

* How long ... ?

Indefinite Past Time vs. Definite Past Time

▶ 2   Because present perfect sentences do not indicate a definite time, use the present perfect only to talk about an indefinite time. Use the simple past to talk about a definite time.

Present Perfect **(Indefinite Past Time)**	**Simple Past** **(Definite Past Time)**
Have you **visited** Maria lately?	**When did** you **visit** Maria?

Just, Already, and *Yet*

▶ 3   It is common to use *just*, *already*, and *yet* with the simple past. The following sentences have the same meaning.

Present Perfect	**Simple Past**
A: You should call Jada. B: I**'ve just called** her.	A: You should call Jada. B: I **just called** her.
A: Don't forget to buy some milk. B: I**'ve already bought** some.	A: Don't forget to buy some milk. B: I **already bought** some.
A: **Have** you **eaten yet**? B: No, not yet.	A: **Did** you **eat yet**? B: No, not yet.

E1 Listening for Meaning and Use

▶ Note 1

CD1 T26   Listen to each situation and choose the sentence you hear. Pay attention to the second sentence in each situation to help you understand the context.

1. **a.** I've lived there for a year.
   (b.) I lived there for a year.

2. **a.** We've worked with him for six months.
   b. We worked with him for six months.

3. **a.** He's kept the secret all week.
   b. He kept the secret all week.

4. **a.** She's studied physics for two years.
   b. She studied physics for two years.

5. **a.** I've had a parrot for a long time.
   b. I had a parrot for a long time.

6. **a.** I've owned a car for years.
   b. I owned a car for years.

7. **a.** They've worked there for three years.
   b. They worked there for three years.

8. **a.** I've played the piano for years.
   b. I played the piano for years.

E2 Choosing the Simple Past or the Present Perfect ▶ Notes 1, 2

Choose the simple past or present perfect forms that best complete the conversation.

Jeff: How long (have you had / did you have) this computer?

Kim: Let's see. (I've bought / I bought) it when (I've moved / I moved) here, so (I've owned / I owned) it for a long time.

Jeff: Well, (I've had / I had) mine for two years, and it already seems to be outdated. (It's been / It was) very slow lately. Do you think it needs more memory?

Kim: I don't know. (Have you called / Did you call) Janet lately? She knows everything about this stuff. (She's worked / She worked) for Computing World since (she's graduated / she graduated).

Jeff: Well, actually, I have tried to reach her. (I've phoned / I phoned) her last night, but (she was / she's been) out for the evening.

Kim: What about your roommate? (Hasn't he taken / Didn't he take) all kinds of engineering and computing courses last year?

Jeff: Yeah, but he doesn't know much about personal computing. Anyway, (he's left / he left) town yesterday because his uncle (has died / died) suddenly on Monday. (He lived / He's lived) with his uncle for two years. They were very close.

Kim: Oh, I'm sorry to hear that. Why don't you call the Computer Center on campus? (They were / They have been) very helpful last week when I called them.

Jeff: That's a good idea.

E3 Asking for Information

▶ Note 3

Work with a partner. Take turns as Student A and Student B. Imagine today is the town festival.

Student A: Ask about the festival events using the words in parentheses.
Student B: Answer the questions using the schedule.

GALESBURG TOWN FESTIVAL SCHEDULE

12:00–12:30	Welcome Speech by Mayor Ferrara
12:30–1:00	Jerry's Juggling Show
1:00–1:30	The Melodians Barbershop Quartet
1:30–2:00	Storytellers
2:00–2:30	Three-legged Race
2:30–3:00	Pie-eating Contest
3:00–3:30	Line Dancers from Green Apple Ranch
3:30–4:00	Folk-Dancing Club: Dances from Around the World
4:00–4:30	Jazz from the Blues Men
4:30–7:30	Picnic Dinner
7:30–8:00	Request-a-Song Sing-Along
8:00–8:45	Fireworks

1. It's 2:00 P.M. (the juggler/perform)

   A: *Has the juggler already performed?*   OR   A: *Did the juggler perform already?*
   B: *Yes, he has. He finished an hour ago.*   B: *Yes, he did. He finished an hour ago.*

2. It's 3:00 P.M. (the jazz band/play)

   A: *Has the jazz band played yet?*   OR   A: *Did the jazz band play yet?*
   B: *No, they haven't. They play at four.*   B: *No, they didn't. They play at four.*

3. It's 11:00 A.M. (the mayor/speak)

4. It's 5:00 P.M. (the picnic/start)

5. It's 7:00 P.M. (the fireworks/begin)

6. It's 3:00 P.M. (the three-legged race/happen)

7. It's 3:45 P.M. (the pie-eating contest/end)

8. It's 2:00 P.M. (The Melodians/sing)

9. It's 6:00 P.M. (the sing-along/take place)

10. It's 4:10 P.M. (the line dancers/perform)

Beyond the Sentence

Introducing Topics with the Present Perfect

The present perfect has a special introductory use in larger contexts. It is often used at the beginning of a written text (or conversation) to introduce a general idea with indefinite past time. The text often continues with the simple past to give more specific details about the general idea.

A Newspaper Article

For the second time in two weeks, an inmate **has escaped** from the local prison. Last night at 2:00 A.M., several guards **heard** strange noises coming from an underground tunnel. An investigation **revealed**...

E4 Introducing Topics with the Present Perfect

A. **Read each present perfect introductory sentence. Then write a sentence in the simple past that adds a detail. Tell when the particular experience happened.**

1. Computers have helped me a lot with my schoolwork. For example,

   I did all my assignments on a computer last semester.

2. There have been several disasters in recent years. For example,

   _____

3. I've made many mistakes in my life. For example,

   _____

4. There have been many changes in my country/town/family lately.

   For example, _____

5. I've learned a lot of important things in recent years. For example,

   _____

6. I've taken long trips by bus/train/car. For example,

   _____

B. **Write a paragraph. Choose one of the six items in part A as the beginning of your paragraph. Use the simple past to develop specific examples and details.**

   Computers have helped me a lot with my schoolwork. For example, I did all my assignments on a computer last semester. I was able to type and edit my work quickly. Most importantly, I found a lot of useful information on the Internet without leaving home.

Think Critically About Meaning and Use

A. Read each sentence and the statements that follow. Write *T* if the statement is true, *F* if it is false, or *?* if you do not have enough information to decide.

1. I've studied Russian.

    _F_ **a.** I'm still studying Russian.

    _T_ **b.** I studied Russian at some time in the past.

2. I haven't eaten breakfast this morning.

    _____ **a.** It's still morning.

    _____ **b.** I'm going to eat breakfast.

3. I've worked there for many years.

    _____ **a.** I don't work there anymore.

    _____ **b.** I'm changing jobs next week.

4. I still haven't visited the exhibit.

    _____ **a.** I didn't visit the exhibit.

    _____ **b.** I expect to visit the exhibit.

5. I've owned a house.

    _____ **a.** I still own a house.

    _____ **b.** I bought a house some time in the past.

6. I've had this cold for two weeks already.

    _____ **a.** I don't have this cold anymore.

    _____ **b.** I caught this cold two weeks ago.

7. I lived there for two years.

    _____ **a.** I still live there.

    _____ **b.** I moved two years ago.

8. I've already finished my work.

    _____ **a.** I finished sooner than expected.

    _____ **b.** I finished it a few minutes ago.

Edit

Find the errors in this newspaper article and correct them.

Hubble Celebrates 20 Years in Orbit

CAPE KENNEDY, April 22, 2010—Since 1993, the Hubble Space Telescope has ~~provide~~ *provided*

us with extraordinary pictures of the universe. It has shown us new comets and black

holes. It is found exploding stars. Astronomers have been amazed that the Hubble

Space Telescope have sent back so many spectacular images. But it hasn't always been

this way. The Hubble Space Telescope was actually been in space since 1990. However,

for the first three years, there was a problem with the main mirror. The pictures that it

sent back to earth were not at all clear. In 1993, two astronauts have fixed the problem.

They took a space walk and dropped a special lens over the mirror. Since then, four

other servicing missions helped to upgrade the telescope's scientific instruments and

operational systems. The last of these has been in May of 2009.

Today the world celebrates

Hubble's 20 years in orbit. Its images

have delighted and amazing people

around the world and its many

discoveries have help to advance our

understanding of the universe.

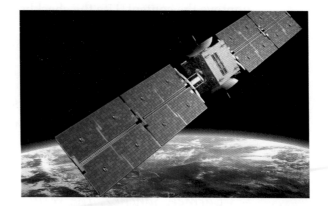

Write

Imagine you are a reporter. Write an article about a recent event or development in your community or country. Use the present perfect and other past, present, and future forms where appropriate.

1. **BRAINSTORM** Think about all the details you might want to include. Use these categories to help you organize your ideas into paragraphs:
   - **Introduce the event:** What has happened? What have one or more people said about the event or development?
   - **Describe the background:** What were things like before the event or development? What happened to bring it about?
   - **Analyze the significance:** Why is the event or development important? How is it affecting people at the current time? What impact will it have on the future?

2. **WRITE A FIRST DRAFT** Before you write your first draft, read the checklist below and look at the example on page 99. Write your draft using the present perfect.

3. **EDIT** Read your work and check it against the checklist below. Circle grammar, spelling, and punctuation errors.

DO I ...	YES
organize my ideas into two or three paragraphs?	☐
use the present perfect to introduce the topic?	☐
use the present perfect for indefinite past time, recent past time, and continuing time up to now?	☐
use the simple past to talk about completed actions and definite past time?	☐
use present and future forms, as needed, to discuss the short- and long-term effects?	☐

4. **PEER REVIEW** Work with a partner to help you decide how to fix your errors and improve the content. Use the checklist above.

5. **REWRITE YOUR DRAFT** Using the comments from your partner, write a final draft.

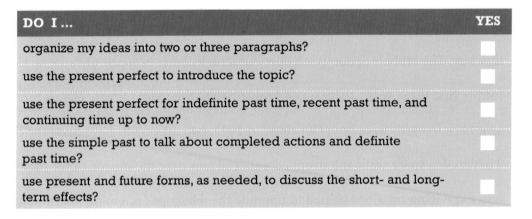

TUTORING PROGRAM A GREAT SUCCESS
For the past five years, secondary schools in our area have conducted a voluntary after-school teen-to-teen tutoring program, and up to now, according to School Superintendent Carmen Sanchez, the results have been amazing...

CHAPTER

5

The Present Perfect Continuous

A. **GRAMMAR IN DISCOURSE: Longer Life in Blue Zones** 102

B. **FORM: The Present Perfect Continuous** 104
   She **has been getting** better.

   Informally Speaking: Omitting *Have*

C. **MEANING AND USE 1: Focus on Continuing or Recent Past Activities** 109

   Focus on Continuing Activities up to Now

   Focus on Recent Past Activities

   Common Uses of the Present Perfect Continuous

D. **MEANING AND USE 2: Contrasting the Present Perfect Continuous and the Present Perfect** 113

   Similar Meanings with Continuing Time up to Now

   Completed vs. Continuing or Recent Past Activities

   Beyond the Sentence: Connecting the Past and the Present in Discourse

   WRITING: Write a Letter to the Editor 118

Longer Life in Blue Zones

A1 Before You Read

Discuss these questions.

Do you look forward to old age? Why or why not? What are some things that people do in order to live longer and stay healthier?

A2 Read

CD1 T27 Read this book review to find out why people in some parts of the world are living longer and healthier lives than the rest of us.

http://www.read-a-lot.us

Longer Life in the Blue Zones

Since 2004, explorer and writer Dan Buettner has been traveling the world with some of the world's best longevity researchers in hopes of identifying the factors that contribute to people leading long healthy lives. The nonagenarians and
5   centenarians he's met and the lessons he's learned from them are at the heart of his best-selling book, *The Blue Zones: Lessons for Living Longer From the People Who've Lived the Longest*.

Here are a few of the amazing people whose stories he tells:

10   One-hundred-year-old Panchita from the Nicoya Peninsula of Costa Rica has been chopping wood and making tortillas by hand every day for as long as she can remember.

Giovanni has spent most of his 103 years walking the rocky mountains of Sardinia as a shepherd. He has also been arm-wrestling for most of that time and hardly ever loses a match.

One-hundred-three-year-old Marge of Loma Linda, California, lifts weights every day and rides an exercise
15   bike for seven or eight miles at a rate of 25 miles per hour. Since her husband passed away after 77 years of marriage, she's been doing volunteer work for no less than seven organizations.

Ushi, from the village of Ogimi on the island of Okinawa in Japan, has been farming her family's land for most of her 104 years. In the afternoons she and Setzu Taira, her 90-year-old friend, bag oranges at a roadside market. They haven't been working there long, but Ushi says her job is one of the things that
20   provides her with *ikigai*, a sense of purpose in life. Her relationships with family and friends are another.

What do Panchita, Giovanni, Marge, and Ushi all have in common? The answer is simple. For their entire lives, they have been living in places that population scientists call Blue Zones—areas of the world where an unusually high percentage of the population live active, healthy lives past the age of 100.

Just how high is unusually high? Well, consider this. Experts estimate that in the United States there are
25 about 10–20 centenarians per 100,000 people. In Okinawa, the ratio is 50 per 100,000, probably the highest in the world. And in general, people in Blue Zones tend to live 10 years longer and experience a sixth the rate of heart disease, a fifth the rate of major cancers, and a third the rate of dementia than people who live elsewhere.

So what are the factors that contribute to greater longevity in the four Blue Zones? People who live in
30 all of these places share specific lifestyle habits that he calls the "Power 9." Among them: walking and getting regular exercise through activities of daily living, having a sense of purpose in life, eating wisely, making time to "de-stress" and relax on a daily basis, and enjoying strong, lifelong ties to one's family and community.

The Blue Zones is a must read for anyone who has ever asked: What can I do to maximize my chances of
35 leading a long, healthy life? Buettner's well-written book offers insight into how making small changes in our lifestyles might add years to our lives.

---

centenarians: people over 100 years old
dementia: medical condition characterized by loss of memory and a decline in mental ability
factors: elements that influence a particular result

longevity: long life
nonagenarians: people between 90 and 99 years old
passed away: died

A3 After You Read

Complete these sentences with appropriate words.

1. The oldest person mentioned in the book review is from _____.

2. _____ recently got a part-time job at a roadside market.

3. Panchita gets her daily exercise by _____.

4. People who live in Blue Zones have lower rates of _____, cancer, and dementia than people from other places around the globe.

5. The Blue Zones covered in Buettner's book are the Nicoya Peninsula of Costa Rica, Sardinia, Loma Linda in California, and the island of _____ in Japan.

6. If you read the book, you will learn about Blue Zone lifestyle habits that Buettner refers to as the _____.

B FORM

The Present Perfect Continuous

⚙ **Think Critically About Form**

A. Look back at the book review on page 102 and complete the tasks below.

1. **IDENTIFY** An affirmative example of the present perfect continuous is underlined. Find five more affirmative examples and one negative example.

2. **RECOGNIZE** How many auxiliaries are there in each example? What ending is added to the main verb? Where is *not* placed in negative forms?

3. **ANALYZE** What are the two forms of *have* in your examples? When is each one used?

B. Discuss your answers with the class and read the Form charts to check them.

ONLINE PRACTICE

AFFIRMATIVE STATEMENTS				
SUBJECT	*HAVE*	*BEEN*	VERB + *-ING*	
I	**have**			
She	**has**	**been**	**working**	there.
They	**have**			

NEGATIVE STATEMENTS					
SUBJECT	*HAVE*	*NOT*	*BEEN*	VERB + *-ING*	
I	**have**				
She	**has**	**not**	**been**	**working**	there.
They	**have**				

YES/NO QUESTIONS				
HAVE	SUBJECT	*BEEN*	VERB + *-ING*	
Have	you			
Has	she	**been**	**working**	there?
Have	they			

SHORT ANSWERS					
YES	SUBJECT	*HAVE*	*NO*	SUBJECT	*HAVE + NOT*
	I	**have**.		I	**haven't**.
Yes,	she	**has**.	**No**,	she	**hasn't**.
	they	**have**.		they	**haven't**.

INFORMATION QUESTIONS					
WH- WORD	*HAVE*	**SUBJECT**	*BEEN*	**VERB + -*ING*	
Who	**have**	you	**been**	**talking**	to?
How	**has**	she		**doing**?	

WH- WORD	*HAVE*		*BEEN*	**VERB + -*ING*	
What	**has**		**been**	**happening**?	
Who				**calling**	you?

- The present perfect continuous has two auxiliary verbs: *have* and *been*. Only *have* and *has* form contractions.
- Verbs with stative meanings are not usually used with the present perfect continuous.

    x I have been knowing her. (INCORRECT)

- See Appendix 3 for spelling rules for verbs ending in *-ing*.
- See Appendix 14 for contractions with *have*.

B1 Listening for Form

CD1 T28   Listen to the sentences and choose the one you hear.

1. **a.** What's been happening this week?

    b. What's happening this week?

2. **a.** Jack has been visiting his grandparents.

    b. Jack has visited his grandparents.

3. **a.** It's rained all day.

    b. It's been raining all day.

4. **a.** They've been living in Florida.

    b. They're living in Florida.

5. **a.** He's been sleeping on the sofa.

    b. He's sleeping on the sofa.

6. **a.** She's been exercising at the gym.

    b. She's exercising at the gym.

B2 Completing Conversations with the Present Perfect Continuous

 Work with a partner. Complete these conversations with the words in parentheses and the present perfect continuous. Use contractions when possible. Then practice the conversations.

Conversation 1

A: What's wrong?

B: I _____'ve been trying_____ (try) to call the doctor for an hour, but the line is
1
still busy.

A: It's not an emergency, is it?

B: No, but I _____ (not/feel) well, and I'm starting to worry.
2

A: You do look tired. _____ (you/get) enough sleep?
3

B: Well, no, I really _____ (not/sleep) very well.
4

Conversation 2

A: I _____ (not/go) to the movies at all this summer.
1

B: Why not?

A: I _____ (help) my parents almost every weekend.
2

We _____ (pack up) their house because they're
3

going to retire to Arizona next month. The house is very large, so it

_____ (take) a lot of my time.
4

Conversation 3

A: We normally don't get any homework in this course, but lately the

instructor _____ (give) us an hour or two each night.
1

B: Maybe you _____ (not/make) enough progress, or maybe
2

the material _____ (get) more difficult.
3

Conversation 4

A: You look wonderful. What _____ (you/do)?
1

B: I _____ (exercise) a lot at the gym, and I
2

_____ (not/eat) junk food.
3

B3 Unscrambling Questions

 A. Work with a partner. Reorder the words to form a question in the present perfect continuous. Make sure you use every word and correct punctuation.

1. you/how/been/have/lately/feeling

   How have you been feeling lately?

2. who/you/writing to/have/lately/been

3. recently/sleeping/you/well/have/been

4. been/you/working/semester/hard/this/have

5. enough/lately/you/exercising/been/have

6. time/what/recently/getting up/have/you/been

7. doing/you/what/in/the/been/have/evening

8. been/have/where/semester/you/eating/this/lunch

B. Now take turns asking and answering the questions. Respond to each question and then ask *What about you?*

A: *How have you been feeling lately?*

B: *I've been feeling fine. What about you?*

A: *I've been feeling great.*

B4 Writing Your Own Sentences

Use these verbs or your own to write two responses for each sentence below.

daydream	read	stand	talk	work
listen	sit	study	think	write

1. Describe something you have been doing since you came to class.

   I've been sitting in the back of the room. I've been…

2. Describe something you haven't been doing since you came to class.

3. Describe what two people in your class have been doing since they came to class.

4. Make questions about what your classmates have been doing since they came to class.

Omitting *Have*

CD1 T29 Look at the cartoon and listen to the conversation. How is each underlined form in the cartoon different from what you hear?

> Have you been going to the study sessions?

> No. I've been writing my English paper all week. It's due tomorrow.

In informal speech, some speakers may omit *have*. Other speakers may say *have* very quickly so that it is difficult to hear. This happens most often in statements with *I* and in questions with *you*. Notice that the subject *you* may also be omitted if it is clear from the context.

Standard Form	What You Might Hear
I **have been** studying so hard.	"I been studying so hard."
Have you **been doing** the homework lately?	"(You) been doing the homework lately?"

B5 Understanding Informal Speech

CD1 T30 Listen and write the standard form of the words you hear.

1. **A:** _What have you been doing_ all day?

2. **B:** _____ my friend.

3. **A:** _____ OK?

4. **B:** No, _____ some problems with my back.

5. **A:** _____ at all?

6. **B:** _____ a lot.

C

Focus on Continuing or Recent Past Activities

Think Critically About Meaning and Use

A. Read the sentences and answer the questions below.

  a. Look at this library book. Someone has been writing all over it.
  b. She's been trying to find information on the Internet, and she's still searching for it.
  c. Look. It's finally done! I've been knitting this sweater for months.

  1. ANALYZE Which sentence focuses on an activity that began in the past and is continuing into the present? b

  2. ANALYZE Which sentence is used to reach a conclusion about a current situation? a

  3. ANALYZE Which sentence expresses an activity that was in progress but just ended? c

B. Discuss your answers with the class and read the Meaning and Use Notes to check them.

Meaning and Use Notes

ONLINE PRACTICE

Focus on Continuing Activities up to Now

▶ **1** The present perfect continuous most often describes activities that began in the past and are continuing at the present time. The present perfect continuous emphasizes that the activity is ongoing. This meaning can be understood in context, but time expressions with *for* and *since* often help to show continuing time up to now.

I've been reading that novel, too. It's so good. (I'm still reading it.)

I've been writing this letter <u>since four o'clock</u>. (I'm still writing it.)

<u>For the past several years</u>, she**'s been knitting** a pair of mittens every day.
    (She's still knitting a pair every day.)

(Continued on page 110)

[handwritten: In progress and maybe just ended]

Focus on Continuing Activities up to Now

▶ **2** The present perfect continuous also describes recent situations or activities that were in progress, but have just ended. To emphasize the recent past, adverbs like *recently*, *just*, and *lately* may be used with the present perfect continuous.

I've been thinking about you <u>recently</u>.

I've <u>just</u> **been reading** the most wonderful book.

What **have** you **been doing** <u>lately</u>?

[handwritten: ___ have you been ___ ing lately?]
[handwritten: What]
[handwritten: How]
[handwritten: What book]

Common Uses of the Present Perfect Continuous

▶ **3** The present perfect continuous is frequently used to make an excuse along with an apology. It is also often used to reach a conclusion about a current situation.

An Excuse: I'm sorry I haven't called you. I **haven't been feeling** well lately.

A Conclusion: Half of my cake is gone. Someone **has been eating** it!

C1 Listening for Meaning and Use

▶ Notes 1–3

🔊 CD1 T31 Listen to the conversations between Max and Helen. Check (✓) the correct column to answer each question.

		MAX	HELEN
1.	Who is reading a John Grisham novel?	✓	
2.	Who is no longer sick?		
3.	Who still volunteers at a hospital?		
4.	Who has been to Chicago more than once this year?		
5.	Who has tried to call Eddie more recently?		
6.	Who is playing chess these days?		

C2 Making Apologies and Excuses

▶ Note 3

Work with a partner. Use the present perfect continuous to make excuses for your behavior. Begin with an apology. Then practice the conversations.

1. **A:** What's the matter? You're not listening to me.

   B: *I'm sorry. I've been thinking about something else.*

2. A: You're really late. What took you so long?

B: Sorry, I have been sitting in a traffic jam. for 2 hours.

3. A: I thought we were going to the movies sometime this week.

B: Sorry, I have been studying for a test. since Tuesday.

4. A: You never come home right after school anymore. What's going on?

B: Sorry, I have been studying in the library (after hours) (since last week.)

5. A: Is something wrong? You keep looking out the window.

B: Sorry, I have been looking at the hot girl (for 30 minutes.)

6. A: It was your turn to go grocery shopping, wasn't it? We're out of milk.

B: Sorry, I have been playing video game (for 3 hours.)

C3 Reaching Conclusions

▶ Note 3

Work in small groups. Look at the picture. What can you conclude about what has just been happening? Write as many sentences as possible.

The TV is on. Someone has been watching TV.

A. Work with a partner. The advertisements below are missing introductory sentences that will attract attention. Write one or two present perfect continuous questions to begin each advertisement.

1

Have you been trying to lose weight without success? Have you been feeling frustrated lately?

Come to
Diet Helpers

We'll help you lose weight easily and healthily.

For more information call 555-2323.

3

_____
_____
_____

Call Apartment Finders Rental Agency at 555-4949.
We'll help you find the kind of apartment you need today.

2

_____
_____
_____

You need MORE EXERCISE!
Join the **Aurora Health & Fitness Club**

Reasonable rates, friendly staff

Stop by for more information about a free trial membership.

298 Ridgewood Road, 555-0908

4

_____
_____
_____

You need to get away!
We offer discounted plane and bus fares for students.

Let us help you plan your trip.

Mills Travel Agency
209 West Main St.

B. Create a newspaper, radio, or TV advertisement for one of the businesses below. Begin your advertisement with one or more attention-getting questions in the present perfect continuous. Be prepared to share your ad with the class.

a clothing store   an ice-cream shop   a photocopy center
a dance studio   an Internet provider   a take-out restaurant

Contrasting the Present Perfect Continuous and the Present Perfect

[handwritten: Since = up to now.   I have worked here since I was 20.]

Think Critically About Meaning and Use

[handwritten diagram: P Start work p.b 2010 ∼∼∼∼∼ now F]

A. Read the sentences and answer the questions below.

1a. Kathy has been reading the book. *[handwritten: (still reading)]* **2a.** I've been working here for ten years.
1b. Vera has read the book. *[handwritten: (finish reading)]* **2b.** I've worked here for ten years.

1. **EVALUATE** Which pair of sentences express the same meaning?

2. **EVALUATE** Which pair express different meanings?

3. **INTERPRET** In sentences 1a and 1b, who has probably finished the book? *[handwritten: 1b]* In which sentence is the activity continuing up to the present? *[handwritten: 1a]*

B. Discuss your answers with the class and read the Meaning and Use Notes to check them.

Meaning and Use Notes

ONLINE PRACTICE

Similar Meanings with Continuing Time up to Now

▶ **1A** Certain common verbs can be used in the present perfect or the present perfect continuous with *for* or *since* with no difference in meaning. These verbs include *live, teach, wear, work, study, stay,* and *feel.*

Present Perfect	**Present Perfect Continuous**
Mr. Ortiz **has lived** here since 1960. =	Mr. Ortiz **has been living** here since 1960.
He's **taught** English for a long time. =	He's **been teaching** English for a long time.
He's **worn** the same jacket for years. =	He's **been wearing** the same jacket for years.

▶ **1B** The meanings of the present perfect and the present perfect continuous are not always the same. Sometimes the focus on the ongoing activity is stronger in the continuous, so you can choose the continuous to emphasize the length of time a situation lasted. Remember, using the continuous can show a more intense or emotional situation.

Present Perfect	**Present Perfect Continuous**
I've **waited** for an hour.	I've **been waiting** for an hour. I'm very annoyed.
I've **thought** about this for days.	I've **been thinking** about this for days. I can't stop.

[handwritten: stronger about]

(Continued on page 114)

Completed vs. Continuing or Recent Past Activities

▶ **2**   The present perfect can express a completed activity that may or may not have been recent. In contrast, the present perfect continuous suggests that an activity is continuing up to the present time or was very recently completed.

Present Perfect	≠	**Present Perfect Continuous**
I**'ve read** a book about astronomy. (I finished it at some indefinite time in the past.) *Don't say when*		I**'ve been reading** a book about astronomy. (I'm not finished. OR I've just finished.) *Up to now because of PPC*

⚠ ❗ A sentence with the present perfect continuous usually does not tell how many times an activity is repeated.

Present Perfect	**Present Perfect Continuous**
I**'ve read** the report three times.	**X** I've been reading the report ~~three times.~~ (INCORRECT)

D1 Listening for Meaning and Use

▶ Notes 1A, 1B, 2

🔊 CD1 T32   **A.** Listen to each situation. Decide whether the situation is completed or continues. Check (✓) the correct column.

	COMPLETED	CONTINUES
1.		✓
2.		
3.		
4.		
5.		
6.		
7.		
8.		

D2 Contrasting the Present Perfect and the Present Perfect Continuous

▶ Notes 1A, 1B, 2

A. Complete this email with the words in parentheses and the present perfect or the present perfect continuous. In some sentences, either one is acceptable.

From: Anne Atherton
To: Ellen Bates
Subject: Hello!

Dear Ellen,

How are you and how's your family? _Has your father been feeling_ [1]
(your father/feel) better? I hope so. I _have been thinking_ [2] (think) about you a lot and
have been wondering [3] (wonder) if everything is OK.

I _have been reading_ [4] (read) the novel that you sent me for my birthday. So far, I
have read [5] (read) about a hundred pages, and I'm really enjoying it. I
have been being [6] (be) so busy lately that I _haven't been having_ [7] (not/have) much
time to read, but I hope to finish it soon.

Right now, I'm writing a paper for my psychology course. I _have been writing_ [8]
(write) it for two weeks. It's going to be long. So far, I _have changed_ [9] (change)
the topic four times, but now I'm finally pleased with it.

What _have you done_ [10] (you/do) during the past few weeks? _Have you been working_ [11]
(you/work) hard? _Have you had_ [12] (you/have) any exams yet? I
have had [13] (have) two so far, and I did pretty well on them.
Have you decided [14] (you/decide) what you're going to do this summer? We really
need to make plans soon! Please write!

Love,
Anne

B. Reread the email in part A. Write a similar email to a family member or friend. Use the present perfect and the present perfect continuous to tell what you have been doing recently and to ask questions, too.

D3 Writing a Conversation

▶ Notes 1A, 1B, 2

Work in small groups. Have you ever exaggerated in order to impress someone or to avoid a problem? Choose one of these situations and write a conversation in which one of the characters exaggerates. Use the present perfect and the present perfect continuous. Act out your conversation to the class.

1. A young man is trying to impress some new friends that he has just met. Although he has just begun a low-paying job at a television station, he exaggerates quite a bit about his job.

    New Friend: *So what do you do?*
    Young Man: *I work for XYZ News. I haven't been there long, but I've been working very hard. I've been writing all of the stories for the news show. I've also been on television three times.*

2. A young woman is at a job interview for a well-paying job. She is not qualified for this job. She has not finished college. She has only worked in her uncle's law office for a few months where she answers the telephone and runs errands.

3. A man is on the phone with his mother, who will soon be celebrating her 50th birthday. He and his brothers and sisters are planning a surprise birthday celebration. The mother is getting suspicious and asking a lot of questions.

4. A teenager promises that she will make dinner while her parents pick up relatives at the airport. They call from the airport to check on her progress. She assures them that she has been very busy. In fact, she hasn't really started dinner yet.

Beyond the Sentence

Connecting the Past and the Present in Discourse

In longer conversations and in writing, it is often important to relate past and present situations and events. Choose between the simple past, the present perfect, and the present perfect continuous to focus on whether a situation is complete or incomplete, recent or distant, whether it happened once or many times, and how long it lasted.

> **A:** I**'ve been working** here for nine years, and that's how long I**'ve known** Jenny. This is where we **met**.
>
> **B:** How long **did** you **know** each other before you **got** married?
>
> **A:** For a year.
>
> **B:** So you**'ve been married** for eight years. It doesn't seem that long.
>
> **A:** Well, we just **celebrated** our eighth wedding anniversary. We **spent** the weekend in the mountains…

D4 Connecting the Past and the Present in Discourse

Complete this conversation by choosing the correct answers in parentheses. In some sentences, either answer is possible.

Daughter: (I've been studying / I studied) French (for / since) six years now, but lately (I thought / I've been thinking) that I don't want to be a French teacher. You see…

Mother: But what about your plans to study in Paris next year? I thought (you made / you've made) your decision a few months ago to apply for the Junior Year Abroad program.

Daughter: Yes, (I've applied / I've been applying) for that, and I'd still like to go! You see…

Mother: But what's the point of going to Paris if you've already (decided / been deciding) not to be a French teacher?

Daughter: (I tried / I've been trying) to tell you… You see, (I took / I've been taking) a course in French Art this term, and I'm really enjoying it. In fact, I want to change my major to Art History and then minor in French.

Mother: And have you (told / been telling) your advisor this?

Daughter: Of course! (I talked / I've talked) to her a month ago when I first started to think about it, and (I spoke / I've spoken) to her every week since then. (She's been / She was) very helpful in showing me how I can combine my two interests.

Mother: So, is it official? Have you (changed / been changing) your major yet?

Daughter: No, (I decided / I've been deciding) to talk to you first. That's why (I've come / I've been coming home) this weekend! So what do you think?

Mother: Well, (I've never seen / I never saw) you so excited, so I think it's a great idea!

Think Critically About Meaning and Use

A. Choose the best response to complete each conversation.

1. **A:** I've been working at this school for 15 years.
   B: a. Why did you leave?
   b. Are you going to retire soon?

2. **A:** Andrew has been visiting us for three days.
   B: a. Is he having a good time?
   b. Did he have a good time?

3. **A:** Cheryl has been going to Vancouver on business.
   B: a. How many times has she been there?
   b. Has she gone there more than once?

4. **A:** Excuse me, Miss. I've been waiting for the doctor for an hour.
   B: a. How long have you been here?
   b. He had an emergency. He'll be with you soon.

5. **A:** Joanna has been coming to work late.
   B: a. It's happened only once. Can't we ignore it?
   b. It's happened more than once. We can't ignore it.

6. **A:** How long have you known about the scandal?
   B: a. A few minutes ago.
   b. Since I saw it in the newspaper.

B. Discuss these questions in small groups.

1. **EVALUATE** Find the conversations that start with the present perfect continuous. In which one of these could speaker A have used the present continuous without changing the meaning of the statement or question?

2. **DRAW A CONCLUSION** Look at conversation 3. How does the meaning change if speaker A had said, "Cheryl has gone to Vancouver on business?"

Edit

Find the errors in this paragraph and correct them. Pay close attention to the context of each sentence.

Life expectancy is the average number of years that a person will live. Two thousand years ago, the Romans have ~~been living~~ *lived* only an average of 22 years. In other words, they have been having a life expectancy of 22. Since the beginning of the twentieth century, life expectancy around the world has been rising dramatically in many parts of the world. It will certainly continue to go up well into the twenty-first century. The rise in life expectancy has been being due to the fact that people have been taking much better care of themselves. Each generation has experienced better nutrition and medical care than the one before. In 1900 people in the United States have been living to an average age of 47. All that has changed, however: The life expectancy in 2009 was 78.7, and it may be even higher today.

Write

More and more people have been living to the age of 80 and beyond. Do you think your country has been doing a good job of taking care of its elderly population? Write a letter to the editor of your local newspaper expressing your opinion. Use the present perfect continuous and other past, present, and future forms where appropriate.

1. **BRAINSTORM** Use these questions to help you organize your letter into paragraphs.
   - What has the government been doing to help elderly people in recent years? (Think about services such as housing, finances, health, and recreation.)
   - What problems have elderly people and their younger relatives been experiencing with these services? How will the situation worsen in the future?
   - What do you think the role of the government should be in the future?

2. **WRITE A FIRST DRAFT** Before you write your first draft, read the checklist below and look at the examples on page 119. Write your draft using the present perfect continuous.

3. **EDIT** Read your work and check it against the checklist below. Circle grammar, spelling, and punctuation errors.

DO I...	YES
organize my ideas into paragraphs?	☐
use affirmative and negative statements in the present perfect continuous?	☐
use the present perfect continuous for continuing time up to now and recent past activities?	☐
use other tenses as necessary to talk about the present and future?	☐

4. **PEER REVIEW** Work with a partner to help you decide how to fix your errors and improve the content. Use the checklist above.

5. **REWRITE YOUR DRAFT** Using the comments from your partner, write a final draft.

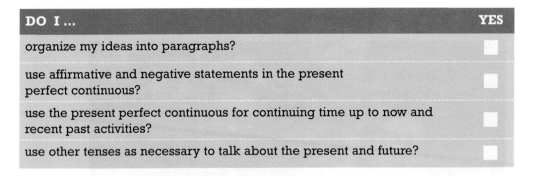

Dear Editor,

I am writing to express my concerns about the services that the government provides for the elderly. While it is true that our culture has a long tradition of caring for the elderly, people have been living longer and...

A. **GRAMMAR IN DISCOURSE: Wild Thing** 122

B. **FORM: The Past Perfect and the Past Perfect Continuous** 124

The Past Perfect	**The Past Perfect Continuous**
They **had hiked** for hours by then.	They **had been hiking** for hours by then.

Informally Speaking: Reduced Forms of *Had*

C. **MEANING AND USE 1: The Past Perfect** 130

Order of Events in the Past

The Past Perfect and Past Time Clauses

Expressions Used with the Past Perfect

D. **MEANING AND USE 2: The Past Perfect Continuous** . . . 135

Order of Events in the Past with Continuing Actions

Contrasting the Past Perfect and the Past Perfect Continuous

Adding Background Information to a Sentence

Beyond the Sentence: Adding Background Information in Longer Discourse

WRITING: Write a Biographical Essay About a Famous Person's Career 140

PART 2 TEST: Connecting The Present, Past, and Distant Past 143

Wild Thing

A1 Before You Read

Discuss these questions.

Have you ever wanted to do something different or unusual, such as climbing a mountain or bungee jumping? Name some challenges that you would like to face. Why do some people like to face great challenges?

A2 Read

CD1 T33 **Read this book excerpt to find out why a young woman wanted to participate in an educational program called Outward Bound.**

Wild Thing

With the wind biting my face and rain soaking through my clothes, it didn't seem like July. I watched a puddle form at the foot of my

5　sleeping bag as the 10-foot plastic sheet above me gave way to the wind. I hadn't eaten for almost a day, and a rumble in my stomach demanded to know why I was in the

10　Northern Cascades of Oregon—alone, soaked—in the first place. With two more days alone in the wilds ahead of me, I had plenty of time to think about that question.

15　　I'd always admired people who had been in Outward Bound, basically because I'd always lumped myself in the I-could-never-do-that category. For one thing, I just assumed I was

20　too small and urban… I also wasn't a big risk-taker. I'd always relied a lot on my family and friends, and I evaluated myself on how well I met their expectations of me.

25   Signing up for an Outward Bound course the summer after my junior year in high school was a chance to break away from that. After all, the courses are described as "adventure-
30 based education programs that promote self-discovery through tough outdoor activities." Exactly what I needed; I would be facing challenges away from my usual supporters. As
35 the starting date approached, though, I became increasingly terrified. I'd never attempted mountain climbing, white-water rafting, backpacking, rappelling, or rock climbing, and I
40 was plagued by fears that I would fail at one or all of them. I begged my mother to cancel for me. No such luck…

Adapted from *Chicken Soup for the Teenage Soul*

lump: to put many things into one category	**rely on:** to depend on
plagued: continuously upset or troubled	**rumble:** a deep, rolling sound
rappelling: using ropes to climb down a steep mountain	**wilds:** wilderness; a natural area with few people

A3 After You Read

Write *T* for true or *F* for false for each statement.

___T___ **1.** The young woman was going to spend two more days alone in the wilderness.

_____ **2.** She came from the city.

_____ **3.** She had always been very self-confident.

_____ **4.** It was summer.

_____ **5.** She was an expert mountain climber.

_____ **6.** Her mother wanted her to stay home.

B FORM

The Past Perfect and the Past Perfect Continuous

Think Critically About Form

A. Look back at the book excerpt on page 122 and complete the tasks below.

1. **IDENTIFY** An example of the past perfect is underlined. Find four more examples. What is the contracted form of *had* in the past perfect?

2. **COMPARE AND CONTRAST** Look at the following example of the past perfect continuous. Underline the two auxiliaries and circle the main verb. How does it differ from the past perfect?

   She had been searching for a way to challenge herself.

B. Discuss your answers with the class and read the Form charts to check them.

▶ The Past Perfect

AFFIRMATIVE STATEMENTS

SUBJECT	HAD	PAST PARTICIPLE	
I			
He	**had**	**hiked**	for hours by then.
They			

CONTRACTION			
He**'d**		**hiked**	for hours by then.

NEGATIVE STATEMENTS

SUBJECT	HAD	NOT	PAST PARTICIPLE	
I				
He	**had**	**not**	**hiked**	before.
They				

CONTRACTION			
He	**hadn't**	**hiked**	before.

▶ The Past Perfect Continuous

AFFIRMATIVE STATEMENTS

SUBJECT	HAD	BEEN	VERB + -ING	
I				
He	**had**	**been**	**hiking**	for hours by then.
They				

CONTRACTION			
He**'d**		**been**	**hiking**	for hours by then.

NEGATIVE STATEMENTS

SUBJECT	HAD	NOT	BEEN	VERB + -ING	
I					
He	**had**	**not**	**been**	**hiking**	before.
They					

CONTRACTION			
He	**hadn't**	**been**	**hiking**	before.

▶ The Past Perfect

YES/NO QUESTIONS

HAD	SUBJECT	VERB	
Had	you		
	he	**hiked**	before?
	they		

SHORT ANSWERS

YES	SUBJECT	HAD	NO	SUBJECT	HAD + NOT
Yes,	I		**No,**	I	
	he	**had.**		he	**hadn't.**
	they			they	

INFORMATION QUESTIONS

WH-WORD	HAD	SUBJECT	PAST PARTICIPLE	
Where	**had**	you	**hiked**	before?
What		he	**done?**	

WH-WORD	HAD		PAST PARTICIPLE
What	**had**		**happened?**

▶ The Past Perfect Continuous

YES/NO QUESTIONS

HAD	SUBJECT	BEEN	VERB + -ING	
Had	you			
	he	**been**	**hiking**	before?
	they			

SHORT ANSWERS

YES	SUBJECT	HAD	NO	SUBJECT	HAD + NOT
Yes,	I		**No,**	I	
	he	**had.**		he	**hadn't.**
	they			they	

INFORMATION QUESTIONS

WH-WORD	HAD	SUBJECT	BEEN	VERB + -ING	
Why	**had**	you	**been**	**hiking**	before?
Where		he		**doing?**	

WH-WORD	HAD			VERB + -ING
What	**had**		**been**	**happening?**

The Past Perfect

- The past perfect has the same form with all subjects.
- The past participle of regular verbs is the same as the simple past form (verb + -ed). See Appendices 4 and 5 for spelling and pronunciation rules for verbs ending in -ed.
- Irregular verbs have special past participle forms. See Appendix 6 for irregular verbs and their past participles.
- See Appendix 14 for contractions with *had*.
- Note that the past perfect form of *have* is *had had*. It is an irregular form.

    It was 2:00 P.M. We **had had** a busy day at the store, and I was exhausted.

(Continued on page 126)

The Past Perfect Continuous

- The past perfect continuous has two auxiliary verbs: *had* and *been*. Only *had* forms contractions.

- Verbs with stative meanings are not usually used with the past perfect continuous.

  I **had** already **known** him for many years.

  x I had already been knowing him for many years. (INCORRECT)

- See Appendix 3 for spelling rules for verbs ending in *-ing*.

B1 Listening for Form

CD1 T34　Listen and write the simple past, past perfect, or past perfect continuous verb forms you hear. Use full forms or contractions.

In 1928, Amelia Earhart ___became___ the first woman to fly across the Atlantic. Ten years before, she ___'d been working___ as a nurse's aide when she ___visited___ an airfield near Toronto. She ___made up___ her mind that she ___wanted___ to fly an airplane right then. After her trans-Atlantic flight, Ms. Earhart ___became___ an instant heroine, although she really ___hadn't flown___ the plane. Her two male companions ___hadn't let___ her touch any of the controls. But the world ___didn't care___.

Charles Lindbergh ___had crossed___ the Atlantic a year earlier, and many aviators ___had been trying___ to repeat his successful flight since then. Sadly, fourteen pilots, including three women, ___had died___ since Lindbergh's triumph. Because Ms. Earhart ___had been___ embarrassed about her role in her first trans-Atlantic flight, she ___seemed___ more determined than ever to fly across the Atlantic alone. And that's exactly what ___happened___ in 1932 when she finally ___flew___ over the Atlantic by herself.

B2 Working on Verb Forms

Complete the chart.

	SIMPLE PAST	PAST PERFECT	PAST PERFECT CONTINUOUS
1.	I flew home.	I had flown home.	I had been flying home.
2.	We went	We had gone to school.	had been going
3.	tried	had tried	They had been trying hard.
4.	I held my keys.	had held	had been holding
5.	had	had had	You had been having fun.
6.	He made a mess.	had maken	had been making
7.	thought	They had thought about it.	had been thinking
8.	did	had down	We had been doing nothing.
9.	What happened?	had happened	had been happening
10.	got	It had gotten harder.	had been getting

B3 Building Sentences

Build as many meaningful sentences as possible. Use an item from each column.
Punctuate your sentences correctly.

Had you been working?

		working
had you	been	left
she	had	lunch
who	had been	sick
		taken a walk

B4 Asking and Answering Questions

 A. Work with a partner. Take turns asking and answering questions using the phrases below and the past perfect. Start your questions with *Before you started this course* and use *ever*. Respond with short answers and an explanation.

1. take any other English courses

   A: *Before you started this course, had you ever taken any other English courses?*

   B: *Yes, I had. I'd studied English for a year in high school.* OR
   No, I hadn't. I'd never taken any English courses.

2. study English grammar

3. speak on the phone in English

4. write any letters in English

5. see any English-language movies

 B. Now take turns asking and answering questions using the phrases below and the past perfect continuous. Start your questions with *Before you started this course.* Respond with short answers and an explanation.

1. read any English-language newspapers

   A: *Before you started this course, had you been reading any English-language newspapers?*

   B: *Yes, I had. I'd been reading The New York Times almost every day.* OR
   No, I hadn't.

2. learn any songs in English

3. practice English with friends

4. watch any TV programs in English

5. listen to English-language news broadcasts

B5 Transforming Sentences

Change the past perfect continuous to the past perfect. Where possible, change the past perfect to the past perfect continuous. Which sentences cannot change? Why?

1. We had been standing outside for a long time.

   We had stood outside for a long time.

2. I had never had a car with so many problems.

3. She had been limping for the last mile.

4. How long had they known about the accident?

5. Where had everybody been?

6. Had anyone been looking for us?

7. They had been trying to call for help.

8. What had happened?

💬 Informally Speaking

Reduced Forms of *Had*

🔊 CD1 T35 Look at the cartoon and listen to the conversation. How is the underlined form in the cartoon different from what you hear?

Especially in fast speech, *had* is usually reduced with subject nouns. *Had* is also reduced with many information question words.

> Did you see Dana and Maria at the library last night?
>
> Dana had already left by the time I got there, but I saw Maria.

Standard Form	What You Might Hear
Dana had already left.	"/ˈdænəd/ already left."
The **cars had** stopped.	"The /ˈkɑrzəd/ stopped."
Who had already left?	"/hud/ already left?"
What had you been doing?	"/ˈwʌtəd/ you been doing?"

B6 Understanding Informal Speech

🔊 CD1 T36 Listen and write the standard form of the words you hear.

1. She ___had___ never ___been___ alone in the woods before.

2. Her family ___had___ ___gone___ camping when she was young.

3. Her father ___had___ ___told___ her the skills she needed.

4. No one ___had___ ___prepared___ her for this experience, though.

5. Why ___had___ she ___signed___ for this program?

6. Who ___had___ she ___been trying___ to impress?

C

The Past Perfect

Think Critically About Meaning and Use

A. Read the sentences and complete the tasks below.

  a. I called for help because a tree had fallen across my driveway.
  b. She wanted to withdraw from the course after she had enrolled.
  c. He'd been on a mountain climbing expedition before he wrote the article.
  d. Although I'd been terrified, I felt quite brave the next morning.

Think about the two events in each sentence.

  1. IDENTIFY Underline the clause that expresses the earlier event.

  2. RECOGNIZE What verb form is in the clause that expresses the earlier event?

  3. RECOGNIZE What verb form is in the clause that expresses the later event?

B. Discuss your answers with the class and read the Meaning and Use Notes to check them.

Meaning and Use Notes

ONLINE PRACTICE

Order of Events in the Past

▶ **1A** The past perfect expresses the relationship in time between two past events. It shows that one action or state occurred before another action or state in the past. The past perfect expresses the first (or earlier) event. The simple past often expresses the second (or later) event.

Past Perfect (1st Event)	**Simple Past (2nd Event)**
I **had** just **completed** the exam.	I **felt** so relieved.

complete exam ——— *relieved* ———⟶

▶ **1B** The past time can be recent or distant.

go to meeting   call ———⟶

Recent Time

Miguel called me <u>this morning</u>, but I wasn't there. **I'd gone** to a meeting.

Distant Time

Miguel wrote me <u>last year</u>, but I never got the letter. (**I'd**) **moved** away.

I missed the class because I had gone to market.

The Past Perfect and Past Time Clauses

▶ **2A** The past perfect is often used in sentences containing past time clauses. The past perfect is used to indicate the first event. The simple past is used to indicate the second event. *Before*, *by the time*, *when*, *until*, and *after* introduce the time clause.

Past Perfect (1st Event)	Simple Past (2nd Event) *CLAUSE*
The thief **had escaped**	before I **called** the police.
We **had calmed** down	by the time the police **came**.
He **had been** upstairs	when we **came** home.
We **hadn't noticed**	until we **heard** the footsteps.
CLAUSE After I **had called** the police,	we **realized** the thief was gone.

▶ **2B** In sentences with *before*, *after*, *by the time*, and *until*, the past perfect is sometimes replaced by the simple past with no difference in meaning. This is especially common with *before* and *after*.

go inside   coat off

Past Perfect and Simple Past	=	Simple Past Only
I'**d gone** inside before I **took off** my coat.	=	I **went** inside before I **took off** my coat.
After I'**d gone** inside, I **took off** my coat.	=	After I **went** inside, I **took off** my coat.

Expressions Used with the Past Perfect

▶ **3A** The past perfect is often used with the same adverbs and prepositions that are used with the present perfect: *already*, *yet*, *still*, *ever*, *never*, *for*, *since*, and *just*. These expressions help to clarify the sequence of past events.

By lunchtime, we **had** already **discussed** the new budget and written a report. We **hadn't written** the new vacation policy yet.

I **had lived** in Texas for 12 years before I moved to California.

A: **Had** she *hold life* ever **traveled** abroad before she went to college?

B: No, she'**d** never **left** her hometown.

▶ **3B** *By* + a time can be used with the past perfect to express the later time in the sentence.

We **had finished** by then.

By noon, we **had hiked** two miles.

C1 Listening for Meaning and Use ▶ Notes 1A, 1B, 2A, 2B, 3B

CD1 T37 Listen to the sentences. For each pair of past events below, choose the event that happened first.

1. **(a.)** The patient's condition improved.

   b. The doctor came.

2. **(a.)** We got to the airport.

   b. The plane landed.

3. **(a.)** I entered the building.

   b. I took off my hat.

4. **a.** The emergency crew arrived.

   (b.) The building collapsed.

5. **(a.)** I saw Betty.

   b. She heard the news.

6. **a.** He became vice president.

   (b.) He worked hard.

7. **(a.)** I called my mother.

   b. I spoke to my sister.

8. **(a.)** She hurt her wrist.

   b. She went to work.

C2 Expressing the Order of Past Events ▶ Notes 1A, 1B, 2A, 2B

Read the pairs of sentences and order the events. Number the first event with a *1* and the second with a *2*. Then make a sentence with the word(s) in parentheses that includes both events. Use the past perfect and the simple past where appropriate.

1. __2__ The sink overflowed.   __1__ I left the water running.

   (after) _The sink overflowed after I had left the water running._

2. __2__ He graded the exam.   __1__ He read the answers carefully.

   (before) _Before he passed the exam he had read the answers carefully._

3. ____ They were married for five years.   ____ They had a child.

   (when) _____

4. __1__ The car collided with a truck.   __2__ Someone called the police.

   (after) _After the car had collided .. Someone ----_

5. __2__ The doctor said she was very healthy.   ____ She was worried.

   (until) _Before `` she had worried_

6. __1__ She slept for ten hours.   __2__ I decided to wake her up.

   (by the time) _After she slept .. I had decided ``_

C3 Discussing Previous Accomplishments

▶ Notes 1A, 3A

Work with a partner. Read each situation and look at the picture. Tell what things had been done already and what had not been done yet. Use the expressions in parentheses and the past perfect with *already* and *not … yet*.

1. Sonia was hoping to move into her new apartment a few days early. Yesterday she went to see if it was ready yet.

   (paint the apartment)   *They had already painted the apartment.*

   (clean the carpet)   *They hadn't cleaned the carpet yet.*

   (fix the window)

   (repair the lock)

2. Martin checked to see if he had completed the requirements for graduation.

   (complete the English requirement)

   (take the math courses)

   (pass the writing test)

   > Requirements for high school graduation:
   > ✓ 3 Math courses
   > ✓ 4 English courses
   >   Writing test

3. Your cousin has been looking for a job for a month. You spoke to her a few days ago.

   (look at the classified ads)

   (go to an employment agency)

   (write her résumé)

C4 Describing New Experiences

▶ Notes 1A, 3A

A. These situations describe new experiences. Use the phrases below and the past perfect with *never* and *before* to describe the things that the people had never done before. Then add one of your own ideas.

1. Brian and Jo Ann have just had their first child.

   a. diaper a baby _They had never diapered a baby before._

   b. bathe a baby _They had never bathed a baby before._

   c. _They had never played with a baby before._

2. Irina started college last fall.

   a. live on her own _She had never lived on her own before_

   b. sleep in a dormitory _She had never slept in a dormitory before_

   c. _She had never cleaned her room before._

3. Dominick got his first summer job at a supermarket.

   a. use an electronic cash register _He had never used an ... before._

   b. get a paycheck _He had never gotten a paycheck before._

   c. _He had never worked before._

4. Nora took her first driving lesson.

   a. drive a car _She had never driven a car before._

   b. be so scared _She had never been so scared._

   c. _She had never washed a car before._

B. Think of something you did for the first time. Describe the aspects of the experience that were new to you. Write four sentences using the past perfect and *never*. Then tell your class about your new experience.

New Experience: _I decided to go to Europe for my summer vacation._

1. _I had never flown on a plane before._

2. _I had never taken a trip with friends before._

3. _____

4. _____

D MEANING AND USE 2

The Past Perfect Continuous

Think Critically About Meaning and Use

A. Read the sentences and complete the task below.

_____ **a.** We arrived at 9:30 P.M. Julia
had been eating her dinner.
(Dinner was just ending.)

_____ **b.** We arrived at 9:30 P.M.
Julia had eaten her dinner.
(Dinner was over.)

ORGANIZE Match each illustration to the sentence that best describes it.

B. Discuss your answers with the class and read the Meaning and Use Notes to check them.

Meaning and Use Notes

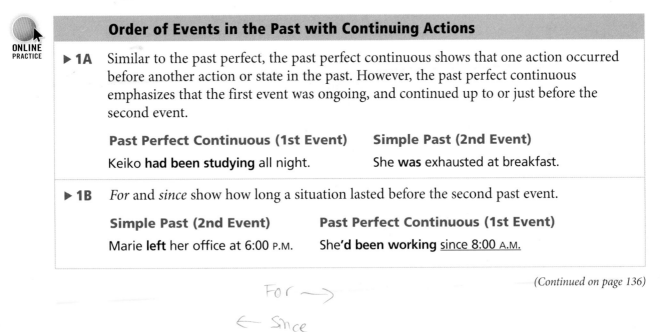

ONLINE PRACTICE

Order of Events in the Past with Continuing Actions
▶ **1A** Similar to the past perfect, the past perfect continuous shows that one action occurred before another action or state in the past. However, the past perfect continuous emphasizes that the first event was ongoing, and continued up to or just before the second event.

Past Perfect Continuous (1st Event)	**Simple Past (2nd Event)**
Keiko **had been studying** all night.	She **was** exhausted at breakfast.

▶ **1B** *For* and *since* show how long a situation lasted before the second past event.

Simple Past (2nd Event)	**Past Perfect Continuous (1st Event)**
Marie **left** her office at 6:00 P.M.	She**'d been working** <u>since 8:00 A.M.</u>

(Continued on page 136)

For ➝

⬅ Since

> **1C**   The past perfect continuous is often used in sentences containing past time clauses.

Past Perfect Continuous (1st Event)	**Simple Past (2nd Event)**
Marie **had been working** for nine and a half hours	<u>by the time</u> she **left** her office.

Contrasting the Past Perfect and the Past Perfect Continuous

> **2A**   Certain common verbs can be used with the past perfect and past perfect continuous with little or no difference in meaning. Remember, though, that using the continuous can show a more intense or emotional situation.

Past Perfect	**Past Perfect Continuous**
Mr. Ortiz **had lived** there since 1960.	Mr. Ortiz **had been living** there since 1960.
I**'d waited** for an hour.	I**'d been waiting** for an hour! I was so angry.

> **2B**   The past perfect can express a completed action that may or may not have occurred recently. In contrast, the past perfect continuous suggests that an action was continuing up to or ended just before a specific time in the past.

Past Perfect	**Past Perfect Continuous**
Hiro **had watered** the garden before I arrived. (Hiro may have watered it a few minutes or many hours before I arrived.)	Hiro **had been watering** the garden before I arrived. (Hiro watered the garden a few minutes before I arrived.)

> ! A sentence with the past perfect continuous usually does not tell how many times an action is repeated.
>
> | **Past Perfect** | **Past Perfect Continuous** |
> | --- | --- |
> | I**'d read** it three times before. | **X** I'd been reading it three times before. (INCORRECT) |

Adding Background Information to a Sentence

> **3**   Both the past perfect continuous and the past perfect are often used to provide background information about earlier events. They are used to give reasons with *because* and express contrasts with *although* or *even though*. They are also used to draw conclusions.

Reasons

She looked very tired	<u>because</u> she **had been studying** all night.
	<u>because</u> she **had studied** all night.

> **Contrasts**
>
> She looked very tired   <u>although</u> she **had been sleeping** for 12 hours.
>
>   <u>even though</u> she **had slept** for 12 hours.
>
> **Conclusions**
>
> I realized that   he **had been** criticizing my work.
>
>   he **had** just criticized my work.

D1 Listening for Meaning and Use

▶ Note 2B

CD1 T38   Listen to the two events in each sentence. Check (✓) *Just Before* if the context makes it clear that the first event happened right before the second. Check (✓) *Unclear* if the context does not specify how close together in time the two events were.

	JUST BEFORE	UNCLEAR
1.	✓	
2.		✓
3.	✓	
4.	✓	✗
5.		✓
6.	✓	
7.		✓
8.		✓

D2 Talking About Continuing Past Actions

▶ Note 1A–1C

Write two different sentences that tell how long each situation lasted. Use the past perfect continuous with *for* and *since* and simple past time clauses with *when*.

1. Elena worked from 2006 to 2008. Then she went back to school.

    When Elena went back to school, she had been working for two years.
    When Elena went back to school in 2008, she had been working since 2006.

2. Brigitte began to work at C & M in 2009. Her husband joined the company in 2011.

3. The chicken started baking at 5:30. The electricity went off at 5:45.

4. Lisa went to sleep at 11:00 P.M. The phone woke her up at 2:00 A.M.

5. Paulo and Celia got married in 2009. They had their first child in 2011.

6. Kate studied from 2005 to 2011. She graduated from medical school in 2011.

7. Carlos lived in Mexico City from 2008 to 2010. He moved to Paris in 2010.

8. Eric started taking piano lessons in January of 2010. He gave his first recital in July of that year.

D3 Expressing Reasons and Results

▶ Notes 2A, 2B, 3

A. Work with a partner. Complete each sentence with a *because* clause in the past perfect or the past perfect continuous. Then write one more main clause in the simple past and ask your partner to complete it using *because*.

1. He looked very tired _because he had been sleeping poorly._

2. The student was expelled from school _because he had been cheating_

3. She quit her job _because she had been feeling bored._

4. _____

B. Now complete each sentence with a main clause in the simple past. Then write one more *because* clause and ask your partner to complete it with a main clause.

1. _He didn't hear the doorbell_ because he had been listening to music.

2. _We had been tired_ because we had been exercising.

3. Because she hadn't listened to her parents, _she hurt herself._

4. _____

D4 Expressing Contrasts

▶ Notes 2A, 2B, 3

A. Complete each sentence with a clause using *although* or *even though* in the past perfect or the past perfect continuous.

1. I passed the exam _although I hadn't studied._

2. She was able to answer the question _although she hadn't brought the book._

3. _Although we had weared the mask_, everyone became sick.

4. _Although he had gotten high salary_, he wanted to quit his job.

B. Complete each sentence with a main clause in the simple past.

1. Even though I had been calling for days, _she never called me back._

2. _I finished all the food_ although I had gone grocery shopping two days before.

3. Although we had been good friends, _he break his feeling_

4. Even though I had been trying as hard as I could, _I failed_

Beyond the Sentence

Adding Background Information in Longer Discourse

Both the past perfect and the past perfect continuous are often used in a story to give details and background information about an earlier past time. These verb forms usually appear near the beginning of the story. Then the story often continues in the simple past.

> We finally landed in London at 9:30 A.M. We **had been traveling** for thirteen hours and the whole family was exhausted and cranky, especially me. The seat **had been** uncomfortable, and I **hadn't slept** at all. I tried not to be too unpleasant, but it was difficult because nothing seemed to be going right. When we got to the baggage claim area, two suitcases came through quickly, but the other two were missing…

D5 Adding Background Information

A. Read each introductory statement. Then write two or three past perfect or past perfect continuous sentences that provide background information.

1. I was in my favorite restaurant that Sunday afternoon.

   We had gathered for a family reunion in honor of my parents' 25th wedding anniversary. My brother and I had been planning this event for months.

2. I remember the day I moved here.

3. I'll never forget that afternoon. We were stuck in heavy traffic on a bridge.

4. I entered my apartment and immediately felt that something was strange.

B. Write a paragraph. Choose one of the items in part A as the beginning of your paragraph. Add some background information in the past perfect or the past perfect continuous. Then complete the paragraph using the simple past to explain more about what happened in the first sentence.

   I was in my favorite restaurant that Sunday afternoon. We had gathered for a family reunion in honor of my parents' 25th wedding anniversary. My brother and I had been planning this event for months. We had been emailing each other almost daily with plans, menus, and guest lists. As they had been doing for 25 years, my parents arrived exactly on time. When they saw everyone…

Think Critically About Meaning and Use

A. Read each sentence and the statements that follow. Write *T* if the statement is true, *F* if it is false, or *?* if you do not have enough information to decide.

1. After he had eaten a sandwich, he ate a salad.

___F___ **a.** He ate the salad first. Then he ate the sandwich.

___F___ **b.** He ate the salad and sandwich together.

2. He had left before the play ended.

___F___ **a.** The play ended. Then he left.

___T___ **b.** He was gone by the end of the play.

3. He had known her for many years when they started to work together.

___F___ **a.** He met her at work.

___T___ **b.** He knew her a long time.

4. Tom didn't lose weight until he went on a diet.

___F___ **a.** Tom didn't lose weight.

___T___ **b.** Tom went on a diet.

5. It was lunchtime. I looked out the window, and I saw that it had rained.

___?X___ **a.** It had rained just before I looked out the window.

___T___ **b.** I looked out the window after the rain stopped.

6. He left his job because he had found a better one.

___F___ **a.** He left his job. Then he looked for a better job.

___T___ **b.** He left his job after he found another job.

7. The hospital didn't lose power, although there had been a power failure in the city.

___F___ **a.** The hospital had a power failure.

___T___ **b.** The city lost power.

8. The two men had been working on a project together when I met them.

___T___ **a.** They worked together before I met them.

___?X___ **b.** They finished the project.

B. Discuss the questions in small groups.

1. **PREDICT** In sentence 4, if we change *until* to *when*, how does it affect the answers to statements a and b?

2. **PREDICT** In sentence 8, if we change *had been working* to *had worked*, how does it affect the answers to statements a and b?

Edit

Find the errors in these paragraphs and correct them, using either the simple past or the present perfect.

In 1953, Edmund Hillary and Tenzing Norkay ~~had been~~ *were* the first climbers to reach the top of Mount Everest. Since then, many people ~~had~~ *have* climbed Mount Everest, especially in recent years. Before 1953, no human had ever stood on top of the world's highest peak, although some had tried. George Mallory and Sandy Irvine, for example, had died almost 30 years earlier on a perilous path along the North Ridge.

Since 1953, many more people ~~had~~ *have* set world records. In 1975, Junko Tabei of Japan ~~had become~~ *became* the first woman on a mountaineering team to reach the top. In 1980, Reinhold Messner of Italy ~~had become~~ *became* the first person to make the climb to the top alone, without other people and without oxygen. In 1995, Alison Hargreaves of Scotland ~~had~~ duplicated Messner's triumph. She became the first woman to climb Mount Everest solo and without oxygen.

Each climber faces frigid winds, storms, avalanches, and most dangerous of all, the serious effects of the high altitude on the heart, lungs, and brain. So why ~~had~~ *have* many hundreds of people tried to climb Mount Everest in recent years? The only way to explain these numbers is to understand that the climb up Mount Everest represents the ultimate challenge of reaching the "top of the world."

Write

Write an essay about a major event in a famous person's career. Use the past perfect, past perfect continuous, and time clauses to provide background.

1. **BRAINSTORM** Think of a famous person and research his or her life in the library or on the Internet. Decide on the event you will focus on and make a timeline leading up to it. Use these categories to help you organize your ideas into paragraphs.

    - **Introduce the event:** What happened and when?
    - **Discuss background events leading to the event:** What had happened and what had the person been doing before?
    - **Describe and comment on the event:** What happened during the period of the event? What was its significance of the event? How did it affect the rest of the person's career?

2. **WRITE A FIRST DRAFT** Before you write your first draft, read the checklist below and look at the example on page 126. Write your draft using the past perfect and the past perfect continuous.

3. **EDIT** Read your work and check it against the checklist below. Circle grammar, spelling, and punctuation errors.

DO I...	YES
organize my ideas into paragraphs?	☐
use the simple past and past continuous to announce and describe the event?	☐
use the past perfect for completed actions/states that occurred before another past action/state?	☐
use the past perfect continuous for ongoing actions that continued up to or just before another past action/state?	☐
use time clauses and time expressions to clarify the order and duration of past events?	☐

4. **PEER REVIEW** Work with a partner to help you decide how to fix your errors and improve the content. Use the checklist above.

5. **REWRITE YOUR DRAFT** Using the comments from your partner, write a final draft.

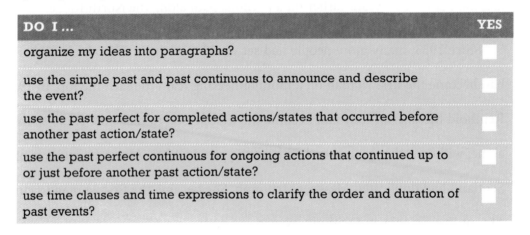

On May 16, 1975, 26-year-old Junko Tabei of Japan became the first woman to reach the top of Mount Everest. Junko had been attracted to mountain climbing since she climbed up Mount Nasu on a school trip at the age of 10. By the time she graduated from university...

Choose the correct word or words to complete each sentence.

1. Where _____ sending her patients for rehabilitation since the nearby facility closed?

   a. has the doctor been

   b. the doctor has

   c. the doctor has been

   d. is the doctor

2. Scientists have _____ specimens from the rain forest in order to study their medicinal properties.

   a. take   **b.** took   **c.** taking   **d.** taken

3. The room became quiet when the teacher entered. The students had _____ been talking about her.

   a. yet   **b.** when   **c.** before   **d.** just

4. Why _____ before the end of last year?

   a. unemployment hadn't risen

   b. hasn't unemployment risen

   c. hadn't unemployment risen

   d. hasn't unemployment been rising

Choose the correct response to complete each conversation.

5. **A:** I haven't eaten breakfast yet this morning.

   B: _____

   a. Well, there's still time.

   b. It's 1:45 P.M. Let's have lunch.

   c. It was delicious, wasn't it?

   d. What about tomorrow?

6. **A:** I've lived in the same apartment for ten years.

   B: _____

   a. Why did you leave it?

   b. Do you ever feel like moving?

   c. That was a long time ago.

   d. I hadn't been before.

7. **A:** Your boss has been calling all day.

   B: _____

   a. I'm surprised he called only once.

   b. What time did he call?

   c. I'm glad he hasn't called.

   d. How many times did he call?

8. **A:** I've been playing in the same band for eight years.

   B: _____

   a. Why did you quit?

   b. How long ago did you join?

   c. Are you going to stay with them?

   d. Had you been together that long?

9. **A:** I've been sleeping late this week.

   B: _____

   a. Had you been going to sleep early? **c.** Are you going to take a vacation?

   b. Are you on vacation? **d.** Why haven't you been sleeping?

Reorder each set of words to make a statement or question in the present perfect continuous.

10. jogging/just/you/been/have/?

   _____

11. been/it/long/raining/has/how/?

   _____

Match the response to the statement or question below.

_____ 12. How long have they been married?

_____ 13. Have you taken a vacation lately?

_____ 14. When did you last see Jack?

_____ 15. We had a long list of things to do.
   What have we done so far?

   a. I haven't seen him for a while.

   b. For about a year.

   c. I'm surprised that they haven't called you.

   d. No, but I really need one.

   e. Yes, yesterday.

   f. No, but I hear it's very good.

   g. Well, we've made a lot of progress.

   h. Two years ago.

Complete each sentence with the past perfect form of the words in parentheses. Do not use contractions.

16. After _____ (we/buy) all the ingredients, we made dinner.

17. When the season ended, our team _____ (not/lose) a single game.

Write a question for each response. Use the words in parentheses. Do not use contractions.

18. **A:** (How long) _____

   B: I've been in this room for 30 minutes.

19. **A:** (Where/your sister/lately) _____

   B: She has been on vacation.

20. **A:** (How long) _____

   B: I've been a student for two years.

Modals of Possibility

A. **GRAMMAR IN DISCOURSE: Doctor Fran's
    Fitness Forum** **146**

B. **FORM: Modals of Present and Future Possibility** **148**
    Present Modals
        He **may/might/could/should/must be** home.
    Future Modals
        He **may/might/could/should/will be** home soon.
    Present Phrasal Modals
        He **ought to be** home.
        She **has to/has got to be jogging** in the park.
    Future Phrasal Modals
        He **ought to be** home soon.
        She **has to/has got to be coming** home soon.

C. **MEANING AND USE 1: Modals of Present Possibility** **153**
    Overview
    Guessing with *Could, Might,* and *May*
    Expectations with *Should* and *Ought To*
    **Strong Certainty and Understanding with *Must, Have To,*
    and *Have Got To***
    Strong Certainty with *Can't* and *Couldn't*

D. **MEANING AND USE 2: Modals of Future Possibility** **160**
    Overview
    Guessing with *Could, Might,* and *May*
    Expectations with *Should* and *Ought To*
    Strong Certainty with *Will* and *Won't*

    **WRITING: Write an Article for Your School's
    Online Newspaper** **165**

Doctor Fran's Fitness Forum

A1 Before You Read

Discuss these questions.

What do you and your friends do to stay fit? What benefits can you get from regular exercise? Do you think exercise could be bad for you?

A2 Read

CD1 T39 Read this post from an online fitness forum to find out about a fitness expert's perspective on the possible dangers of overexercising.

Doctor Fran's Fitness Forum

TODAY'S TOPIC:

Could Too Much Exercise Hurt You?

Q: Is it possible to exercise too much? My sister runs several marathons a year. She should be the healthiest person I know, but she isn't. Almost every time she takes part in an event,

5 she gets sick with a cold or virus or respiratory infection. I'm starting to think that there might be a link between her training and her illnesses.
Carol *from Portland*

A: You're right, Carol. Too much exercise could have harmful effects. Your sister may
10 be showing the effects of what the experts call overtraining. All that physical stress on her body might be having a negative effect on her immune system. A recent study of 2,000 runners in the Los Angeles Marathon showed that 13% of the runners became ill the following week. Researchers concluded that marathon runners are six times more likely to get sick after a race and their immune systems may take longer to recover
15 than non-runners. According to experts, moderate exercise should normally strengthen our immune systems but too much exercise could have the opposite effect. It may be hard to believe, but a number of studies on physical education teachers and on former high-school, college, and professional athletes have shown that too much of certain

kinds of exercise might lead to painful and potentially disabling conditions. These, in
20   turn, could result in hip and knee replacements, not to mention broken bones and
years of discomfort.

But, while excessive amounts of exercise and sport may turn out to be bad for you,
most experts agree on one thing. No exercise at all could prove to be even more
harmful in the long run.

▼

---

excessive: more than is necessary or normal
immune system: system of the body that helps you
   fight against infection and disease
in the long run: over a long period of time

moderate: not too much or too little, average
potentially: likely to be or develop in the future
respiratory: of or related to the organs of breathing

A3 After You Read

Choose the answer that best completes each sentence.

1. Carol suspects that her sister's
   frequent illnesses are caused by
   _____.

   a. the environment

   b. her lack of exercise

   c. training

2. Doctor Fran suggests that
   overtraining may have a bad
   effect on _____.

   a. mental readiness

   b. endurance

   c. the immune system

3. Research shows that marathon
   runners often _____ right
   after a race.

   a. have heart attacks

   b. become ill

   c. break bones

4. Moderate exercise normally has
   _____ effect on the
   immune system.

   a. a positive

   b. a negative

   c. no

5. Studies show that, over time, excessive
   exercise can lead to _____ .

   a. bone and joint problems

   b. stronger bones and joints

   c. early retirement

6. Doctor Fran believes that getting
   no exercise is _____
   excessive exercise.

   a. even more harmful than

   b. not as harmful as

   c. equally as harmful as

B FORM

Modals of Present and Future Possibility

Think Critically About Form

A. Look back at the article on page 146 and complete the tasks below.

1. **IDENTIFY** Look at the three underlined examples of modals of present and future possbility. Find six more examples.

2. **CATEGORIZE** Sort your examples into modals followed by:
   a. *be*   **b.** *be* + verb + *-ing*   **c.** a different main verb

B. Discuss your answers with the class and read the Form charts to check them.

▶ **Present Modals**

ONLINE
PRACTICE

AFFIRMATIVE STATEMENTS			
SUBJECT	MODAL	MAIN VERB OR *BE* (+ VERB + *-ING*)	
He	may	have	a car.
	might		
She	could	be meeting	him now.
They	should	be	home.
	must		

NEGATIVE STATEMENTS			
SUBJECT	MODAL + *NOT*	MAIN VERB OR *BE* (+ VERB + *-ING*)	
He	may not	have	a car.
	might not		
She	couldn't	be meeting	him now.
	can't		
They	shouldn't	be	home.
	must not		

▶ **Future Modals**

AFFIRMATIVE STATEMENTS			
SUBJECT	MODAL	MAIN VERB OR *BE* (+ VERB + *-ING*)	
He	may	get	a car soon.
	might		
She	could	be meeting	him later.
They	should	be	home soon.
	will		

NEGATIVE STATEMENTS			
SUBJECT	MODAL + *NOT*	MAIN VERB OR *BE* (+ VERB + *-ING*)	
He	may not	get	a car soon.
	might not		
She	couldn't	be meeting	him later.
	can't		
They	shouldn't	be	home yet.
	won't		

Modals of Present Possibility

- Modals have only one form with all subjects.

- *Must not*, *may not*, and *might not* have no contracted forms as modals of possibility.

> ⚠ Do not confuse the two words *may be* (modal + *be*) with *maybe*, a one-word adverb that often begins a sentence.
>
> He **may be** late. **Maybe** he's late.

- *Could* and *can* are used to ask questions about present possibility. *Might* is very uncommon. Use *be* in short answers to questions containing *be*.

  A: **Could** he **be sleeping**?   A: **Can** it **be true**?

  B: He **might be**.   B: It **must not be**.

- See Appendix 14 for contractions with *should*, *could*, and *can*.

Modals of Future Possibility

- *Must (not)*, *can't*, and *couldn't* are not usually used to express future possibility unless they are combined with the continuous.

  She **must not be getting** a new car next month.

- *Could* may be used to ask questions about future possibility. Notice the short answers.

  A: **Could** he **arrive** before we get home?   B: Yes, he **might**. / No, he **won't**.

- See Appendix 14 for contractions with *will*.

▶ Present Phrasal Modals

AFFIRMATIVE STATEMENTS

SUBJECT	MODAL	MAIN VERB OR *BE* (+ VERB + *-ING*)	
He	**ought to**	**be**	home.
She	**has to** **has got to**	**be riding**	her bike.
They	**have to** **have got to**	**have**	a car.

CONTRACTIONS

She**'s** They**'ve**	**got to**	**have**	a car.

▶ Future Phrasal Modals

AFFIRMATIVE STATEMENTS

SUBJECT	MODAL	MAIN VERB OR *BE* (+ VERB + *-ING*)	
He	**ought to**	**be**	
She	**has to** **has got to**	**be coming**	home soon.
They	**have to** **have got to**		

CONTRACTIONS

She**'s** They**'ve**	**got to**	**to be coming**	home soon.

(*Continued on page 150*)

B1 Listening for Form

CD1 T40 **Listen to this story and write the modals or phrasal modals you hear. Use contractions if you hear them.**

The Abominable Snowman of the Himalayas and the Loch Ness Monster of Scotland are two creatures that _____ *may* _____ or

1

_____ *may not* _____ be real—that depends

2

on your beliefs. If you ask someone about them,

they _____ respond, "That

3

_____ be true," or they

4

_____ respond, "That

5

_____ be true." Over the years,

6

it has been difficult to separate fact from fiction

as stories about these creatures continue.

The Loch Ness Monster or a hoax?

_____ it be true that an ape-like creature with long hair lives high

7

in the Himalayas? _____ the large footprints found there belong to

8

such a creature? While many scientists say this _____ be a myth, others

9

claim that there _____ be some kind of creature out there. But no one

10

knows for sure.

In Scotland, _____ there really be a mysterious water monster
with a long neck and a large body like a brontosaurus? Many claim that there

_____ be some truth to this story that's been around since the fifteenth
century. Just ask the two million tourists who visit the area each year, hoping to see
the monster.

B2 Completing Conversations with Modals

**Work with a partner. Complete the conversations with the words in parentheses.
Use contractions when possible. Then practice the conversations.**

Conversation 1

A: That number _____may not be_____ (be/not/may) right.

B: Don't worry. It _____ (be/not/can) wrong. The computer doesn't
make mistakes!

Conversation 2

A: They _____ (arrive/should) soon.

B: I doubt it. They probably _____ (arrive/not/will) until later.

A: No, I spoke to them a half hour ago. They _____ (be/ought to) here
in 20 minutes.

Conversation 3

A: This _____ (be/have to) a mistake. My phone bill
_____ (be/not/could) $300 for just one month!

B: Don't worry about it. Just call up the phone company. There _____
(be/must) an explanation.

Conversation 4

A: Why isn't Sasha home yet? The movie _____ (be/have got to)
over by now.

B: Actually, it just ended. He _____ (be/should) here soon.

B3 Using Short Answers with Modals

Work with a partner. Switch roles for each question.

Student A: Ask a question about healthy living.

Student B: Answer the question with your beliefs. Use positive or negative short answers with *may*, *might*, *must*, or *could*. Use *be* where necessary.

1. Do carrots improve your eyesight?

   A: Do carrots improve your eyesight?
   B: They may. OR *They may not.*

2. Is moderate exercise good for everyone?

   A: Is moderate exercise good for everyone?
   B: It must be. OR *It couldn't be.*

3. Do eggs cause heart disease?

4. Is coffee good for your memory?

5. Do cell phones cause cancer?

6. Are microwave ovens bad for you?

7. Does table salt lower your blood pressure?

8. Are full-time jobs bad for you?

B4 Building Sentences with Modals

Build as many meaningful sentences as possible. Use an item from each column. Punctuate your sentences correctly.

John must be sleeping.

John it	must might can't has to	be have	sleeping true a problem broken

B5 Writing Your Own Sentences with Modals

Think about a distant city where you have relatives or friends. Use modals of present possibility to do the tasks below.

1. Write three sentences about the weather in the city you are thinking about.

   It must be raining in Rio.
   It may be cool...

2. Write three sentences describing what you think your friends or relatives are doing right now.

   Carla must be traveling.
   Marco might be teaching a class, or he could be...

MEANING AND USE 1

Modals of Present Possibility

Think Critically About Meaning and Use

A. Read the sentences and answer the questions below.

   a. He must be telling the truth. He never lies.
   b. He may be telling the truth. I'm not sure.
   c. He can't be telling the truth. His story doesn't make sense.
   d. He could be telling the truth. It's possible, I guess.
   e. He might be telling the truth. I don't know.
   f. He should be telling the truth. He usually does.

   1. **ANALYZE** In which sentences is the speaker more certain?

   2. **ANALYZE** In which sentences is the speaker less certain?

B. Discuss your answers with the class and read the Meaning and Use Notes to check them.

Meaning and Use Notes

ONLINE PRACTICE

	Overview	
▶ 1	Modals and phrasal modals of possibility are used to express guesses, expectations, or inferences about present situations. The modal you choose shows how certain you are that something is true.	

Less Certain	• could, might, might not	Jim **could be** upstairs, or he **might be** outside.
↑	• may, may not	He **may not be** awake yet. I'm not sure.
	• should, shouldn't, ought to	Jim **should be** upstairs. I saw him go up a few minutes ago.
↓	• must, must not, have to, have got to	I don't see Jim. He **must not be feeling** well. He **has to be** upstairs.
More Certain	• can't, couldn't	Jim **couldn't be** upstairs. I saw him go out.

(Continued on page 154)

Guessing with *Could*, *Might*, and *May*

▶ 2 Use *could*, *might (not)*, and *may (not)* to guess about a present situation when you don't have much proof. *Could* and *might* sometimes show less certainty than *may*, especially when they express more than one possibility.

More Certain	Less Certain
A: Where's Jim?	A: Where's Jim?
B: He **may be** upstairs.	B: He **could be** upstairs, or he **might be** outside.

Expectations with *Should* and *Ought To*

▶ 3 Use *should(n't)* and *ought to* when you have an expectation about a present situation based on proof or experience.

A: Where's Jim?

B: He **should be** upstairs. I saw him go up a few minutes ago.

> Expectations expressed with *should* and *ought to* may be confused with the meanings of advisability and necessity that are also expressed by these modals. To make the meaning clear, the context must be stated or understood.
>
> Jim **ought to be** in bed. I thought I saw him go upstairs before. (*ought to* = expectation)
>
> Jim **ought to be** in bed. He looks very sick. (*ought to* = advisability)

Strong Certainty and Understanding with *Must*, *Have To*, and *Have Got To*

▶ 4A Use *must (not)*, *have to*, and *have got to* to draw conclusions when you are certain of something, and you believe there is only one logical explanation.

A: We can't find Jim.

B: He ⎧ **must** ⎫ **be** upstairs. We've looked everywhere else.
⎨ **has to** ⎬
⎩ **has got to** ⎭

▶ 4B In conversation, *must be* or *must feel* with an adjective often show understanding of someone's feelings.

A: I hardly slept at all last night. My neighbors had a party.

B: You **must be** very annoyed at them.

C: You **must feel** tired. Do you still want to go out later?

	Strong Certainty with *Can't* and *Couldn't*

▶ **5A** Use *can't* and *couldn't* when you are certain something is unlikely or impossible. Notice that in the affirmative, however, *could* expresses less certainty.

A: I think Jim is upstairs.

B: He **couldn't be** upstairs. I saw him go out. (*couldn't* = strong certainty)

A: Well, I **could be** wrong. (*could* = less certainty)

▶ **5B** *Can't* and *couldn't* sometimes express surprise or disbelief.

A: I heard that you're going to be promoted.

B: That **can't be** true. The boss doesn't like me. (*can't* = disbelief)

C1 Listening for Meaning and Use

▶ Notes 1–3, 4A, 4B, 5A, 5B

CD1 T41 Listen to each situation. Is the speaker expressing less certainty or more certainty about the situation? Check (✓) the correct column.

	LESS CERTAINTY	MORE CERTAINTY
1.	✓	
2.		
3.		
4.		
5.		
6.		
7.		
8.		

C2 Expressing Degrees of Certainty

▶ Notes 1–3, 4A

Work with a partner. Read each question and the two responses. Then complete each response with a modal that expresses the appropriate degree of certainty. More than one answer may be possible for each item.

Conversation 1

A: What's wrong with Alice? She has been looking strange ever since class ended.

B: She ___might___ be upset. I don't think she did very well on the exam.
   1

C: She ___must___ be upset. I saw her exam. She got a very low grade.
   2

Conversation 2

A: Are the clothes dry yet?

B: They _____ be dry by now. They usually take 45 minutes to dry, and they've
   1

been in the dryer almost 40 minutes.

C: They _____ be dry by now. They usually take 45 minutes, and they've been in
   2

the dryer for almost an hour.

Conversation 3

A: Do you think they've finished repairing your car by now?

B: It _____ be ready. It's 2:00 P.M., and they said it'd be ready at noon.
   1

C: It _____ be ready. It's noon. They said it would probably be ready by noon.
   2

Conversation 4

A: Whose black jacket is this? Someone forgot to take it after the meeting.

B: It _____ be Diane's. I saw her wearing a black jacket earlier.
   1

C: It _____ be Diane's. She wears a lot of black.
   2

Conversation 5

A: It's 10:30 P.M. Who could be calling so late?

B: It _____ be Chris. She said she wanted to talk to me today.
   1

C: It _____ be Chris. She said she was going to call after ten o'clock.
   2

C3 Guessing with *Could, Might,* and *May* ▶ Note 2

 Work in small groups. Describe what you think the people in the pictures are doing. Use *could, might,* and *may* to make as many guesses as you can.

They could be watching a car show.
They might be looking at…

C4 Making Guesses and Drawing Conclusions ▶ Notes 1, 2, 4A

Work in small groups. Write guesses and conclusions about each situation below. Use *could, must, may, might, has to,* and *has got to.* Add one or two more sentences to explain what you mean. Discuss your answers.

1. The teacher is absent today.

   She must be sick. She wasn't feeling well yesterday. OR
   She might be out of town, or she could be sick. Nobody knows. OR
   She might not be feeling well again. She was sick a few weeks ago.

2. The fire alarm is ringing.

3. Your new neighbor never smiles.

4. Everyone's eating chocolate cake for dessert except Tina.

5. You've been sneezing all morning.

6. Your sister has just received a dozen long-stemmed roses with no card.

7. Jenny isn't answering the telephone.

8. Sam always looks tired.

C5 Stating Expectations and Drawing Conclusions ▶ Notes 3, 4A

 Work with a partner. Terry is a nurse. Read Terry's work schedule and complete each sentence below. Give your conclusions or expectations using *must be* or *should be* + a continuous verb or a time of day.

Day Shift Schedule	
6:45 A.M.	meet with night nurses
7:15 A.M.	check vital signs of patients (temperature, pulse, blood pressure)
7:45 A.M.	meet with doctors
8:30 A.M.	give patients medicine
10:00 A.M.	write notes on charts
11:00 A.M.	discharge patients
12:30 P.M.	attend meeting
1:00 P.M.	admit new patients
2:45 P.M.	take a break
4:30 P.M.	go home

1. If it's 7:20, *Terry must be checking the patients' vital signs.*

   OR *Terry should be checking the patients' vital signs.*

2. If Terry is meeting with the doctors, *it must be 7:45.* OR *it should be 7:45.*

3. If it's 1:10, _____

4. If Terry is going home, _____

5. If it's 8:30, _____

6. If it's 11:00, _____

7. If it's 6:50, _____

8. If Terry is writing notes on charts, _____

9. If Terry is taking a break, _____

10. If it's 12:30, _____

C6 Expressing Understanding ▶ Note 4B

Work with a partner. Take turns reading these statements. Answer with *you must be* or *you must feel* + an adjective to show your understanding of each situation.

1. I studied all night for my exam.

   You must be exhausted. OR *You must feel tired.*

2. I didn't eat breakfast or lunch today.

3. Tomorrow is my first job interview.

4. My English teacher canceled our midterm exam.

5. My friends are going to visit me next week. I haven't seen them for six months.

6. My car broke down again. I just spent $300 on it last week.

7. I didn't get accepted to graduate school.

8. My parents are going to go on a cruise next month.

C7 Expressing Strong Certainty and Disbelief ▶ Notes 4A, 4B, 5A, 5B

A. Work with a partner. Write a dialogue in which the speakers express strong certainty and surprise or disbelief about one of the topics below. Use some of these modals: *can't, couldn't, must, have to, have got to.*

1. A young person is trying to make excuses to his or her parents about not doing well in school.

   Young person: *There's got to be a mistake. My grades can't be that bad.*

   Parent: *You must be kidding! What about the homework that you didn't do, and the classes that you missed?*

   Young person: *Well,…*

2. Two friends are discussing the surprising behavior of a mutual friend.

3. Two co-workers are discussing some rumors that are going around the office.

4. Two teachers are discussing a student's work, which has suddenly improved.

B. Practice your dialogue. Be prepared to present it to the class.

Modals of Future Possibility

Think Critically About Meaning and Use

A. Read the sentences and answer the questions below.

a. The plane might be on time. It's not clear yet.
b. The plane should be on time. It left on time.
c. The plane could be on time. They sometimes make up time in the air.
d. The plane will be on time. They just announced it.

1. ANALYZE In which sentences is the speaker less certain?

2. ANALYZE In which sentences is the speaker more certain?

3. INTERPRET Which sentences have about the same meaning?

B. Discuss your answers with the class and read the Meaning and Use Notes to check them.

Meaning and Use Notes

ONLINE PRACTICE

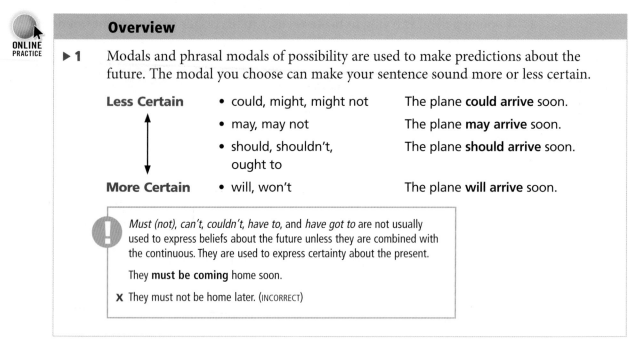

Overview

▶ **1** Modals and phrasal modals of possibility are used to make predictions about the future. The modal you choose can make your sentence sound more or less certain.

Less Certain	• could, might, might not	The plane **could arrive** soon.
	• may, may not	The plane **may arrive** soon.
	• should, shouldn't, ought to	The plane **should arrive** soon.
More Certain	• will, won't	The plane **will arrive** soon.

> ! *Must (not), can't, couldn't, have to,* and *have got to* are not usually used to express beliefs about the future unless they are combined with the continuous. They are used to express certainty about the present.
>
> They **must be coming** home soon.
>
> ✗ They must not be home later. (INCORRECT)

Guessing with *Could, Might,* and *May*

▶ **2** Use *could, might (not),* and *may (not)* to guess about a future situation when you don't have much proof. *Could* and *might* sometimes show less certainty than *may,* especially when they are used to express more than one possibility.

More Certain	**Less Certain**
A: When is Liz arriving?	A: When is Liz arriving?
B: She **may be arriving** soon.	B: She **could arrive** at 7:30, but she **might be** late.

Expectations with *Should* and *Ought To*

▶ **3** Use *should(n't)* and *ought to* when you have an expectation about a future situation based on proof or experience. *Should* and *ought to* are used to indicate future expectations more frequently than present expectations.

A: When is she coming?

B: She **should be** here at 7:30. That's what she told me yesterday.

> ⚠ Expectations expressed by *should* and *ought to* can become confused with the meanings of advisability and necessity that are also expressed by these modals. To make the meaning clear, the context must be stated or understood.
>
> Liz **ought to be** here on Monday. She said she's coming. (*ought to* = possibility)
>
> Liz **ought to be** here on Monday. I told her to come. (*ought to* = advisability)

Strong Certainty with *Will* and *Won't*

▶ **4A** Use *will* and *won't* to express strong certainty about the future.

She**'ll come** soon. I'm not worried. (very likely)

She **won't be coming**. (very unlikely)

▶ **4B** *Will* is often weakened with adverbs of possibility such as *maybe, perhaps,* and *probably. Probably* is the strongest of these adverbs, although it still expresses a small amount of doubt.

Maybe she**'ll come**. (= She **might come.**)

Perhaps she**'ll come**. (= She **might come.**)

She**'ll probably come**. (= She **should be coming.**)

D4 Making Predictions About Your Lifetime ▶ Notes 1–3, 4A, 4B

A. **Complete each sentence with an affirmative or negative modal to make a prediction about your lifetime.**

1. During my lifetime, more people _____ will _____ live to the age of 100.

2. People _____ may not _____ visit other planets.

3. Researchers _____ find a cure for cancer.

4. Astronomers _____ solve the mysteries of the universe.

5. People _____ live on Mars.

6. I _____ ride in a spaceship.

7. Robots _____ do all of our housework.

8. Countries _____ stop producing nuclear weapons.

9. Scientists _____ find ways to predict earthquakes.

10. There _____ be another world war.

B. **Now write five more predictions about things that *could*, *might*, *may*, or *will* happen in your lifetime. Use adverbs of possibility in at least two of your sentences.**

In the future, robots may assist the elderly with all of their household chores.

Maybe everyone will be driving electric cars.

My country will probably host the Olympics.

C. **Follow these steps to write a paragraph about one of your predictions from parts A or B.**

1. Write down some details about the prediction.

2. Use the prediction to write a clear introductory sentence and a paragraph explaining what might or might not happen.

3. Make sure to use various modals and adverbs of possibility, but don't use them in every sentence.

During my lifetime, people may not visit other planets, but unmanned space vehicles will certainly continue to visit them. People might be able to…

Think Critically About Meaning and Use

A. Work with a partner. Read each situation. Choose the sentence that is the most certain.

1. The key is missing.
- **a.** It may be on the table.
- **b.** It must be on the table. *(circled)*
- **c.** It ought to be on the table.

2. A letter has just arrived.
- **a.** It can't be from Mary.
- **b.** It must not be from Mary.
- **c.** It might not be from Mary.

3. Thomas is doing his homework.
- **a.** He might finish by four o'clock.
- **b.** He could finish by four o'clock.
- **c.** He won't finish by four o'clock.

4. The answer is 25.
- **a.** That may not be right.
- **b.** That couldn't be right.
- **c.** That might not be right.

5. The doorbell is ringing.
- **a.** It has to be the mail carrier.
- **b.** It should be the mail carrier.
- **c.** It ought to be the mail carrier.

6. My car is at the service station.
- **a.** It won't be ready soon.
- **b.** It will probably be ready soon.
- **c.** It ought to be ready soon.

B. Discuss these questions in small groups.
   1. **GENERATE** Look at sentence 1. Imagine you know for sure that the key is <u>not</u> on the table. What two modal forms could you use to replace *must be*?
   2. **PREDICT** Look at sentence 6a. What might the speaker say next to support the idea?

Edit
Find the errors in this paragraph and correct them.

A migraine is a severe headache that can ~~to~~ affect your quality of life. Migraine sufferers often experience symptoms such as zigzag flashing lights or blind spots in their vision. However, there are other symptoms that could signaling that a migraine is coming. You maybe sensitive to light, sound, or smells, or you might be feel overly tired. The good news is that treatment must often relieve the pain and symptoms and prevent further attacks.

Write

Imagine that you are the health editor of your school's online newspaper. Write an article discussing ways that students might stay fit while they are studying at your school. Use modals and phrasal modals of present and future possibility.

1. **BRAINSTORM** Think about all the problems that students face and the solutions that you might include. Use these categories to help you organize your ideas into three or four paragraphs.

   - **Problems:** Why might students find it difficult to stay fit while they are studying (e.g., sitting for too many hours, study/sleep habits, food)?
   - **Solutions/Advice:** What are some of the things that students might do to stay fit (e.g., exercise, eat properly, get enough sleep)?
   - **Conclusion:** What may happen if they don't follow your advice? What benefits might they experience if they follow your suggestions?

2. **WRITE A FIRST DRAFT** Before you write your first draft, read the checklist below and look at the examples on pages 146–147. Write your draft using modals of possibility.

3. **EDIT** Read your work and check it against the checklist below. Circle grammar, spelling, and punctuation errors.

DO I...	YES
give my article a title?	☐
organize my ideas into paragraphs?	☐
use a variety of modals of possibility to speculate about the problems students may be facing now and the solutions they might consider in the near future?	☐
use adverbs such as *maybe*, *perhaps*, and *probably* to soften my ideas?	☐

4. **PEER REVIEW** Work with a partner to help you decide how to fix your errors and improve the content. Use the checklist above.

5. **REWRITE YOUR DRAFT** Using the comments from your partner, write a final draft.

● ● ●

STUDENT HEALTH LINE   ▲

Don't just sit there!

Let's face it! If you're a serious student, you're probably doing a lot of sitting—in class, in the library, in your room. You might also be living away from home for the first time, so you may not be thinking about good nutrition or your sleep habits…

8

Past Modals

A. **GRAMMAR IN DISCOURSE: The Really Early Birds** 168

B. **FORM: Past Modals** 170

Past Modals
> I **may/might/could/should/must have passed** the test.

Past Phrasal Modals
> He **ought to have come**.
> She **has to/has got to have known**.

Informally Speaking: Reducing Past Modals

C. **MEANING AND USE 1: Modals of Past Possibility** 176

Overview

Guessing with *May Have*, *Might Have*, and *Could Have*

Strong Certainty with *Must Have*, *Have to Have*, and *Have Got to Have*

Strong Certainty with *Can't Have* and *Couldn't Have*

D. **MEANING AND USE 2: Other Functions of Past Modals** 180

Past Ability and Opportunity

Advice, Obligations, and Regrets About the Past

Past Permission and Necessity

WRITING: Write a Review of a Movie, TV Show, or Short Story 186

PART 3 TEST: Modals 189

The Really Early Birds

A1 Before You Read

Discuss these questions.

Have you ever thought about how birds are able to fly? Do you know what makes it possible? Have you ever dreamed or wished you could fly?

A2 Read

CD1 T43   Read this magazine article to find out what new evidence has been found about how birds first learned to fly.

The Really Early Birds

A new theory explains how the first feathered creatures to fly <u>may have gotten</u> off the ground. Researchers believe that a prehistoric
5 bird that descended from dinosaurs, archaeopteryx (pronounced "ar-kee-op-te-riks"), had a good wingspan for a half-pound bird—more than 20 inches. That has to have been enough
10 to enable the crow-sized bird to fly, or at least glide, through the Jurassic skies. But the toughest part of flying is the takeoff. And the first birds and their dinosaur ancestors just didn't
15 have the same specialized muscle power for liftoff that their modern descendants do. It's a question that scientists have been arguing about for

more than 200 years. How did the
20 first fliers get into the air? A study in the journal Nature shows how it could have happened.

Fly or die? According to this popular theory, a tree-dwelling
25 prehistoric bird could have launched itself—or could have fallen—from its perch and managed to stay up by flapping its wings. That solves the gravity issue, but Luis Chiappe, a
30 palaeontologist at the Natural History Museum of Los Angeles County, points out a problem. "We don't know of any bird ancestors that lived in trees."

35   **A running start?** This could have helped a bird like archaeopteryx into

the air, but the ancient bird's estimated speed wasn't fast enough for liftoff. Chiappe worked with an 40 expert in aerodynamics, Phillip Burgers, to simulate the takeoff of the archaeopteryx. They found that the bird's wings were able to rotate in a way that may have provided the extra 45 burst of speed needed to outrun a hungry predator or catch a quick-running lizard. And, the new calculations show, the wing flapping could have generated sufficient speed 50 for takeoff. During the early phase of liftoff, archaeopteryx's wings must have acted more like an airplane's engines, providing extra speed. Then, when the archaeopteryx was in the 55 air, it must have rotated its wings back to horizontal position, to maintain altitude.

Modern birds do exactly the same thing, so why hasn't anyone noticed 60 until now? Experts have been fascinated by lift, probably because it's something humans can't do. Chiappe and Burgers have shown that the archaeopteryx could have 65 taken off from the ground, but whether or not it actually did may never be known. According to the researchers, the answer to this question is not really important. 70 Rather, the importance of their discovery is that the wings could have helped the archaeopteryx gain speed. Flying might have developed as the archaeopteryx ran faster and faster 75 while flapping its wings, not by falling out of trees. Perhaps flying is just the continuation of running by other means.

Adapted from *Newsweek*

---

aerodynamics: the science that studies forces that act on things moving through air

altitude: height in the air

Jurassic: the time period when dinosaurs and the earliest birds lived

paleontologist: a scientist who studies fossils to learn about the history of life on earth

predator: an animal that lives by killing and eating other animals

wingspan: measurement across the wings when the wings are extended

A3 After You Read

Check (✓) the facts that scientists who study prehistoric birds are certain about.

_✓_ **1.** They had feathers.

_____ **2.** They descended from dinosaurs.

_____ **3.** They had wings.

_____ **4.** They were much smaller than modern birds.

_____ **5.** They could fly.

_____ **6.** They lived in trees.

B FORM

Past Modals

Think Critically About Form

A. Look back at the article on page 168 and complete the tasks below.

1. **IDENTIFY** An example of a past modal is underlined. Find six more examples.

2. **COMPARE AND CONTRAST** Find two past modals with singular subjects and two with plural subjects. Is there any difference in form between them?

3. **EVALUATE** What auxiliary follows the modals? What is the form of the main verbs?

B. Discuss your answers with the class and read the Form charts to check them.

▶ Past Modals

ONLINE
PRACTICE

AFFIRMATIVE STATEMENTS						NEGATIVE STATEMENTS				
SUBJECT	MODAL	*HAVE*	PAST PARTICIPLE			SUBJECT	MODAL + NOT	*HAVE*	PAST PARTICIPLE	
I	may might could should must	have	passed	the test.		I	may not might not couldn't can't shouldn't must not	have	passed	the test.

- Past modals have only one form with all subjects.
- Past modals have two auxiliary verbs: a modal and *have*. Only the modal forms contractions.
- *May not have*, *might not have*, and *must not have* have no contracted forms as past modals.
- *Could have* and *should have* may be used to ask questions with past modals. Notice that short answers contain modal + *have* and optional main verb *be* if appropriate.

  A: **Could** they **have called**?   A: **Should** she **have been** at the meeting?

  B: No, they **must not have**.   B: Yes, she **should have been**.

- See Appendix 14 for contractions with *can*, *could*, and *should*.
- See Appendix 6 for irregular verbs and their past participles.

▶ Past Phrasal Modals

AFFIRMATIVE STATEMENTS			
SUBJECT	MODAL	*HAVE*	PAST PARTICIPLE
He	**ought to**	**have**	**come**.
She	**has to** **has got to**	**have**	**known**.
You	**have to** **have got to**		

NEGATIVE STATEMENTS			
SUBJECT	MODAL + NOT	*HAVE*	PAST PARTICIPLE
He	**ought not to**	**have**	**come**.

CONTRACTIONS		
She's You've	got to	have	known.

- *Ought to have* has only one form. *Have to have* and *have got to have* have different third-person singular forms.
- *Ought to have* can be used in the affirmative or negative. *Have to have* and *have got to have* are used only in the affirmative.
- *Have got to have* has contracted forms. *Have to have* and *ought to have* do not.
- *Had to have* + past participle can often replace *have to have* + past participle.

You { have to have / had to have } known the answer.

B1 Listening for Form

CD1 T44 **Listen to this podcast and write the past modals you hear.**

Most scientists now agree that an asteroid collision or a similar event ____must have____ been responsible for
1
starting the mass extinction of dinosaurs and other animals about 65 million years ago. But there is still disagreement about another wave of extinction that occurred more recently, just 13,000 years ago. That's

when great woolly mammoths, mastodons, saber-tooth tigers, and other large animals known as megafauna died off in northern Eurasia and the Americas.

What _____ caused the disappearance of these great beasts? Some
2
say that human colonizers from Siberia _____ done the damage over a
3
period of a thousand years. But others disagree. In their opinion, a relatively small group of hunters _____ killed off so many animals across three whole
4
continents. As one researcher told me, "We _____ found evidence of
5
such overhunting, but we haven't. So humans _____ been the cause."
6

Others think it _____ been climate change. Scientists know that
7
there was a cold snap that led to a partial return to Ice Age conditions between 12,900 and 11,500 years ago, and some believe that this _____ put stress on
8
the megafauna. Again, for the theory to be true, they _____ found
9
proof, but so far they haven't.

The most recent theory is that a major cosmic catastrophe such as an airburst or impact from a comet _____ caused the extinctions. Evidence to
10
support this _____ already been found in soil samples at more than
11
50 sites across North America, and glacier scientists think they _____
12
found signs in the Greenland ice sheet as well.

B2 Completing Conversations

Work with a partner. Complete these conversations using the past modal form of the words in parentheses. Then practice the conversations using contractions where appropriate.

Conversation 1

A: I ___could have gone___ (could/go) to the movies with you, but I decided to
              1
study instead.

B: You didn't miss anything. You _____ (might/not/like) it anyway.
                                                2
There _____ (must/be) ten different violent scenes!
              3

Conversation 2

A: I _____ (should/not/drive) to work this morning. There was so
          1
much traffic.

B: You _____ (should/take) the bus. It was empty.
                      2

Conversation 3

A: She _____ (could/not/leave) yet. We're not that late.
                    1

B: But she _____ (might/forget) to wait for us.
                        2

Conversation 4

A: You _____ (must/not/got) much sleep last night.
                    1

B: You're right. I was up coughing and sneezing most of the night. I
_____ (should/go) to the doctor yesterday, He _____
          2   3
(could/write) me a prescription for some cold medicine.

Conversation 5

A: I lost my keys last night. I _____ (might/leave) them at your house.
                                                1

B: No, you _____ (could/not). You drove home with them.
                        2

A: That's right. Then I _____ (must/drop) them after I parked the car.
                                    3

B: You _____ (might/lock) them in your car. Have you checked?
                    4

B3 Asking and Answering Questions with Past Modals

Work with a partner. Switch roles for each question.

Student A: Ask a question about prehistoric birds. Use the words below with *could have.*

Student B: Answer the question in your own opinion. Use short answers with modals.

1. have feathers

    A: Could prehistoric birds have had feathers?

    B: Yes, they could have. OR *They must have.*

2. descend from dinosaurs

    A: Could prehistoric birds have descended from dinosaurs?

    B: No, they couldn't have.

3. have wings

4. jump from trees

5. run fast

6. live on the ground

7. eat smaller animals .

8. eat seeds

B4 Forming Past Modals

Rewrite these sentences. Change the modals to past modals.

1. The researchers might be wrong. There may be some data they ignored.

    The researchers might have been wrong. There may have been some data they ignored.

2. The report should be available on April 12.

3. He ought to study more for the test.

4. I could work harder.

5. She has to be home.

6. I should do things differently. I should exercise more. I know I could find the time.

7. I should relax more. Perhaps I could learn yoga.

8. I shouldn't worry so much. Worrying couldn't be good for my health.

Informally Speaking

Reducing Past Modals

CD1 T45 Look at the cartoon and listen to the conversation. How is each underlined form in the cartoon different from what you hear?

This traffic is terrible. We <u>should have</u> stayed in the office!

Yeah. We <u>could have</u> left after rush hour.

In informal speech, affirmative and negative past modals are often reduced. Have may sound like /əv/. If it is reduced even more, it sounds like /ə/.

Standard Form	What You Might Hear		
I **could have** come.	"I /ˈkʊdəv/ come."	OR	"I /ˈkʊdə/ come."
They **must have** come.	"They /ˈmʌstəv/ come."	OR	"They /ˈmʌstə/ come."
He **may not have** come.	"He /ˈmeɪnɑtəv/ come."	OR	"He /ˈmeɪnɑdə/ come."
We **should not have** come.	"We /ˈʃʊdntəv/ come."	OR	"We /ˈʃʊdndə/ come."

B5 Understanding Informal Speech

CD1 T46 Listen and write the standard form of the words you hear.

A: I'm sorry I'm late. I ___*should have*___ called you. Then you
1

_____ met me downtown.
2

B: That _____ worked anyway. I didn't get out of work until six.
3

And then there _____ been fifty people waiting for the elevator.
4

It took me ten minutes to get out of the building.

A: So where's Linda? She _____ been here by now. She
5

_____ forgotten.
6

B: I doubt that. She _____ gotten stuck in traffic, or she
7

_____ left work late, too. Let's sit down over there and wait for her.
8

Modals of Past Possibility

Think Critically About Meaning and Use

A. Read the sentences and answer the questions below.

  a. Prehistoric birds must have been able to fly. They had wings.
  b. Prehistoric birds could have been able to fly. They were small.
  c. Prehistoric birds might have been able to fly. They were light enough.
  d. Prehistoric birds couldn't have been able to fly. They had no way of getting into the air.

  1. EVALUATE In which sentences is the speaker more certain?

  2. EVALUATE In which sentences is the speaker less certain?

B. Discuss your answers with the class and read the Meaning and Use Notes to check them.

Meaning and Use Notes

ONLINE
PRACTICE

Overview

▶ **1**   Modals of past possibility are used to make guesses or inferences about the past. The modal you choose shows how certain you are that something was true.

		A: Where was Jim this morning?
Less Certain	• might have, might not have, could have	B: He **might have been** outside. I'm not sure.
	• may have, may not have	C: He **may not have been** awake yet.
	• must have, must not have, have to have, have got to have	D: He **must have been** in bed. He never gets up before noon.
More Certain	• can't have, couldn't have	E: He **can't have been** upstairs. He wasn't home.

Guessing with *May Have*, *Might Have*, and *Could Have*

▶ **2**   Use *may (not) have*, *might (not) have*, and *could have* to guess about a past situation when you don't have much proof.

  Dinosaurs **may have perished** because of a climate change, or they **might have** perished because of disease. Some people think they **could have perished** because a large meteor hit Earth.

Strong Certainty with *Must Have*, *Have to Have*, and *Have Got to Have*

▶ 3   Use *must (not) have*, *have to have*, and *have got to have* to draw conclusions about the past when you are certain of something, and you believe there is only one logical explanation.

Problem: Someone stole the money from the drawer. No one was in the room except Sally.

Conclusion: Sally **must have taken** it.

Sally **has (got) to have taken** it.

Strong Certainty with *Can't Have* and *Couldn't Have*

▶ 4A   Use *can't have* and *couldn't have* when you are certain something was unlikely or impossible.

No one believes him. He **can't have been** home at the time of the crime. The police have evidence that he was at the crime scene.

▶ 4B   *Can't have* and *couldn't have* sometimes express surprise or disbelief about the past.

A: You got an A on the exam.

B: I **couldn't have gotten** an A! That's impossible. Didn't I get the last question wrong?

C1 Listening for Meaning and Use

▶ Notes 1–3, 4A, 4B

CD1 T47   Listen to the different opinions among archaeologists about Neanderthals. Is each speaker expressing less certainty or more certainty? Check (✓) the correct column.

	LESS CERTAINTY	MORE CERTAINTY
1.	✓	
2.		
3.		
4.		
5.		
6.		
7.		
8.		

C2 Understanding Degrees of Certainty

▶ Notes 1–3, 4A

Work with a partner. Read what two different archaeologists (A and B) have said about the "Iceman," a 5,000-year-old frozen mummy that was discovered in 1991 in the Alps. Rewrite their opinions with modals of possibility.

1. **A:** Maybe the Iceman was a shepherd.

   B: We don't believe he was a shepherd.

   A: The Iceman may have been a shepherd.
   B: He couldn't have been a shepherd.

2. **A:** It was impossible for him to build a fire.

   B: Perhaps he built a fire.

3. **A:** It is possible he froze to death.

   B: He almost certainly froze to death.

4. **A:** We can conclude that he lived in a valley.

   B: It's not likely he lived in a valley.

5. **A:** Perhaps he wasn't older than 25.

   B: We can assume he wasn't older than 25.

C3 Making Guesses and Drawing Conclusions

▶ Notes 1–3, 4A

Work in small groups. Read about a mysterious incident and discuss what might have happened. Use different affirmative and negative past modals.

Unfriendly Native Americans may have killed the first group.
The Croatoans were friendly. They can't have killed the second group.

The "Lost Colony of Roanoke" is one of the great mysteries of early American history. When John White and a group of English settlers arrived on Roanoke Island in July 1587, the only sign they found of the previous colonists were some bones. What happened is still a mystery. White quickly established good relations with the Native Americans on the nearby island of Croatoan, but a second group remained unfriendly. The settlers convinced White to sail back to England to arrange for food and supplies, but war with Spain delayed him. When he arrived three years later, in August 1590, there was no sign of the 118 settlers. Even their homes had disappeared. The only clue was the word "Croatoan" carved into a post of the fort and "Cro" carved into a tree.

Many questions remain. What happened to the first settlers? Did the second group go to live with the Croatoans? Did unfriendly natives kill them? Did they die of disease? Why was there no sign of their houses? Did they split up and go off to live in different areas?

C4 Expressing Impossibility and Disbelief

▶ Notes 4A, 4B

Work with a partner. Switch roles for each statement.

Student A: Read a statement.

Student B: Express disbelief with *couldn't have*. Give a reason for your disbelief.

1. You just won the game.

   A: You just won the game.

   B: I couldn't have won the game. I didn't even buy a ticket.

2. Your great-great-grandfather sent you a letter.

3. Your Rolls Royce ran out of gas.

4. You grew three inches taller this week.

5. You lost a million dollars yesterday.

6. You swam the English Channel last week.

C5 Writing About Impossibility and Disbelief

▶ Notes 4A, 4B

A. Do you believe everything you read in the news or on the Internet? Make a list of events or situations that you have read about that seem unbelievable. Why do you think they are unbelievable?

B. Choose one of your events or situations from part A. Write a paragraph expressing your disbelief. Tell why you think the incident couldn't have happened the way it was described. Describe what you think must have happened instead.

I found a website about the "Lost Colony of Roanoke" on the Internet yesterday. It said the colonists may have died of starvation, but I don't think this could have happened. Many historians say that the island must have had a lot of wild game, seafood, and edible plants in the late 1500s. With so much food around, the colonists couldn't have gone hungry...

MEANING AND USE 2

Other Functions of Past Modals

Think Critically About Meaning and Use

A. Read the sentences and answer the questions below.

a. Paul lived near his office. He could walk there every morning. He liked the exercise.

b. Paul lived near his office. He could have walked there every morning, but he broke his leg.

c. Paul lived near his office. He should have walked there every morning, but he was too lazy.

1. **EVALUATE** Which sentences suggest that Paul didn't walk to work every day?

2. **EVALUATE** Which one suggests that he did?

3. **EVALUATE** Which sentence expresses the speaker's opinion and advice about a past situation?

B. Discuss your answers with the class and read the Meaning and Use Notes to check them.

Meaning and Use Notes

ONLINE PRACTICE

Past Ability and Opportunity

▶ 1   *Could have* suggests that a person had the ability or opportunity to do something in the past but <u>did not</u> do it. *Could* suggests that a person had the ability or opportunity to do something and <u>was able to</u> or <u>did</u> do it.

***Could Have* (Did Not Do It)**

I **could have walked** to school, but I got a ride instead. (I didn't walk to school.)

You **could have spoken** French with her, but you were too shy. (You didn't speak French with her.)

***Could* (Did It)**

I lived near the school, so I **could walk** there. (I walked to school.)

You **could speak** French at an early age. (You spoke French at an early age.)

Advice, Obligations, and Regrets About the Past

▶ **2A** *Should(n't) have* expresses advice about past situations. *Should(n't) have* and *ought (not) to have* express past obligations (what you were or were not supposed to do). Compare the actions that the speakers actually <u>did</u> do and the actions that the speakers <u>did not</u> do.

Did Not Do It

You **should have asked** for help. (Asking for help was a good idea, but you <u>didn't</u> do it.)

She **ought to have registered** on Monday. (She was supposed to register on Monday, but she <u>didn't</u>.)

He **should have visited** his aunt in the hospital. (Visiting his aunt was the right thing to do, but he <u>didn't</u> do it.)

Did It

You **shouldn't have driven** in bad weather. (It was a bad idea to drive, but you <u>did</u> it anyway.)

He **shouldn't have taken** the money. It's illegal. (He wasn't allowed to take the money, but he <u>did</u> it anyway.)

▶ **2B** In the first person, *should(n't) have* shows regret. It means that you think that something you did or did not do was a mistake.

Did Not Do It

I **should have accepted** the job offer. (I didn't accept the job. Now I am sorry.)

Did It

I **shouldn't have lost** my temper. (I lost my temper. It was a mistake.)

Past Permission and Necessity

▶ **3** *May (not)* for expressing permission and *must* for expressing necessity do not have past modal forms. Several different past expressions are used instead.

Present Modals	Past Expressions		
Seniors **may have** cars.	Seniors	were permitted to were allowed to	**have** cars.
Freshmen **may not have** cars.	Freshmen	were not permitted to were not allowed to	**have** cars.
All visitors **must register**.	All visitors	were required to were supposed to had to	register.

D1 Listening for Meaning and Use

▶ Notes 1, 2A, 2B, 3

🔊 CD1 T48 Listen to the statements. Choose the sentence that best expresses the meaning of the situation that you hear.

1. **a.** John should have applied for the scholarship.

    b. John must have applied for the scholarship.

2. **a.** John could have left early.

    b. John should have left early.

3. **a.** John shouldn't have asked for help.

    b. John ought to have asked for help.

4. **a.** John must have taken two English courses.

    b. John had to take two English courses.

5. **a.** John may have registered late.

    b. John was permitted to register late.

6. **a.** John shouldn't have called his parents yesterday.

    b. John was supposed to call his parents yesterday.

7. **a.** John had to work in a department store.

    b. John could have worked in a bank.

8. **a.** I should have called John last night.

    b. I shouldn't have called John last night.

D2 Contrasting *Could* and *Could Have*

▶ Note 1

Read each situation. Choose *could* + verb or *could have* + verb.

1. When I worked downtown, I ((could buy)/ could have bought) fresh coffee on my way to the office, so I never made any at home in the morning.

2. I (could ride / could have ridden) my bicycle to school every day, but I never did because I was afraid of the traffic.

3. We always knew when my father got off the bus because we (could see / could have seen) the bus stop from our window.

4. Why didn't anyone tell me? I (could take / could have taken) my vacation last week.

5. You (could call / could have called) me when the car broke down. Why did you leave the car on the side of the road instead?

D3 Talking About Past Opportunities

▶ Note 1

A. Work with a partner. Make up sentences about each situation using *could have* and the expressions that follow to express the different opportunities that were available to the person. Then think of one more opportunity for each situation.

Situation 1
Paul went to college. He majored in biology and education. He became a teacher, but there were other possibilities that he considered.

1. work in a lab

   He could have worked in a lab.

2. go to medical school

3. teach science in a high school

Situation 2
Lee went to cooking school. He became a chef on a cruise ship after he considered several other careers.

1. become a cook in a restaurant

2. open a restaurant

3. work in a hotel

Situation 3
Ella majored in English. She became an editor after she considered some other choices.

1. be a fiction writer

2. go to law school

3. work for a newspaper

Situation 4
Ed majored in art. He thought about other careers before he decided to paint on his own.

1. become an art teacher

2. get a job in advertising

3. do graphic design

B. On your own, think about some opportunities you had for jobs, schools, or places to live. What did you decide to do? Write four sentences describing what you could have done and a description of what you decided to do instead.

I could have lived in London, but I decided to move to New York instead.

C. Tell the class about one of your opportunities.

D4 Talking About Advice in the Past

▶ Note 2A

Work in small groups. Ask questions about each situation using *should have* and the possibilities that follow. Then give short answers with *should have* or *shouldn't have*. You can also use *could have* to express other possibilities. Explain your answers and discuss any differences in opinion you may have.

Situation 1
Ko is a foreign student who recently arrived in the United States. Last night he was invited to an American friend's house for dinner. He didn't know what to bring.

1. flowers

   A: *Should he have brought flowers?*

   B: *Yes, he should have. It's polite.* OR *He could have. Flowers are always nice.*

2. an expensive gift

3. a traditional food from his country

4. five friends with him

Situation 2
At the dinner table, he started eating before the host sat down. Then he ate his food quickly and he was still hungry.

1. wait for the host

2. eat more slowly

3. ask for more

4. wait for someone to offer him more

Situation 3
In a restaurant a few days later, Ko wanted to speak to his waiter. He didn't know how to get the waiter's attention.

1. whistle

2. snap his fingers

3. clap loudly

4. raise his hand when the waiter was looking at him

Situation 4
There was a mistake on Ko's bill at the restaurant. He didn't know what to do.

1. ignore it

2. tell the waiter

3. call the manager immediately

4. shout at the waiter

D5 Expressing Regret

▶ Note 2B

Work with a partner. Imagine that you each made these mistakes. Take turns making sentences using *should have* and *shouldn't have* to express your regret.

1. You didn't go to the movies with your friends. Everyone enjoyed the film.

   I should have gone to the movies with my friends.
   I shouldn't have stayed home last night.

2. You cooked the rice too long. It burned.

3. You left your car windows open during a rainstorm.

4. You were in a hurry at the post office. You sent an expensive birthday gift to your aunt. She never received it, and you did not insure it.

5. You didn't apply for a summer job. Now it's too late.

6. You drove over the speed limit. You got a traffic ticket.

D6 Writing About Regrets

▶ Note 2B

A. Work in small groups. Read this list of the top ten regrets that many people have. Do you agree with the list? What other regrets would you add to the list?

B. Make a list of your biggest regrets. Then write a paragraph describing a few things you think you should have done differently and tell why you feel that way. Remember to begin your paragraph with a clear topic sentence.

   My biggest regrets are all related to the fact that I moved so far away from my family. Because of the distance, I often missed holiday gatherings and last-minute lunches I could have had with my sisters. I should have stayed closer to home, and I should have visited more often. I shouldn't have...

Life's Top Ten Regrets	
1	Not apologizing when you've done something wrong
2	Not traveling enough
3	Losing touch with good friends from childhood
4	Not taking time to exercise and keep fit
5	Not saving enough money for the future
6	Taking a job you knew wasn't right for you
7	Not being self-disciplined
8	Not taking your education more seriously
9	Moving away from your hometown
10	Not being more active in your town's community

Think Critically About Meaning and Use

A. Work with a partner. Read each sentence and the statements that follow. Write *T* if the statement is true or *F* if it is false.

1. I shouldn't have gone to the movies.

   __F__ **a.** I didn't go to the movies.

   __T__ **b.** I am sorry that I went to the movies.

2. He couldn't have been at work.

   _____ **a.** I don't believe that he was at work.

   _____ **b.** It's very unlikely that he was at work.

3. She ought to have called first.

   _____ **a.** She called first.

   _____ **b.** She should have called first.

4. Students may not chew gum in class.

   _____ **a.** Students are not allowed to chew gum in class.

   _____ **b.** Students were allowed to chew gum in class.

5. I should have told you.

   _____ **a.** I think I made a mistake.

   _____ **b.** I'm sorry that I didn't tell you.

6. There is only one flight from Centerville per day. They have got to be on that plane.

   _____ **a.** They can't be on the plane.

   _____ **b.** They must be on the plane.

7. I couldn't have passed my driver's test. I didn't practice at all!

   _____ **a.** I'm surprised that I passed.

   _____ **b.** I didn't pass.

8. I could go to the beach every day when I lived in Florida.

   _____ **a.** I wanted to go to the beach, but I didn't do it.

   _____ **b.** I went to the beach a lot.

B. Discuss these questions in small groups.

   1. **EVALUATE** Which sentence expresses strong possibility?

   2. **ANALYZE** Look at 2 and 7. Which expresses disbelief? Which expresses impossibility?

Edit

Find the errors in these sentences and correct them.

1. They *may not* ~~mayn't~~ have called yet.

2. When he could have called?

3. He might a been late.

4. I ought to visited him at the hospital.

5. May he have taken the train instead of the bus?

6. She must have a cold yesterday.

7. I should have asked him. I'm sorry that I did.

8. He should have taking the exam.

9. You could of called me. I was home.

10. She have to have arrived yesterday.

11. The letter might arrived this afternoon.

12. He must had a cold yesterday.

Write

Write a review of a movie, a TV show, or a short story. Briefly summarize it and say what you liked about it. Then use past modals to discuss what you think could have or should have happened differently.

1. **BRAINSTORM** Use these categories to help you organize your ideas into three paragraphs.
    - **Summary:** What was it about? What were the important events?
    - **Strong Points:** What did you like about it?
    - **Critique:** What do you think could have or should have happened differently? What should the characters/author/producer have done differently?

2. **WRITE A FIRST DRAFT** Before you write your first draft, read the checklist below. Write your draft using past modals.

3. **EDIT** Read your work and check it against the checklist below. Circle grammar, spelling, and punctuation errors.

DO I...	YES
organize my ideas into paragraphs?	☐
use the simple past and other past forms, as appropriate, to summarize the story and say what I liked about it?	☐
use past modals to speculate about what could have happened or been done differently?	☐

4. **PEER REVIEW** Work with a partner to help you decide how to fix your errors and improve the content. Use the checklist above.

5. **REWRITE YOUR DRAFT** Using the comments from your partner, write a final draft.

> Last night I watched a fascinating documentary on TV about the disappearance of mammoths and other megafauna in the Americas about 13,000 years ago. The show focused on four different theories about how the extinction might have occurred...

Choose the correct word or words to complete each sentence.

1. Although many linguists think there are about four or five thousand languages in the world today, others believe that there _____ many more.

   a. mustn't be

   b. maybe

   c. might be

   d. has got to

2. They _____ not be at home. All of the lights are out.

   a. must

   b. couldn't

   c. has got to

   d. don't have to

3. _____ it be snowing in New York City at the beginning of June?

   a. Could

   b. May

   c. Must

   d. Have to

4. They could _____ a lot of traffic. Maybe that's why they were so late.

   a. of had

   b. have had

   c. had had

   d. have been

5. How _____ air pollution over the past fifty years?

   a. should have controlled

   b. we should control

   c. we should have controlled

   d. should we have controlled

Choose the correct response to complete each conversation.

6. **A:** We should have registered for the yoga class.

   B: _____

   a. I'm really glad we did.

   b. It's too bad that we didn't.

   c. When did we register?

   d. You're right. We have to.

7. **A:** How much did they charge you?

   B: Last month, _____

   a. I must pay twenty-five dollars.

   b. I've got to pay twenty-five dollars.

   c. I might pay twenty-five dollars.

   d. I had to pay twenty-five dollars.

8. **A:** Did you take pictures in the museum?

   B: No, _____

   a. we must not use our cameras.

   b. we had to use our cameras.

   c. we were not allowed to use our cameras.

   d. we shouldn't have used our cameras.

Choose the correct response to complete each conversation below.

9. **A:** You may be getting a call later.

   B: _____

   a. May I?   **b.** That's good.   **c.** You won't be home.   **d.** Yes, you may.

10. **A:** I didn't sleep all night. I have a bad cough.

    B: You must be _____

    a. coughing.   **b.** sleeping.   **c.** exhausted.   **d.** at the doctor's.

11. **A:** Is the roast beef ready yet?

    B: It _____ be. It's only been in the oven for 15 minutes.

    a. ought to   **b.** mustn't   **c.** has got to   **d.** can't

Match the response to the question or statement below.

_____ **12.** Did you see that huge diamond ring?

_____ **13.** Mia lost her wallet yesterday.

_____ **14.** He hasn't returned my calls.

a. He must be exhausted.   **d.** I know. You may not like it.

b. It can't be real.   **e.** She could be on her way here.

c. She must be really upset.   **f.** He may be out of town.

Match the response to the question or statement below.

_____ **15.** You should have taken that medication.

_____ **16.** Sally arrived three hours early.

_____ **17.** When you were in high school, did you drive to school?

a. Don't worry. You'll get another one.   **e.** She must have taken the early flight.

b. No. I wasn't allowed to.   **f.** My bag was too large. I had to check it.

c. Why didn't you?   **g.** Yes, I could.

d. I'm sorry I didn't.

Complete each sentence using the past form of the modal and the verb in parentheses.

18. The mechanic _____ (ought to/check) that noise.

19. No one is answering the phone. They _____ (must/go) out.

20. _____ (I/may/leave) my ATM card at the bank. It's not in my wallet.

Passive Sentences (Part 1)

A. **GRAMMAR IN DISCOURSE: The Expression
    of Emotions** 192

B. **FORM: The Present and Past Passive** 194

Simple Present Passive
The directions **are explained** by the teacher.

Simple Past Passive
The directions **were explained** by the teacher.

Present Continuous Passive
The directions **are being explained** by the teacher.

Past Continuous Passive
The directions **were being explained** by the teacher.

C. **MEANING AND USE 1: Changing Focus from
    Active to Passive** 198

Contrasting Active and Passive Sentences

Choosing Active or Passive Sentences

Vocabulary Notes: Verbs with No Passive Forms

D. **MEANING AND USE 2: Reasons for Using
    the Passive** 202

Focus on Results or Processes

Omitting the Agent

Beyond the Sentence: Keeping the Focus

**WRITING: Write an Email Informing Your Professor
About Your Lab Project for a Science Course** 208

The Expression of Emotions

A1 Before You Read

Discuss these questions.

Look at the photographs below. Discuss what emotion you think each person is expressing. Do you agree with your classmates?

A2 Read

CD2 T2 Read this excerpt from a psychology textbook to find out if the expression of emotions is universal.

The Expression of Emotions

The four basic emotions

Joy and sadness are found in diverse cultures around the world, but how can we tell when other people are happy or despondent? It turns out that
5 the expression of many emotions may be universal (Rinn 1991). Smiling is apparently a universal sign of friendliness and approval. Baring the teeth was noted by Charles Darwin
10 (1872) as a possible universal sign of anger. Darwin believed that the universal recognition of facial expressions would have survival value. For example, facial expressions could
15 signal the approach of enemies (or friends) in the absence of language.

Most investigators (e.g., Brown 1991, Buss 1992, etc.) agree that certain facial expressions suggest the
20 same emotions in all people. Moreover, people in diverse cultures recognize the emotions that are signaled by the facial expressions. In classic research, Paul Ekman (1980) took photographs of
25 people exhibiting the emotions of anger, disgust, fear, happiness, sadness, and surprise. He then asked people around the world to indicate what emotions were being shown in the
30 photos. Ekman's results suggested that the expression of several basic emotions such as happiness, anger, surprise, and fear is universally recognized. The subjects of the study ranged from
35 European college students to members of the Fore, a New Guinea highlands tribe that had had almost no contact with Western culture. It was found that all groups, including the Fore,
40 agreed on the emotions the pictures expressed.

Ekman and his colleagues obtained similar results in a study of ten different cultures. In this study, the

participants were permitted to report whether they thought that more than one emotion was shown by a facial expression. The participants generally agreed on which two emotions were
50 being expressed and which emotion was the most intense.

Emotions are also being studied from other perspectives. For example, although it is generally recognized that
55 facial expressions reflect emotional states, it is not unreasonable to ask whether feelings must always come before facial expressions. Are positive feelings ever produced by smiling? Is

60 anger ever produced by frowning? Psychological research has shown in experiments that when participants are induced to smile first, they rate cartoons as funnier. When they are
65 induced to frown first, they rate cartoons as more aggressive. Psychologists have a number of complicated explanations for these results, but not surprisingly, they have
70 also concluded that none of the theories of emotion apply to all people in all situations. Our emotions are not quite as easily understood as some theories have suggested.

Adapted from *Essentials of Psychology*

---

baring the teeth: showing the teeth by moving one's lips
despondent: sad and without hope

diverse: different from each other
induce: to make someone do something
perspective: view; a way of judging something

A3 After You Read

Choose the answer that best completes each sentence.

1. The expression of many of our emotions appears to be _____.

   a. universal

   b. limited by culture

2. Psychologists would be surprised to find a culture with people who _____.

   a. never smile

   b. frown

3. Darwin was interested in emotions and their relationship to _____.

   a. love

   b. survival

4. Ekman showed _____ to people around the world.

   a. photos

   b. reports

5. The reactions of the Fore are important because _____.

   a. they show Western influence

   b. they suggest similarity across cultures

6. Other research has shown that _____ may produce _____.

   a. facial expressions; emotions

   b. emotions; facial expressions

B FORM

The Present and Past Passive

> ⚙ **Think Critically About Form**
>
> **A.** Look back at the excerpt on page 192 and complete the tasks below.
>
> 1. **CATEGORIZE** An example of the simple present passive is underlined. Find three more examples. Sort them into singular and plural.
>
> 2. **CATEGORIZE** An example of the simple past passive is circled. Find three more examples. Sort them into singular and plural.
>
> 3. **APPLY** Look at the examples of the present continuous and past continuous passives below. Find one example of each of these forms in the text.
>   **a.** A great deal of research **is being done**.
>   **b.** A great deal of research **was being done**.
>
> **B.** Discuss your answers with the class and read the Form charts to check them.

▶ The Present Passive

▶ The Past Passive

ONLINE PRACTICE

SIMPLE PRESENT PASSIVE
AM / IS / ARE + PAST PARTICIPLE (+ *BY* + NOUN)
The directions **are explained (by the teacher)**.
The answer **isn't explained**.
Is the study **published** yet?   **Yes**, it **is**. / **No**, it **isn't**.
When are the results **announced**?

SIMPLE PAST PASSIVE
WAS / WERE + PAST PARTICIPLE (+ *BY* + NOUN)
The directions **were explained (by the teacher)**.
The answer **wasn't explained**.
Was the study **published**?   **Yes**, it **was**. / **No**, it **wasn't**.
Where were the results **announced**?

▶ The Present Passive

PRESENT CONTINUOUS PASSIVE
AM / IS / ARE + *BEING* + PAST PARTICIPLE (+ *BY* + NOUN)
The directions **are being explained (by the teacher)**. The answer **isn't being explained**. **Is** the study **being published**? 　**Yes**, it **is**. / **No**, it **isn't**. **How are** the results **being announced**?

▶ The Past Passive

PAST CONTINUOUS PASSIVE
WAS / WERE + *BEING* + PAST PARTICIPLE (+ *BY* + NOUN)
The directions **were being explained (by the teacher)**. The answer **wasn't being explained**. **Was** the study **being published**? 　**Yes**, it **was**. / **No**, it **wasn't**. **Why were** the results **being announced**?

- Only transitive verbs can be in the passive. A transitive verb is a verb that is followed by an object. For example: **give** <u>an exam</u>, **throw** <u>a baseball</u>, **cook** <u>a meal</u>.

- *By* + a noun phrase is optional at the end of passive sentences.

    The directions **were explained (by the teacher)**.

    The study **is being published (by *Psychology Today*)**.

- See Appendices 4 and 5 for spelling and pronunciation rules for verbs ending in *-ed*.

- See Appendix 6 for irregular verbs and their past participles.

B1 Listening for Form

CD2 T3　Listen to this information about facial expressions and write the passive forms you hear.

1. Last year some research ____was being done____ on smiling across cultures.

2. I _____ to join the study after it began.

3. A number of questions _____ at the same time.

4. For example, _____ the general meaning of a smile always _____?

5. Why _____ the mouth _____ in some cultures?

6. Is it true that smiles _____ for friends and family in some cultures?

7. The results of this research _____ at a psychology conference.

8. The results _____ also _____ in a popular psychology magazine.

B2 Asking and Answering Questions with Simple Present Passives

Work with a partner. Complete this conversation with the words in parentheses and the simple present passive. Then practice the conversation.

A: When ____is the trash collected____ (the trash/collect) in your neighborhood?
                    1

B: It _____ (pick up) on Mondays, but we don't have much
              2

trash anymore. Almost everything we use _____
                                                              3

(recycle).

A: And _____ (the recycled items/collect) too?
              4

B: Some of them _____ (collect). Newspapers, glass, and
                          5

cans _____ (take away) by a private recycling company.
          6

A: And then what _____ (do) with all of that stuff?
                          7

B: It _____ (sell) to other companies for further recycling.
              8

B3 Working on Simple Past Passives

Work with a partner. Complete this paragraph about how glass was made in the picture. Use the words in parentheses and the simple past passive.

When the glass ____was made____ (make),
                        1
certain materials _____ (melt)
                        2
together and then they _____ (cool).
                                    3
The materials _____ (heat) in large
                        4
furnaces that _____ (build) of ceramic
                        5
blocks. When the bubbles _____
                                    6
(remove) from the hot mixture, the hot liquid
_____ (pour) into molds, and it
        7
_____ (form) into different shapes.
        8

B4 Working on Present and Past Continuous Passives

A. Complete this paragraph with the words in parentheses and the present continuous passive.

The building where I work _____is being renovated_____ (renovate) right
                                              1
now, and a number of changes _____ (make). For
                                                2
example, all of the offices _____ (paint), and the
                                         3
carpeting _____ (replace). New shelves _____
                      4
_____ (build), and the computer system _____
         5   6
(upgrade). Finally, a new kitchen _____ (add) for the
                                                   7
staff. A refrigerator, microwave, and sink _____ (install)
                                                              8
in the new kitchen.

B. Now rewrite the paragraph in the past continuous passive.

*The building where I work was being renovated last month, and a number
of changes…*

B5 Working on Passive Questions

A. Imagine you are interviewing the director of the computer lab at your school about changes that are taking place. For items 1–4 write information questions with the present continuous passive. For items 5–8 write *Yes/No* questions with the present continuous passive.

1. what kind of computers/buy

    What kind of computers are being bought?

2. how many computers/not replace

3. which software program/install

4. how much money/spend

5. more employees/hire

6. new furniture/purchase

7. the old equipment/throw away

8. the hours of operation/expand

B. Change questions 1–4 to the past continuous passive.

What kind of computers were being bought?

C. Change questions 5–8 to the simple past passive. End each question with *last semester.*

Were more employees hired last semester?

Changing Focus from Active to Passive

Think Critically About Meaning and Use

A. Read the sentences and answer the questions below.

1a. High winds damaged the bridge.
1b. The bridge was damaged by high winds.
2a. The state inspects the bridge once a year.
2b. The bridge is inspected by the state once a year.

1. **EVALUATE** Do the sentences in each pair have about the same meaning or different meanings?

2. **ANALYZE** Which sentences focus more on a noun that is performing an action or causing something to happen?

3. **ANALYZE** Which sentences focus more on a noun that receives an action?

B. Discuss your answers with the class and read the Meaning and Use Notes to check them.

Meaning and Use Notes

ONLINE PRACTICE

Contrasting Active and Passive Sentences

▶ 1A The passive form changes the usual order of the subject and object of an active sentence. The object of an active sentence becomes the subject of a passive sentence.

Active Sentence:	Jonah	sent	the letter.

Passive Sentence:	The letter **was sent by** Jonah.

▶ 1B In active sentences, the agent (the noun that is performing the action) is in subject position. In passive sentences, the receiver (the noun that receives or is the result of an action) is in the subject position. Passive sentences often do not mention the agent.

	Agent		**Receiver**
Active Sentence:	Jonah	sent	the letter.

	Receiver		**Agent**
Passive Sentence:	The letter	**was sent**	by Jonah.
	The letter	**was sent.**	

Choosing Active or Passive Sentences

▶ 2   Choosing the active or the passive form of a sentence does not change the meaning, but it does affect the way you think about the information in the sentence. Use an active sentence to focus on who or what performs the action. Use a passive sentence to focus on the receiver or the result of an action.

Active Sentence

<u>We</u> **tried** to get help during the storm, but <u>we</u> **couldn't get through** on the phone, so <u>we</u> **waited** until the next morning.
(The focus is on us—the speakers—and what <u>we did</u> during the storm.)

Passive Sentence

The next morning, <u>our roof</u> **was damaged** and <u>the basement</u> **was flooded**. Next door, <u>the porch</u> **was ruined** and <u>several windows</u> **were broken**.
(The focus is on the <u>results</u> of the storm. The sentences describe the damage caused by the storm.)

C1 Listening for Meaning and Use

▶ Notes 1A, 1B

CD2 T4   Listen to this description of a research study. Check (✓) whether each sentence is active or passive.

	ACTIVE	PASSIVE
1.		✓
2.		
3.		
4.		
5.		
6.		
7.		
8.		

C2 Using Agents and Receivers

▶ Notes 1A, 1B

Create meaningful active or passive sentences in the simple past. Use the words given. The first words in each item must be the subject of your sentence.

1. the medicine/take/the patient _The medicine was taken by the patient._

2. the patient/take/the medicine _The patient took the medicine._

3. the window/break/the child _____

4. the concert/attend/many people _____

5. she/make/the cake _____

6. we/cancel/the appointment _____

7. the car/repair/two mechanics _____

C3 Focusing on Receivers

▶ Note 2

Work with a partner. Use the words in parentheses and the past continuous passive to tell what was happening. Then add another idea of your own.

1. Your friend's wedding reception started at 2:00 P.M. When you arrived at 2:15,

   a. (the guests/greet) _the guests were being greeted._

   b. (the bride and groom/photograph) _____

   c. (appetizers/serve) _____

   d. _____

2. When your dinner guests arrived, you were still getting ready and

   a. (the roast beef/slice) _____

   b. (the salad/make) _____

   c. (the table/set) _____

   d. _____

3. When you arrived at the scene of the accident,

   a. (one person/lift into an ambulance) _____

   b. (a man/give oxygen) _____

   c. (two witnesses/question) _____

   d. _____

Vocabulary Notes

Verbs with No Passive Forms

Intransitive Verbs Verbs that cannot be followed by objects are called intransitive verbs. They have no passive forms. Here are some common intransitive verbs:

appear	come	die	go	look	rain	stay
arrive	cry	emerge	happen	occur	sleep	walk

See Appendix 7 for a list of more intransitive verbs.

Transitive Nonpassive Verbs Verbs that can be followed by objects are called transitive verbs. Most transitive verbs have passive forms, but some do not. Notice how the passive form of *fit* does not make sense in English.

Active	**Passive**
The dress fits Valerie.	x Valerie is fit by the dress. (INCORRECT)

Here are some more transitive verbs that have no passive forms:

Ben **has** a CD player. Jenny **resembles** her father. She **became** a doctor.

We **lack** funds. The test **consists of** two parts. The book **costs** ten dollars.

The dress **suits** her. Ten pounds **equal** 4.5 kilos. He **weighs** 150 pounds.

Verbs That Are Intransitive or Transitive Some verbs can be transitive or intransitive. When they are intransitive they do not have passive forms. Here are some examples:

begin   break   close   end   freeze   open   start   stop

C4 Choosing Verbs with Active or Passive Forms

Change these active sentences to passive sentences if possible. Some of the sentences cannot be changed. Explain why some of the sentences have no passive form.

1. A graduate student is gathering data for a study on emotions.

   Data is being gathered by a graduate student for a study on emotions.

2. A psychologist proposed a new theory about facial expressions.

3. Some interesting results are emerging from cross-cultural data.

4. The research team was considering the new theory.

5. They already have 75 participants for the study.

6. The psychology department is paying each participant.

7. Some new equipment for the project arrived yesterday.

8. The researchers still need more equipment for data analysis.

D

Reasons for Using the Passive

Think Critically About Meaning and Use

A. Read the sentences and answer the questions below.

A radio broadcast
1a. A former employee robbed the C&R bank at about 8:00 P.M. last night.
1b. The C&R bank was robbed at about 8:00 P.M. last night.

A sign in a doctor's office
2a. Patients are requested to pay before leaving.
2b. Dr. Lewis requests that patients pay before leaving.

1. **ANALYZE** In which sentence is the agent probably unknown?

2. **EVALUATE** In sentences 2a and 2b, which sign is more impersonal and indirect?

B. Discuss your answers with the class and read the Meaning and Use Notes to check them.

Meaning and Use Notes

ONLINE PRACTICE

Focus on Results or Processes

▶ **1** Use the passive when the receiver or result of an action is more important than the agent. The passive is often used in descriptions of results or processes involving things rather than people.

Many homes **were damaged** by the flood. (The result is more important than the agent.)

The mixture **is boiled** before it **is poured** into the bowl. (The focus is on the process.)

Omitting the Agent

▶ **2A** Passive sentences that do not mention the agent are called agentless passives. They are used when the agent is unimportant, unknown, or obvious.

Unimportant Agent	**Unknown Agent**
Supercomputers **were developed** to solve complex problems.	This package **was left** on my desk. Do you know who left it?

Obvious Agent

The mail **is delivered** at noon. (It is obvious that a mail carrier delivers the mail.)

> **2B**   The agentless passive is used to avoid very general subjects such as *people*, *someone*, *we*, *one*, and impersonal *you* and *they*. The passive often sounds more indirect or impersonal.

Agentless Passive	Active
ID photos **are being taken** today.	<u>They</u> are taking ID photos today.
Calcium **is needed** for strong bones.	<u>People</u> need calcium for strong bones.
Reservations **are required**.	<u>We</u> require reservations.
Parsley is an herb that **is used** as a garnish.	Parsley is an herb that <u>one</u> uses as a garnish.

> **2C**   Sometimes the agentless passive is used to avoid taking responsibility for an action or to avoid blaming another person.

A Boss Speaking to His Employees

A serious error **was made** in the payroll.
(The boss deliberately doesn't say who made the error.)

D1 Listening for Meaning and Use

> Notes 1, 2A, 2B

CD2 T5   Listen to each situation. Check (✓) the sentence that has approximately the same meaning as the passive sentence you hear.

1. _____ **a.** You can park in front of the building.

    __✓__ **b.** We ask visitors not to park in front of the building.

2. _____ **a.** They speak French in Quebec.

    _____ **b.** Nobody speaks French in Quebec.

3. _____ **a.** We permitted Julie to speak.

    _____ **b.** They permitted Julie to speak.

4. _____ **a.** A falling tree injured several people.

    _____ **b.** Several people injured a tree.

5. _____ **a.** The author wrote the book in 1966.

    _____ **b.** My friend wrote the book in 1966.

6. _____ **a.** You appreciate our assistance.

    _____ **b.** We appreciate your assistance.

Beyond the Sentence

Keeping the Focus

You can choose between an active or passive sentence in order to keep the focus on a noun that was mentioned in a previous sentence. To keep the focus, make the noun the subject of the next sentence. Sometimes you will need an active sentence to do this; sometimes you will need a passive sentence. It is easier to follow ideas from sentence to sentence when the focus is understood.

Active Sentence Followed by Passive Sentence

Yesterday, the old man lost <u>his wallet</u>. Fortunately, <u>it</u> **was found** by a police officer a few hours later.

Active Sentence Followed by Active Sentence

Yesterday, the old man lost his <u>wallet</u>. Fortunately, <u>it</u> **had** no money inside.

D5 Keeping the Focus

A. Choose the active or passive sentence that best completes each item. Your answer will depend on the underlined focus.

1. <u>Charlotte</u> opened the door to her house,

   a. and she was greeted by an unknown child.

   b. and an unknown child greeted her.

2. When <u>we</u> lived in that house,

   a. a garden was never planted.

   b. we never planted a garden.

3. <u>Golf</u> is one of the most popular sports in the United States.

   a. It is played by people of all ages.

   b. People of all ages play it.

4. My uncle got <u>a new car</u>.

   a. It was purchased in New Jersey.

   b. He bought it in New Jersey.

5. In 1994, <u>she</u> wrote a best-selling novel.

   a. After that, many offers were received to write more fiction.

   b. After that, she received many offers to write more fiction.

6. Bhutan and Nepal have many <u>mountains</u>.

    a. In those countries, transportation is difficult.

    b. They make transportation difficult in those countries.

7. <u>The Great Lakes</u> are the largest group of freshwater lakes in the world.

    a. They were formed by glaciers about 250,000 years ago.

    b. Glaciers formed them about 250,000 years ago.

8. As soon as <u>the robber</u> tried to leave the bank,

    a. he was arrested by a detective waiting outside.

    b. a detective waiting outside arrested him.

B. Each of these sentences has an underlined noun indicating the focus. For each noun, write an appropriate active or passive sentence that gives additional information about the focus. Use nouns or pronouns.

    1. <u>Sushi</u> is a rice delicacy in Japan. *It is often filled or topped with raw fish.*

    Sushi is a rice <u>delicacy</u> in Japan. *Another popular delicacy is sashimi.*

    2. <u>Antibiotics</u> kill certain bacteria. _____

    Antibiotics kill <u>certain bacteria</u>. _____

    3. <u>French</u> is a Romance language. _____

    French is a <u>Romance language</u>. _____

    4. <u>Music</u> used to be recorded on cassettes. _____

    Music used to be recorded on <u>cassettes</u>. _____

    5. <u>Psychologists</u> are interested in facial expressions. _____

    Psychologists are interested in <u>facial expressions</u>. _____

    6. <u>Rice</u> is a staple in many countries around the world. _____

    Rice is a <u>staple</u> in many countries around the world. _____

C. Choose one of the sentences from part B and expand it into a short paragraph of four or five sentences. Work on maintaining the focus between sentence pairs. Use active or passive sentences where appropriate.

    Sushi is a rice delicacy in Japan. Another popular delicacy is sashimi. While both delicacies are made from very thinly sliced raw fish, sushi is served with…

Think Critically About Meaning and Use

A. Read each sentence and the statements that follow. Choose the statement that best explains the meaning of the sentence.

1. Students are required to take the final exam.
   a. The students require the final exam.
   b. The professor requires the final exam.

2. Student photos are being taken in the gym.
   a. Students are taking pictures.
   b. Students are being photographed.

3. He has been called a liar by the manager.
   a. The manager has called him a liar.
   b. He has called the mayor a liar.

4. Laser beams are used in surgery.
   a. Laser beams use surgery.
   b. Surgeons use laser beams.

5. He was asked to resign by the board of directors.
   a. He asked the board of directors to resign.
   b. The board of directors asked him to resign.

6. It is believed that she will run for president.
   a. It is certain that she will run for president.
   b. People think that she will run for president.

7. The letter was sent to all patients by the doctor.
   a. The patients sent the letter.
   b. The doctor sent the letter.

8. He is not being hired for the job.
   a. He is not going to get the job.
   b. He is not hiring us for the job.

B. Discuss these questions in small groups.

1. **EVALUATE** Why is it important to include the agent in sentences 3 and 5?

2. **COMPARE AND CONTRAST** Look at sentences 2 and 6. In which is the agent obvious? In which is the agent unimportant?

Edit

Find the errors in these paragraphs and correct them.

It is ~~claiming~~ ^{claimed} by psychologists that everyone lies at some time or other. Moreover, many people can lie without showing it in their facial expressions or body language. For this reason, lie detector tests are frequently use in police investigations. The use of such tests to detect lies is many hundreds of years old.

For example, it is believe that in China suspected liars were forced to chew rice powder and then spit it out. If the powder was dry, the suspect is considered guilty. In Spain, another variation for lie detection used. The suspect was being required to swallow a slice of bread and cheese. It was believed that if the bread stuck inside the suspect's mouth, then he or she was lying. Psychologists report that these strange methods actually show a basic principle that is know about lying: Anxiety that is related to lying is linked to lack of saliva, or dry mouth.

Modern lie detectors, which are calling polygraphs, are used to indicate changes in heart rate, blood pressure, breathing rate, and perspiration while a person is be examined. Questions about the validity of the polygraph, however, are frequently raising. Consequently, results from polygraphs are often thrown out in legal cases.

Write

Imagine you and two of your classmates are doing a lab project for a science course. Write an email informing your professor of your progress. Use present and past passives.

1. **BRAINSTORM** Decide on the project you will describe. Make a list of what you have already done and what you are currently working on. Use these categories to help you organize your ideas into paragraphs:
   - **Opening:** Say why you're writing (e.g., to update your professor on your progress).
   - **Stage 1:** What things were done? What problems were encountered? What solutions were found?
   - **Stage 2:** What things are being done now? How are problems being dealt with?
   - **Closing**: Assure the instructor that everything is going. If desired, suggest a meeting to discuss your progress.

2. **WRITE A FIRST DRAFT** Before you write your first draft, read the checklist below and look at the sentences you wrote for D2 and D3 on pages 204–205. Write your draft using present and past passives.

3. **EDIT** Read your work and check it against the checklist below. Circle grammar, spelling, and punctuation errors.

DO I...	YES
use active sentences to focus on who or what is performing an action?	☐
use passive sentences to talk about a process or to focus on the receiver or result?	☐
omit the agent in passive sentences when it is unimportant, unknown, or obvious or when I want to avoid blame?	☐

4. **PEER REVIEW** Work with a partner to help you decide how to fix your errors and improve the content. Use the checklist above.

5. **REWRITE YOUR DRAFT** Using the comments from your partner, write a final draft.

From:	Helga Schmidt
To:	Mr. Tanaka
Subject:	Lab Project

I'm happy to report that my team and I are making good progress on our lab project. Last week all major work on the research phase was completed, and this week our lab results are being written up. Here is a quick update of the first two stages…

Passive Sentences (Part 2)

A. GRAMMAR IN DISCOURSE: At-Risk Students Can Be Helped, But Not by Budget Cuts... 212

B. FORM: The Future, Present Perfect, and Modal Passive 214

Future Passive With *Will*

The teacher **will be fired**.

Future Passive *With Be Going To*

The teacher is **going to be fired**.

Present Perfect Passive

The teacher **has been fired**.

Modal Passive

The teacher **must be fired**.

Phrasal Modal Passive

The teacher **has (got) to be fired**.

C. MEANING AND USE 1: The Role of the Agent 218

Including the Agent

D. MEANING AND USE 2: The Passive in Academic and Public Discourse 221

Common Uses of the Passive in Academic Discourse

Common Uses of the Passive in Public Discourse

Informally Speaking: Using Passives with *Get*

WRITING: Write a Letter to the Editor About How Education Could Be Improved in Your Country 226

At-Risk Students Can Be Helped, But Not by Budget Cuts...

A1 Before You Read

Discuss these questions.

What are some reasons why students drop out of high school in your country? What do you think could be done to stop students from dropping out of school?

A2 Read

CD2 T6 Read this letter to the editor to find out what one student thinks must be done to help at-risk students stay in school and finish their high-school education.

LETTER TO THE EDITOR

At-Risk Students Can Be Helped, but Not by Budget Cuts...

Dear Editor:

I'm writing to congratulate you on your excellent article about the rise in high school dropout rates. This issue
5 has been ignored for far too long, and I'm glad that the silence has finally been broken. If enough people speak out, perhaps the message will be heard. Over a third of all high school students
10 drop out before graduation, and the situation simply cannot be allowed to continue.

I consider myself lucky, and I hope others can be helped by my story. I
15 grew up in a "bad" neighborhood. Most of the adults around me were high school dropouts, and education wasn't important to them. Nobody took time to read stories to me or help me with
20 my homework, and my elementary school teachers weren't much help

either. By the time I was ten, I could barely read and I hated school. Luckily, a caring middle-school teacher took an
25 interest in me and got me into an after-school tutoring program and a free summer reading camp. Within a year, I was making great progress and, to the amazement of family and friends, I

30 have just been given a full scholarship
    to a local college. Sadly, however,
    many of my classmates have not had
    the same good fortune.
       I have recently been told that due
35 to budget cuts, a certain caring middle
    school teacher has been forced into
    early retirement, and a certain after-
    school tutorial program will be
    canceled. In addition, our school's
40 work-study program will be shut down
    and a new community job center won't
    be built. Why? Because the government
    says that teaching staff and special
    programs must be cut back until the

45 economy improves.
       How many more teachers will be
    fired? How many more job-skills
    programs will be closed? How many
    more students are going to be forced to
50 lead a life of poverty because the
    system has failed them?
       I'm living proof that at-risk
    students can be helped. That's why I
    feel strongly that ways must be found
55 to protect the people and programs that
    have been designed to help them.

    Sincerely,
    Tony Diaz

---

at-risk student: a student in danger of dropping out or having other problems at school

be condemned to: be forced to experience something difficult or unpleasant

budget cut: decrease or reduction in the amount of money that a government or other organization plans to spend

caring: kind and understanding

ignore: not pay attention to

poverty: the state of being poor

scholarship: money given by a school or organization to help a student pay for his or her education

tutoring program: program that gives extra, usually one-on-one, help to students who are not doing well in one or more school subjects

A3 After You Read

Choose the answer that best completes each sentence.

1. At the beginning of his letter, Tony mentions an article about _____.

   a. budget cuts   **b.** student ignorance   **c.** the high dropout rate

2. According to Tony, _____ saved him from dropping out of high school.

   a. a journalist   **b.** a middle school teacher   **c.** his family

3. Tony is concerned that budget cuts will negatively affect the future of _____.

   a. at-risk students   **b.** the economy   **c.** high-school dropouts

4. The main point of Tony's letter is that at-risk students _____.

   a. are going to fail   **b.** come from poor families   **c.** ought to be helped

B FORM

The Future, Present Perfect, and Modal Passive

Think Critically About Form

A. Look back at the article on page 212 and complete the tasks below.

1. **IDENTIFY** An example of the present perfect passive has been underlined. Find five more examples. What are the three parts of the present perfect passive?

2. **IDENTIFY** An example of the future passive with *will* is circled. Find three more examples. What are the three parts of the future passive with *will*? Can you think of another way to form the future passive?

3. **ANALYZE** Look at this example sentence. What are the three parts of the modal passive?

   "The situation simply cannot be allowed to continue."

B. Discuss your answers with the class and read the Form charts to check them.

▶ The Future Passive

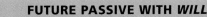

ONLINE PRACTICE

FUTURE PASSIVE WITH *WILL*
WILL + *BE* + PAST PARTICIPLE (+ *BY* + NOUN)
The teacher **will be fired**.
The job center **won't be built**.
Will the programs **be cut**?
Yes, they **will**. / **No**, they **won't**.
Why will the teachers **be fired**?

FUTURE PASSIVE WITH *BE GOING TO*
BE GOING TO + *BE* + PAST PARTICIPLE (+ *BY* + NOUN)
The teacher **is going to be fired**.
The job center **isn't going to be built**.
Are the programs **going to be cut**?
Yes, they **are**. / **No**, they **aren't**.
Why are the teachers **going to be fired**?

▶ The Present Perfect Passive

PRESENT PERFECT PASSIVE
HAS / HAVE + *BEEN* + PAST PARTICIPLE (+ *BY* + NOUN)
The teacher **has been fired**.
The job center **hasn't been built**.
Have the programs **been cut**?
Yes, they **have**. / **No**, they **haven't**.
Why have the teachers **been fired**?

▶ The Modal Passive

MODAL PASSIVE
MODAL + *BE* + PAST PARTICIPLE (+ *BY* + NOUN)
The teacher **must be fired**.
The job center **should not be built**.
Could the programs **be cut**?
Yes, they **could be**. / **No**, they **couldn't be**.
Why should the teachers be **fired**?

PHRASAL MODAL PASSIVE
MODAL + *BE* + PAST PARTICIPLE (+ *BY* + NOUN)
The teacher **has (got) to be fired**.
The job center **ought to be built**.
Do the programs **have to be cut**?
Yes, they do. / **No**, they don't.
Why do the teachers **have to be fired**?

Future, Present Perfect, and Modal Passive

- In passives with more than one auxiliary verb (*will be built, is going to be built, has been built, should be built*), only the first auxiliary changes position or combines with *not* in questions and negative sentences.

  Isn't it going to be built?

  It **isn't** going to be built.

Phrasal Modal Passive

- The negative and question forms of *have to* and *need to* use *do*.

  It **doesn't** have to be built.

  Does it have to be built?

- *Have got to* is not used with negatives or questions.

B1 Listening for Form

CD2 T7   Listen to each sentence. Is it active or passive? Check (✓) the correct column.

	ACTIVE	PASSIVE
1.		✓
2.		
3.		
4.		
5.		
6.		
7.		
8.		

B2 Working on Future and Modal Passives

A. Complete these sentences with the words in parentheses and the future passive with *will*.

Community Center Policies

1. New courses _____will be offered_____ (offer) every six weeks.

2. Instructor schedules _____ (post) at the front desk.

3. Schedule changes _____ (not/announce) until the first day of classes.

4. Classes with fewer than five participants _____ (cancel).

Online Shopping

1. Your order _____ (ship) within 48 hours.

2. Shipping and handling _____ (add) to all orders.

3. Refunds for credit card purchases _____ (credit) to your account.

4. Refunds _____ (not/made) for goods that are returned after 30 days of receipt.

B. Complete these sentences with the words in parentheses and a modal passive.

Product Instructions

1. This product _should be refrigerated_ (should/refrigerate) after opening.

2. This prescription _____ (can/not/refill).

3. This product _____ (should/keep) out of the reach of children.

4. After opening, this product _____ (may/store) for up to three months in a cool, dry place.

Online Returns Policy Information

1. Your package _____ (need to/insure) before mailing.

2. Any damage _____ (have to/report) within two weeks.

3. Each return _____ (must/accompany) by the return form.

4. Returns _____ (should/send) to the address below.

B3 Working on Present Perfect Passives

Complete each sentence with the words in parentheses and the present perfect passive.

1. The exam _has been canceled by the teacher._____
(cancel/the teacher)

2. These products _____
(manufacture/the company/for three years)

3. This book _____
(translate/into many languages)

4. The furniture _____
(move/to the new house)

5. The recipes _____
(create/a famous chef)

6. A new prescription _____
(recommend/the doctor)

B4 Asking and Answering Passive Questions

A. Work in small groups. Take turns asking and answering questions using the words below and the modal *should*. Then make up two more questions to ask the class.

1. cars/permit/town center

> A: *Should cars be permitted in the town center?*
> B: *Yes, they should.* OR *No, they shouldn't.*

2. bicyclists/allow/on busy streets

3. violent films/ban/from television

4. a new community center/build/downtown?

5. men/give/parental leave for childcare

6. women/pay/the same wages as men

7. children/punish/for coming home late

8. animals/use/for medical research

B. Which issues did your group agree on? Which ones didn't you agree on?

The Role of the Agent

Think Critically About Meaning and Use

A. Read the sentences and complete the tasks below.

1a. The course will be given by the instructor on Mondays.
1b. The course will be given by a team of experts via satellite on Mondays.
2a. The article was written by Gregory Marks in one day.
2b. The article was written by the author in one day.

1. **IDENTIFY** Underline the agent in each sentence.

2. **ANALYZE** Which agents give important or unexpected information?
   Which ones seem unnecessary?

B. Discuss your answers with the class and read the Meaning and Use Notes to check them.

Meaning and Use Notes

ONLINE PRACTICE

Including the Agent

▶ **1A** Passives are often used without agents if the agent is unimportant, unknown, or obvious. However, the agent is necessary when it is surprising or unexpected.

Agentless Passive	**Passive with an Agent**
The mail **has been delivered**.	The mail **has been delivered** <u>by an experimental robot</u>. (The agent is surprising.)
We **were given** six pages of homework.	We **were given** six pages of homework <u>by a substitute teacher</u>. (The agent is unexpected.)

▶ **1B** An agent is used to provide additional or new information.

Agentless Passive	**Passive with an Agent**
You **will be notified** about the exam date.	You **will be notified** about the exam date <u>by email</u>.

▶ **1C** An agent is used to complete the meaning of the sentence or to add important information—especially a proper noun, such as the name of an author, artist, composer, inventor, or designer.

Agentless Passive	**Passive with an Agent**
Washington, D.C. **was designed**.	Washington, D.C. **was designed** <u>by Pierre L'Enfant</u>.

C1 Listening for Meaning and Use

▶ Notes 1A–1C

🔊 CD2 T8 Listen to each sentence. Does the agent complete the meaning and/or provide necessary information? Check (✓) whether the agent is necessary or unnecessary.

	NECESSARY AGENT	UNNECESSARY AGENT
1.		✓
2.		
3.		
4.		
5.		
6.		
7.		
8.		

C2 Including or Omitting Agents

▶ Notes 1A–1C

💬 Work with a partner. Change each sentence to the passive. Decide whether to keep or omit the agent. Be prepared to explain your decision.

1. Next week a painter will paint our house.

   Next week our house will be painted.
   (The agent is omitted because it is obvious.)

2. Pablo Picasso painted *The Three Musicians.*

   The Three Musicians *was painted by Pablo Picasso. (The agent is included because it adds important information.)*

3. Teenage drivers have caused many car accidents in this community.

4. Parents shouldn't allow children to watch too much television.

5. Lawmakers will pass new tax law soon.

6. Winston Churchill led the British government during World War II.

7. Will the city council pass stronger environmental laws this year?

8. A young child has written this incredible story.

C3 Including or Omitting Agents

▶ Notes 1A–1C

Rewrite these active descriptions using the future passive. Then work in small groups and discuss whether or not you needed to use the agent in any of your sentences. What is the difference between the active and passive descriptions?

At the Hospital

1. When Derek arrives at the emergency room, they are going to examine his arm.

   When Derek arrives at the emergency room, his arm is going to be examined.

2. Then they will send him for an X-ray.

   Then he'll be sent for an X-ray.

3. They will tell him whether it is broken.

4. If his arm is broken, they will send him back to the emergency room.

5. First they will put his arm in the proper position.

6. Then they will put a cotton sleeve over his arm, and they will wrap it with wet bandages.

7. After it sets, they will tell him how to care for the cast.

At School

1. Please listen carefully. The teacher is going to read the instructions only once.

2. He will give each student a test booklet and a pencil.

3. He will ask the students to turn to the first page.

4. Then he will show them a set of pictures.

5. He will tell them to check the correct answer in the booklet.

6. After the last picture, he will collect the booklets.

7. Finally, he will dismiss the students.

The Passive in Academic and Public Discourse

Think Critically About Meaning and Use

A. Read the sentences and complete the tasks below.

a. Sulfur dioxide is used to produce sulfuric acid.

b. As a special benefit to online customers, orders will be shipped free of charge.

c. Your vehicle must be insured. Proof of insurance must be presented.

1. GENERATE Change each sentence to an active sentence.

2. EVALUATE Think about the differences between the active and passive sentences. Which type of sentence sounds more formal and impersonal? Why?

3. PREDICT In what context would you expect to find each of the passive sentences?

B. Discuss your answers with the class and read the Meaning and Use Notes to check them.

Meaning and Use Notes

ONLINE
PRACTICE

Common Uses of the Passive in Academic Discourse

▶ **1** Academic discourse, such as textbooks and other factual materials, tends to focus on objects, processes, and results. Such materials try to present an objective and impersonal perspective to convey a sense of authority. To express this tone, writers often use passive expressions with *it*-subjects (e.g., *It is expected that*) as well as other passive constructions.

Psychology Text

It **is** generally **agreed** that people can learn something much more rapidly the second time.

Encyclopedia

Dams **may be built** on main streams or their branches. They **are** usually **built** at a spot where the river becomes narrow.

Computer Programming Book

Subprograms **are defined** between SUB and END SUB statements.

(Continued on page 222)

Common Uses of the Passive in Public Discourse

▶ 2 In public discourse, such as newspaper headlines, public announcements, and signs, the passive is used to convey an objective or impersonal tone. The passive often sounds more formal, factual, or authoritative. Note that newspaper headlines and signs often omit forms of *be*.

Newspaper Headlines

Over 100 People **Injured** by Aftershocks

News Report

More than a hundred people **have been injured** by the aftershocks.

Sign

No Pets **Allowed**

Telephone Recording

Please continue to hold. Your call **will be answered** by the next available agent.

Rules at a Health Club

Handball courts **may be reserved** one week in advance.

Announcement on an Airplane

Passengers **are requested** to remain seated.

D1 Listening for Meaning and Use

▶ Notes 1, 2

CD2 T9 **A.** Listen to each example. Is it from academic discourse (e.g., college lectures), public discourse (e.g., ads, announcements, TV broadcasts), or personal discourse (e.g., conversations between friends)? Check (✓) the correct column.

	ACADEMIC DISCOURSE	PUBLIC DISCOURSE	PERSONAL DISCOURSE
1.		✓	
2.			
3.			
4.			
5.			
6.			
7.			
8.			

B. Work in groups. Listen to each example again. Discuss what specific features of each announcement influenced your choice.

D2 Understanding News Headlines

▶ Note 2

A. Change each news headline into two full sentences, one using the present perfect passive and one using the simple past passive. If necessary, add articles and other missing words.

> **Two Children Injured in Train Accident**

1. _Two children have been injured in a train accident._ OR _Two children were injured in a train accident._

> **Site Selected for Recycling Plant**

4. _____

> **New Cancer Treatment Discovered**

2. _____

> **Restaurant Closed by Health Department**

5. _____

> **Presidents's Trip Delayed by Weather**

3. _____

> **Golfer Struck by Lightning**

6. _____

B. Think about the active forms of each of the headlines. Why do you think the passive was used instead? Why was the agent used in certain headlines?

Using Passives with *Get*

CD2 T10 Look at the cartoon and listen to the conversation. How is the underlined form in the cartoon different from what you hear?

> Guess what? I'm going to <u>be promoted</u> to district manager.

> Congratulations!

Get commonly replaces *be* in informal conversation. *Get* passives are often more dynamic and emotional than *be* passives. Sentences with *get* passives are usually about people rather than objects and especially about situations people can't control.

STANDARD FORM	WHAT YOU MIGHT HEAR
Tran **was accepted** by several colleges, but his best friend **was rejected** by the same ones.	"Tran got accepted by several colleges, but his best friend got rejected by the same ones."

D3 Understanding Informal Speech

CD2 T11 Listen and write the standard form of the words you hear.

1. Do you think you __'ll be sent__ to the convention in Hawaii?

2. I _____ soon.

3. John _____ to the Boston office.

4. He _____ by Harvard Business School.

5. The manager _____ breaking the rules.

6. He _____.

7. Steve finally _____ for all of his extra work.

8. He _____ for a special award yesterday.

D4 Writing Rules

A. Change the rules on the first sign to a more formal, impersonal style by using passive instead of active sentences. Write your rules on the second sign.

SWIMMING POOL RULES

1 Members must show their membership passes at the gate.
2 Members can purchase guest passes at the main office.
3 We may limit the number of guests on weekends.
4 We do not admit children under 12 unless an adult accompanies them.
5 You must supervise small children at all times.
6 You must take a shower before entering the pool.
7 You must obey the lifeguard at all times.
8 We permit diving in designated areas only.
9 We prohibit eating, gum chewing, and glass bottles in the pool area.
10 You may eat food in the picnic area only.

SWIMMING POOL RULES

1 <u>Membership passes must be shown at the gate.</u>
2 _____
3 _____
4 _____
5 _____
6 _____
7 _____
8 _____
9 _____
10 _____

B. Now write a set of rules for one of these topics or a topic of your choice: (a) course requirements at your school, (b) rules for using books and other materials at the library, (c) rules for living in an apartment building, or (d) rules for members of a health club. Use the passive to give your rules a more formal, impersonal tone.

Think Critically About Meaning and Use

A. Read each sentence. Check (✓) the sentences that have approximately the same meaning.

1. Your application should be sent to us by email.

   ____✓____ **a.** You should email us your application.

   _____ **b.** We will email an application to you.

2. The problem could be solved.

   _____ **a.** The problem will be solved.

   _____ **b.** Someone might solve the problem.

3. He got robbed twice last year.

   _____ **a.** He has robbed two people.

   _____ **b.** On two different occasions, someone robbed him.

4. All reservations must be accompanied by a 25 percent deposit.

   _____ **a..** Deposit some money in the bank in order to make a reservation.

   _____ **b.** Customers need to pay a 25 percent deposit when they make a reservation.

5. No one will be hired by the company.

   _____ **a.** No one will get fired by the company.

   _____ **b.** The company won't be hiring anyone.

6. Your prescription can be refilled three times.

   _____ **a.** You will be able to get three refills.

   _____ **b.** You must get three refills.

7. Passengers have been requested to check in at the gate.

    ____ **a.** Passengers have requested to check in at the gate.

    ____ **b.** We have requested that passengers check in at the gate.

8. Several factors need to be considered by the judge.

    ____ **a.** The judge needs to consider several factors.

    ____ **b.** We need to consider several factors.

B. Discuss these questions in small groups.

1. **PREDICT** Which sentence would most likely be heard over a loudspeaker system? Why?

2. **PREDICT** Which sentence would most likely be heard in a conversation between two friends? Why?

Edit

Find the errors in these sentences and correct them.

1. These pills should be ~~take~~ _taken_ every four hours.

2. The letter ought to delivered in the afternoon.

3. The bell will be rang several times.

4. A young man has seriously injured in a car accident. That's terrible!

5. The mail has sent to the wrong address.

6. Will a new road build soon, or will the old one be repaired?

7. It will be not needed any longer.

8. All online orders must get paid by credit card.

Write

Write a letter to the editor of a national newspaper proposing steps that should be taken to improve education. Use future, present perfect, modal, and other passive forms where appropriate.

1. **BRAINSTORM** Makes notes about (a) improvements that have been made in education in recent years and (b) problems that still need to be solved. Use these categories and questions to help you organize your ideas into paragraphs:
   - **Opening:** What improvements have been made in recent years? What areas have been ignored and still need improvement?
   - **Body:** What problems need to be solved? What steps should be taken?
   - **Closing:** How urgent is the situation? What will happen if improvements aren't made? What actions should be taken?

2. **WRITE A FIRST DRAFT** Before you write your first draft, read the checklist below and look at the example on pages 212–213. Write your draft using passive forms.

3. **EDIT** Read your work and check it against the checklist below. Circle grammar, spelling, and punctuation errors.

DO I...	YES
use a range of present perfect, future, and modal passives to make my writing sound more formal and objective?	☐
use active forms, where appropriate, to keep the focus on an agent?	☐
use at least one example of a passive expression with an *it-subject* (e.g., *It is expected/generally agreed that...*)?	☐
use or omit agents as appropriate?	☐

4. **PEER REVIEW** Work with a partner to help you decide how to fix your errors and improve the content. Use the checklist above.

5. **REWRITE YOUR DRAFT** Using the comments from your partner, write a final draft.

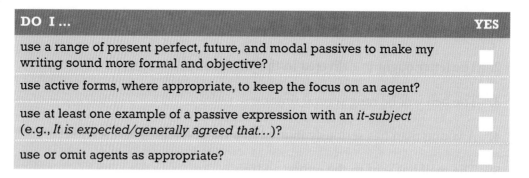

Dear Editor,

I'm proud to say that education in our country has improved greatly in recent years. Hundreds of new schools have been built in rural areas, and many more students are being given the opportunity to complete high school and college...

11

Contrasting Gerunds and Infinitives

A.   **GRAMMAR IN DISCOURSE: Become a Less Aggressive Driver** . . 230

B.   **FORM 1: Gerunds and Infinitives** **232**

Gerunds	**Infinitives**
I hate **driving in traffic.**	I hate **to drive in traffic.**
Gerunds As Subjects	*It* **Subject . . . + Infinitive**
Owning a car costs a lot.	It costs a lot **to own a car.**
Gerunds After Verbs	**Infinitives After Verbs**
Experts suggest **driving slowly.**	Drivers agree **to slow down.**

Vocabulary Notes: Short Answers to Questions with Infinitives

C.   **MEANING AND USE 1: Verbs Used with Gerunds**
and Infinitives **238**

Same Meanings with *Begin*, *Start*, and *Continue*

Similar Meanings with *Like*, *Love*, *Hate*, and *Prefer*

Different and Similar Meanings with *Try*

Different Meanings with *Remember*, *Stop*, *Forget*, and *Regret*

D.   **FORM 2: More About Gerunds and Infinitives** **243**

Verb Phrase + Gerund	**Be + Adjective + Preposition + Gerund**
She is busy **talking**	We were afraid of **driving in the snow.**
Preposition + Gerund	**Adjective + Infinitive**
Without **realizing it,** drivers speed.	She was ready **to talk.**
Verb + Preposition + Gerund	**In Order + Infinitive**
Think about **slowing down.**	Put on some music (in order) **to relax.**

E.   **MEANING AND USE 2: Interpreting Gerunds**
and Infinitives **247**

The Performer of Gerund Actions

The Performer of Infinitive Actions

WRITING: Write a Persuasive Essay About Ways to
Reduce Stress **250**

PART 4 TEST: The Passives, Gerunds, and Infinitives **253**

Become a Less Aggressive Driver

A1 Before You Read

Discuss these questions.

Driving aggressively means driving in an unsafe and angry manner. How safe do you feel on the road? Do you ever see angry drivers? What do you do?

A2 Read

CD2 T12 Read this book excerpt to find out what psychologist Richard Carlson has suggested for aggressive drivers.

Become a Less Aggressive Driver

Where do you get the most uptight? If you're like most people, (driving in traffic) is probably high on your list. Most major highways these
5 days are more like racetracks than like roadways.

There are three major reasons for becoming a less aggressive driver. First, when you are aggressive, you put
10 yourself and everyone around you in extreme danger. Second, driving aggressively is extremely stressful. Your blood pressure goes up, your grip on the wheel tightens, your eyes are
15 strained, and your thoughts are spinning out of control. Finally, you end up saving no time at all.

Recently, I was driving south from Oakland to San Jose. Traffic was
20 heavy, but it was moving. I noticed an extremely aggressive and angry driver who kept weaving in and out of his lane. He was constantly speeding up and slowing down. Clearly, he was in
25 a hurry. For the most part, I remained in the same lane for the entire 40-mile journey. I was listening to a new audio tape and daydreaming along the way. I enjoyed the trip a great deal because
30 driving gives me a chance to be alone. As I was exiting off the highway, the aggressive driver came up behind me and raced on by. His weaving, rapid acceleration, and putting families at
35 risk had earned him nothing except perhaps some high blood pressure. On average, he and I had driven at the same speed.

The same principle applies when you see drivers who are speeding past you in order to beat you to the next stoplight. It simply doesn't pay to speed.

When you make the conscious decision to become a less aggressive driver, you begin using your time in the car to loosen up. Instead of tensing your muscles, try to relax them. I even have a few audio tapes that are specifically for muscular relaxation. Sometimes I put one in and listen. By the time I reach my destination, I feel more relaxed than I did before getting into the car. During the course of your lifetime, you'll probably spend a great deal of time driving. You can spend those moments being frustrated, or you can use them wisely. If you do the latter, you'll be a more relaxed person.

Adapted from *Don't Sweat the Small Stuff … And It's All Small Stuff*

---

grip: a strong hold or grasp
it doesn't pay: it's not worth doing
latter: the second of two things just mentioned
sweat: (informal) to worry about something

uptight: (informal) tense
weave: to move around things and change directions quickly

A3 After You Read

Write *T* for true and *F* for false for each statement about the author.

___F___ **1.** He is always in a hurry.

_____ **2.** He gets angry at other drivers when they pass him.

_____ **3.** He sees a direct relationship between stress and driving.

_____ **4.** He tries to find ways to relax in the car.

_____ **5.** He probably follows and honks at aggressive drivers.

_____ **6.** He probably allows himself extra time in order to get to places on time.

FORM 1

Gerunds and Infinitives

Think Critically About Form

A. Look back at the excerpt on page 230 and complete the tasks below.

1. **IDENTIFY** A gerund can act as the subject of a sentence. An example is circled. Find another example.

2. **IDENTIFY** A gerund can directly follow a verb. An example is underlined. Find another example.

3. **RECOGNIZE** Look in the last paragraph. Find an infinitive that directly follows a verb.

4. **EVALUATE** Look at the example sentence below. The infinitive appears at the end of the sentence. What word is in the subject position?

   "It simply doesn't pay to speed."

B. Discuss your answers with the class and read the Form charts to check them.

▶ Overview

AFFIRMATIVE AND NEGATIVE GERUNDS	
	GERUND
I hate	driving. driving slowly. driving in traffic. driving a big car.
I prefer	not driving.

AFFIRMATIVE AND NEGATIVE INFINITIVES	
	INFINITIVE
I hate	to drive. to drive slowly. to drive in traffic. to drive a big car.
I prefer	not to drive.

ONLINE PRACTICE

▶ Gerunds

GERUNDS AS SUBJECTS	
GERUND	VERB PHRASE
Owning a car	costs a lot. is expensive.

GERUNDS AFTER VERBS		
SUBJECT	VERB	GERUND
Drivers	should consider	**slowing down.**
Experts	suggest	**driving slowly.**

▶ Infinitives

IT SUBJECT… + INFINITIVE		
IT	VERB + NOUN	INFINITIVE
It	costs a lot	**to own a car.**

IT	VERB + ADJECTIVE	INFINITIVE
It	is expensive	**to own a car.**

INFINITIVES AFTER VERBS			
	VERB	INFINITIVE	
Drivers	agree	**to slow down.**	

	VERB	OBJECT	INFINITIVE
Experts	warn	people	**to drive slowly.**

	VERB	(OBJECT)	INFINITIVE
I	want		**to drive carefully.**
I	want	him	**to drive carefully.**

Overview

- All verbs, except modal auxiliaries, have gerund and infinitive forms.
- A gerund can be one word (*driving*) or part of a longer phrase, with an adverb (*driving slowly*), a prepositional phrase (*driving in traffic*), or an object (*driving a big car*).
- All verbs, except modal auxiliaries, have infinitive forms.
- An infinitive can be two words (*to drive*) or part of a longer phrase with an adverb (*to drive slowly*), a prepositional phrase (*to drive in traffic*), or an object (*to drive a big car*).

Gerunds as Subjects

- A gerund can function as the subject of a sentence. Gerunds function as singular nouns and take singular verbs. A gerund can be replaced by the pronoun *it*.

    Owning a car costs a lot.   (**It** costs a lot.)

Gerunds After Verbs

- Here are some examples of verbs followed by gerunds (see Appendix 8 for a list of more verbs):

advise	consider	deny	enjoy	go	miss	practice	suggest
avoid	delay	dislike	finish	mind	postpone	recommend	

It Subject … + Infinitive

- Although an infinitive can function as the subject of a sentence (*To own a car is expensive*), this is not common. Instead, the pronoun *it* begins the sentence. It has the same meaning as the infinitive it replaces.

    It costs a lot **to own a car.** (It = to own a car)

- *It* is followed by *be* or one of a limited group of verbs. For example:

appear	be	cost	look	pay	seem	take

(Continued on page 234)

Infinitives After Verbs

- Infinitives after verbs appear in one of three patterns:

Verb + Infinitive

agree	decide	learn	plan	refuse
appear	hope	offer	seem	wait

Verb + Object + Infinitive

advise	force	invite	remind	teach	urge
cause	get	order	require	tell	warn

Verb + (Object) + Infinitive

(These verbs can be followed by the infinitive with or without an object.)

ask	expect	need	promise	wish
choose	help	pay	want	would like

- See Appendix 9 for a list of more verbs followed by infinitives.

B1 Listening for Form

🔊 CD2 T13 Listen to each sentence. Do you hear an infinitive or a gerund? Check (✓) the correct column.

	GERUND	INFINITIVE
1.		✓
2.		
3.		
4.		
5.		
6.		

B2 Rephrasing Subject Gerunds as *It* ... + Infinitive

Rewrite each of these opinions. Change the subject to *It* and the gerund to an infinitive. Remember to put the infinitive at the end of the sentence.

1. Raising children is not easy.   It's not easy to raise children.

2. Studying all night is not a good idea. _____

3. Walking to work takes too much time.   _____

4. Getting exercise is important. _____

5. Owning a house costs a lot of money. _____

6. Knowing a foreign language can be useful. _____

B3 Working on Subject Gerunds and *It* ... + Infinitive

A. **Work with a partner. Choose one of the topics below and make a list of five common problems related to that topic. Use affirmative and negative gerunds.**

Living in a big city   Owning a car

Learning a language   Living in a foreign country

Problems with living in a big city: parking, making friends, not having a garden,…

B. **Write two sentences about each of the problems you listed, one with a subject gerund and one with *it* + an infinitive.**

Parking is difficult in a big city.

It is difficult to park in a big city.

B4 Building Sentences with Gerunds and Infinitives

Build as many meaningful sentences as possible. Use an item from each column, or from the first and third columns only. Punctuate your sentences correctly.

He told me to go more slowly.

he told she expects he learned they advised don't delay	me	to go more slowly to speak Spanish leaving taking a driving class

B5 Distinguishing Gerunds and Infinitives After Verbs

Imagine that some people are discussing a controversial new movie. Complete each sentence with *seeing it* or *to see it*.

1. I'm planning _to see it._

2. Do you recommend _____

3. You should consider _____

4. I've decided _____

5. I suggest _____

6. Don't expect me _____

7. He refuses _____

8. I warn you not _____

9. You should avoid _____

10. I urge you _____

Vocabulary Notes

Short Answers to Questions with Infinitives

Short answers in response to questions with infinitives can contain the main verb + *to*.

> Do you plan to take a vacation soon? Yes, **I plan to**. / No, **I don't expect to**.

If you begin a short answer with an infinitive, *to* is omitted.

> What do you want to do later? **Take a walk**.

When you join two or more infinitives with *and* or *or*, *to* appears only with the first infinitive.

> Do you want **to eat out** or **make dinner at home**?

B6 Using Short Answers to Questions with Infinitives

Take turns asking and answering questions. Use the verbs in parentheses to form affirmative or negative short answers with infinitives.

1. **A:** Are you going to graduate in June?

   B: Yes, _____I hope to_____. (hope)

2. **A:** Are your parents taking a vacation this summer?

   B: No, they _____. (expect)

3. **A:** Do you think you'll go to the wedding?

   B: Yes, we _____. (would like)

4. **A:** Is she interested in going with us?

   B: No. She _____. (want)

5. **A:** Are you going to buy a house?

   B: Yes, we _____ soon. (plan)

6. **A:** Please ask him not to leave so early.

   B: I'm sorry, but he really _____. (need)

B7 Asking Information Questions with Gerunds and Infinitives

A. Work with a partner. Ask questions using *What* and these words and phrases + the verb *do* as a gerund or an infinitive. Answer the questions and then ask *What about you?*

1. expect/this weekend

   A: *What do you expect to do this weekend?*
   B: *Sleep late. What about you?*
   A: *I expect to study most of the time.*

2. enjoy/in your free time

3. suggest/after dinner

4. would like/on your birthday

5. want/during your vacation

6. avoid/on the weekend

7. hope/next summer

8. dislike/in the morning

B. Now write three sentences that compare your partner's answers with yours. Use the appropriate verbs or phrases with gerunds or infinitives.

Anna expects to sleep late this weekend, but I expect to study most of the time.

B8 Asking *Yes/No* Questions with Gerunds and Infinitives

Work with a partner. Take turns asking and answering questions with gerunds or infinitives.

1. expect/travel/stay home/next summer

   A: *Do you expect to travel or stay home next summer?*
   B: *Stay home.*

2. suggest/stay home/see a movie/tonight

3. hope/live in a big city/a small town

4. need/study a lot/a little

5. recommend/eat breakfast/skip breakfast

6. want/stay in your apartment/find a new apartment

Verbs Used with Gerunds and Infinitives

Think Critically About Meaning and Use

A. Read the sentences and answer the questions below.

1a. I stopped to shop at London's Bakery. It's so inexpensive.
1b. I stopped shopping at London's Bakery. It's so expensive.
2a. He started to talk as soon as he saw me. He's not shy.
2b. He started talking as soon as he saw me. He's very friendly.

EVALUATE Which pair has the same meaning? Which pair has a different meaning?

B. Discuss your answers with the class and read the Meaning and Use Notes to check them.

Meaning and Use Notes

ONLINE
PRACTICE

Same Meanings with *Begin*, *Start*, and *Continue*
Some verbs are used with both infinitives and gerunds. See Appendix 10 for a list of these verbs.

▶ 1   After *begin*, *start*, and *continue*, the infinitive and the gerund have the same meaning. If the main verb is in the continuous, use the infinitive, not the gerund.

Infinitive	Gerund
He <u>started</u> **to laugh**.	He <u>started</u> **laughing**.
We <u>continued</u> **to read**.	We <u>continued</u> **reading**.
It <u>began</u> **to snow**.	It <u>began</u> **snowing**.
It <u>was beginning</u> **to snow**.	**x** It was beginning snowing. (INCORRECT)

Similar Meanings with *Like*, *Love*, *Hate*, and *Prefer*

▶ **2**   After *like*, *love*, *hate*, and *prefer*, the infinitive and the gerund are similar in meaning. However, sometimes it is more common to use an infinitive to talk about an activity at a specific time, and a gerund to talk about an activity in general.

Infinitive	Gerund
I <u>like</u> **to swim** early in the morning.	I <u>like</u> **swimming** and **boating**.
Would you <u>prefer</u> **to play tennis** or **swim** today?	Do you <u>prefer</u> **playing tennis** or **swimming**?

Different and Similar Meanings with *Try*

▶ **3A**   After *try*, the infinitive and the gerund are similar in meaning.

Infinitive	Gerund
<u>Try</u> **to relax** more.	<u>Try</u> **relaxing** more.

▶ **3B**   When *try* is in the past, the infinitive often implies that an action did not occur. The gerund implies that an action occurred but may or may not have been successful.

Infinitive (Didn't Occur)	Gerund (Did Occur)
I <u>tried</u> **to take some aspirin** for the pain, but I couldn't open the bottle. (I didn't take any aspirin.)	I <u>tried</u> **taking some aspirin** for the pain, but it didn't help. (I took some aspirin.)

Different Meanings with *Remember*, *Stop*, *Forget*, and *Regret*

▶ **4A**   After *remember*, *stop*, *forget*, and *regret*, the infinitive refers to an action that happens after the action of the main verb. The gerund refers to an action that happened before the action of the main verb.

Infinitive Action Happens After Verb	Gerund Action Happened Before Verb
I <u>remembered</u> **to mail the letter**. (I remembered the letter. Then I mailed it.)	I <u>remembered</u> **mailing the letter**. (I mailed the letter. Later I remembered doing it.)
I <u>stopped</u> **to listen** to him. (I stopped what I was doing. Then I listened to him.)	I <u>stopped</u> **listening** to him. (I was listening to him. Then I stopped listening.)

(Continued on page 240)

▶ **4B** *Forget* is more commonly used with an infinitive. With a gerund, it occurs mostly in sentences with *will never*.

Infinitive Action Happens After Verb	Gerund Action Happened Before Verb
I <u>forgot</u> **to pay my telephone bill**. (I forgot, so then I didn't pay the bill.)	I <u>will never forget</u> **living in Ecuador**. (I lived there. Now I'll never forget it.)

▶ **4C** *Regret* can take either an infinitive or a gerund with verbs such as *inform*, *tell*, *say*, and *announce*. With all other verbs, *regret* takes a gerund.

Infinitive Action Happens After Verb	Gerund Action Happened Before Verb
I <u>regret</u> **to inform you** that I'm leaving. (I feel regret. Then I inform you.)	I <u>regret</u> **informing you** that I'm leaving. (I informed you. Now I regret it.)
x I regret to leave. (INCORRECT)	I <u>regret</u> **leaving**.

C1 Listening for Meaning and Use
▶ Notes 3A, 3B, 4A, 4B

CD2 T14   Listen to each situation. Choose the sentence that is more likely to follow it.

1. **a.** He was rude to me.

    b. He was so grateful to me.

2. **a.** It's a good thing I did, though.

    b. That was a terrible mistake.

3. **a.** But I couldn't stand the smell.

    b. It really helped me feel better.

4. **a.** But I had no choice.

    b. But I have no choice.

5. **a.** I like the editorials.

    b. It's not well written.

6. **a.** It's on my calendar for tomorrow.

    b. It was so exciting.

C2 Rephrasing Gerunds and Infinitives
▶ Notes 1, 2

Work with a partner. Change each gerund to an infinitive, and each infinitive to a gerund. Then practice the conversations.

1. **A:** I love skiing. What about you?

    B: I like skiing, but I prefer staying indoors in the winter.

    A: *I love to ski. What about you?*

    B: *I like to ski, but I prefer to stay indoors in the winter.*

2. **A:** I hate to drive in traffic.

    B: Then you should continue to take the bus home.

A: _____

B: _____

3. **A:** It started to rain a few minutes ago.

   B: Then let's wait here for a while. I don't like to walk in the rain.

   A: _____

   B: _____

4. **A:** I hate waiting in line.

   B: So do I. That's why I prefer to shop late at night.

   A: _____

   B: _____

C3 Making Suggestions

▶ **Notes 3A, 4A, 4B**

Work in small groups. Choose one of the topics below. Make suggestions by completing each sentence with a gerund or infinitive. Then read your suggestions to the class without mentioning your topic. The class guesses what topic the advice is for.

Reducing stress

Cleaning your apartment

Studying for a test

Finding a job

Improving your English

Making more friends

Suggestions for reducing stress

1. Try _to get more sleep._

2. Consider _taking a yoga class._

3. Avoid _____

4. Don't forget _____

5. Plan _____

6. Don't delay _____

7. Aim _____

8. Volunteer _____

C4 Expressing Feelings and Preferences ▶ Notes 1, 2, 3A, 4A

 A. Work with a partner. Jay is visiting his cousin Joe in Chicago. Complete these conversations with the words in parentheses and gerunds or infinitives. In some cases, you may use either one.

1. **Joe:** Another beautiful day! I love ___*getting up/to get up*___ (get up) in
   the morning.

   Jay: You're kidding! I really dislike _____₂_____ (get up) in the
   morning. I immediately start _____₃_____ (worry) about
   all of the things I need _____₄_____ (do).

2. **Joe:** Let's go _____₁_____ (shop). I like _____₂_____
   (watch) the crowds, and I'd like _____₃_____ (buy)
   some gifts.

   Jay: Do we have to? I don't like _____₄_____ (fight) my way
   through crowds.

   Joe: Well, would you like _____₅_____ (go) to the top of the Sears
   Tower? The view is great. You can see the lake from there.

   Jay: I remember _____₆_____ (go) up there once. It was terrible.
   I prefer _____₇_____ (have) both of my feet on the ground.

3. **Joe:** I'm beginning _____₁_____ (feel) hungry. Let's try
   _____₂_____ (find) a good restaurant.

   Jay: I try _____₃_____ (avoid) eating out. You wouldn't mind
   _____₄_____ (cook) something at home, would you?

B. Now work on your own and write a paragraph about a person that you know. Use gerunds and infinitives to discuss the person's feelings and likes or dislikes.

My friend Alex is hoping to be a food critic someday, so he loves to eat at new restaurants. He prefers going to five-star French restaurants. That's fine, except that he always wants me to go with him, and he refuses to listen to my objections. He considers...

D FORM 2

More About Gerunds and Infinitives

Think Critically About Form

A. Read the sentences and complete the tasks below.

    a. Instead of <u>tensing your muscles</u>, try to relax them.

    b. During your lifetime, you'll probably spend a lot of time <u>driving on the highway</u>.

    c. You end up <u>saving no time at all</u>.

    d. Some drivers are too anxious <u>to reach their destinations</u>.

    1. ANALYZE Write the letter of the sentence that contains one of these forms before a gerund:

        _____ a verb phrase ending in a noun   _____ a phrasal verb (verb + particle)

        _____ a preposition or prepositional phrase

    2. DIFFERENTIATE Which sentence has a phrase containing an infinitive? What part of speech does it follow?

B. Discuss your answers with the class and read the Meaning and Use Notes to check them.

▶ Gerunds

ONLINE PRACTICE

VERB PHRASE + GERUND		
	VERB PHRASE	**GERUND**
She	is busy	**talking**.
He	spent some time	**relaxing**.

PREPOSITION + GERUND		
PREPOSITION	**GERUND**	
Without	**realizing it**,	drivers speed.
In addition to	**swimming**,	we played tennis.

	PREPOSITION	**GERUND**
Drivers speed	without	**realizing it**.

VERB + PREPOSITION + GERUND	
VERB + PREPOSITION	**GERUND**
Think about	**slowing down**.

	PHRASAL VERB	**GERUND**
We	ended up	**waiting an hour**.

BE + ADJECTIVE + PREPOSITION + GERUND		
	***BE* + ADJECTIVE + PREPOSITION**	**GERUND**
We	were afraid of	**driving in the snow**.

(Continued on page 244)

- Some common verb phrases that end in adjectives or nouns can be followed by gerunds:

be busy	have a good time	it's no use	spend an hour	waste time
have fun	have trouble	it's (not) worth	spend time	

- Examples of one-word prepositions and longer phrases followed by gerunds:

after	besides	in	instead of
before	by	in addition to	without

- Examples of verb + preposition combinations followed by gerunds:

approve of	depend on	insist on	talk about	work on
believe in	disapprove of	look forward to	think about	worry about

- Examples of *be* + adjective + preposition combinations followed by gerunds:

be accustomed to	be good at	be surprised at	be used to
be afraid of	be interested in	be tired of	be worried about

- Phrasal verbs (*end up*, *call off*) can be followed by gerunds.
- See Appendix 8 for a list of more combinations with prepositions followed by gerunds.
- See Appendix 15 for a list of common phrasal verbs.

▶ Infinitives

ADJECTIVE + INFINITIVE			
	VERB	**ADJECTIVE**	**INFINITIVE**
She	was	ready	**to talk**.

IN ORDER + INFINITIVE	
	(*IN ORDER* +) **INFINITIVE**
Put on some music	(in order) **to relax**.

(*IN ORDER* + *NOT*) **INFINITIVE**	
In order not **to panic**,	take a deep breath.

- Many adjectives can be followed by infinitives.

afraid	eager	excited	hesitant	sorry
determined	embarrassed	happy	ready	surprised

- See Appendix 9 for a list of more adjectives followed by infinitives.
- Infinitives do not directly follow prepositions.
- Infinitives may follow the expression *in order*. They are called purpose infinitives.

- In affirmative purpose infinitives, *in order* may be omitted. In negative purpose infinitives, *in order* is necessary.

> ⓘ Do not confuse expressions ending in the preposition *to* followed by gerunds with verbs followed directly by the infinitive.
>
> I <u>look forward to</u> **leaving** soon.   I <u>expect</u> **to leave** soon.

D1 Listening for Form

CD2 T15   Listen to this conversation. Write the gerunds or infinitives you hear.

A: You should consider ___taking___ a vacation. You could spend some time
₁

_____.
₂

B: I can't. I'm busy _____ on a project that's due soon. My boss has told me
₃

_____ it as quickly as possible.
₄

A: I know. That's the point. Aren't you sick of _____?
₅

B: Well, instead of _____ a long vacation, I might be interested in
₆

_____ away for a weekend. But I'd have trouble _____ before noon
₇   ₈

on Saturday. I save Saturday morning for _____ on my office email.
₉

A: Didn't you promise _____ more?
₁₀

D2 Using Gerunds After Prepositions

Follow each preposition with the gerund form of the expressions below. Then complete each sentence.

clean your apartment	do the laundry	look for an apartment	take a trip
cook dinner	find a job	reduce stress	use a computer

1. Before _taking a trip, check your car carefully._ _____

2. After _____

3. Instead of _____

4. Besides _____

5. By _____

6. In addition to _____

7. Before _____

8. After _____

D3 Choosing Between Gerunds and Infinitives

 A. Work with a partner. Switch roles for each question.

Student A: Ask a *What* question using the phrase and the verb *do* as a gerund or an infinitive.

Student B: Answer and then ask *What about you?*

1. be hesitant

   A: *What are you hesitant to do?*

   B: *I'm hesitant to take too many classes. What about you?*

   A: *I'm hesitant to look for a part-time job.*

2. be good at

3. be eager

4. be afraid of

5. be ready/right now

6. be accustomed to

7. be determined/before you are 50

8. look forward to/next year

 B. Report three of your partner's answers to the class using full sentences with gerunds or infinitives.

Leroy is hesitant to take too many classes.

D4 Working on Purpose Infinitives

A. Complete these sentences about errands with affirmative purpose infinitives. Use your own ideas. You can omit *in order*.

1. First I went to the bank _to get some money._

2. Then I stopped at the dry cleaners _____

3. Next I went to the drugstore near my home _____

4. After that I stopped by the library _____

5. On the way home, I stopped at the gas station _____

 B. Work with a partner. Choose two items from the suggested topics below and write simple instructions for each. Use affirmative and negative purpose infinitives.

how to open a jar of jelly, a can of beans, a box of crackers, or a carton of juice
how to operate your DVD player or computer
how to start your car, drive safely in traffic, fix a flat tire, or fill your car with gas

To open a jar of jelly, grip the jar tightly and twist the lid.
In order to loosen the top, run it under hot water.

Interpreting Gerunds and Infinitives

Think Critically About Meaning and Use

A. Read the sentences and answer the questions below.

1a. Tom worries about Jane's driving at night.
1b. Tom worries about driving at night.
2a. Susan wants Sam to come early.
2b. Susan wants to come early.

1. **ANALYZE** Compare 1a and 1b. In each sentence, who is driving?

2. **ANALYZE** Compare 2a and 2b. In each sentence, who might come early?

B. Discuss your answers with the class and read the Meaning and Use Notes to check them.

Meaning and Use Notes

ONLINE
PRACTICE

The Performer of Gerund Actions

▶ **1A** Like other actions, the actions expressed by gerunds are performed by someone. Sometimes the performer of the gerund action is the sentence subject. Sometimes the performer of the gerund action is not the subject. In these cases, a possessive adjective is used to indicate the performer.

Gerund Only

We were surprised at **passing the exam**.
(We passed the exam.)

Possessive Adjective + Gerund

We were surprised at <u>Tim's/his</u> **passing the exam**. (Tim passed the exam.)

▶ **1B** When a gerund occurs after a verb, an object pronoun can replace the possessive adjective. Sentences with object pronouns convey a less formal tone than those with possessive adjectives.

Verb + Object Pronoun + Gerund

We were surprised at <u>him</u> **passing the exam**.

(Continued on page 248)

The Performer of Infinitive Actions

▶ **2A** Like other actions, the actions expressed by infinitives are performed by someone. When an infinitive directly follows a verb, the performer of the infinitive action is the sentence subject. When an infinitive follows an object, the performer of the infinitive action is the object.

Verb + Infinitive Only	**Verb + Object + Infinitive**
I <u>want</u> **to take a different route**.	I <u>want him</u> **to take a different route**.
(I may take a different route.)	(He may take a different route.)

▶ **2B** *Help* + object can be followed by an infinitive or a base form with no change in meaning. The verbs *make*, *have*, and *let* + object are followed by the base form of a verb, but not the infinitive. Like all objects before infinitives, the objects of these verbs perform the action expressed by the base form.

Verb + Object + Base Form of Verb	**Verb + Object + Infinitive**
He <u>helped me</u> **get** there safely.	He <u>helped me</u> **to get** there safely.
He <u>made me</u> **get** some rest.	
He <u>had me</u> **call** the doctor.	
He <u>let me</u> **call** the hospital.	

E1 Listening for Meaning and Use

▶ Notes 1A, 1B, 2B

🔊 CD2 T16   Listen to each situation and choose the statement that is true.

1. **a.** My friend shouldn't work so hard.

   b. The doctor shouldn't work so hard.

2. **a.** I recommended some exercises.

   b. The doctor recommended some exercises.

3. **a.** She called a health club.

   b. We called a health club.

4. **a.** We called in the evening.

   b. They called us in the evening.

5. **a.** We made arrangements.

   b. The manager made arrangements.

6. **a.** We invited him.

   b. He invited us.

7. **a.** He drove in the rain.

   b. I drove in the rain.

8. **a.** The manager left a deposit.

   b. We left a deposit.

E2 Expressing Intentions and Desires

▶ Notes 1A, 1B, 2A

Choose either Situation A or B and complete the sentences that you might say.
Use sentences with appropriate infinitives or gerunds. Add an object before infinitives
or a possessive adjective before gerunds, if possible.

Situation A: You are going to run for president.

Situation B: You are going to resign from your position because of a scandal.

1. I have decided _to run for president._

2. I appreciate _your encouraging me so much._

3. I expect _____

4. I invite _____

5. I'm concerned about _____

6. I urge _____

7. I want _____

8. I don't mind _____

E3 Talking About Teaching

▶ Notes 2A, 2B

A. In small groups, discuss the best way to teach someone to do something. Choose
one of the suggested topics below. Use the verbs *make*, *let*, *help*, and *have* followed
by an infinitive or base form where possible.

teaching a foreign friend how to speak your language
teaching a friend how to drive
teaching a child how to cook

A: *To teach a foreign friend your language, you need to be very patient.*

B: *It is important to practice as much as possible.*

C: *Yes. Also, let him make mistakes. That's how you help him make progress.*

B. Write a summary of your discussion and read it to the class. Find out whether the
class agrees with your methods.

Think Critically About Meaning and Use

A. Read each sentence and the statement that follows. Write *T* if the statement is true and *F* if it is false.

1. I forgot to mail the letter.

   __F__ I mailed the letter.

2. I didn't remember to take out the garbage.

   _____ I took out the garbage.

3. I'll never forget opening that letter.

   _____ I opened the letter.

4. I always avoid eating sweets.

   _____ I eat sweets.

5. They permitted me to leave.

   _____ I left.

6. She stopped to eat lunch.

   _____ She didn't eat lunch.

7. I tried soaking my ankle, but it still hurts.

   _____ I soaked my ankle.

8. I heard about his winning the race.

   _____ He won the race.

9. He was surprised at my failing the exam.

   _____ I failed the exam.

10. I had him complain to the manager.

    _____ I complained to the manager.

B. Discuss these questions in small groups.

1. **PREDICT** Look at sentence 2. How would the meaning change if the speaker had said, "I didn't remember taking out the garbage"?

2. **PREDICT** Look at sentence 6. How would the meaning change if the speaker had said, "She stopped eating lunch."

Edit

Find the errors in these paragraphs and correct them.

Unfortunately, it is very common _to_ encounter aggressive drivers every day. They are usually trying to getting somewhere in a hurry. Them speeding can cause them follow too closely or change lanes frequently without signaling.

In order avoid becoming an aggressive driver, there are a number of rules following. First, allow enough time to reaching your destination. Second, change your schedule to keep from drive during rush hours. Third, call ahead for explain if you are going to be late. Then you can relax.

If you see an aggressive driver, try get out of the way safely. Never challenge an aggressive driver by speed up or attempting to hold your position in your lane. Don't let others make you driving dangerously. You need be in control at all times.

Write

Write a persuasive essay advising readers how to manage the stress in their lives. Use gerunds and infinitives.

1. **BRAINSTORM** Research your topic on the Internet or at the library. Make a list of all the different ways to manage stress (e.g., using relaxation techniques, doing leisure-time activities, and so on.) Use these categories to help you organize your ideas into paragraphs.
   - **Introduction:** What role does stress play in our lives? Why is it important that people learn how to manage stress?
   - **Analysis/Advice:** Choose 2–3 methods and devote a paragraph to each. What is the method? Why do you think it is effective? Why should readers try it?
   - **Conclusion:** What "call to action" can you give readers to persuade them to take your ideas seriously?

2. **WRITE A FIRST DRAFT** Before you write your first draft, read the checklist below and look at the examples in A2 on pages 230–231 and C3 on page 241. Write your draft using gerunds and infinitives.

3. **EDIT** Read your work and check it against the checklist below. Circle grammar, spelling, and punctuation errors.

DO I...	YES
use gerunds and gerund phrases as subjects and objects, and after prepositions or common verb phrases?	☐
use the correct gerund or infinitive form after specific verbs?	☐
use at least one example of a sentence with *It...* + infinitive?	☐
make suggestions with imperatives + appropriate gerunds or infinitives?	☐

4. **PEER REVIEW** Work with a partner to help you decide how to fix your errors and improve the content. Use the checklist above.

5. **REWRITE YOUR DRAFT** Using the comments from your partner, write a final draft.

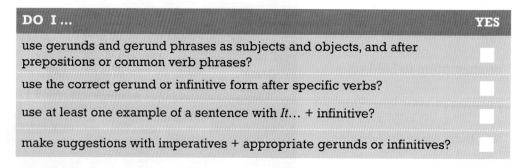

Dealing with stress is a fact of living in the modern world. Our lives are all about keeping the bills paid, juggling career and family, and generally never having enough hours in the day. The bad news is that living with a high level of stress can lead to...

Choose the correct word or words to complete each sentence.

1. _____ repairing a twenty-five year old television set.

   a. I decided

   b. We refused

   c. It's not worth

   d. They asked me

2. Would you mind _____ me the time, please?

   a. tell

   b. to tell

   c. told

   d. telling

3. Why _____ believed that infants should be read aloud to often?

   a. is it

   b. there is

   c. do we

   d. should it

4. When _____ substituted for gasoline in automobiles?

   a. other fuels are going to be

   b. are other fuels going to be

   c. are other fuels going

   d. other fuels are going

5. Typewriters _____ in offices any longer.

   a. not used

   b. are used

   c. are being used

   d. are not being used

Choose the best answer to complete each conversation.

6. **A:** I stopped to listen to his advice.

   B: Oh, I'm glad you did. _____

   a. He has bad ideas.

   b. He has good ideas.

   c. What did you recommend?

   d. He's a good listener.

7. **A:** The doctor permitted Tanya to fly to New York.

   B: Really? _____

   a. Has she considered coming by train?

   b. It pays to be cautious sometimes.

   c. What flight did the doctor take?

   d. What flight did she take?

8. **A:** I avoid cooking with butter.

   B: Me, too. _____

   a. I love using it.

   b. Unfortunately, I've run out.

   c. I've stopped using it.

   d. I used to hate it.

Choose the most likely source of each item.

9. Karl Marx was born in Germany on May 5, 1818.

    a. encyclopedia   **c.** formal letter

    b. public notice   **d.** newspaper headline

10. Congratulations. You have been accepted to City College.

    a. sign   **c.** recorded announcement

    b. formal letter   **d.** textbook

11. Credit Cards Not Accepted

    a. rule book   **c.** newspaper

    b. formal letter   **d.** sign

Complete each sentence with the correct form of the word or words in parentheses.

12. I'm on vacation next week. I'm planning _____ (not/do) any work.

13. He isn't accustomed _____ (eat) spicy food.

14. The children had fun _____ (ride) on the roller coaster.

Match each sentence ending to the correct beginning.

_____ **15.** We're interested   **a.** in buying a hybrid car.

_____ **16.** He insists   **b.** of driving on icy roads.

_____ **17.** She's not used   **c.** obeying speed limits.

                              d. about selling his car.

                              e. parking such a big car.

                              f. on being a back-seat driver.

                              g. to driving in bad weather.

                              h. at backing up.

Change each sentence from active to passive. Use the agent only if needed.

18. If it snows, the coach will cancel the game.

_____

19. Someone has seen the mayor at that restaurant.

_____

20. Pablo Picasso painted *The Three Musicians*.

_____

Indefinite and Definite Articles; Review of Nouns

A. GRAMMAR IN DISCOURSE: Chicken Soup,
Always Chicken Soup 256

B. FORM: Indefinite and Definite Articles;
Review of Nouns 258

Count Nouns	**Noncount Nouns**
banana	soup
physicians	research

Indefinite Articles	**Definite Articles**
I ate **a banana**.	I ate **the banana**.
I ate **an apple**.	I ate **the apple**.
Did you eat **Ø apples**?	Did you eat **the apples**?
I didn't eat **Ø fruit**.	I didn't eat **the fruit**.

C. MEANING AND USE 1: The Indefinite Article 262

Introducing Nouns with Indefinite Articles

Classifying and Describing Nouns

D. MEANING AND USE 2: The Definite Article 265

Identifying Nouns with the Definite Article

Vocabulary Notes: *Another* vs. *The Other*

Beyond the Sentence: Connecting Information

E. MEANING AND USE 3: Article Use with Generic Nouns . . . 271

Overview of Generic Nouns	**Using No Article (Ø)**
Using *A/An*	**Using** *The*

Beyond the Sentence: Indefinite Generic Nouns in Discourse

WRITING: Write a Pamphlet About Healthy Eating 276

Chicken Soup, Always Chicken Soup

A1 Before You Read

Discuss these questions.

What do you do when you have a cold? Do you take medicine? vitamins? herbs? What special treatments are used in your family? Do they work?

A2 Read

CD2 T17 Read this book excerpt to find out about the special medicinal properties of old-fashioned chicken soup.

Chicken Soup,
Always Chicken Soup

Have you ever wondered why chicken soup is such a popular remedy for the common cold? The first authority to recommend chicken soup
5 was the distinguished twelfth-century physician Moses Maimonides. According to the story, when Sultan Saladin, a powerful Muslim military leader, begged Maimonides for a cure
10 for his son's asthma, Maimonides prescribed chicken soup. The prescription was probably effective because chicken soup is now known to have medicinal properties.
15 Scientific research has begun to explain why age-old food remedies, passed down for centuries by medical sages and grandmothers, have been effective against respiratory problems
20 such as colds and the flu. The doctor who knows most about this is Irwin Ziment, M.D., a lung specialist at the

University of California at Los Angeles. Dr. Ziment has concluded
25 from a study of early medical literature that foods used to fight diseases for centuries are very similar to many of the drugs we now use. Chicken, for example, contains a
30 certain chemical which is released when you make the soup. This substance is remarkably similar to a common drug for bronchitis and respiratory infections. In fact, the
35 drug was originally made from chicken feathers and skin. The substance in chicken soup has been shown to help clear the lungs of

▶ Definite Articles

SINGULAR COUNT NOUNS	PLURAL COUNT NOUNS	NONCOUNT NOUNS
THE + SINGULAR COUNT NOUN	*THE* + PLURAL COUNT NOUN	*THE* + NONCOUNT NOUN
I ate **the banana**.	I ate **the bananas**.	I didn't eat **the fruit**.
Did you eat **the apple**?	Did you eat **the apples**?	Did you eat **the fruit**?

Nouns
- Common nouns can be count or noncount.
- Count nouns can be used with numbers. They have both singular and plural forms.
- Noncount nouns cannot be used with numbers. They do not have plural forms.
- Common nouns that occur with an indefinite article or no article (Ø) are indefinite nouns.
- Common nouns that occur with a definite article are definite nouns.

Indefinite Articles with Singular Count Nouns
- Indefinite articles can occur before a singular count noun (*an apple*) or before an adjective + singular count noun (*a green apple*).
- Use *an* before words that begin with a vowel sound; use *a* before all others.

  If a noun begins with the letter *h*, use *an* if the *h* is not pronounced. Use *a* if the *h* is pronounced.

  > **an** hour   **an** honor   **a** house   **a** human

- If a noun begins with the letter *u*, use *an* if the *u* is a short vowel. Use *a* if the *u* is pronounced like the *y* in yellow.

  > **an** umbrella   **an** understanding   **a** unit   **a** utensil

Indefinite Articles with Plural Count and Noncount Nouns
- Do not use indefinite articles before plural count nouns or noncount nouns.
- *Some* and *any* often act like indefinite articles with plural count nouns or noncount nouns. We often use *some* in affirmative sentences and questions and *any* in negative sentences and questions.
- Indefinite articles, *some*, and *any* do not have to be repeated when nouns are combined with *and*.

  > **a** banana and **(an)** apple   **some** fruit and **(some)** cereal

Definite Articles with Count and Noncount Nouns
- The definite article *the* can be used before all common nouns—singular and plural count nouns and noncount nouns.

(Continued on page 260)

- Definite articles can occur before a noun (*the apple*) or before an adjective + noun (*the green apple*).
- Definite articles do not have to be repeated when nouns are combined with *and*.

> **the** bananas and **(the)** apples

B1 Listening for Form

🔊 CD2 T18   Listen to these facts about the common cold. Write the articles you hear. Write Ø if there is no article. After you finish, check the capitalization.

Although ___the___ common cold is generally not serious, it causes _____
               1   2

people to be absent from _____ work and go to _____ doctor more often than
                               3   4

_____ other illnesses. _____ majority of colds come from _____ contact
     5   6   7

with _____ surfaces that _____ people touch frequently. People transmit
        8   9

_____ cold viruses on these surfaces to their eyes, noses, and mouths. Once
   10

_____ symptoms appear, there are many treatments for relieving _____
   11   12

discomfort. Whatever _____ person does, unfortunately, _____ cold will
                         13   14

probably still last from six to ten days.

B2 Identifying Indefinite and Definite Articles

Read the passage and underline all the common nouns, along with their articles and adjectives. Then write *D* for definite or *I* for indefinite to indicate whether the noun is used definitely or indefinitely in its context.

                                 I

Have you ever eaten <u>coconut</u>? You probably have, but you may not be very familiar with coco palms. Coconuts come from coco palms, which are trees that grow in tropical regions. Coco palms are very unusual because all of the parts of the tree have a commercial value. For example, coconuts are an important food in tropical regions, and coconut milk, which comes from inside the coconut, is a nutritious drink. Coconut oil, the most valuable product of all,

also comes from coconuts. Some of the other parts of the tree that are eaten include the buds and young stems. Besides food, the tree is also used for manufacturing commercial products. The leaves are used for making fans and baskets, and the fibers from the husks and trunks are made into mats, cord, and rope. Even the hard shells and the husks are used to make fuel, and the trunks are used for timber.

B3 Building Sentences with Indefinite and Definite Articles

Build as many meaningful sentences as possible. Use an item from each column. Punctuate your sentences correctly.

I ate some rice.

| I ate
they had | a
an
some
Ø
the | pencil
rice
fun
vegetables
idea |

B4 Transforming Sentences

A. Change the underlined singular nouns to plural nouns, and the underlined plural nouns to singular nouns. You may also need to change pronouns and verbs.

1. I took <u>a book</u> and <u>a pen</u> with me.

   I took books and pens with me. OR
   I took some books and pens with me.

2. Take a <u>peach</u>.

3. Those are <u>herbs</u>.

4. <u>Children</u> get more colds than <u>adults</u>.

5. We need <u>some magazines</u> with more information.

6. I watched <u>a movie</u> last night.

B. Change the underlined definite articles to indefinite articles, and the indefinite articles to definite articles.

1. I went to <u>a</u> bank and took out <u>some</u> money.

   I went to the bank and took out the money.

2. Take <u>the</u> sheet of paper and <u>the</u> pen.

3. Did you eat <u>some</u> cookies or <u>Ø</u> cake?

4. I'm taking <u>the</u> medication and eating <u>the</u> yogurt twice a day.

5. Did you see <u>a</u> movie last week?

6. I went to <u>a</u> store yesterday.

C MEANING AND USE 1

The Indefinite Article

Think Critically About Meaning and Use

A. Read the sentences and answer the questions below.

1a. My friend wants to marry <u>a millionaire</u>. She met him last year.
1b. My friend wants to marry <u>a millionaire</u>. She hasn't found one yet.
2a. <u>Bananas</u> are tropical fruits.
2b. Please buy <u>some bananas</u> on your way home.

1. **ANALYZE** Compare the meanings of 1a and 1b. In which sentence does the speaker have a specific mental picture of the underlined noun?

2. **DIFFERENTIATE** Compare the meanings of 2a and 2b. Which sentence refers to a small quantity of the underlined noun? Which sentence describes or classifies the underlined noun?

B. Discuss your answers with the class and read the Meaning and Use Notes to check them.

Meaning and Use Notes

ONLINE PRACTICE

	Introducing Nouns with Indefinite Articles
▶ **1A**	Use *a/an* or no article (Ø) to introduce a common noun when it is first mentioned.

First Mentioned

A: What did you do last night?

B: I watched **a movie**. What did you do?

A: I had **Ø friends** over and made **Ø dinner**.

▶ **1B**	Usually when a common noun is introduced, it is specific for the speaker, but not specific for the listener. This means that the speaker has an idea or a mental picture of the noun, but the listener does not. Sometimes the noun is not specific for the speaker or the listener.

Specific for the Speaker Only	**Not Specific for the Speaker or Listener**
Jill: I bought **a new coat** yesterday. (Jill has a specific coat in mind, but the listener doesn't.)	Joe: I need **new shirts**. (Joe doesn't have any specific shirts in mind, and the listener doesn't either.)

▶ **1C** When introducing singular count nouns, *a* and *an* often express the quantity "one." When introducing plural count and noncount nouns, some and any are often used to express a small quantity.

Singular Count Nouns	Plural Count and Noncount Nouns
Would you like **a cookie**?	Would you like **some cookies**?
I'd like to order **a steak**, please.	I'd like to order **some steaks**, please.
	Do you have **any information** about this medicine?

Classifying and Describing Nouns

▶ **2** Common nouns with *a*, *an*, and Ø are often used in sentences with *be* to classify or describe nouns. *Some* and *any* are not used this way.

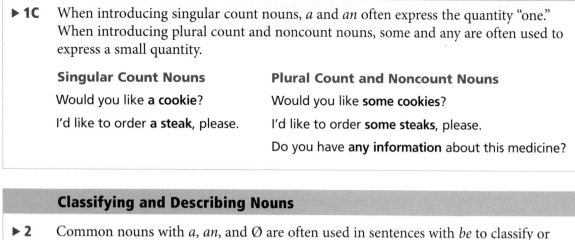

My father is **a teacher**.

What are those? They're **vitamins**.   **x** They're some vitamins. (INCORRECT)

C1 Listening for Meaning and Use

▶ Notes 1A–1C

CD2 T19   Listen to each situation. Is the noun specific or not specific for the speaker? Check (✓) the correct column.

		SPECIFIC	NOT SPECIFIC
1.	orange juice	✓	
2.	apples		
3.	a new doctor		
4.	a friend		
5.	some soup		
6.	an appointment		
7.	a book		
8.	cough medicine		

C2 Introducing New Information

▶ Notes 1A–1C

Complete these conversations with a sentence that introduces new information with three indefinite nouns. Use *a/an, some,* or Ø.

1. **A:** What did you do last night?

   B: _I read a book, watched a movie, and took a bath._

2. **A:** What did you buy at the supermarket?

   B: _____

3. **A:** What do you take on a trip?

   B: _____

4. **A:** What do you want for your birthday?

   B: _____

5. **A:** What do you keep in your pockets?

   B: _____

6. **A:** What can you buy at a hardware store?

   B: _____

C3 Classifying Nouns

▶ Note 2

A. Make a list of all the foods you have eaten in the last two days. Do not list specific quantities. Use *a/an, some,* or Ø next to each noun that you list. Then sort the nouns into three categories: Healthy, Unhealthy, or Not Sure.

HEALTHY	UNHEALTHY	NOT SURE
an apple	potato chips	eggs
milk	a candy bar	
cereal		

B. Share your list with a partner. Discuss whether you agree with the way your partner has classified each item. What foods are you not sure about? Why?

A: *Do you think eggs are healthy or unhealthy?*

B: *I think they're healthy.*

D MEANING AND USE 2

The Definite Article

A. Read the sentences and answer the questions below.

  a. Did you hear what <u>the mayor</u> said this morning on <u>the news</u>?
  b. I bought a sweater and a shirt but <u>the sweater</u> was too small.
  c. Please pass the <u>salt</u>.

  1. ANALYZE In which sentence does the speaker mention the underlined noun more than once?
  2. ANALYZE In which sentence are the speaker and the listener from the same geographic area?
  3. ANALYZE In which sentence can the listener see the underlined noun?

B. Discuss your answers with the class and read the Meaning and Use Notes to check them.

Meaning and Use Notes

ONLINE
PRACTICE

Identifying Nouns with the Definite Article

The is used with a common noun when it is specific for both the speaker and the listener because of information they share. Following are some different ways that speakers and listeners share information about a noun.

▶ 1A The listener can identify the noun if it has already been mentioned in a conversation or text. When it is mentioned again, the speaker uses *the*. Notice that the exact words do not have to be repeated.

First Mentioned	**Mentioned Again**
I ordered <u>a steak</u> and <u>a salad</u> for lunch.	**The steak** was great, but **the salad** was awful.
<u>A kitten</u> was found in a box near my house.	**The poor creature** was cold and hungry.

▶ 1B The listener can identify the noun if he or she can see or hear it.

Visual Context

Mother: Watch out! Don't shake **the table**. You'll spill **the milk**.

Son: OK. Could you please pass **the rice**?

(Continued on page 266)

▶ 1C The listener can identify the noun from the situation or from general knowledge.

General Knowledge

I went to <u>an unusual wedding</u>. **The bride** and **groom** wore jogging clothes.
    (The listener knows that a wedding has a bride and a groom.)

▶ 1D The listener can identify the noun if the listener and speaker share geographic or social information.

Shared Information

A: Do you think **the secretaries** make enough money?

B: Yes. I think they do.
    (The listener assumes that this means the secretaries who work with them.)

▶ 1E Certain names of places and things that are very familiar to the speaker almost always use *the*. The listener may not know the specific identity of the noun but assumes that it refers to a place that the speaker habitually goes to, an object the speaker habitually uses, and so on.

Familiar Nouns

the bank	the doctor	the library	the office	the radio
the beach	the gym	the mall	the park	the store
the dentist	the hospital	the movies	the post office	the TV

When you go to **the store**, could you buy some milk? And turn off **the TV** before
    you go.

▶ 1F The listener can identify the noun if the noun is unique (there is only one).

Unique Nouns

I took my guests to **the best restaurant** in town, and they chose **the most expensive**
    item on the menu.

Earth rotates around **the sun** once every 365 days.

Please look at **the top** of this page.

▶ 1G The listener can identify the noun with the help of modifiers in the noun phrase.

Noun Modifiers

I took my guests to **the best restaurant** in town, and they chose **the most expensive**
    item on the menu.

The book <u>that's on sale</u> is on the counter. (*that's on sale* tells which book)

The <u>red</u> **book** is mine. (*red* tells which book)

D1 Listening for Meaning and Use

▶ Notes 1A–1C, 1F, 1G

CD2 T20   Listen to each sentence. Would the sentence that follows use a definite or indefinite article? Choose the sentence that is more likely to follow.

1. **a.** I bought a blue shirt.

   b. I bought the blue shirt.

2. **a.** The poor child lost all the money.

   b. A poor child lost all the money.

3. **a.** Does anyone know a writer?

   b. Does anyone know the writer?

4. **a.** Did the bride wear a long gown?

   b. Did a bride wear the long gown?

5. **a.** A steering wheel.

   b. The steering wheel.

6. **a.** Not anymore. I lent the CD to Joan.

   b. Not anymore. I lent a CD to Joan.

7. **a.** A doorbell is ringing.

   b. The doorbell is ringing.

8. **a.** Should I send a new one?

   b. Should I send the new one?

D2 Choosing Definite or Indefinite Articles

▶ Notes 1A–1G

Work with a partner. Read each situation and decide whether to use *a*, *an*, or *the*. Then discuss the reasons why you chose your answers.

1. If there are no chairs left in this classroom, you'll have to sit on __the__ floor.
   ₁

   Or maybe you should go next door and ask if you can borrow _____ chair from
   ₂

   that classroom.

2. _____ apartment that I live in now is too small. I have to start looking for
   ₁

   _____ new one. I'd really like to find _____ apartment with
   ₂   ₃

   _____ garden.
   ₄

3. There's _____ interesting exercise in your textbook. Please look at _____
   ₁   ₂

   bottom of page 10.

4. Did you read _____ magazine that I sent you last week? It had _____
   ₁   ₂

   interesting story about _____ mayor of Philadelphia.
   ₃

5. Would you answer _____ telephone, please? I'm trying to diaper _____ baby.
   ₁   ₂

Vocabulary Notes

Another vs. The Other

Another is indefinite like *a/an*. It means "one more" or "a different one."

There are several cookies on a plate. Your friend asks:

Do you want **another** cookie?

The other is definite. It refers to a specific alternative when you are choosing between two things.

There are only two cookies on a plate. Your friend takes one and asks:

Do you want **the other** cookie?

D3 Using *Another* and *The Other*

Work with a partner. Make up two short conversations for each of these contexts. Use another in one conversation and the other in the second conversation.

1. at a friend's house

   Conversation 1
   A: *There are a few cookies left. Would you like another one?*
   B: *No thanks. I've already had several.*

2. at the supermarket

3. at school

4. at a restaurant

5. at a department store

D4 Making Inferences Based on General Knowledge ▶ Note 1C

Read each sentence and then write a related sentence with a definite noun that you can identify based on the context. Use these nouns:

the author	the mechanic	the bank teller
the driver	the receptionist	the waiter

1. Last summer I took a bus ride through a terrible storm.

   The driver was excellent, and we reached our destination safely.

2. I had lunch at the Pinewood Restaurant yesterday.

3. My car began making a strange noise, so I took it to a garage.

_____

4. I went to deposit some money at the bank this morning.

_____

5. I read a great book during my vacation.

_____

6. I called my doctor's office yesterday afternoon.

_____

Beyond the Sentence

Connecting Information

Like pronouns, articles help make sentences clear and connect ideas in a paragraph or conversation. Indefinite nouns are used to introduce new information. Definite nouns are used to refer to old information, which is more specific.

We've just bought **a new rabbit**. We brought her home last week, and **she**'s doing fine. **My son** is so protective of **the rabbit** that **he** insisted on getting up to check on **her** for the first few nights. But now that **he** is convinced that **the rabbit** can stay alone, **he** doesn't get up to check on **her** anymore. **He** sleeps through the night in the comfort of **his own room**, and the rabbit spends **her nights** in **her little house** in the backyard.

D5 Connecting Information

A. Work with a partner. Number these sentences to make a meaningful paragraph. Pay attention to the articles and pronouns to help you decide on the order.

_____ He cut the wire and jumped from the window into a creek.

_____ No one knows exactly where he found the ladder.

__1__ Another prisoner has escaped from the local prison.

_____ He was able to reach a high window covered with wire.

_____ He swam across the creek, climbed over a wall, stole a car, and drove away.

_____ Sometime during the night, the prisoner climbed up a ladder.

B. Read the story aloud to see if it sounds right. Be ready to explain your choices.

D6 Talking About Familiar Nouns

▶ Note 1E

Work with a partner. Take turns saying each of these sentences. Add a specific identity for each underlined noun. Do any of the nouns have different identities for you and your partner? Why?

1. I went to <u>the supermarket</u> last night.

   I went to the A & P supermarket near my house last night.

2. I went to <u>the bank</u> before I came to class.

3. I bought <u>the newspaper</u> before I came to class.

4. <u>The mayor</u> is going to speak on television tonight.

5. I didn't feel well yesterday, so I went to <u>the doctor</u>.

D7 Understanding Shared Information

▶ Notes 1A–1D, 1G

A. Work in small groups. Imagine that you overhear the conversations below. Think about each situation and try to figure out what information the speaker and listener(s) share. Use your imagination.

1. Two women are talking. One of them says, "Did you order <u>the flowers</u> yet?"

   The women are sisters. They're sending a gift to their mother. OR

   The women are friends. One of them is getting married soon and they're discussing the wedding.

2. Two young men are talking. One says, "<u>The car</u> costs $2,500." The other says, "I don't know how I'll be able to afford it."

3. A woman approaches a man and says, "I got <u>the money</u>."

4. Three women are talking. One asks, "Did you bring <u>the photographs</u>?"

5. A woman is talking to a man. The woman says, "How could you forget to pay <u>the bill</u>?"

6. Two men are talking. One says, "Oh, by the way, I <u>got the tickets</u>."

B. Choose one of the situations from part A. Make a list of details about the situation. Then write a paragraph about it. Begin with a clear topic sentence.

   Two sisters are talking about a gift that they have planned to send their mother for her birthday. The gift is a large bouquet of her favorite flowers. After the flowers arrive, they are going to take their mother to an elegant restaurant for to celebrate. She doesn't know that all of her friends will be there.

Article Use with Generic Nouns

Think Critically About Meaning and Use

A. Read the sentences and answer the questions below.

1a. Unfortunately, my children have <u>colds</u> at the moment.
1b. <u>Colds</u> cannot be cured by antibiotics.
2a. <u>Garlic</u> can help fight certain diseases.
2b. I put <u>garlic</u> in the soup.
3a. I have <u>a mango</u> in the refrigerator.
3b. <u>A mango</u> is a sweet-tasting fruit.
4a. <u>The typewriter</u> is not used much anymore in most offices.
4b. I put <u>the typewriter</u> away because we never use it.

1. ANALYZE Which underlined noun in each pair refers to a whole class or group of nouns?

2. ANALYZE Which underlined noun in each pair refers to a specific noun or nouns?

B. Discuss your answers with the class and read the Meaning and Use Notes to check them.

Meaning and Use Notes

ONLINE
PRACTICE

	Overview of Generic Nouns
▶1	We don't always use a noun to refer to a specific object, event, or concept. Sometimes we use the noun to refer to a whole class or group of objects, events, or concepts. This noun is called a generic noun, and statements about a generic noun are called generic statements.

Ø

Flies are insects.

I like **rice**.

A/An

A bird can fly, but **a reptile** can't.

The

The laser has become an important tool in surgery.

(Continued on page 272)

Using No Article (Ø)

▶ **2** Plural count nouns and noncount nouns are the most common type of generic nouns. No articles are used with them. They are often used in generic statements to classify nouns, express likes or dislikes, and give opinions.

Classification	**Likes and Dislikes**	**Opinions**
Flies are insects.	I don't like **rice**.	**Carrots** are good for you.

Using *A/An*

▶ **3** Singular count nouns with *a/an* can also be used as generic nouns to represent all members of a class. The nouns are often used in definitions and in sentences expressing general factual information.

Definitions

A locksmith is **a person** who makes and repairs locks and keys.

A penguin is **a black and white bird** that lives in the Antarctic.

Factual Information

A bird can fly.

A child has six to ten colds per year. **An adult** has two colds per year.

Using *The*

▶ **4A** The use of generic nouns with *the* is less common than the use of other types of generic nouns. Definite generic nouns express a more formal tone and are used more often in scientific and technical writing. They usually refer to plants, animals, mechanical objects, and other scientific phenomena.

More Formal Writing	**Less Formal Writing**
The mosquito can spread malaria.	Mosquitoes can spread malaria.
The computer has changed our lives.	Computers have changed our lives.

> **!** Remember that *the* with a plural noun is not used generically. It refers to specific plural nouns.
>
> **The computers** that we bought last year have helped our business.

▶ **4B** Musical instruments are often referred to generically with the definite article.

I used to play **the piano** and **the violin**.

E1 Listening for Meaning and Use

▶ Notes 1–3, 4A

CD2 T21   Listen to each situation. Check (✓) *Generic* if the noun refers to a class of things or *Specific* if the noun refers to a particular thing.

		GENERIC	SPECIFIC
1.	the carrot		✓
2.	almonds		
3.	garlic		
4.	food		
5.	the onion		
6.	a cold		
7.	vitamins		
8.	a headache		

E2 Defining Nouns with *A/An*

▶ Notes 1, 3

Work with a partner. Make up a simple generic statement that defines each noun below. Use singular count nouns with *a/an*. You may need a dictionary.

A spatula is a cooking utensil.

1

spatula

3

iris

5

elm

7

pineapple

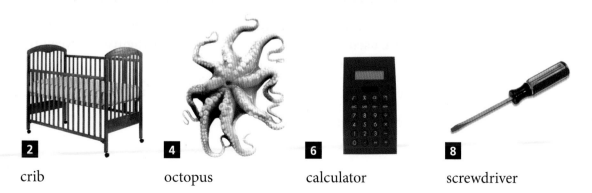

2

crib

4

octopus

6

calculator

8

screwdriver

E3 Rephrasing Formal Generic Sentences

▶ Note 4A

A. Rewrite this paragraph as a less formal version. Use plural generic nouns instead of definite generic nouns. Change pronouns and verbs when necessary. Start your paragraph with *Kangaroos are…*

> The kangaroo is an Australian animal with very distinctive physical features. It has large back legs that are used for hopping very fast, and it has a very large tail that helps it maintain its balance. The female kangaroo carries her young around in a special pocket of skin on her stomach that is called a pouch.

B. Read these statements. Rewrite one of them as a less formal sentence and use it to introduce a short, informal explanation that you will present to the class.

> The computer doesn't always make life easier.
> The trumpet is important in orchestras as well as jazz bands.
> The human heart is like a machine.
> The digital camera has revolutionized popular photogaphy.

> *Computers don't always make life easier. Sometimes they actually make life more frustrating when they break down. For example, last week at the bank…*

Beyond the Sentence

Indefinite Generic Nouns in Discourse

An indefinite generic noun (with *a, an, Ø*) can remain indefinite throughout a paragraph or conversation as long as it continues to refer to a whole class or group of nouns instead of to a specific noun.

> **An onion** is a small white vegetable with a strong smell and a strong taste. Researchers have found that it is actually the strong taste that makes **an onion** good for your blood. Unfortunately, sweet or mild **onions** do not have this effect on your blood. Someday, according to researchers, **an onion** will taste sweet and benefit your health at the same time.

E4 Choosing Between Generic and Specific Nouns

A. In these following sentences, some nouns are used generically with no article, and others are used to refer to a specific thing. Distinguish between these generic and specific uses by writing *a, an, the,* or *Ø*.

1. I don't really like ____Ø____ desserts, but my neighbor makes _____
   ₁   ₂

   dessert that I'm very fond of.

2. _____ cell phone is useful in an emergency. However, in many places, it is
   unlawful to use _____ cell phone while driving.
      1   2

3. It's hard to find _____ inexpensive clothing. _____ clothing in the
                          1   2
   stores is so expensive these days.

4. I eat _____ rice at almost every meal. _____ rice that I buy is usually
               1   2
   on sale downtown. It's _____ very flavorful kind of rice.
                               3

5. _____ camels are animals with long necks and humps on their back. In
         1
   desert areas, people ride on _____ camels and use them for transportation.
                                      2

6. He's allergic to _____ cats. When he goes near _____ cat, he starts
                          1   2
   to sneeze.

B. **Choose one of these sentences as the introduction to a paragraph. Write a
description that continues to refer to the underlined generic noun.**

I don't usually like <u>fancy restaurants</u>.
<u>A vacation</u> isn't always relaxing.
<u>Teachers</u> have to be patient.
<u>A laptop computer</u> is useful in college.

> *I don't usually like fancy restaurants. Sometimes they have good food, but most of
> the time the food is drowned in exotic sauces and the portions are very small. The
> worst thing about them is that the atmosphere is always very stuffy and pretentious,
> and I never feel at home in them. They also have outrageously expensive prices.*

Think Critically About Meaning and Use

A. Read each sentence and the statements that follow. Write *T* if the statement is true or *F* if it is false.

1. I bought a tennis racket last night.

   _T_ **a.** The speaker has a specific tennis racket in mind.

   _F_ **b.** The listener has a specific tennis racket in mind.

2. I looked at an apartment last night, but the kitchen was too small.

   _____ **a.** The listener has seen the kitchen.

   _____ **b.** The listener has just heard about this apartment.

3. Please take the other cookie.

   _____ **a.** The speaker is referring to the last cookie.

   _____ **b.** Someone already took a cookie.

4. I'd like some cheese, please.

   _____ **a.** The speaker is referring to a small quantity of cheese.

   _____ **b.** The listener knows exactly which cheese the speaker wants.

5. Open a window, please.

   _____ **a.** The speaker wants a particular window to be opened.

   _____ **b.** There are at least two windows.

6. **Mother:** Wear the dress to school.
   Daughter: No, not today.

   _____ **a.** The mother has a specific dress in mind.

   _____ **b.** The daughter has a specific dress in mind.

7. I saw Maria at the post office yesterday.

_____ **a.** The speaker usually goes to that post office.

_____ **b.** The listener may not know that post office.

8. The snake is frightening that little girl.

_____ **a.** The speaker is referring to a particular snake.

_____ **b.** The sentence is about all snakes.

B. Discuss these questions in small groups.

1. **ANALYZE**   Look at sentence 2. What can we assume about the listener if the speaker had said, "I looked at the apartment last night…"

2. **PREDICT**   Look at sentence 8. What would the speaker have said if he or she wanted to make a statement about the effect that snakes generally have on the little girl?

Edit

Some of these sentences have errors. Find the errors and correct them.

1. I need new coat. Please help me find one.
    a

2. When you get to my house, you don't have to ring doorbell. Just walk in.

3. We have plenty of sandwiches. Please take the another one.

4. My grandparents were some immigrants. They came to this country in 1920.

5. She graduated with a major in the mathematics and physics.

6. The life is not always easy.

7. Calcium is mineral.

8. Please pass the rice and the salt.

9. Book I bought was on sale.

10. Let's sit in a last row so that we can leave quickly when the play is over.

Write

Imagine you work as a writer for a public relations firm that does work for a family health clinic. Write the first page of a pamphlet about healthy eating. Use count, noncount, and generic nouns with definite, indefinite, and no articles, as needed.

1. **BRAINSTORM** Think of all the ways that food contributes to good/poor health. Make a list of healthy/unhealthy foods. Then use these categories to help you organize your ideas into paragraphs:
   - **What is the relationship between food and good health?** What lessons should parents teach their children about eating well and maintaining a healthy weight?
   - **What kinds of foods keep us healthy?** What health benefits do these foods offer? How often should we eat them?
   - **What foods should we avoid?** What are the bad effects of these foods? What advice can you give to parents and children?

2. **WRITE A FIRST DRAFT** Before you write your first draft, read the checklist below and look at the examples of how writers discuss certain foods on pages 256–257 and 274. Write your draft using indefinite and definite articles.

3. **EDIT** Read your work and check it against the checklist below. Circle grammar, spelling, and punctuation errors.

DO I ...	YES
use indefinite articles (*a/an, some/any*) for nonspecific nouns?	☐
use no article (Ø) for nonspecific plural count nouns and noncount nouns?	☐
use the definite article *the* with specific nouns?	☐
use plural count nouns and noncount nouns without articles to make generic statements?	☐

4. **PEER REVIEW** Work with a partner to help you decide how to fix your errors and improve the content. Use the checklist above.

5. **REWRITE YOUR DRAFT** Using the comments from your partner, write a final draft.

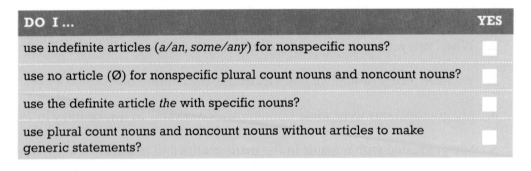

FAMILY FOOD FACTS We Are What We Eat

Providing our children with nutritious meals is one of the greatest responsibilities of parenthood. It's also one of the greatest gifts we can give our families...

Relative Clauses with Subject Relative Pronouns

A. **GRAMMAR IN DISCOURSE: Office Outfits That Work** . . 280

B. **FORM: Relative Clauses with Subject Relative Pronouns** 282

Restrictive Relative Clauses

I know a woman **who/that works at Jones & Roe.**
The rules **which/that require suits** are strictly enforced.

Nonrestrictive Relative Clauses

I know Sue Dunn, **who works at Jones & Roe.**
The rules, **which are strictly enforced**, require business suits.

C. **MEANING AND USE 1: Identifying Nouns with Restrictive Relative Clauses** 288

Identifying Nouns

Reducing Restrictive Relative Clauses

Beyond the Sentence: Combining Sentences with Relative Clauses

D. **MEANING AND USE 2: Adding Extra Information with Nonrestrictive Relative Clauses** 294

Adding Extra Information About Nouns

Contrasting Restrictive and Nonrestrictive Relative Clauses

Reducing Nonrestrictive Relative Clauses

WRITING: Write a "For and Against" Essay 298

Office Outfits That Work

A1 Before You Read

Discuss these questions.

What kind of clothes do you think professional people and their staffs should wear to work: more formal or less formal? Do you think clothing affects job performance?

A2 Read

CD2 T22 Read this newspaper article to find out what advice an employment expert gives to a male college student and a female executive.

OFFICE OUTFITS THAT WORK
Advice for Dressing Successfully in the Workplace

Q: *I'm a male college student who is starting to job hunt. What advice can you give me about clothes that are suitable for interviews? I'm hoping to*
5 *talk to a number of major software companies, which supposedly have "business casual" dress codes. Does that mean I don't have to wear a suit?*

A: Let's start with your second
10 question. "Business casual" means

different things at different companies. Generally speaking, it *doesn't* mean dressing in formal business wear, which for men means suits and ties.
15 What it *does* mean is dressing in a relaxed, yet neat and professional-looking style. At some companies this might include cotton pants and knit shirts with collars, while other
20 companies might even allow jeans and T-shirts.

But does that mean you should leave your suit and tie in the closet on the day of a big interview? Most
25 managers would say, "Well, it *may* be OK, but it's not worth the risk." Interviewers are more likely to be impressed by job candidates who dress in a neat, professional way. If you're a
30 male college grad who wants to make the best possible impression, you can't go wrong with a classic business suit.

Ideally, you should look for a suit that looks good and feels good. This will help you project the image of a person who is confident and capable. Suit colors like navy blue or gray are always a good choice. Then you can complete the look with a matching tie, a well-ironed, long-sleeved white shirt, and well-shined shoes.

Q: *I'm a fashion-conscious female executive who doesn't have a lot of time to worry about her wardrobe. Can you recommend any books or websites for women like me?*

A: I'm glad you asked! There are several sites for female executives who want to show their stylish side. One of my favorites is a blog called "execu-chic," which is written by a top-level woman consultant. For example, this week's entry recommends classic but trendy low-heeled shoes for the busy female executive who is on her feet all day.

Our column next week will feature advice on pants suits and skirt suits, so I'm sure you'll find it useful.

---

capable: having the right skills and abilities
confident: sure of oneself and one's abilities
executive: top-level manager

fashion-conscious: interested in wearing stylish clothes
supposedly: according to what people say
wardrobe: all of a person's clothing

A3 After You Read

Write *T* for true or *F* for false for each statement. Then change the false statements to true ones.

___F___ **1.** The person who sent in the first question is a college graduate.

The person who wrote the first question is still in college.

_____ **2.** Companies do not always agree on the meaning of "business casual."

_____ **3.** The writer of the column thinks the man should definitely wear a suit to his interviews.

_____ **4.** The woman who submitted the second question is not interested in dressing fashionably.

_____ **5.** The writer of the column also writes a blog called "execu-chic."

_____ **6.** The writer's next column will probably appeal to the woman who submitted the second question.

B FORM

Relative Clauses with Subject Relative Pronouns

▶ Restrictive Relative Clauses

ONLINE PRACTICE

RELATIVE CLAUSES AFTER THE MAIN CLAUSE				
MAIN CLAUSE		RELATIVE CLAUSE		
	NOUN	SUBJECT RELATIVE PRONOUN	VERB	
I know	a woman	who / that	works	at Jones & Roe.
They have	rules	which / that	require	business suits.

RELATIVE CLAUSES INSIDE THE MAIN CLAUSE				
MAIN CLAUSE				
RELATIVE CLAUSE				
NOUN	SUBJECT RELATIVE PRONOUN	VERB		
A woman	who / that	works	there	won't wear a suit.
The rules	which / that	require	suits	are strictly enforced.

▶ Nonrestrictive Relative Clauses

info

RELATIVE CLAUSES AFTER THE MAIN CLAUSE				
MAIN CLAUSE		**RELATIVE CLAUSE**		
	NOUN	SUBJECT RELATIVE PRONOUN	VERB	
I know	Sue Dunn,	**who**	**works**	**at Jones & Roe.**
No one likes	the rules,	**which**	**are**	**strictly enforced.**

RELATIVE CLAUSES INSIDE THE MAIN CLAUSE				
MAIN CLAUSE				
	RELATIVE CLAUSE			
NOUN	SUBJECT RELATIVE PRONOUN	VERB		
Sue Dunn,	**who**	**works**	**at Jones & Roe,**	won't wear a suit.
The rules,	**which**	**are**	**strictly enforced,**	require business suits.

Restrictive and Nonrestrictive Relative Clauses

point to

- Relative clauses (also called adjective clauses) modify nouns (or noun phrases). There are two types of relative clauses: restrictive and nonrestrictive.

- Restrictive relative clauses distinguish one noun from another.

   I know <u>the woman</u> **who works at Jones & Roe**. I don't know <u>the woman</u> **who works at Transco**.

- Nonrestrictive relative clauses give extra information about a noun and are separated from that noun by commas. (In speech, a pause signals the commas.)

   <u>Sue Dunn</u>, **who works at Jones & Roe**, won't wear a suit.

- As with all clauses, relative clauses have a subject and verb. They are dependent clauses. They cannot stand alone as complete sentences. They must be attached to a main clause.

- A relative clause can occur anywhere in a sentence but it must follow the noun it refers to.

   I know <u>a woman</u> **who works at Jones & Roe**.

   <u>A woman</u> **who works at Jones & Roe** won't wear a suit.

Subject Relative Pronouns

- When *who*, *which*, or *that* is the subject of a relative clause, it is a subject relative pronoun.

(Continued on page 284)

- In restrictive clauses, *who* and *that* are used for people. *Which* and *that* are used for things and animals.
- In nonrestrictive clauses, *who* is used for people and *which* is used for things.
- A subject relative pronoun is followed by a verb. The verb agrees with the noun that the subject relative pronoun refers to.

    I know <u>a man</u> **who** <u>works</u> at Jones & Roe.

    I know two <u>men</u> **who** <u>work</u> at Jones & Roe.

- A subject relative pronoun always has the same form, whether or not it refers to a singular noun (a man) or a plural noun (men).
- Sentences with subject relative pronouns can be thought of as a combination of two sentences.

    I know a woman. <u>She</u> works there. = I know a woman **who** works there.

- Do not repeat the noun or pronoun in the relative clause.

    x I know a woman who she works there. (INCORRECT)

B1 Listening for Form

CD2 T23   Listen to these comments about dress codes. Choose the main clause or relative clause that you hear. (Not every sentence contains a relative clause.)

1. **a.** clothes that express my individuality

   b. clothes express my individuality

2. **a.** the dress code, which is very casual

   b. the dress code is very casual

3. **a.** Ms. Chang, who is the manager

   b. Ms. Chang is the manager

4. **a.** the dress code is still very conservative

   b. the dress code that is still very conservative

5. **a.** Barker Bank has a strict dress code

   b. Barker Bank, which has a strict dress code

6. **a.** clothes were more formal

   b. clothes that were more formal

7. **a.** the men, who don't have to wear ties anymore

   b. the men don't have to wear ties anymore

8. **a.** my boss dresses very casually

   b. my boss, who dresses very casually

B2 Identifying Relative Clauses

Work with a partner. Find the relative clauses in the conversation. Underline them and circle the noun phrases that they modify. Then practice the conversation.

Paul: What should I wear to my job interview, Dad?

Dad: How about your gray suit and (the shirt) that matches it?

Paul: Do you mean my new blue shirt, which is at the cleaners?

Dad: Oh. Well, what about the shirts that are hanging here on the door?

Paul: Hmm . . . should I wear the white one or the one that has pinstripes?

Dad: Wear the one that feels more comfortable. What time is the interview?

Paul: The boss's secretary, who called to confirm yesterday, said 10:15, although the manager who originally contacted me said 10:30. I'd better be there at 10:15.

Dad: By the way, was the Department of Labor booklet helpful?

Paul: Yes, especially part 3, which had a lot of practical advice.

Dad: Is the position that's open a new one?

Paul: No. I know the person who has it now. She's leaving to work at the Boston branch, which opens after the first of the year.

B3 Building Sentences with Subject Relative Pronouns

Build as many meaningful sentences as possible. Use an item from each column. Punctuate your sentences correctly.

We like the man that works in the bakery.

we like	the man Gary, the new phone cards, cars	that who which	works in the bakery are affordable

B4 Working on Placement of Relative Clauses

A. Rewrite these sentences about dress codes, inserting the restrictive relative clause in parentheses after the appropriate noun.

1. Dress codes can make employees unhappy. (that are too strict)

   Dress codes that are too strict can make employees unhappy.

2. Some employers won't hire applicants. (who dress too casually)

3. Employees believe that clothing is a form of free expression. (who oppose dress codes)

4. Some companies restrict clothing. (that has sports logos on it)

5. A company dress code may not allow women to wear skirts. (that are very short)

B. Rewrite these sentences, inserting the nonrestrictive relative clause in parentheses after the appropriate noun. Remember to add commas.

1. This T-shirt is inappropriate for work. (which has slogans on it)

   This T-shirt, which has slogans on it, is inappropriate for work.

2. What do you think about rule number 3? (which restricts very tight clothing)

3. My nephew Dan often wears very unusual clothing. (who works for a high-tech company)

4. My boss is trying to enforce a new dress code. (who has been here only for a year)

5. Casual dress has become the new standard in many companies. (which is hard to define)

B5 Working on Verb Agreement in Relative Clauses

Work with a partner. Complete each sentence with an appropriate subject relative pronoun and the correct form of the verb in parentheses. (Some items will have two possible answers.) Then practice the conversations with a partner.

1. **A:** Who is the person _____ who sits _____ (sit) next to you in English class?

   B: I don't know her name, but she's also in our chemistry class. She's the woman _____ who ask _____ (ask) a lot of questions.

2. **A:** My notebook, _____ which was _____ (be) on the table before, is missing.

   B: There's one over there _____ that looks _____ (look) like your notebook.

3. **A:** Sami, ___who___ ___lives___ (live) across the street, plays with my son. Do you
   ₁

   know his family?

   B: No. I thought that the people ___who___ ___own___ (own) that house didn't have
   ₂

   any children.

4. **A:** I need to see a doctor ___who___ ___treats___ (treat) skin problems. Do you
   ₁

   know any?

   B: Yes. Dr. Wu, ___who___ ___has___ (have) an office near here, is a dermatologist.
   ₂

5. **A:** Koji and Susan, ___who___ ___finished___ (finish) the project yesterday, can leave
   ₁

   early today. Everyone else must stay in class until they finish.

   B: But what about the people ___who___ ___were___ (be) not in class yesterday?
   ₂

6. **A:** AC Express, ___which___ ___has___ (have) an office downtown, can probably ship
   ₁

   that package overseas. You should call them.

   B: OK. I will. But first I need to finish packing the items ___that___ ___are___ (be)
   ₂

   on this list.

B6 Combining Sentences with *Who*, *That*, or *Which*

Combine each pair of sentences to make a restrictive relative clause using *who*, *that*, or
which. There are two possible answers for each item.

1. I picked up the package. It was lying on the front step.

   I picked up the package that/which was lying on the front step.

2. The professor ^who emailed me. He teaches Russian.

3. My sister has a cat. ^that It has three kittens.

4. Did you buy the socks? ^which They were on sale.

5. The little girl ^who was crying. She hurt her knee.

6. They gave us an exam. ^which It lasted an hour.

7. I spoke to two women. ^who They saw the accident.

8. The child ^who went home. He was sick.

Identifying Nouns with Restrictive Relative Clauses

Think Critically About Meaning and Use

A. Read the sentences and answer the questions below.

1a. <u>A man</u> wore a tuxedo today.
1b. <u>A man</u> who works with me wore a tuxedo today.
2a. A dress code is a <u>set of rules</u>.
2b. A dress code is a <u>set of rules</u> that describes the appropriate kind of clothing for work.

1. **ANALYZE** Compare 1a and 1b. Which sentence gives information that identifies the underlined noun?

2. **ANALYZE** Which sentence is a more complete definition, 2a or 2b?

B. Discuss your answers with the class and read the Meaning and Use Notes to check them.

Meaning and Use Notes

**ONLINE
PRACTICE**

	Identifying Nouns

▶ **1A** Restrictive relative clauses identify nouns. They distinguish one person or thing from other people or things. They answer the question *Which one(s)?* Restrictive relative clauses express necessary information. They cannot be omitted without affecting the meaning of the sentence.

With a Relative Clause

A: Are your children in that group over there?

B: Yes, <u>the girl</u> **that's wearing the red sweater** and <u>the boy</u> **who's wearing the gray sweatshirt** are mine.
(The relative clauses clearly identify B's children and distinguish them from the other children.)

Without a Relative Clause

A: Are your children in that group over there?

B: Yes, <u>the girl</u> and <u>the boy</u> are mine.
(B's children have not been clearly identified. The meaning is incomplete.)

▶ **1B**   Restrictive relative clauses are used in definitions.

A locksmith is <u>a person</u> **who makes and repairs locks and keys**.

A penguin is <u>a black and white bird</u> **which lives in the Antarctic**.

▶ **1C**   Restrictive relative clauses are often used to provide information about a noun when it is first mentioned. If the information is new to the listener, the relative clause quickly identifies the noun. If the information is shared with the listener, it reminds the listener of the noun.

New Information

Guess what? <u>A guy</u> **who works with me** bought a house on our street.

Shared Information

Look. There are <u>the dresses</u> **that are on sale**.

Reducing Restrictive Relative Clauses

▶ **2**   Subject relative pronouns + be are often omitted from restrictive relative clauses.

Full Form	**Reduced Form**
Take the food **that/which is on the table**.	Take the food **on the table**.
Look at the man **who/that is wearing a tuxedo**.	Look at the man **wearing a tuxedo**.

C1 Listening for Meaning and Use

▶ Notes 1A, 1C

🔊 CD2 T24   Listen to the questions. Choose the most appropriate answer.

1. **a.** The woman who is near the window.
    b. The one which is near the window.

2. **a.** The rules are too strict.
    b. The rules that are too strict.

3. **a.** The one that's over there.
    b. The one who's over there.

4. **a.** The man who called yesterday.
    b. The man called yesterday.

5. **a.** The man is working downstairs.
    b. The man who is working downstairs.

6. **a.** The guy who fixes up old cars.
    b. The guy fixes up old cars.

7. **a.** The ones that got wet.
    b. The ones who got wet.

8. **a.** A suit is worn on formal occasions.
    b. A suit that is worn on formal occasions.

C2 Identifying Nouns

▶ **Notes 1A, 1C**

Work with a partner. In each picture one object belongs to you. Describe it using a restrictive relative clause.

1. You're at the airport, and you're looking for your luggage. There are four suitcases that look like yours.

   My suitcase is the one that has a round luggage tag.

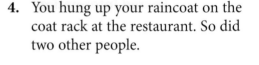

2. It's dark, and you can't find your car in the parking lot. There are some cars in a row that look like yours.

3. You took off your snow boots when you entered the doctor's office. As you're leaving, you notice that there are three other pairs of boots similar to yours.

4. You hung up your raincoat on the coat rack at the restaurant. So did two other people.

5. All the students left their backpacks outside the language lab. Several students have backpacks just like yours.

6. You've lost your keys in a department store. When you go to the lost and found, the clerk shows you three sets of keys.

C3 Identifying and Defining with Subject Relative Pronouns

▶ Notes 1A–1C

Work with a partner. Read each passage and use the information to answer each question with a sentence containing a relative clause.

1. Georgia O'Keeffe was a twentieth-century American artist. She painted well into her eighties. She is famous for painting flowers. The flowers were colorful.

   a. Who was Georgia O'Keeffe?

      Georgia O'Keeffe was a twentieth-century American artist who painted well into her eighties.

   b. What is she famous for?

2. Cancer is a serious condition. It causes tumors to grow in the body. Radiation is a cancer treatment. It can shrink tumors and prevent them from spreading.

   a. What is cancer?

   b. What is radiation?

3. Martin Luther King, Jr., was an African American. He led the civil rights movement in the 1960s. He fought for equal rights through passive resistance. This nonviolent method of protest was previously used by Mahatma Gandhi in the 1940s.

   a. Who was Martin Luther King, Jr.?

   b. What is passive resistance?

4. Phobias are exaggerated fears. These fears can prevent a person from leading a normal life. Some people suffer from agoraphobia. They have a fear of being in open places. Others suffer from claustrophobia. They have a fear of being in closed places.

   a. What is a phobia?

   b. Which people suffer from agoraphobia? Which suffer from claustrophobia?

C4 Defining Words with Relative Clauses

▶ Note 1B

Work with a partner. Describe these different types of doctors by writing sentences with relative clauses. If necessary, use a dictionary.

1. A dermatologist *is a doctor who treats skin problems.*

2. A neurologist _____

3. A pediatrician *is a doctor who treats children.*

4. A dentist *is a doctor who treats teeth*

5. A cardiologist *is a doctor who treats heart.*

6. A podiatrist *is a doctor who*

C5 Distinguishing Between Two Nouns

▶ Note 2

Work with a partner. Look at each picture and answer the question using full and reduced relative clauses. Make up as many answers as possible for each item.

1. Which pair of shoes did you buy?

The shoes that were made in Italy.
The shoes made in Italy.

4. Which man is your father?

2. Which one is your son?

5. Which hat are you going to wear?

3. Which woman is the office manager?

6. Which iced tea mix do you prefer?

Beyond the Sentence

Combining Sentences with Relative Clauses

A paragraph with many short sentences may seem disconnected and hard to understand. You can use a relative clause to combine sentences that refer to the same noun or noun phrase. Relative clauses help avoid repetition and make the information flow more smoothly.

A Paragraph Without Relative Clauses

This story is about a young woman. She graduated from college with an engineering degree. After college, she worked for a small Internet company. The company sold books. Her friends, on the other hand, worked for well-known companies. These companies paid high salaries. She was frustrated and thought about quitting her job, but she didn't. That decision paid off. That small Internet company was one of the first "dot-coms." It became popular worldwide. Today, she is worth millions of dollars.

A Paragraph with Relative Clauses

This story is about a young woman **who graduated from college with an engineering degree**. After college, she worked for a small Internet company **that sold books**. Her friends, on the other hand, worked for well-known companies **that paid high salaries**. She was frustrated and thought about quitting her job, but she didn't. That decision paid off. That small Internet company was one of the first "dot-coms" **that became popular worldwide**. Today, she is worth millions of dollars.

C6 Connecting Ideas with Relative Clauses

A. Rewrite the following paragraph using relative clauses to make the information flow more smoothly. Make any changes that you think will improve the paragraph.

School dress codes are becoming popular again, although this doesn't necessarily mean that students have to wear uniforms. A school dress code is a set of rules. The rules restrict certain types of clothing. Some dress codes prohibit certain T-shirts. The T-shirts have offensive writing or pictures on them. Other dress codes prohibit certain types of pants or shirts. They prohibit very baggy pants, very tight pants, and very tight shirts. Many others prohibit certain types of skirts and dresses, too. The skirts and dresses are several inches above the knee. Some dress codes go even further. They don't allow sports clothing. This clothing has logos on it.

B. In small groups, compare your rewritten paragraphs. Discuss any differences between your paragraphs. Decide which changes you prefer and why. Combine your paragraphs into one version that you all agree on.

Adding Extra Information with Nonrestrictive Relative Clauses

Think Critically About Meaning and Use

A. Read the sentences and answer the questions below.

    a. <u>My brother who lives in Maine loves to fish.</u> My other brother loves to ski.

    b. <u>My brother, who lives in Maine, loves to fish.</u> He takes us fishing when we visit.

    1. ANALYZE Which relative clause gives necessary information that identifies my brother? Which relative clause adds information that is not essential?

    2. ANALYZE Which underlined sentence implies that the speaker has only one brother?

B. Discuss your answers with the class and read the Meaning and Use Notes to check them.

Meaning and Use Notes

ONLINE PRACTICE

Adding Extra Information About Nouns

▶ **1A**   A nonrestrictive relative clause adds extra information about a noun, but it is not needed to identify the noun. This information is often new to the listener, but it isn't essential; it can be omitted without affecting the meaning of the sentence.

Without a Relative Clause

My son Scott always wears a baseball cap. My son Greg doesn't.

With a Relative Clause

<u>My son Scott</u>, **who is 11**, always wears a baseball cap. <u>My son Greg</u>, **who is 13**, doesn't.
(The relative clauses give extra information about Scott and Greg but do not change the meaning of the sentences.)

▶ **1B**   Nonrestrictive relative clauses can add extra information about proper nouns and other unique nouns. They can also add information about a definite noun that has already been identified.

Proper Noun

<u>Boston</u>, **which is in Massachusetts**, has many colleges and universities.

Noun Already Identified

<u>My antique desk</u> was damaged by the flood. <u>The desk</u>, **which is worth a lot of money**, can probably be repaired.

Unique Noun

<u>My sister</u>, **who is 17**, is in high school.

Contrasting Restrictive and Nonrestrictive Relative Clauses

▶ 2 Restrictive relative clauses provide essential information in order to distinguish one noun from other similar nouns. Nonrestrictive relative clauses are used when there is only one particular noun or set of nouns. They do not distinguish nouns or provide essential information.

Restrictive Relative Clause	**Nonrestrictive Relative Clause**
<u>My brother</u> **who lives in Baltimore** calls me every weekend. (The relative clause distinguishes my brother from a brother who lives elsewhere. It implies that the speaker has more than one brother.)	<u>My brother</u>, **who lives in Baltimore**, calls me every weekend. (The relative clause is not used to distinguish my brother from anyone else. It implies that the speaker has only one brother.)

Reducing Nonrestrictive Relative Clauses

▶ 3 Subject relative pronouns + *be* are often omitted from nonrestrictive relative clauses.

Full Form	**Reduced Form**
I spoke to Pedro, **who is the boss**.	I spoke to Pedro, **the boss**.

D1 Listening for Meaning and Use

▶ Notes 1A, 1B, 2

CD2 T25 **Listen to these situations. Choose the sentence that you hear.**

1. **(a.)** My sister, who lives in New York, has two children.

   b. My sister who lives in New York has two children.

2. **a.** Have you met her brother, who works at the bank?

   b. Have you met her brother who works at the bank?

3. **a.** Give me the sheet of paper, which has the list of names.

   b. Give me the sheet of paper which has the list of names.

4. **a.** The man, who is talking, is my boss.

   b. The man who is talking is my boss.

5. **a.** She showed me her necklace which had beautiful stones.

   b. She showed me her necklace, which had beautiful stones.

6. **a.** Her grandmother, who lived until 80, was a teacher.

   b. Her grandmother who lived until 80 was a teacher.

D2 Adding Extra Information

▶ Notes 1A, 1B

A. Complete each main clause with a proper noun or other unique noun. Then add more information with a nonrestrictive relative clause at the end of the sentence.

1. I come from _____Queens_____, which __is in New York City.__

2. I once visited _____UAB_____, which __is in BHM__
   _____

3. I've never met _____Bryan_____, who __makes lots of noise__
   _____

4. I'd like to meet _____Monte_____, who __is my grammar teacher__
   _____

B. Complete these sentences by first adding a nonrestrictive relative clause, and then completing the main clause.

1. My next vacation, __which will be in March, is for one week.__

2. My best friend, __who is 25 ___, is going to New York.__

3. My birthday, __when is on Jan 1st, is tomorrow.__

4. My home, __which is new, is going fine.__

D3 Choosing Restrictive or Nonrestrictive Relative Clauses

▶ Note 2

Work with a partner. Read each situation and related statement. Decide whether the relative clause in each statement is restrictive or nonrestrictive. If the clause is nonrestrictive, add commas to the sentence.

1. **Situation:** My parents moved to Toronto a few years ago. They used to live in Montreal.

   Statement: My parents, who used to live in Montreal, moved to Toronto a few years ago. nonrestrictive

2. **Situation:** I have two aunts on my mother's side. One of them lives in Rio. The other one lives in São Paulo. One of them invited me to her son's wedding.

   Statement: My aunt who lives in Rio invited me to her son's wedding.

3. **Situation:** We live in Panama City. It's very warm and humid here.

   Statement: We live in Panama City, which is very warm and humid.

4. **Situation:** My father lives next to a golf course. He loves to play golf.

   Statement: My father who loves to play golf lives next to a golf course.

5. **Situation:** My dentist has several dental hygienists. The same one always cleans my teeth. A different one cleans my son's teeth.

   Statement: The dental hygienist who cleans my teeth doesn't clean my son's teeth.

6. **Situation:** One of my sons is in the second grade, one is in the fourth grade, and one is a sophomore in high school.

   Statement: My son who is in the second grade loves math.

7. **Situation:** You've invited your friends Jane and Tina to dinner. Jane and Tina work at the same company. You tell this to Tina.

   Statement: I've invited my friend Jane who works in the legal division at your company.

8. **Situation:** A newspaper article describes pollution.

   Statement: Pollution which is still a major problem was an issue in the last election.

D4 Describing People

Write two sentences about each person. In the first sentence, identify the person with a restrictive relative clause. In the second sentence, provide further information using a nonrestrictive relative clause. Be ready to tell the class about one of these people.

1. an aunt

   My aunt that lives in San Francisco loves antiques.
   Her daughter, who was just married, has a lot of antiques, too.

2. an uncle

3. a friend

4. a teacher

5. a neighbor

6. a classmate

Think Critically About Meaning and Use

A. Read each sentence and the statements that follow. Write *T* if the statement is true or *F* if it is false.

1. The woman who works for my mother bought a new car.

   __T__ **a.** A woman works for my mother.

   _____ **b.** My mother bought a new car.

2. My brother, who just called my father, lives in Dallas.

   _____ **a.** My brother lives in Dallas.

   _____ **b.** My father called my brother.

3. The man who looked at my car was very old.

   _____ **a.** My car was very old.

   _____ **b.** A man looked at my car.

4. An explosion, which injured 20 people, occurred at about 11:00 last night.

   _____ **a.** An explosion injured 20 people.

   _____ **b.** An explosion occurred at about 11:00.

5. I spoke to my brother, who is very worried about something.

   _____ **a.** I have a brother.

   _____ **b.** I am very worried about something.

6. My son who talked to Mary looks like John.

   _____ **a.** I have more than one son.

   _____ **b.** Mary looks like John.

7. The milk, which is still on the first shelf, is spoiled.

   _____ **a.** The milk is spoiled.

   _____ **b.** There's probably milk on another shelf, too.

8. I took the umbrella, which was in the car.

   _____ **a.** There was only one umbrella.

   _____ **b.** The umbrella was in the car.

B. Discuss these questions in small groups.

1. **EVALUATE** Look at sentence 1. What can we conclude about the number of women on the mother's staff? How does the meaning differ if the sentence had read, "A woman who works for my mother…"

2. **PREDICT** Look at sentence 8. If we change the sentence to read, "I took the umbrella that was in the car," how does it affect your answers to statements a and b?

Edit

Find the errors in these paragraphs and correct them. There may be more than one way to correct an error.

What kind of clothing should people ~~which~~ *who* are going on a job interview wear? Is it ever acceptable to wear jeans to an interview? Should job candidates wear something, that is sporty and comfortable? Or should they wear something what is more professional-looking? These are some of the questions concern many high school and college students which has never been on a job interview before.

Most people agree about the type of clothing is appropriate for interviews nowadays. Many employment websites advise that job applicants should try to dress in clothing is appropriate for a particular job. For example, a man who applying for an entry-level food service or factory job doesn't need to appear for an interview in a three-piece business suit and an expensive silk tie. He should wear sensible, clean, and well-pressed clothing that show a readiness to roll one's sleeves up and get the job done. Someone is applying for a managerial position will obviously need to dress more professionally to make a good first impression. Remember, too, that personal cleanliness is something who can impress an interviewer as much as your clothes. Candidates that shows up for an interview with bad breath or messy hair or fingernails are dirty are not going to make a good impression.

Write

Some people think primary and secondary students in your country should wear school uniforms, while others are strongly against it. Write a "for and against" essay presenting both sides of the issue. Use relative clauses with subject relative pronouns.

1. **BRAINSTORM** Think of all the arguments for and against students wearing school uniforms. Then use these categories to help you organize your ideas into paragraphs.
   - **Introduction:** What is the current situation? Do students wear uniforms? Can they wear what they like? Are there other rules about clothing?
   - **Arguments for:** What are the 2–3 main arguments for wearing school uniforms?
   - **Arguments against:** What are the 2–3 main arguments against wearing uniforms?
   - **Conclusion:** After considering both sides, which side do you support?

2. **WRITE A FIRST DRAFT** Before you write your first draft, read the checklist below and look at the sentences you wrote in C6 on page 293. Write your draft using relative clauses.

3. **EDIT** Read your work and check it against the checklist below. Circle grammar, spelling, and punctuation errors.

DO I ...	YES
organize my ideas into paragraphs?	☐
use relative clauses to connect ideas and combine sentences?	☐
use correct subject relative pronouns and verb forms that agree with the nouns that are modified?	☐
use commas, as needed, to set off nonrestrictive relative clauses?	☐

4. **PEER REVIEW** Work with a partner to help you decide how to fix your errors and improve the content. Use the checklist above.

5. **REWRITE YOUR DRAFT** Using the comments from your partner, write a final draft.

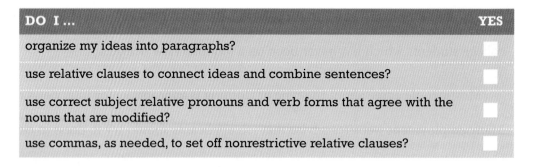

I come from a country that has a long tradition of students wearing school uniforms, but now some people are questioning the tradition. On one hand, there are people who want to see the tradition continue. On the other hand, there are people who believe that...

C H A P T E R

14

Relative Clauses with Object Relative Pronouns

A. **GRAMMAR IN DISCOURSE: The New Face of a Role Model** 302

B. **FORM 1: Relative Clauses with Object Relative Pronouns** 304

Restrictive Relative Clauses
Mia Hamm is an athlete **who/whom/that/Ø I admire**.
The game **which/that/Ø the girls won** was on TV.

Nonrestrictive Relative Clauses
I met Mia Hamm, **who/whom I admire a lot**.
The World Cup, **which we saw on TV**, was a big media event.

Vocabulary Notes: Object Relative Pronouns

C. **MEANING AND USE 1: Identifying Nouns and Adding Extra Information** 309

Identifying Nouns

Adding Extra Information

D. **FORM 2: Object Relative Pronouns with Prepositions** 313

Relative Clauses Ending In Prepositions
There's the coach **who/whom/that/Ø I spoke to**.
He coaches the Liberty team, **which she plays on**.

Relative Clauses Beginning With Prepositions
There's the coach **to whom I spoke**.
He coaches the Liberty team, **on which she plays**.

E. **MEANING AND USE 2: Reducing Relative Clauses** 317

Reducing Relative Clauses

Avoiding Repetition

Vocabulary Notes: *When* and *Where* in Relative Clauses

WRITING: Write a Report About Women's Sports in Your Country 322

PART 5 TEST: Modifying Nouns 325

A GRAMMAR IN DISCOURSE

The New Face of a Role Model

A1 Before You Read

Discuss these questions.

A role model is a person who is an example for other people to follow. What are some qualities of a role model?

A2 Read

CD2 T26 Read this magazine article about soccer star Mia Hamm to find out what she thinks about being a role model.

THE NEW FACE OF A ROLE MODEL

In women's soccer, girls finally get the role model they deserve: Mia Hamm

The Women's World Cup, which the media called the biggest female sporting event in history, arrived for the first time in the United States in 1999. Three television
5 networks televised all 32 games, with an estimated one billion viewers. One of the stars was Mia Hamm, who many people call the Michael Jordan of women's soccer.

Though her ballerina mom tried to
10 interest her in dance, it was her father's soccer passion that she followed. Hamm led the University of North Carolina to four championships in the early nineties, won Olympic gold in 1996, won the U.S.
15 Soccer Player of the Year award many times, and broke the international goal-scoring record for males and females.

None of this would have been possible without a law called Title IX, which the
20 U.S. government passed in 1972. This law requires equal funding for girls' school sports. Until 1972, the only role models that female athletes had were female

skaters, female gymnasts, and male
25 athletes. Now, more than seven million girls play soccer, and they all want to be like Mia.

Hamm retired from professional soccer in 2004, but she continues to
30 inspire. She has created the Mia Hamm Foundation, which she has dedicated to two causes that are very important to her: encouraging young female athletes and research on bone marrow diseases.
35 (Her brother Garrett died from aplastic anemia.)

Hamm juggles her personal relationships with her busy career. Here are some things that she says about life as

40 sport's newest kind of role model:

Q: Girls today have a wider variety of role models than ever before and you're one of them. What's it like to be a role model?

A: I take it very seriously. I didn't have

45 the role models these girls have. Most of my athletic role models were men.

Q: Will playing team sports help girls as they grow up? How has it helped you?

A: Sports can do so much. It's given me a

50 framework: meeting new people, confidence, self-esteem, time management, discipline, motivation. I learned all these things, whether I knew I was learning them or not, through sports.

55 **Q:** What's the most important thing your mother taught you?

A: Everyone has goodness. It's just a matter of how it's nurtured. Hopefully, I can do the same thing, nurture my children

60 to grow up with love in their hearts for everyone...

---

anemia: a disease of the blood

bone marrow: the soft tissue in the center of the bone

foundation: an organization that gives out money for special purposes (e.g., research)

juggle: to do many things at once

the media: television, radio, and newspapers

nurture: to encourage to develop

A3 After You Read

Choose the answer that best completes each sentence.

1. The Women's World Cup _____.

   a. began in the United States

   b. became well known through television

   c. started in 1999

2. Mia Hamm developed her love for soccer because of _____.

   a. her mother

   b. her father

   c. her brother

3. Mia Hamm has won _____ only once.

   a. an Olympic gold medal

   b. a college championship

   c. the Soccer Player of the Year award

4. Hamm broke the international goal-scoring record for _____.

   a. women

   b. men

   c. men and women

5. Title IX is a law that requires equal _____ for girls' and boys' sports.

   a. athletes

   b. stadiums

   c. money

6. Mia Hamm grew up without _____.

   a. an opportunity to dance

   b. a female role model

   c. a busy career

Relative Clauses with Object Relative Pronouns

Think Critically About Form

A. Look back at the article on page 302 and complete the tasks below.

   1. IDENTIFY Look at the underlined relative clauses. Circle the object relative pronoun in each clause (*who*, *which*, or *that*) and the noun or noun phrase it modifies.

   2. EVALUATE Look at the circled relative clauses. These clauses do not have object relative pronouns. Which object relative pronoun is omitted from each clause?

B. Discuss your answers with the class and read the Form charts to check them.

▶ Restrictive Relative Clauses

ONLINE PRACTICE

RELATIVE CLAUSES AFTER THE MAIN CLAUSE				
— MAIN CLAUSE —		— RELATIVE CLAUSE —		
	NOUN	**OBJECT RELATIVE PRONOUN**	**SUBJECT**	**VERB (PHRASE)**
Mia Hamm is	an athlete	**who/whom that/Ø**	**I**	**admire**.
Mia didn't have	the opportunities	**which/that/Ø**	**girls**	**have now**.

RELATIVE CLAUSES INSIDE THE MAIN CLAUSE				
— MAIN CLAUSE —				
	— RELATIVE CLAUSE —			
NOUN	**OBJECT RELATIVE PRONOUN**	**SUBJECT**	**VERB (PHRASE)**	
An athlete	**who/whom that/Ø**	**I**	**admire a lot**	is Mia Hamm.
The game	**which/that/Ø**	**the girls**	**won**	was on TV.

▶ Nonrestrictive Relative Clauses

RELATIVE CLAUSES AFTER THE MAIN CLAUSE				
MAIN CLAUSE		RELATIVE CLAUSE		
	NOUN	OBJECT RELATIVE PRONOUN	SUBJECT	VERB (PHRASE)
I met	Mia Hamm,	**who/whom**	**I**	**admire a lot**.
Mia was at	the World Cup,	**which**	**we**	**saw on TV**.

RELATIVE CLAUSES INSIDE THE MAIN CLAUSE				
MAIN CLAUSE				
	RELATIVE CLAUSE			
NOUN	OBJECT RELATIVE PRONOUN	SUBJECT	VERB (PHRASE)	
Mia Hamm,	**who/whom**	**I**	**admire**,	is a soccer player.
The World Cup,	**which**	**we**	**saw on TV**,	was a big media event.

Restrictive and Nonrestrictive Relative Clauses

• Relative clauses (restrictive and nonrestrictive) modify nouns (or noun phrases). They have a subject and a verb and cannot stand alone as complete sentences.

• Relative clauses can be thought of as a combination of two sentences.

   Mia Hamm is an athlete. I admire <u>her</u>. = Mia Hamm is an athlete **who** I admire.

• Restrictive clauses distinguish one noun from another. Nonrestrictive relative clauses add extra information about a noun and are separated by commas.

Object Relative Pronouns

• When *who*, *whom*, *which*, or *that* is the object of a relative clause, it is an object relative pronoun.

• In restrictive clauses, *who*, *whom*, and *that* are used for people. *Which* and *that* are used for things and animals. In nonrestrictive clauses, *who* or *whom* is used for people and *which* is used for things.

• Object relative pronouns are followed by a subject + verb (phrase). The verb agrees with the subject before it. It does not agree with the noun that the clause refers to.

   Mia Hamm is an athlete **who I admire a lot**.

• Object relative pronouns can be omitted from restrictive relative clauses.

   A swimmer **who I know** won a medal. = A swimmer **Ø I know** won a medal.

(Continued on page 306)

- Object relative pronouns are never omitted from nonrestrictive relative clauses.

    x I met Mia Hamm, I admire a lot. (INCORRECT)

- Do not repeat the object noun or pronoun in the relative clause.

    x I met Mia Hamm, who I admire her. (INCORRECT)

B1 Listening for Form

CD2 T27　**Listen to these sentences and choose the sentence you hear.**

1. a. The team that we played didn't do very well.

   b. The team that played didn't do very well.

2. a. The equipment we broke is expensive to repair.

   b. The equipment which broke is expensive to repair.

3. a. Did you hear about the team that we beat?

   b. Did you hear about the team that beat us?

4. a. We didn't know about the rules that changed.

   b. We didn't know about the rules they changed.

5. a. I didn't meet the player they called.

   b. I didn't meet the player that called.

6. a. The man he called wanted to join the team.

   b. The man who called wanted to join the team.

B2 Examining Relative Clauses with Object Relative Pronouns

Read the paragraphs and look at the underlined relative clauses. Circle the noun or noun phrase that each clause modifies and write *S* over the subject of each relative clause.

Kay Valera used to be a "soccer mom." But now the 40-year-old mom has become a soccer player in a women's league <u>which she joined last spring</u>. One of the things <u>that she has learned</u> is how challenging it is to play a sport that requires players to think, kick, and run at the same time. As she plays, she recalls all the advice <u>that she has given her kids</u>. Everything that looked so easy from the sidelines is now so challenging.

Many kids come to the games to cheer on the moms. They can be very encouraging, but they also love to discuss the mistakes <u>that mom made</u> and the moves <u>that she should have made</u>. They might say, "Don't feel bad, you did your best, but you know that kick <u>that you tried in midfield</u>, well…"

Vocabulary Notes

Object Relative Pronouns

Who and Whom In restrictive and nonrestrictive relative clauses, *whom* expresses a much more formal tone than *who*. It is less common than other relative pronouns.

> **Formal Speech:** Let me introduce you to the person **whom I admire most**, my friend and colleague, Stanley Chen.

That and Ø In restrictive relative clauses, *that* is used more often than *who*, *whom*, and *which*. Omitting the object relative pronoun (Ø) is also very common in speech and writing.

> **News Broadcast:** The judge **(that) the president will appoint next week** is a woman.

B3 Using Object Relative Pronouns

Complete the sentences by circling all the words (and Ø) that can form correct sentences.

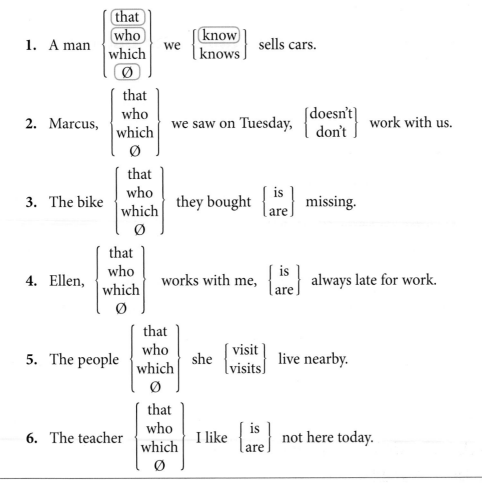

1. A man { that / who / which / Ø } we { know / knows } sells cars.

2. Marcus, { that / who / which / Ø } we saw on Tuesday, { doesn't / don't } work with us.

3. The bike { that / who / which / Ø } they bought { is / are } missing.

4. Ellen, { that / who / which / Ø } works with me, { is / are } always late for work.

5. The people { that / who / which / Ø } she { visit / visits } live nearby.

6. The teacher { that / who / which / Ø } I like { is / are } not here today.

B4 Combining Sentences Using Relative Clauses

Work in small groups. Imagine that you are visiting your 45-year-old aunt, who is showing you family photos and souvenirs. Combine the sentences below to describe the underlined noun phrase. Use restrictive or nonrestrictive relative clauses with an object relative pronoun. Practice different alternatives.

1. Let's look at some things. I've been saving them for a long time.

   Let's look at some things that I've been saving for a long time. OR

   Let's look at some things which I've been saving for a long time. OR

   Let's look at some things I've been saving for a long time.

2. Here is a photo of your grandfather. I still miss him so much.

3. Our great grandfather Gus is in this picture. We loved him a lot.

4. The dress is in this box. I wore it to my wedding.

5. I'll never forget the guests. I invited them to my wedding.

6. I remember my high school teacher Miss Pullman. I liked her so much.

7. Here is a poem. I wrote it in her class.

8. This is an award. I received it for my poem.

B5 Asking and Answering Questions with Object Relative Pronouns

Work with a partner. Take turns asking and answering *what* or *who* questions with restrictive relative clauses, using the words given. Practice different alternatives in your questions and answers.

1. a person/you call every day

   A: *Who is a person (that/who) you call every day?*

   B: *My sister is a person (that/who) I call every day.*

2. a game/you liked to play as a child

3. the relative/you look like most

4. the person/you call when you're in trouble

5. a food/you have never tasted

6. a teacher/you will always remember

7. a book/you like to read over and over again

8. a thing/you can't live without

Identifying Nouns and Adding Extra Information

Think Critically About Meaning and Use

A. Read the sentences and complete the tasks below.

1a. The coat that costs $200 is on sale now.
1b. The coat you wanted is on sale now.
2a. Megan Quann, who was only 16, was on the Olympic swimming team.
2b. Megan Quann, who I know, was on the Olympic swimming team.

1. **IDENTIFY** Underline the relative clause in each sentence. Circle the noun that each clause refers to.

2. **EVALUATE** In which pair of sentences do the relative clauses help identify the noun? In which pair do they add extra information about the noun?

B. Discuss your answers with the class and read the Meaning and Use Notes to check them.

Meaning and Use Notes

ONLINE PRACTICE

Identifying Nouns

▶ **1A** Restrictive relative clauses with object relative pronouns distinguish one person or thing from other similar people or things. They cannot be omitted without affecting the meaning of the sentence.

With a Relative Clause	**Without a Relative Clause**
Three women tried out. <u>The woman</u> **that I met** made the team. (The relative clause clearly identifies which woman made the team.)	Three women tried out. <u>The woman</u> made the team. (It is unclear which woman made the team. The meaning is incomplete.)

▶ **1B** Restrictive relative clauses are often used to provide information about a noun when it is first mentioned, or to remind the listener about previously mentioned information. The relative clause immediately identifies the noun to the listener.

First Mentioned (New Information)
<u>A man</u> **Ø I know** is a champion swimmer.

Previously Mentioned (Shared Information)
<u>The tennis racket</u> **that we saw yesterday** is now on sale.

(Continued on page 310)

▶ 2A Nonrestrictive relative clauses with object relative pronouns add extra information about a noun but aren't needed to identify it. They can be omitted without affecting the meaning of the sentence.

With a Relative Clause

<u>The woman's decathlon world record</u>, **which Austra Skujyte set in 2005**, had previously been set in 2004. (The relative clause gives extra information about the record.)

Without a Relative Clause

<u>The woman's decathlon world record</u> had previously been set in 2004. (Without the relative clause, the meaning of the sentence is still complete.)

▶ 2B Especially at the end of a sentence, nonrestrictive relative clauses with object relative pronouns are a simple way to add extra information to a sentence without starting a new one.

Many young girls now play soccer, **which most high schools didn't offer when I was a student**.

C1 Listening for Meaning and Use

▶ Notes 1A, 1B, 2A, 2B

CD2 T28   Listen to the situations carefully. Then choose the sentence that would most appropriately follow each one.

1. **a.** Really? Do you know her?

   (b.) Really? How did you meet her?

2. **a.** Why did she quit the girls' team?

   b. What was the name of the girls' team?

3. **a.** She was lucky.

   b. That's too bad.

4. **a.** What sports did they play?

   b. Too bad you didn't know them.

5. **a.** That's not good!

   b. That's surprising!

6. **a.** Was that before the laws were changed?

   b. Why didn't they offer sports in your high school?

C2 Identifying Nouns

▶ Notes 1A, 1B

A. Add a restrictive relative clause with an object relative pronoun to complete the meaning of each sentence.

1. I once had a teacher _who I admired a great deal._

2. My neighbor is a person _____

3. I know a man _____

4. I'd like a job _____

5. Someday I'm going to live in a house _____

6. I have a friend _____

7. I shop in stores _____

8. My father is someone _____

B. Choose one of your sentences as the first sentence of a paragraph describing that person, place, or thing. First make a list of five or six characteristics or details that you will include. Then use your list to write a descriptive paragraph with at least two more relative clauses with object relative pronouns.

> *I once had a teacher who I admired a great deal. He was my role model. He taught history classes that everyone enjoyed...*

C3 Adding Extra Information

▶ Notes 2A, 2B

A. Write five simple sentences about specific people, places, or objects related to sports.

> *1. My brother is the captain of our high school baseball team.*
>
> *2. A popular women's sport is soccer.*

B. Work with a partner. Exchange papers and add extra information to your partner's sentences. Use nonrestrictive relative clauses with object relative pronouns.

> *1. My brother, who is going to college next year, is the captain of our high school baseball team.*
>
> *2. A popular women's sport is soccer, which most of the world calls football.*

C4 Expressing Your Opinion

▶ Notes 1A, 1B,

Write two sentences that give your opinion about the nouns in parentheses. Begin one sentence with *I like* and the other sentence with *I don't like*. Use restrictive relative clauses with object or subject relative pronouns.

1. (cars) I like cars that go fast.

   I don't like cars (that) you have to fix all the time.

2. (teachers) _____

   _____

3. (clothes) _____

   _____

4. (newspapers) _____

   _____

5. (friends) _____

   _____

6. (TV shows) _____

   _____

7. (foods) _____

   _____

8. (music) _____

   _____

9. (books) _____

   _____

10. (cell phones) _____

   _____

D FORM 2

Object Relative Pronouns with Prepositions

 Think Critically About Form

A. Read the sentences and complete the tasks below.

    a. We saw the movie that everyone is talking about.
    b. We saw the movie about which everyone is talking.

    1. IDENTIFY The relative pronoun in each relative clause is the object of a preposition. Underline each object relative pronoun and circle each preposition.

    2. COMPARE AND CONTRAST Compare a and b. Where does the preposition occur in each relative clause? What other difference do you see?

B. Discuss your answers with the class and read the Form charts to check them.

▶ Relative Clauses Ending in Prepositions

ONLINE PRACTICE

RESTRICTIVE RELATIVE CLAUSES					
MAIN CLAUSE		RELATIVE CLAUSE			
	NOUN	**OBJECT RELATIVE PRONOUN**	**SUBJECT**	**VERB**	**PREPOSITION**
There's	the coach	**who/whom that/Ø**	**I**	**spoke**	**to.**
He coaches	the team	**which/that/Ø**	**she**	**plays**	**on.**

NONRESTRICTIVE RELATIVE CLAUSES					
MAIN CLAUSE		RELATIVE CLAUSE			
	NOUN	**OBJECT RELATIVE PRONOUN**	**SUBJECT**	**VERB**	**PREPOSITION**
There's	Coach Smith,	**who/whom**	**I**	**spoke**	**to.**
He coaches	the Liberty team,	**which**	**she**	**plays**	**on.**

(Continued on page 314)

Relative Clauses Ending in Prepositions

- An object relative pronoun (*who*, *whom*, *that*, or *which*) can be the object of a preposition.

    There's the coach. I spoke <u>to him</u>. = There's the coach **who** I spoke **to**.

- Relative clauses ending in prepositions are usually used in spoken English and less formal written English.

- In restrictive relative clauses that end in prepositions, the object relative pronoun can be omitted.

▶ Relative Clauses Beginning with Prepositions

<table>
<tr><td colspan="6" align="center">RESTRICTIVE RELATIVE CLAUSES</td></tr>
<tr><td colspan="2" align="center">MAIN CLAUSE</td><td colspan="4" align="center">RELATIVE CLAUSE</td></tr>
<tr><td></td><td>NOUN</td><td>PREPOSITION</td><td>OBJECT RELATIVE PRONOUN</td><td>SUBJECT</td><td>VERB</td></tr>
<tr><td>There's</td><td><u>the coach</u></td><td>to</td><td>whom</td><td>I</td><td>spoke.</td></tr>
<tr><td>He coaches</td><td><u>the team</u></td><td>on</td><td>which</td><td>she</td><td>plays.</td></tr>
</table>

<table>
<tr><td colspan="6" align="center">NONRESTRICTIVE RELATIVE CLAUSES</td></tr>
<tr><td colspan="2" align="center">MAIN CLAUSE</td><td colspan="4" align="center">RELATIVE CLAUSE</td></tr>
<tr><td></td><td>NOUN</td><td>PREPOSITION</td><td>OBJECT RELATIVE PRONOUN</td><td>SUBJECT</td><td>VERB</td></tr>
<tr><td>There's</td><td><u>Coach Smith</u>,</td><td>to</td><td>whom</td><td>I</td><td>spoke.</td></tr>
<tr><td>He coaches</td><td><u>the Liberty team</u>,</td><td>on</td><td>which</td><td>she</td><td>plays.</td></tr>
</table>

Relative Clauses Beginning with Prepositions

- In very formal English, a preposition can begin a relative clause. The preposition is followed by either *whom* for people or *which* for things. It cannot be followed by *who* or *that*.

- *Whom* and *which* are never omitted after prepositions.

D1 Listening for Form

CD2 T29 Listen and choose the sentences you hear.

1. **a.** Do you know the woman he's married to?

   b. Do you know the woman to whom he's married?

2. **a.** The man he spoke to helped quite a bit.

   b. The man who he spoke to helped quite a bit.

3. **a.** Let's look at the book I brought in.

   b. Let's look at the book. I brought it in.

4. **a.** Did you meet the people he works with?

   b. Did you meet the people who we work with?

5. **a.** Did you see the doctor I was waiting for?

   b. Did you see the doctor? I was waiting for her.

D2 Building Relative Clauses Ending in Prepositions

Work in small groups. Add the information that follows each sentence, using a relative clause ending in a preposition.

1. A woman called me last night.
   (My sister works with her.)

   A woman who my sister works with called me last night. OR

   A woman that my sister works with called me last night. OR

   A woman my sister works with called me last night.

   (I always talk to her at the supermarket.)
   (I went to high school with her.)
   (I used to live next door to her.)

2. The movie was great.
   (We went to the movie last night.)
   (You told us about the movie.)
   (I didn't want to go to it.)
   (You reported on it in class.)

3. Do you know the doctor?
   (Young-soo lives across from her.)
   (Eva plays tennis with her.)
   (Luisa works for her.)
   (I was waiting for her.)

4. Have you read the book?
   (The whole class is interested in it.)
   (The teacher looked for it last week.)
   (Julie wrote about it.)
   (I brought in the book.)

5. Today we're going to read the story.
   (You've heard a lot about it.)
   (You listened to a recording of it.)
   (I was working on it.)
   (The lecturer talked about it.)

D3 Working on Relative Clauses Ending in Prepositions

 A. Work in small groups. Read these situations. Use restrictive relative clauses ending in prepositions to distinguish between the people or things.

1. Bill needs to ask one of his neighbors to water his plants while he's away. He works with one of them, but he doesn't work with the other one.

   He decides to ask the person _(who/that) he works with._

2. You know that your friend was born in one small town, but that she grew up in a different small town.

   You ask her the name of the town _____

3. Martha and Luisa are in a store looking for a new desk chair. Martha is sitting on one of them, and Luisa is sitting on another one.

   A salesman recommends the one _____

4. Anna has called her doctor's office twice this week. She spoke to one nurse on Tuesday and another nurse on Wednesday.

   Today she asked for the nurse _____

5. Two movies are playing nearby. Martin has heard about one of them, but he hasn't heard about the other one.

   He decides to see the movie _____

6. Your friend borrowed two CDs from the library. She listened to one of them last night, and she will listen to the other one tomorrow.

   She decided to return the one _____

7. Two players on the soccer team were carded for bad language. The coach talked to one right after the game, but didn't get a chance to talk to the other.

   Today he will talk to the player _____

8. I saw two new ads for teachers in the paper yesterday. I'm more interested in one, but I'm more qualified for the other.

   I think I'll apply for the one _____

B. Now rewrite items 1–4 from part A in very formal English. Use restrictive relative clauses beginning with prepositions.

   1. He decides to ask the person with whom he works.

MEANING AND USE 2

Reducing Relative Clauses

Think Critically About Meaning and Use

A. Read the sentences and answer the question below.

    a. Give the names of two professors who you have taken courses with.
    b. Give the names of two professors with whom you have taken courses.
    c. Give the names of two professors you have taken courses with.

    ANALYZE Which sentence sounds the most formal?

B. Discuss your answers with the class and read the Meaning and Use Notes to check them.

Meaning and Use Notes

ONLINE PRACTICE

	Reducing Relative Clauses

▶ 1A In both conversation and writing, object relative pronouns are often omitted from restrictive relative clauses. Remember, a preposition must follow the verb in a reduced relative clause. (It cannot go at the beginning of the clause).

Conversation

The meal **Ø we ate yesterday evening** was delicious. I'm going to write down the name of the restaurant **Ø we went to**. You should try it.

Newspaper Article

The suspect **Ø the police caught this morning** remains in custody.

▶ 1B When relative clauses with prepositions are <u>not</u> reduced, they sometimes sound very formal if the preposition precedes the relative pronoun.

Sounds Formal

Write the name and address of the hotel **in which you are staying**.

Doesn't Sound Formal

Write the name and address of the hotel **which you are staying in**.

(Continued on page 318)

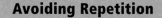

Avoiding Repetition

▶ **2**   Object relative pronouns are often omitted when many restrictive relative clauses are used in one context. When two restrictive relative clauses occur next to each other, the first object relative pronoun is often omitted. The second is not.

Interview Question

What is the most important thing ⑴ Ø her mother taught her ⑵ that she can teach her children?

Textbook

One issue ⑴ Ø the study mentioned ⑵ that researchers need to consider further is the effect of changing climate.

E1 Listening for Meaning and Use   ▶ Notes 1A, 1B

 CD2 T30   Listen to each situation and check (✓) whether you think it has a formal or informal tone. Then listen again and think of an appropriate context for each situation.

	FORMAL	INFORMAL	CONTEXT
1.		✓	a conversation between two students
2.			
3.			
4.			
5.			
6.			

E2 Rephrasing Formal Relative Clauses   ▶ Notes 1A, 1B

Work with a partner. Take turns changing the formal tone of each sentence to a conversational tone. Use relative clauses ending in prepositions.

Application for Travel Insurance

1.   List the names of the family members with whom you will be traveling.

   List the names of the family members who/that/Ø you'll be traveling with.

2.   List the city from which you will depart and the city to which you will return.

3. List the name of the tour operator with whom you will be traveling.

_____

4. List the hotel in which you will be staying.

_____

5. List the code numbers of any extra tours for which you have registered.

_____

Job Application

1. Name two colleagues with whom you have worked closely.

_____

2. Name one supervisor for whom you have worked.

_____

3. List two different projects on which you have worked.

_____

4. Name two decisions in which you have played an important role.

_____

5. Name the job for which you would like to apply.

_____

E3 Reducing Relative Clauses Ending in Prepositions ▶ Notes 1A, 1B

Work with a partner. Take turns finding out information about each other. Match a noun from the left box with a verb + preposition from the right box to form reduced relative clauses. Use appropriate tenses.

A: *Name a restaurant you've eaten at recently.*

B: *The Noodle House. It's really good. Now it's your turn. Name a sport…*

NOUN		VERB + PREPOSITION	
a restaurant	a friend	vote for	disagree with
a sport	a CD	eat at	rely on
a politician	a relative	listen to	work on
an assignment	a magazine	participate in	subscribe to

E4 Writing an Email Message

▶ Notes 1A, 1B

Your company has sent you to another country for a long training program. You have been there for a week. Write an email message to your family asking them to send five different items that you left at home. Describe the items carefully using relative clauses. Tell your family why you need them.

From:	Emma
To:	Mom and Dad
Subject:	Things I need

… It's warm here during the day, but it gets cool at night. The jacket I brought is not warm enough. Please send the one that you gave me for my birthday. It's hanging in my closet next to…

Vocabulary Notes

When and *Where* in Relative Clauses

Where and *when* can replace object relative pronouns to introduce relative clauses.

Where is used to express location. It can modify a noun that refers to a place. It can replace *which*, *that*, or Ø and the prepositions *in* or *at*.

That's the building **where** my father lives. = That's the building **in which** my father lives.

= That's the building **that/Ø** my father lives **in**.

When is used to express time. It can replace *that*, Ø, or *during which* to refer to a period of time.

The year **when** I lived in Vancouver = The year **that/Ø/during which** I lived in was very special.   Vancouver was very special.

E5 Using *Where, When,* and Object Relative Pronouns

A. Complete the sentences below. Use *where, when, that, which, in which,* or Ø to introduce the relative clauses. More than one answer is possible. Discuss which alternatives you prefer in small groups.

Baseball, _____which_____ is the "national pastime" of the United States,
                            1

is also popular in the Dominican Republic. This small country is a place

_____ a large number of famous major-league baseball players
            2

have been born. In fact, one of its small cities, San Pedro de Macoris, is described as the city _____ more

players have been born than anywhere else in the world. According to the record books, from 1960 to the present day, no fewer than 79 major leaguers have come from the tiny Dominican town _____ people refer to as San Pedro.

Baseball star Robinson Cano is one of San Pedro's most-loved native sons. He says he'll never forget his childhood, _____ his father José (another San Pedroan who played briefly in the major leagues) taught him how to play the game. In his early teens, Cano spent three years in New Jersey, during _____ he attended his first New York Yankee baseball game and became convinced that the Yankees were the team _____ he wanted to play for. The year 2005 was the year _____ his dream came true. The champion hitter still visits San Pedro in winter, _____ he enjoys spending his time being a role model and helping as many kids as he can. He is also the head of the Robinson Cano Foundation, _____ he founded to raise money to help Dominican children with heart diseases.

B. Write three sentences each about a place and a time from your past. Use **where** and **when** to introduce a relative clause in each sentence.

The house where I grew up was very small for my big family.
Dinnertime, when all of us tried to eat together, was chaotic.

C. Exchange papers with a partner. Pick two of your partner's sentences to rewrite using object relative pronouns (**who, that, which, Ø**). Make any necessary changes.

The house (that) I grew up in was very small for my big family.
Dinnertime, during which all of us tried to eat together, was chaotic.

Think Critically About Meaning and Use

A. Read each sentence and the statements that follow. Write *T* if the statement is true or *F* if it is false.

1. My brother, who I resemble, lives in Jordan.

    _F_   **a.** I live in Jordan.

    _____   **b.** I resemble my brother.

2. The man my sister works with has a sailboat.

    _____   **a.** My sister has a sailboat.

    _____   **b.** My sister works on a sailboat.

3. The team I wanted to win lost in the semifinals.

    _____   **a.** The team lost.

    _____   **b.** I wanted to win.

4. Andrei still loves playing hockey, which he learned when he was five.

    _____   **a.** Andrei is five years old.

    _____   **b.** Andrei plays hockey.

5. I looked at some equipment that my neighbors were selling at a garage sale.

    _____   **a.** I sold some equipment at a garage sale.

    _____   **b.** My neighbors looked at some equipment at a garage sale.

6. Ms. Wang wrote the book I heard about on a radio show.

    _____   **a.** I listened to a radio show.

    _____   **b.** Ms. Wang heard about a book.

7. The professor assigned a book in which the history of baseball is discussed.

    _____   **a.** The professor gave an assignment.

    _____   **b.** The professor discussed the history of baseball.

8. Charlotte, who I once worked for, took over the company.

    _____   **a.** I once worked for Charlotte.

    _____   **b.** Charlotte took over the company.

Discuss these questions in small groups.

1. **IDENTIFY** Which three sentences contain reduced relative clauses that end with prepositions?

2. **GENERATE** How could you rewrite these three sentences to make them sound more formal?

Edit

Find the errors in these paragraphs and correct them.

Sisleide Lima do Amor, ~~which~~ *who* soccer fans know as Sissi, was not discouraged as a child by the boys who wouldn't let her play the game with which she loved most. Eventually, she got her way on the streets of Salvador, Brazil, because the soccer ball that the boys wanted to play with it was hers. Still, she often ran home with her ball after she grew frustrated with the negative attitudes that the boys displayed. Sissi had learned to play soccer by practicing with all kinds of objects what she found around the house. These included rolled-up socks, oranges, bottle caps, and the heads of dolls that her parents had given her them. It was her father who finally decided that she needed a soccer ball to keep her from destroying her dolls.

Sissi showed her admiration for Brazil's male soccer heroes by choosing the jersey number who Romario once wore and by shaving her head to resemble the style in which Ronaldo made famous. During the 1999 Women's World Cup, Sissi displayed the type of skill fans will long remember. Left-footed Sissi scored seven goals for her team, including a goal that she kicked in with her weaker right foot. According to Sissi, her seventh goal was the one about which she kept thinking about long after the 1999 Women's World Cup was over. During a 3–3 tie, she kicked the ball into a spot the goalkeeper couldn't reach it, and her team's 4–3 victory put them into the semifinals.

Write

Write a report about the status of women's sports in your native country. Use relative clauses with object and subject relative pronouns where appropriate.

1. **BRAINSTORM** Think about all the things you can say about the status of women's sports in your country. Use these categories and questions to help you organize your ideas into sections:
   - **Current Situation:** What athletic training do girls typically receive in childhood? Are things different for boys and men? What professional sports do women play?
   - **Developing Trends:** What successes or setbacks have women athletes experienced? Have people's attitudes changed? Have female athletes appeared as role models?
   - **The Future:** What does the future of women's sports look like? How do you see things developing over the next 10–20 years?

2. **WRITE A FIRST DRAFT** Before you write your first draft, read the checklist below and look at the examples of sports writing on pages 302–303 and 323. Write your draft using relative clauses.

3. **EDIT** Read your work and check it against the checklist below. Circle grammar, spelling, and punctuation errors.

DO I ...	YES
use headings to help readers see how the information is organized?	☐
use relative clauses to connect ideas and combine sentences?	☐
use correct relative pronouns?	☐
use at least one object relative pronoun with a preposition?	☐
use appropriate verb forms to reflect past, present, and future time?	☐

4. **PEER REVIEW** Work with a partner to help you decide how to fix your errors and improve the content. Use the checklist above.

5. **REWRITE YOUR DRAFT** Using the comments from your partner, write a final draft.

> The Status of Women's Sports in Greece
> OVERVIEW
> Greece is a country that most people identify with the Olympic Games. But did you know that in ancient times, the Olympics were a competition that women did not take part in? ... In fact, women athletes in Greece really weren't taken seriously until 1992. That was the year that track star Voula Patoulidou won an Olympic gold medal. Since then, ...

Choose the correct word or words to complete each sentence.

1. No one is really sure how the huge stones of Stonehenge, _____, were moved to the south of England thousands of years ago.

   a. that is an ancient monument   **c.** an ancient monument

   b. it is an ancient monument   **d.** is an ancient monument

2. I spoke to the man _____ by the door.

   a. he was sitting   **c.** who sits

   b. who was sitting   **d.** sat

3. Do you know anything about the new requirements _____?

   a. that announced   **c.** they announced them

   b. that they announced   **d.** that they announced them

4. The woman _____ gave me a very positive letter of recommendation.

   a. whom I worked   **c.** who I worked

   d. that worked with   **d.** with whom I worked

Choose the correct word to complete each sentence. Choose X when an indefinite or definite article is not necessary in the sentence.

5. _____ microscope was invented in the seventeenth century by a Dutch scientist named Anton van Leeuwenhoek.

   a. The   **b.** One   **c.** Some   **d.** X

6. During the spring semester, _____ chemistry will not be offered.

   a. the   **b.** a   **c.** X   **d.** any

7. Her parents were professors at _____ small university.

   a. a   **b.** the   **c.** any   **d.** X

Choose the correct response to complete each conversation.

8. **A:** The woman who called Helen is a famous athlete.

   B: _____

   a. I didn't know Helen was famous.   **c.** What is the woman's name?

   b. Why did Helen call her?   **d.** I didn't know Helen was an athlete.

9. A: I bought some rice.

B: _____

    a. How many?   **c.** Should I cook them?

    b. Where is it?   **d.** How much did they cost?

10. A: There were two witnesses, and I spoke to one of them.

B: _____

    a. What about another one?   **c.** What about the other one?

    b. What about the others?   **d.** What about another?

11. A: The book she ordered hasn't arrived.

B: _____

    a. When did she order it?   **c.** Who ordered the book?

    b. Why hasn't she arrived?   **d.** Where did she put it?

Rewrite each sentence using the reduced relative clause.

12. I bought the shoes that were made in Italy.

_____

13. Look at the man who is wearing a tuxedo.

_____

14. There are the dresses that are on sale.

_____

Match the sentence ending to the correct beginning.

_____ **15.** French is a language   **a.** that she has to iron.   **e.** whom I've never met.

_____ **16.** He sent her an email   **b.** he can finish quickly.   **f.** she hates to eat.

_____ **17.** He's marrying a woman   **c.** which she hopes to attend.   **g.** which his father built.

                                    d. I've never studied.   **h.** that she never answered.

Complete each sentence with *a* or *an*.

18. Sheila has _____ unique singing voice, doesn't she?

19. I don't think there's _____ hospital in his town that can perform open-heart surgery.

20. Mr. Porter will be coming back in about _____ hour.

15

Real Conditionals, Unreal Conditionals, and Wishes

A. **GRAMMAR IN DISCOURSE:** **Reflections on Life** 328

B. **FORM: Real Conditionals, Unreal Conditionals, and Wishes** 330

Present and Future Real Conditionals
If I**'m** on time, (then) I **walk** to work.
If it**'s** not too late, (then) I**'ll walk** to work.

Present and Future Unreal Conditionals
If I **had** the time, (then) I**'d walk** to work.
If I **left** on time, (then) I **could walk** to work.

Wishes about The Present And Future
I **wish** (that) I **were** older.
I **wish** (that) you **were going** to the wedding.

Informally Speaking: Using *Was*

C. **MEANING AND USE 1: Real Conditionals** 335

Overview of Real Conditionals   **Expressing Advice, Warnings, and Instructions**
Expressing Certainty
Expressing Predictions and Promises   **Vocabulary Notes: *If* and *Unless***

D. **MEANING AND USE 2: Unreal Conditionals** 340

Unreal Conditionals   **Asking Permission**
Giving Advice and Opinions   **Beyond the Sentence: Omitting *If* Clauses**

E. **MEANING AND USE 3: Wishes** 344

Making Wishes   **Using *If Only***
Expressing Complaints and Regrets

WRITING: Write a Public Service Announcement 348

Reflections on Life

A1 Before You Read

Discuss these questions.

Do you ever make wishes? What do you wish for? Discuss your wishes and decide whether it is possible to achieve them.

A2 Read

CD2 T31 Read these different perspectives on life. Which selection best reflects your outlook on life?

CHINESE PROVERB

If there is light in the soul,
there will be beauty in the person.

If there is beauty in the person,
there will be harmony in the house.

If there is harmony in the house,
there will be order in the nation.

If there is order in the nation,
there will be peace in the world.

—Anonymous

If I Had My Life to Live Over

I'd dare to make more mistakes next time. I'd relax, I would limber up. I would be sillier than I have been this trip. I would take fewer things seriously. I would
5 take more chances. I would climb more mountains and swim more rivers. I would eat more ice cream and fewer beans. I would perhaps have more actual troubles, but I'd have fewer imaginary ones.
10 You see, I'm one of those people who lives sensibly and sanely hour after hour, day after day. Oh, I've had my moments, and if I had it to do over again, I'd have more of them. In fact, I'd try to have
15 nothing else.
If I had my life to live over, I would start barefoot earlier in the spring and stay that way later in the fall. I would go to more dances. I would ride more merry-go-
20 rounds. I would pick more daisies.

—Nadine Stair (85-year-old woman)

You have to count on living every single day in a way you believe will make you feel good about your life so if it were over tomorrow, you'd be content with yourself.

—Jane Seymour (actress)

Wishes of an Elderly Man
Wished at a Garden Party,
June 1914

I wish I loved the human race;
I wish I loved its silly face;
I wish I liked the way it walks;
I wish I liked the way it talks,
And when I'm introduced to one
I wish I thought, what jolly fun!

—Sir Walter Alexander Raleigh
(essayist/critic)

harmony: agreement, peaceful cooperation
jolly: cheerful, happy

limber up: to make the body more flexible, to stretch the muscles so that they move easily

A3 After You Read

Match each reading selection on the left with its main idea on the right.

_d_ **1.** Chinese proverb

____ **2.** *If I Had My Life to Live Over*

____ **3.** Quotation by Jane Seymour

____ **4.** *Wishes of an Elderly Man*

a. The writer regrets not taking advantage of more of the joys in life.

b. The writer doesn't like people very much.

c. It is important to be satisfied with the kind of life you lead.

d. There is a logical connection between the individual and the rest of the world.

B FORM

Real Conditionals, Unreal Conditionals, and Wishes

Think Critically About Form

A. Look back at the selections on pages 328–329 and complete the tasks below.

1. **IDENTIFY** An example of the simple present in an *if* clause is underlined in selection 1. Find three more examples.

2. **RECOGNIZE** Find two sentences that show the simple past in an *if* clause in selections 2 and 3. What verb form do you find in each main clause?

3. **RECOGNIZE** Look at the sentences that contain *wish* in selection 4. What is the tense of *wish*? What verb form is used in each clause that follows *wish*?

B. Discuss your answers with the class and read the Form charts to check them.

ONLINE PRACTICE

PRESENT AND FUTURE REAL CONDITIONALS		
⌐ **IF CLAUSE** ⌐		⌐ **MAIN CLAUSE** ⌐
IF + SIMPLE PRESENT	*(THEN)*	SIMPLE PRESENT
If I**'m** on time,	(then)	I **walk** to work.
IF + SIMPLE PRESENT	*(THEN)*	FUTURE
If it**'s** not too late,	(then)	I**'ll walk** to work. I**'m going to walk** to work.
IF + SIMPLE PRESENT	*(THEN)*	MODAL
If I **leave** on time,	(then)	I **may walk** to work.
IF + SIMPLE PRESENT	*(THEN)*	IMPERATIVE
If you **have** time,	(then)	**walk** with me.

PRESENT AND FUTURE UNREAL CONDITIONALS		
⌐ **IF CLAUSE** ⌐		⌐ **MAIN CLAUSE** ⌐
IF + SIMPLE PAST	*(THEN)*	*WOULD* + VERB
If I **had** the time,	(then)	I **would walk** to work. I**'d walk** to work.
IF + SIMPLE PAST	*(THEN)*	*COULD* + VERB
If I **left** on time,	(then)	I **could walk** to work.
IF + SIMPLE PAST	*(THEN)*	*MIGHT* + VERB
If I **left** on time,	(then)	I **might walk** to work.

Real and Unreal Conditionals

• Conditional sentences have a dependent *if* clause and a main clause.

- When the *if* clause comes first, it is followed by a comma. *Then* is usually omitted before the main clause, but it is always implied.

    If I'm on time, (then) **I walk** to work.　　**If I had** the time, (then) **I'd walk** to work.

- When the main clause is first, there is no comma and *then* is not used. The meaning is the same.

    I walk to work **if I'm** on time.　　**I'd walk** to work **if I had** the time.

- In conditional sentences, either clause or both clauses can be negative.

    If I'm not on time, **I take** the bus.　　**If I'm not** on time, **I won't walk** to work.

- Questions with conditionals are formed by putting the main clause in question word order.

    If it's not too late, **are you going to walk** to work?

    If you had the time, **would you walk** to work?

Real Conditionals

- In real conditionals, the verb in the *if* clause is in the present, even if it has future meaning.

    If you go tomorrow, **call** me.

- Real conditionals can also be formed with the present continuous in the *if* clause.

    If you're going tomorrow, **call me.**　　**If it's raining, I might take** the bus.

Unreal Conditionals

- When an unreal conditional *if* clause contains the verb *be*, use *were* for all subjects.

    If I were on time, **I'd walk** to work.

- Unreal conditionals can also be formed with the past continuous in the *if* clause.

    If I were leaving now, **I might walk** to work.

- See Appendix 14 for contractions with *would*.

WISHES ABOUT THE PRESENT AND FUTURE	
WISH CLAUSE	*THAT* CLAUSE
SIMPLE PRESENT	(*THAT* +) PAST FORM
I wish	(that) I **were** older. (that) I **didn't have** a cold. (that) you **were going** to the wedding. (that) you**'d help** me. (that) you **could come** with me.

(Continued on page 332)

- In sentences with *wish*, the *wish* clause is the main clause. The *that* clause is the dependent clause.
- In *that* clauses with the verb *be*, *were* is used for all subjects.
- *Could* and *would* (the simple past of *can* and *will*) are often used in the *that* clause.
- *That* is often omitted after *wish*, but it is always implied.
- Short answers with *wish* consist of a subject + *wish* clause + subject + *were/did*.

> A: Are you ready yet? A: Does he have any money?
>
> B: No, I **wish I were**. B: No, but I **wish he did**.

B1 Listening for Form

CD2 T32 Elena and Irina are twin sisters who attend college in different cities. Listen to some sentences from their phone conversation. Choose the verb forms that you hear.

1. **a.** could spend
   b. spent

2. **a.** 'd live
   b. lived

3. **a.** will finish
   b. finish

4. **a.** 'll spend
   b. 'd spend

5. **a.** attended
   b. would attend

6. **a.** wouldn't matter
   b. doesn't matter

7. **a.** didn't want
   b. don't want

8. **a.** do you want
   b. would you want

B2 Working on Real and Unreal Conditionals

A. Work in small groups. Start a real conditional sentence chain with *If the teacher cancels class*, and finish it with a result clause. Use the end of the last person's sentence to begin your own sentence.

A: If the teacher cancels class, there will be more time to study.

B: If there's more time to study, we'll do better on the exam.

C: If we do better on the exam,…

B. Now start an unreal conditional chain with *If I had the day off, I'd….* As before, use the end of the last person's sentence to begin your own sentence.

A: If I had the day off, I'd go shopping.

B: If I went shopping, I'd spend a lot of money.

C: If I spent a lot of money, I'd feel bad the next day.

B3 Building Conditional and *Wish* Sentences

Build as many meaningful sentences as possible. Use an item from each column or from two columns only. Punctuate your sentences correctly.

If I were ready, I'd leave.

| if
I wish | I were ready
she is sick
they were driving | I'd leave
call for help
he'll take over
you could come later |

B4 Working on *Wish* Sentences and Unreal Conditionals

A. Work with a partner. Complete these conversations using the appropriate form of the verbs. Add *would* when necessary. Then practice the conversations.

1. **A:** I wish I ____had____ (have) more money to spend.
   ₁

   B: If you _____ (do), you _____ (buy) things you don't need.
   ₂   ₃

2. **A:** I wish this place _____ (be/not) so crowded. If there _____ (be)
   ₁   ₂

   fewer people, we _____ (get) better service.
   ₃

   B: I know. I wish we _____ (can leave), but it's too late to go anywhere else.
   ₄

3. **A:** Do you ever wish you _____ (have) a different job?
   ₁

   B: Yes, quite often. If I _____ (have) a different job, I _____ (have)
   ₂   ₃

   more free time.

4. **A:** Can you help me fix my car?

   B: I wish I _____ (can), but I'm late. If I _____ (have/not) an
   ₁   ₂

   appointment at three, I _____ (stay) to help.
   ₃

B. Write four wishes. Then write a second sentence explaining each one with a related unreal conditional.

I wish it weren't so hot. If it weren't so hot, we could go for a walk.

B5 Completing Real and Unreal Conditionals

A. Complete these sentences with your own ideas. Use an appropriate verb form in the *if* clause or the main clause.

1. If I missed the bus, _I'd have to walk to work._

2. If I'm late for an appointment, _____

3. If I were sick, _____

4. I'm embarrassed if _____

5. I'd quit my job if _____

6. I'll buy a new computer if _____

B. Now write two real and two unreal *if* clauses or main clauses on a separate sheet of paper. Give them to a classmate to complete.

Informally Speaking

CD2 T33

Using *Was*

Look at the cartoon and listen to the conversation. How is each underlined form in the cartoon different from what you hear?

In informal speech, *was* is often used instead of *were* for unreal conditionals and wishes with *I*, *he*, *she*, and *it*.

I need a jacket, but nothing fits me. I wish I were taller.

If it were earlier, we could go to another store. Let's do that tomorrow.

SALE

Standard Form	What You Might Hear
If I **weren't** so busy, I'd go out tonight.	"If I wasn't so busy, I'd go out tonight."
I wish I **weren't** so busy.	"I wish I wasn't so busy."

B6 Understanding Informal Speech

CD2 T34 Listen and write the standard form of the words you hear.

1. If _____I weren't so tired_____, I'd go out for a cup of coffee with you.

2. What would you do if it _____ to take the bus?

3. I wish my boss _____.

4. If he _____, we could leave now.

5. She'd tell you if she _____ at you.

6. Don't you wish he _____ with us?

MEANING AND USE 1

Real Conditionals

Think Critically About Meaning and Use

A. Read the sentences and answer the questions below.

  a. If two hydrogen atoms combine with one oxygen atom, they form a water molecule.
  b. If you help me, I'll help you.
  c. If you finish the test early, turn over your paper.
  d. If you don't hurry, you'll miss the train.

  EVALUATE Which real conditional sentence do you think is a promise? a statement of fact? a warning? an instruction to do something?

B. Discuss your answers with the class and read the Meaning and Use Notes to check them.

Meaning and Use Notes

ONLINE
PRACTICE

Overview of Real Conditionals

▶ **1** In real conditional sentences, the *if* clause and main clause have a cause-and-effect relationship. The *if* clause introduces a possible condition or event (it may or may not happen). The main clause expresses a possible result (what happens or may happen after the *if* clause).

```
         ─── Possible Condition ───        Possible
                                      /    Result  \
If she finds another apartment, she'll move.
```
  (She may find an apartment. Under those circumstances, she'll move. Otherwise, she won't.)

Expressing Certainty

▶ **2A** Some conditionals are used to express results that the speaker is certain of. These sentences are sometimes called factual conditionals; the speaker thinks the results will occur whenever the condition in the *if* clause is true.

If you **lose** your credit card, the bank **replaces** it in a day.
  (This is a fact you are certain of.)

(Continued on page 336)

▶ 2B   When the result clause is in the simple present, real conditionals can express the kinds of routines and habits, facts, or general truths usually found in simple present sentences.

Routines and Habits

If I **take** the 8:05 train, **I get** to work at 8:50.

If I **drive**, **I get** to work earlier.

Facts or General Truths

If air **is heated**, it **rises**.

If you **overcook** fish, it **dries out**.

▶ 2C   Facts or general truths can also be expressed with the *will* future.

Facts or General Truths

If air **is heated**, it **will rise**.

If you **overcook** fish, it **will dry out**.

Expressing Predictions and Promises

▶ 3   When the result clause is in a future form, real conditionals can express predictions with varying degrees of certainty. In the first person, they can also express promises.

Predictions

If it **rains** tonight, the game **may be canceled**.

If it **rains** tonight, the game **will be canceled**.

Promises

If you **come over** tomorrow, **I'll help** you.

Expressing Advice, Warnings, and Instructions

▶ 4   Real conditionals are often used to give advice, warnings, and instructions. The result clause may use the imperative, a modal, or the future.

Advice

If your **throat** hurts, **try** salt water.

If your **throat** hurts, you **should try** salt water.

If you **gargle** with salt water, you**'ll get** immediate relief.

Warnings

If you **don't get** enough sleep, you**'ll get** sick.

Instructions

If the printer **runs out** of paper, **refill** it immediately.

C1 Listening for Meaning and Use

▶ Notes 1, 2A, 2B, 3, 4

CD2 T35 Listen to these sentences. How is each conditional sentence used? Check (✓) the correct column.

	FACTS OR GENERAL TRUTHS	ADVICE, WARNINGS, INSTRUCTIONS	PROMISES
1.		✓	
2.			
3.			
4.			
5.			
6.			
7.			
8.			

C2 Describing Factual Conditions

▶ Notes 2A–2C

Work with a partner and read this chart about fees at a ski resort. Use factual conditional sentences to describe the different conditions for membership and discounts.

If you're between 7 and 15, it costs $50 to buy a full-season pass.
If you're a member, you get a 15 percent discount on equipment rentals

WINTER SEASON
Membership Prices (per person)

Age	Full-Season Pass	Half-Season Pass
7–15*	$150	$95
16 & up	$200	$125

* Children 6 and under ski free when accompanied by an adult ticket holder.

Members receive the following year-round:
- 15% discount on equipment rentals
- Two free days of skiing: once before December 23, once after March 6 (One guest allowed each time)

On Membership Appreciation Days (dates to be announced):
- 50% discount on lift tickets for members
- Free lift ticket for one guest per member

C3 Making Promises

▶ Note 3

Work with a partner. Imagine you are a candidate running for mayor. Make promises using the words and phrases in real conditional sentences.

1. create jobs

   If I am elected mayor, I will create jobs. OR
   If you vote for me, I will create jobs. OR
   If I become mayor, I will create jobs.

2. improve education

3. build new schools

4. reduce crime

5. hire more police

6. expand health care

7. open more hospitals

8. cut taxes

9. employ more women

10. employ more minorities

C4 Rephrasing Advice with Conditional Sentences

▶ Note 4

Work in small groups. Read these statements of advice and think of different ways to rephrase them using real conditional sentences. Try to use the future, modals, or the imperative in your different result clauses.

1. Turn down your thermostat at night. You won't use so much fuel.

   If you turn down your thermostat at night, you won't use so much fuel.
   If you don't want to use so much fuel, (you should) turn down your thermostat at night.

2. Study hard, and you won't fail the test.

3. Make calls at night, and your telephone bill won't be so high.

4. Don't eat so much. You won't get indigestion.

5. Read a book for a while. You'll fall asleep easily.

6. Call the doctor, and you'll get some good advice.

Vocabulary Notes

If and Unless

Sentences with *unless* in the dependent clause often have the same meaning as sentences with negative *if* clauses.

Unless	*If*
Unless the cab **comes** at three, you won't make it to the airport.	**If** the cab **doesn't come** at three, you won't make it to the airport.
Unless you **finish** your work, we'll lose the account.	**If** you **don't finish** your work, we'll lose the account.

C5 Giving Warnings with *If* and *Unless* Clauses

A. Complete these health warnings. Use *will* or *won't* in the result clause.

1. If you don't eat more vegetables, *you won't have a balanced diet.*

2. _____ if you eat too much fat.

3. If you go to bed too late, _____

4. If you don't get enough calcium, _____

5. If you don't exercise, _____

B. Complete these safety warnings by writing negative conditions in the *if* clauses that could lead to the harmful results.

1. You'll get into an accident if *you don't drive more carefully.*

2. If _____, you'll slip.

3. You'll damage your eyes if _____

4. If _____, you'll get sick.

5. You'll start a fire if _____

C. Look at the warnings your partner wrote in part B. Rewrite the warnings that can be rephrased using *unless* instead of *if*.

You'll get into an accident unless you drive more carefully.

Unreal Conditionals

Think Critically About Meaning and Use

A. Read the sentences and answer the questions below.

1a. If my plane is late, I'll miss the meeting.   **2a.** If I were you, I'd leave now.
1b. If my plane were late, I'd miss the meeting.   **2b.** You should leave now.

1. **ANALYZE** Compare 1a and 1b. Which one expresses something that is more likely to happen? Which one expresses something that is probably imaginary?

2. **DIFFERENTIATE** Compare 2a and 2b. Which sentence sounds more direct? Which one seems more indirect?

B. Discuss your answers with the class and read the Meaning and Use Notes to check them.

Meaning and Use Notes

ONLINE
PRACTICE

	Unreal Conditionals
▶ **1A**	Unreal conditional sentences express imaginary situations. The *if* clause introduces the imaginary condition or event (it is not true at the present time). The main clause expresses the imaginary result (what would or could happen after the *if* clause).

Imaginary Condition   Imaginary Result

If she **found** another apartment, she **would move**.
  (She hasn't found an apartment, so she isn't moving.)

▶ **1B**	In the *if* clause, the simple past or past continuous does not indicate past time; it indicates that the situation is unreal. In the result clause, *would, could/would be able to,* or *might* also indicate that the result is unreal.

If I **had** a problem, I**'d ask** for your help. (I don't have a problem right now, so I don't need help.)

If I **had** the money, I **could buy** a new car. (Right now I don't have the money, so I can't buy a new car.)

If we **were staying in Moscow**, we**'d be able to visit** them. (We're not staying in Moscow, so we can't visit them.)

▶ 1C *Would* in the result clause expresses more certainty than *could* or *might* about the imaginary results. *Could* or *might* indicates one of several possible outcomes.

If I **had** the money, I **would buy** a new car. (*Would* expresses more certainty about the imaginary outcome.)

If I **had** the money, I **might buy** a new car. (*Might* expresses one imaginary outcome. There are other possible outcomes.)

Giving Advice and Opinions

▶ 2 Unreal conditionals beginning with *If I were you* can be used as an indirect way of giving advice. Unreal conditionals sound softer than modals like *should* or *ought to*.

Advice with Unreal Conditionals

If I **were** you, I'**d** speak to the instructor.

Advice with Modals

You **should** speak to the instructor.

Asking Permission

▶ 3 Unreal conditionals with *would you mind, would it bother you,* or *would it be OK* can be used to ask for permission. Notice that a negative response to the first two questions means you are giving permission.

Permission with Unreal Conditionals

A: **Would you mind if I opened** the window?

B: **No**, go right ahead.

A: **Would it bother you if I opened** the window?

B: **No**, not at all.

A: **Would it be OK if I opened** the window?

B: **Yes**, go ahead.

Permission with Modals

A: **May I open** the window?

B: **Yes**, go right ahead.

D1 Listening for Meaning and Use

▶ Notes 1A–1C, 2, 3

CD2 T36   Listen and choose the best response.

1. **a.** Sure, it would be a pleasure.

    b. No, not at all.

2. **a.** I took a taxi.

    b. I'll call you.

3. **a.** I might.

    b. I did.

4. **a.** I'll have dinner with Cleopatra.

    b. I'd choose Pablo Picasso.

5. **a.** I would.

    b. Maybe.

6. **a.** No, go right ahead.

    b. Yes, if no one is using it.

D2 Asking Questions About Unusual Situations

 A. Complete these unreal conditionals. Try to think of unusual or interesting situations that people might like to talk about. Then take turns asking and answering the questions with a partner.

1. What would you do if _you found a million dollars?_

    I'd probably report it to the police and hope to get a reward.

2. What would you say if _____

3. How would you feel if _____

4. Where would you go if _____

5. Who would you invite if _____

6. Who would you ask for help if _____

B. Ask the class one of your questions.

D3 Giving Advice with *If I Were You* ▶ Notes 1A–1C

Work in small groups. Give advice with *If I were you, I'd…* or *If I were you, I wouldn't…* Brainstorm different solutions for each problem.

1. There's a big mistake on my electric bill.

    If I were you, I wouldn't ignore it.
    If I were you, I'd call the electric company and explain the situation.

2. My landlord doesn't repair things when I ask him to.

3. I accepted two invitations to go out, and now I don't know what to do.

4. I get a lot of phone calls, but most of them are wrong numbers.

5. My boss isn't very nice to me.

6. I checked my credit card balance online and discovered some charges for expensive items that I know I didn't buy.

7. I want to buy a computer, but I don't know much about them.

8. I'm not doing very well in my English class.

D4 Asking Permission ▶ Notes 3

Work with a partner. Read each situation and take turns asking for permission in at least two different ways. Use *Would you mind if…*, *Would it bother you if…*, or *Would it be OK if…*, and respond with appropriate positive or negative answers.

1. You're supposed to pick your friend up at eight o'clock, but you'd prefer to pick her up earlier.

   A: Would you mind if I picked you up earlier?
   B: No, not at all.

2. You want to listen to the news while your roommate is studying. You don't want to disturb him.

3. You think it's too hot in the classroom. You want to open the window.

4. Your friend has an interesting book. You want to borrow it.

Beyond the Sentence

Omitting *If* Clauses

When a single condition has many results, the *if* clause is usually stated only once. The imaginary results are expressed in new sentences with *would*.

   If I were the boss, I <u>would</u> try to be considerate of my employees' needs to balance work and family. I <u>would</u> give them more time off for family responsibilities. I <u>would</u> even encourage my employees to volunteer in their children's schools during work hours. I <u>would</u>…

D5 Using Conditionals with Many Results

A. If you could be anyone in the world for one day, who would you like to be? Make a list of things you would do if you were that person.

B. Write a paragraph describing what you would do if you were the person you chose in part A. Start your paragraph with *If I were…, I'd…* Continue expressing imaginary results using sentences with *would*. Do not use any more *if* clauses in your paragraph.

   If I were Bill Gates for one day, I'd fly on one of my private jets to a beautiful tropical paradise. I'd spend the day swimming, relaxing, and having fun with my family. I'd have the finest chefs prepare all of my favorite foods, and…

Wishes

Think Critically About Meaning and Use

A. Read the sentences and answer the questions below.

1a. I wish you'd leave work early tomorrow and come to the picnic.
1b. I wish I were wearing a sweater. It's cold.
2a. I wish you would clean up your room more often.
2b. I wish I could help you, but I don't know the answer.

1. **ANALYZE** Look at sentences 1a and 1b. Which sentence is a wish about the present? Which is a wish about the future?

2. **ANALYZE** Look at sentences 2a and 2b. Which expresses a complaint? Which expresses a regret?

B. Discuss your answers with the class and read the Meaning and Use Notes to check them.

Meaning and Use Notes

ONLINE
PRACTICE

Making Wishes

▶ 1   Use *wish* to express a desire for something that does not exist now. It is a desire to change a real situation into an unreal or impossible one. As in unreal conditional sentences, the past form does not indicate past time; it indicates that the situation is unreal. The past form can be simple past, past continuous, *could*, or *would*.

Wishes About the Present

I live in an apartment, but I **wish I lived** in a house.

I **wish I were living** in Chicago.

I **wish I could swim**, but I can't.

Wishes About the Future

I **wish** you **would come** with me tonight.

I **wish** you **were coming** with me tonight.

I **wish you could come** with me tonight.

Expressing Complaints and Regrets

▶ **2A** Sometimes *wish* sentences with *would* express complaints, especially when you want something to change but think it probably won't.

I **wish** it **would stop** raining. We can't go anywhere in this weather.

I **wish** you **wouldn't leave** the car windows open.

▶ **2B** *Wish* sentences often express regret about a current situation.

A: Can you help me this afternoon?

B: No, I'm sorry. I **wish I could**, but I have a doctor's appointment.

Using *If Only*

▶ **3** Sentences with *if only* often have a similar meaning to sentences with *wish*, but they are more emphatic. *If only* sentences focus on the desire to change a negative situation. Unlike other *if* conditionals, an *if only* clause is often used alone without a result clause.

If Only	**Wish**
If only I **had** a car!	I **wish** I **had** a car.
If only I **felt** better, then I'd go out.	I **wish** I **felt** better. Perhaps I'd go out.
If only it **would stop** raining.	I **wish** it **would stop** raining.

E1 Listening for Meaning and Use

▶ Note 1

⏺ CD2 T37   Listen to each situation and check (✓) whether the item exists or doesn't exist.

		EXISTS	DOESN'T EXIST
1.	a cold	✓	
2.	pictures		
3.	free time		
4.	a car		
5.	a safety lock		
6.	a limit		
7.	a credit card		
8.	your guitar		

E2 Making Wishes About the Present

▶ Note 1

Work in small groups. Take turns making up as many wishes as possible for each situation. Explain your wishes with unreal conditional sentences.

1. Your apartment is too small.

   I wish I had more space. If I had more space, I'd get a pet.
   I wish I could move. If I moved, I'd get a much bigger apartment.

2. You're broke. You have no money.

3. Your new teacher is boring.

4. You're very busy.

5. You live in a big city.

6. You drive to work during rush hour.

7. You need more exercise.

8. You're lost in the woods.

E3 Making Wishes About the Future

▶ Notes 1, 3

Work with a partner. Take turns expressing your wishes for the future by using *wish* and *if only* sentences with *would*.

1. You are waiting to receive your grades in the mail. The mail is late.

   I wish the mail would come!
   If only the mail would come!

2. You want your sister to take better care of herself, but you're afraid that she won't.

3. You want your sister to help you choose a present for your parents' wedding anniversary, but she is always busy. You want her to go shopping with you this weekend.

4. You think that your father is working too hard. You want him to take a vacation.

5. The weather is very bad. Your friend dropped by for a few minutes. You want him to stay until the weather improves, but he seems to be in a hurry.

6. Your brother has just announced that he wants to quit school and go back home. You want him to stay in college.

E4 Complaining with *Wish* and *If Only* Sentences ▶ Notes 2A, 3

Work with a partner. Imagine you are very unhappy with your college roommate for the reasons listed below. Complain about your roommate's bad habits using *wish* and *if only* sentences with *would* or *wouldn't*.

1. makes a lot of noise in the morning

   I wish he wouldn't make so much noise in the morning. OR
   I wish he would be quieter in the morning. OR
   If only he wouldn't make so much noise!

2. uses up all the hot water in the shower

3. uses up the milk and doesn't replace it

4. doesn't talk to my friends when they visit me

5. doesn't clean up the kitchen

6. plays video games for hours

E5 Expressing Regret with *Wish* Sentences ▶ Note 2B

Work with a partner. Complete these conversations with expressions of regret. Use the simple past and then give a reason with *but*, explaining the real situation. Then practice the conversations, switching roles.

1. **Roommate A:** Could you please help me with this?

   Roommate B: I'm sorry, I can't. I wish _I could, but I have to leave right now._

2. **Customer:** Do you have any more wallets?

   Salesclerk: No, I'm sorry. I wish _____

3. **Student A:** Can you lend me yesterday's notes?

   Student B: Well, I wish _____

4. **Friend A:** Do you have any free time later this afternoon?

   Friend B: No, I wish _____

5. **Child:** Are there any more cookies left?

   Parent: No, I wish _____

6. **Friend A:** Is it warm outside this morning?

   Friend B: No, I wish _____

Think Critically About Meaning and Use

A. Read each situation and the statements that follow. Write *T* if the statement is true or *F* if it is false.

1. We'd leave if it stopped raining.

_____F_____ **a.** We left.

_____ **b.** It's raining.

2. I'd go to the meeting if I weren't so busy.

_____ **a.** I'm not very busy.

_____ **b.** I'm going to the meeting.

3. Unless I call, I'll be home at six.

_____ **a.** I might call.

_____ **b.** I plan to be home at six.

4. If it weren't on sale, I couldn't afford it.

_____ **a.** It's on sale.

_____ **b.** I can't afford it.

5. If the light flashes, the bell rings five seconds later.

_____ **a.** The bell won't ring until the light flashes.

_____ **b.** The light flashes before the bell rings.

6. I wish I didn't have to take the exam.

_____ **a.** I've taken the exam.

_____ **b.** I don't have a choice.

7. If you lived in that neighborhood, you'd know Joseph Taylor.

_____ **a.** You know Joseph Taylor.

_____ **b.** You don't live in that neighborhood.

8. If only you spoke more slowly, then I'd understand you better.

_____ **a.** You speak slowly.

_____ **b.** I understand you very well.

Edit

Find the errors in this text and correct them.

What ~~you would~~ *would you* do if there were an earthquake in your area? Would you know what to do? Some people are too frightened to find out about safety precautions. They wish they live somewhere else. If you could, won't you rather find out what to do in advance? Here is some advice about what to do before, during, and after an earthquake.

1. If you don't have a box of emergency equipment and supplies, you will need to prepare one in advance.

2. If you would be indoors during an earthquake, you should stay away from windows, bookcases, and shelves.

3. If it were possible, you should turn off the gas, water, and electricity.

4. After the earthquake, don't walk around unless you are not wearing shoes to protect your feet from broken glass.

Don't wait. Don't wish you are prepared. Be prepared!

Write

Imagine you work for a government agency that produces informational material for publication in newspapers and magazines. Write a one-page public service announcement entitled "Home Safety Tips." Use real and unreal conditionals, where appropriate.

1. **BRAINSTORM** Think of all things that people can do to be safe at home (e.g., installing smoke alarms or child-proof electrical outlets). Write down at least 10 useful ideas.

   Think about how you will introduce your topic and organize your tips: Can you think of unreal conditionals or wishes you might use to catch your readers' attention? Do you want to present tips for different rooms or areas or for different concerns (e.g., children's safety, first aid, fire prevention, home security, emergency response)?

2. **WRITE A FIRST DRAFT** Before you write your first draft, read the checklist below and look at the examples in C4 on page 338 and the editing passage on page 349. Write your draft using real and unreal conditionals.

3. **EDIT** Read your work and check it against the checklist below. Circle grammar, spelling, and punctuation errors.

DO I...	YES
use an unreal conditional or wish to attract my readers' attention?	
use factual conditionals to express safety tips?	
use a mix of real conditionals and imperatives to give advice and instructions?	
give at least one warning with an *if* or *unless* clause?	
take care to use correct verb forms in real and unreal conditionals?	

4. **PEER REVIEW** Work with a partner to help you decide how to fix your errors and improve the content. Use the checklist above.

5. **REWRITE YOUR DRAFT** Using the comments from your partner, write a final draft.

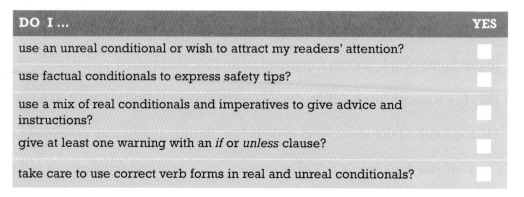

Home Safety Tips

How would you feel if you walked into the bathroom and saw your four-year-old child surrounded by broken glass? Accidents around the home happen, but if you took a few more precautions, many could be avoided...

A. **GRAMMAR IN DISCOURSE: The Ifs of History** 352

B. **FORM: Past Unreal Conditionals and
Past Wishes** 354

  Past Unreal Conditionals

    If I **had known** the answer, (then) I **would have passed** the test.

  Past Wishes

    I **wish** (that) I **had taken** a vacation last year.

  Informally Speaking: Reduced Forms of Past Conditionals

C. **MEANING AND USE 1: Past Unreal
Conditionals** 359

  Past Unreal Conditionals

  Giving Advice

  Restating Past Unreal Conditionals with *But*

D. **MEANING AND USE 2: Past Wishes** 363

  Making Wishes About the Past

  Expressing Regret or Dissatisfaction

  Using *If Only*

  **WRITING: Write an Email Expressing Regret
About Not Meeting a Deadline** 366

  PART 6 TEST: Conditionals 369

The Ifs of History

A1 Before You Read

Discuss these questions.

Think of a decision that you regret. What should you have done differently? Think of a decision that you have never regretted. Why not?

A2 Read

CD2 T38 Read this magazine article to find out about some possible alternatives to actual historical events. Do you agree with this writer's ideas?

> Article

The Ifs of History

by Hans Koning

Franklin Delano Roosevelt

The ifs of history are numberless. For everything that has happened we can, of course, line up infinite alternatives. But not much is gained from this, except for the
5 obvious observation that human history is very iffy.

The ifs I am talking about here are last-minute ifs–that is, I am not going to lose myself and my readers by guessing
10 what would have happened if there had been no Bering Strait or English Channel or no Franklin Delano Roosevelt. A last-minute if is: What would have happened if, in February 1933, Giuseppe Zangara's
15 hand had not been pushed aside in Miami and his bullet had killed Franklin Roosevelt rather than the mayor of Chicago?

This example gets right to the point. Most of my ifs are life-or-death ifs. And
20 that raises the well-known dilemma: Are certain individuals of greater importance to the flow of history? I find it hard to accept that the chance life or death of one person could decide the lives and deaths of millions. But I suspect that the truth lies
25 millions. But I suspect that the truth lies somewhere in between. A few individuals have influenced destiny, but in the long run, history exhibits its own logic.

If that German officer in Hitler's
30 headquarters who moved a briefcase had minded his own business, then the bomb in the briefcase would have killed Hitler. A different government would have taken over in Berlin and World War II would
35 have ended. The Allies would have occupied Germany ten months sooner. As many as a million prisoners' lives would have been saved.

If Cleopatra hadn't lived, Marc Antony
40 would have kept his mind on the affairs of
state and not been eliminated from the
race for Roman emperor. He would have
continued sharing power with his brother-
in-law Octavian, whom he hated, and he
45 would have worked to oppose Octavian's
unjust use of force. If Marc Antony had
done that, it would have hastened the fall
of the Roman Empire by a hundred years.
Everything thereafter would have happened
50 one hundred years sooner.

If Joseph Ginoux, a café owner in
Arles, had allowed Vincent van Gogh to
pay for his lodging in paintings instead of
evicting him, then Vincent would have had
55 some peace and security. His nervous
breakdown might have happened later and
been less severe. He would have painted for
five, perhaps ten years more. The people of
Arles wouldn't have drawn up their petition

60 to have him put in an asylum. In a less
hostile and threatening world, his later
work would have reached an unimaginable
perfection. Gauguin and Picasso would
have been influenced differently; twentieth-
65 century painting would have been different.
(And Ginoux's heirs would have been the
richest people in France.)

Sculpture of Cleopatra Vincent van Gogh,
           Self-Portrait

Adapted from Harper's Magazine

---

asylum: a psychiatric hospital
alternative: a different possibility or choice
dilemma: a difficult choice between alternatives
evict: to force a renter out of his or her apartment

hasten: to cause to happen sooner
iffy: full of uncertainty, doubtful
last-minute: at the final moment before an
 important event

A3 After You Read

Check (✓) the events that actually happened or are true, according to the article.

1. ✓ A man tried to kill Franklin Delano Roosevelt in Miami.

2. _____ Hitler was killed by a bomb in a briefcase.

3. _____ Marc Antony was eliminated from the race for Roman emperor.

4. _____ Van Gogh was evicted from where he was living.

5. _____ Joseph Ginoux received paintings from van Gogh.

B | FORM

Past Unreal Conditionals and Past Wishes

⚙ Think Critically About Form

A. Look back at the article on page 352 and complete the tasks below.

   1. **IDENTIFY** A past unreal conditional sentence is underlined. Find three more examples.

   2. **RECOGNIZE** What form is used in each *if* clause? What form is used in each main clause?

B. Discuss your answers with the class and read the Form charts to check them.

▶ Past Unreal Conditionals

ONLINE PRACTICE

PAST UNREAL CONDITIONALS		
⌐——— *IF* CLAUSE ———⌐		⌐——— MAIN CLAUSE ———⌐
IF + PAST PERFECT	*(THEN)*	*WOULD HAVE* + PAST PARTICIPLE
If I **had known** the answer,	(then)	I **would have passed** the test.
If I**'d known** the answer,	(then)	I**'d have passed** the test.

IF + PAST PERFECT	*(THEN)*	*COULD HAVE* + PAST PARTICIPLE
If I **had known** the answer,	(then)	I **could have passed** the test.

IF + PAST PERFECT	*(THEN)*	*MIGHT HAVE* + PAST PARTICIPLE
If I **had known** the answer,	(then)	I **might have passed** the test.

- The contraction of both *had* and *would* with pronouns is *'d*.
- When the *if* clause comes first, it is followed by a comma. When the main clause is first, there is no comma and *then* is not used.

   If I had known the answer, (then) **I would have passed** the test.

   I would have passed the test **if I had known** the answer.

- Either clause or both clauses can be negative.

   If I hadn't known the answer, **I would have asked** for help.

   If I hadn't known the answer, **I wouldn't have passed** the test.

- Questions are formed by putting the main clause in question word order.

    If you had known the answer, **would you have passed** the test?
- See Appendix 14 for contractions with *had* and *would*.

▶ Past Wishes

PAST WISHES	
WISH CLAUSE	*THAT* CLAUSE
SIMPLE PRESENT	(*THAT* +) PAST PERFECT
I **wish**	(that) I **had taken** a vacation last year.

SIMPLE PRESENT	(*THAT* +) *COULD HAVE* +PAST PERFECT
I **wish**	(that) you **could have come** to the show.

- *That* is often omitted after *wish*, but it is always implied.
- Notice the use of past perfect or past modal short forms when a *wish* clause follows *but*.

    I didn't take a vacation last year, but **I wish I had**.

    I invited Joe to the party, but **I wish I hadn't**.

    I didn't go to the show, but **I wish I could have**.

B1 Listening for Form

CD2 T39   Listen to each conversation and choose the response that you hear.

1. **a.** Not really. If it had been me, I would have interrupted him.

    b. Not really. If it had been me, I wouldn't have interrupted him.

2. **a.** If I had another chance, I'd prepare more for the interview.

    b. If I'd had another chance, I'd have prepared more for the interview.

3. **a.** No, I wouldn't.

    b. No, I wouldn't have.

4. **a.** If I had listened to my roommate, I would have taken it.

    b. If I had listened to my roommate, I wouldn't have taken it.

5. **a.** Yes, if I'd had my way, we would have moved to Seattle.

   b. Yes, if I had my way, we would move to Seattle.

6. **a.** I know. I would have called if it had been so late.

   b. I know. I would have called if it hadn't been so late.

B2 Completing Past Conditional Sentences

A. Complete these sentences with *would have, could have,* or *might have* in a past result clause.

1. If I had studied medicine, _I would have become a doctor._ _____

2. If I had known ten years ago what I know now, _____

3. If I had listened to my parents, _____

4. If I hadn't ever learned to read, _____

5. If I had been born in Australia, _____

6. If I had lived in another century, _____

7. If I hadn't studied English, _____

8. If I hadn't come to school today, _____

 B. On a separate sheet of paper, write three more past *if* clauses. Then trade papers with your partner and complete the sentences.

B3 Working on Past Conditionals

Work in small groups. Start a past unreal conditional sentence chain with *If I hadn't slept well last night*, and finish it with a result clause. Use the end of the last person's sentence to begin your own sentence.

A: *If I hadn't slept well last night, I'd have been exhausted this morning.*

B: *If I'd been exhausted this morning, I would have stayed home from work.*

C: *If I'd stayed home from work,...*

Informally Speaking

Reduced Forms of Past Conditionals

CD2 T40 Look at the cartoon and listen to the conversation. How is each underlined form in the cartoon different from what you hear?

The waiter overcharged me for lunch today, but I didn't say anything.

Well, I <u>would have</u> shown him the mistake. I sure <u>wouldn't have</u> paid the extra money.

In informal speech, would have, could have, and might have are often reduced like other past modals (see Chapter 8, page 175). Have may sound like /əv/. If it is reduced even more, it sounds like /ə/. Notice the reduction of the past perfect in the if clauses as well.

Standard Form	What You Might Hear
If **Tim had** driven, he **would have** arrived earlier.	"If /'tɪməd/ driven, he /'wʊdəv/ arrived earlier." OR "If /'tɪməd/ driven, he /'wʊdə/ arrived earlier."
If **Tim had** driven, he **could have** arrived earlier.	"If /'tɪməd/ driven, he /'kʊdəv/ arrived earlier." OR "If /'tɪməd/ driven, he /'kʊdə/ arrived earlier."
If **Joe had** been there, I **would not have** gone.	"If /'dʒoʊəd/ been there, I /'wʊdntəv/ gone." OR "If /'dʒoʊəd/ been there, I /'wʊdntə/ gone."
If **Joe had** been there, I **might not have** gone.	"If /'dʒoʊəd/ been there, I /'maɪtnɑdəv/ gone." OR "If /'dʒoʊəd/ been there, I /'maɪtnɑdə/ gone."

B4 Understanding Informal Speech

CD2 T41 Listen and write the standard form of the words you hear.

1. _Would you have chosen_ a different career if you hadn't married so young?

2. If I had studied, I _____ much better on the quiz.

3. We _____ so late if the car had been working.

4. If I hadn't been careful, I _____ an accident.

5. I _____ late if I'd missed the bus.

6. If I hadn't scored, we _____ the game.

B5 Working on Past Wishes

A. Work with a partner. Complete these conversations with the appropriate forms of the verbs in parentheses to form past wishes. Then practice the conversations.

1. A: __Does he ever wish__ (he/ever/wish) that he ____had chosen____ (choose)
   ₁ a different career when he graduated?

   B: Yes. Sometimes he _____ (wish) he _____
   ₃ ₄
   (go) to graduate school right after college.

2. A: My sister _____ (wish) she _____ (see) the
   ₁ ₂
   apartment upstairs when she was looking for one.

   B: I didn't know she was interested in a two-bedroom apartment.

   I _____ (wish) I _____ (show) it to her.
   ₃ ₄
   Then we could have been neighbors.

3. A: _____ (you/ever/wish) you _____ (learn) to
   ₁ ₂
   ski when you were younger?

   B: Yes, I _____ (wish) I _____ (be) braver when
   ₃ ₄
   my school offered lessons.

B. Complete these sentences with the short form.

1. I never learned to swim, but I wish __I had.__

2. He didn't graduate this year, but he wishes _____

3. We didn't see that movie, but we wish _____

4. They took the train, but they wish _____

5. She couldn't attend the meeting yesterday, but she wishes _____

Past Unreal Conditionals

Think Critically About Meaning and Use

A. Read the sentences and answer the questions below.

a. If she had been a better student, she would have graduated on time.

b. If she were a better student, she would graduate on time.

1. EVALUATE Which sentence refers to a situation that was not true in the past?

2. EVALUATE Which sentence refers to a situation that is not true in the present?

B. Discuss your answers with the class and read the Meaning and Use Notes to check them.

Meaning and Use Notes

ONLINE PRACTICE

Past Unreal Conditionals

▶ **1A** Past unreal conditional sentences express imaginary situations that were actually not true in the past. In the *if* clause, the past perfect indicates the situation was unreal in the past. In the result clause, *would have*, *could have*, or *might have* also indicate the result was unreal in the past.

If I **had been** the boss, I **would have fired** him. (I wasn't the boss, so I didn't fire him.)

▶ **1B** *Could have* or *might have* in the result clause indicates one of several possible imaginary outcomes. *Would have* indicates that the speaker is more certain about the imaginary results.

If you**'d had** your car, you **could have left** earlier.

If you**'d had** your car, you **might not have left** so late. (*Could have* and *might have* both express one of several possible imaginary outcomes.)

If you**'d had** your car, you **wouldn't have left** so late. (*Would have* expresses more certainty about the imaginary outcome.)

(Continued on page 360)

Giving Advice

▶ 2 Unreal conditionals beginning with *If I had been you* can be used as an indirect way of giving advice. The *if* clause is often omitted. Unreal conditionals sound softer than modals like *should have*.

Advice with Past Unreal Conditionals	**Advice with Modals**
(If I**'d been** you,) I **would have left** early.	You **should have** left early.

Restating Past Unreal Conditionals with But

▶ 3 Often, a sentence with *would have* is used without an *if* condition. Instead, the main clause is joined to a true (not imaginary) sentence with *but*. The true sentence with *but* implies the unreal past condition.

True Sentence with But	**Past Unreal Conditional**
I would have watched the tennis match, **but I had to study**.	I would have watched the tennis match **if I hadn't had to study**.
I would have left earlier, **but my car didn't start**.	I would have left earlier **if my car had started**.

C1 Listening for Meaning and Use

▶ Notes 1A, 1B

CD2 T42 Listen and choose the best answer to each question.

1. **(a.)** I don't know.
   b. I didn't know.

2. **a.** Yes, he did.
   b. He could have.

3. **a.** Maybe, but he'd be quite old.
   b. Maybe he hadn't.

4. **a.** It's hard to say.
   b. They certainly were.

5. **a.** Maybe not.
   b. Yes, they did.

6. **a.** It might be.
   b. It might have.

7. **a.** No, it won't.
   b. No, I doubt it.

8. **a.** No one knows.
   b. No one knew.

C2 Giving Indirect Advice

▶ Note 2

Work with a partner. Take turns giving indirect advice to your partner by telling what you would have done. The *if* clauses may be omitted.

1. **A:** I didn't understand last week's homework, but I didn't do anything about it.

   B: _(If I'd been you,) I would have gone to see the instructor._

2. **A:** My best friend asked to borrow a lot of money. I gave it to him without asking any questions.

   B: _____

3. **A:** A salesperson was rude to me yesterday when I was buying a gift.

   B: _____

4. **A:** My doctor didn't answer all my questions.

   B: _____

5. **A:** My boss didn't offer me the raise that I wanted. I was disappointed.

   B: _____

6. **A:** The airline refused to change my ticket, even though it was an emergency.

   B: _____

C3 Distinguishing Fact and Fiction

▶ Note 3

Work with a partner. List the two facts that each conditional sentence implies. Then paraphrase the conditional sentence using *would have* followed by a true sentence with *but*.

1. If Alexander the Great hadn't died of yellow fever in 532 B.C., he would have attacked Carthage and Rome.

   Facts: 1. _Alexander the Great died of yellow fever in 532 B.C._

            2. _He didn't attack Carthage and Rome._

   Paraphrase: _Alexander the Great would have attacked Carthage and Rome,_

                    but he died of yellow fever in 532 B.C.

(Continued on page 362)

2. If Napoleon's armies had had proper nails for horseshoes, they would have conquered Russia.

       Facts: 1. _____

                 2. _____

   Paraphrase: _____

                       _____

3. If Apollo 13 hadn't had an explosion during its flight, it would have landed on the moon as planned.

       Facts: 1. _____

                 2. _____

   Paraphrase: _____

                       _____

4. If Mozart hadn't died young, he would have finished his famous piece *Requiem*.

       Facts: 1. _____

                 2. _____

   Paraphrase: _____

                       _____

5. If an asteroid or meteorite hadn't crashed into Earth, dinosaurs wouldn't have died out 65 million years ago.

       Facts: 1. _____

                 2. _____

   Paraphrase: _____

                       _____

C4 Describing the Ifs of History

▶ **Notes 1A, 1B**

Work in small groups. Think of five historical events that you know something about. Make up two past unreal conditional sentences about each event.

Apollo 13: If an oxygen tank hadn't exploded during the flight into space, the astronauts' lives wouldn't have been in danger. If the explosion hadn't happened, the astronauts would have landed on the moon.

D

Past Wishes

Think Critically About Meaning and Use

A. Read the sentences and answer the questions below.

1a. I wish the temperature were warmer. I am freezing.
1b. I wish the temperature had been warmer. I was freezing.
2a. If only he didn't have a cold. He really wants to go out.
2b. If only he hadn't had a cold. He really wanted to go out.

1. **ANALYZE** Which sentences are about present situations? Which are about past situations?

2. **ANALYZE** Which pair of sentences seems to express stronger feelings?

B. Discuss your answers with the class and read the Meaning and Use Notes to check them.

Meaning and Use Notes

ONLINE PRACTICE

Making Wishes About the Past

▶ **1** Past *wish* sentences refer to past situations that did not occur. They express a desire to change something that happened in the past.

I **wish** the weather **had been** nice yesterday. (It rained yesterday.)

I **wish** you **could have seen** the movie. (You didn't see the movie.)

Expressing Regret or Dissatisfaction

▶ **2** When you use a past *wish* sentence, you express regret or dissatisfaction about a past situation.

I **wish** I **had gone** to the meeting. I completely forgot about it. I **wish** someone **had called** to remind me.

Using If Only

▶ **3** *If only* is often used in place of a past wish to express strong regret. *If only* sentences focus on the wish to change a negative outcome.

If only I **hadn't lost** my wallet!   **If only** the war **had ended** sooner!

D1 Listening for Meaning and Use

▶ Notes 1–3

CD2 T43 Listen to each situation and choose the sentence that is true.

1. a. I read about World War II.
    b. I saw a movie. *(circled)*

2. a. I wasn't home.
    b. I answered the phone.

3. a. She wasn't elected.
    b. She represents us now.

4. a. You called.
    b. The exam ended.

5. a. They got reservations.
    b. They didn't fly home.

6. a. There was a tree on the driveway.
    b. I wasn't leaving.

7. a. You took a day off last week.
    b. You took today off.

8. a. I didn't have a headache.
    b. I didn't stay.

D2 Expressing Regret

▶ Notes 2, 3

Work with a partner. Take turns making up past *wish* and *if only* sentences that express regret. Think of as many sentences as possible for each situation.

1. You refused to lend your brother money. He had to drop out of school for a semester because he couldn't pay his tuition.

    I wish I'd lent him the money.
    If only I'd helped him.

2. You lost your temper today when you were baby-sitting your nephew. He began to cry.

3. You didn't tell your boss how overworked you've been feeling. Now he has changed your schedule, and you can't take a day off.

4. You didn't call the doctor last week when you got sick. Now you've missed a week of classes.

5. You forgot your best friend's birthday. There was a special dinner for your friend and you didn't go.

6. You accepted a job offer on Monday. On Tuesday you got a better offer from another company.

D3 Expressing Regret or Dissatisfaction

▶ Notes 2, 3

A. Work with a partner. Take turns reacting to the statements by using a past *wish* sentence or *if only* sentence with short forms.

1. **A:** The library was closed yesterday.

   B: <u>I wish it hadn't been.</u>

2. **A:** Our team didn't win first prize.

   B: <u>If only we had.</u>

3. **A:** The president raised taxes again.

   B: _____

4. **A:** My TV stopped working.

   B: _____

5. **A:** The train was late.

   B: _____

6. **A:** I didn't invite Peter.

   B: _____

7. **A:** It snowed a lot.

   B: _____

8. **A:** They didn't call back.

   B: _____

B. With your partner, expand one of the examples above into a longer conversation between two people. (Try to have each person speak three or four times.) Give more details about the situation and try to use at least one more wish sentence, *if only* sentence, or past unreal conditional sentence.

A: The library was closed last night.

B: I know. I wish it hadn't been.

A: I needed to work on my paper. If only I had checked the schedule a few days ago, I would have been able to finish on time.

D4 Explaining Wishes

▶ Note 1

A. Think of two past events in your life that you wish you could have changed. Write a past *wish* sentence about each one. Then write a past *if* sentence to explain your wish.

I wish my family hadn't moved when I was young.
If they hadn't moved, I wouldn't have been so lonely.

B. Now expand one of the events from part A into a paragraph. First, make a list of details that would have been different if your wish had come true. Then use your list to write your paragraph. Use *would have, could have,* and *might have.*

I wish my family hadn't moved when I was young. If we hadn't moved, I wouldn't have been so lonely. I wouldn't have had to leave my best friend. Who knows? We might have remained friends forever. We could have...

Think Critically About Meaning and Use

A. Read each sentence and the statements that follow. Write *T* if the statement is true or *F* if it is false.

1. I would have reached you if the phone had been working.

   ___F___ **a.** The phone was working.

   _____ **b.** I didn't reach you.

2. I wish I had taken a vacation.

   _____ **a.** I should have taken a vacation.

   _____ **b.** I took a vacation.

3. She wouldn't have taken the medication if she had known about the risks.

   _____ **a.** She knew about the risks.

   _____ **b.** She took the medication.

4. If only I hadn't followed his advice.

   _____ **a.** I didn't follow his advice.

   _____ **b.** I shouldn't have followed his advice.

5. I would have come over, but my car broke down.

   _____ **a.** I couldn't come over because my car broke down.

   _____ **b.** If my car hadn't broken down, I would have come over.

6. If I had been there, I'd have complained to the manager.

   _____ **a.** I complained to the manager.

   _____ **b.** I'd have complained to the manager, but I wasn't there.

7. If we hadn't bought our tickets already, we wouldn't have gone to the show.

   _____ **a.** We had already bought our tickets.

   _____ **b.** We went to the show.

8. If only we'd been told about the delay.

   _____ **a.** No one told us about the delay.

   _____ **b.** I regret that we weren't told about the delay.

B. Discuss these questions in small groups. (Try to come up with three answers, using *would*, *could*, and *might* in each main clause.)

1. **GENERATE** What past unreal conditionals can you think of to explain the wish in sentence 2?

2. **GENERATE** What past unreal conditionals can you think of to explain the if only regrets in sentences 4 and 8?

Edit

Find the errors in these paragraphs and correct them.

Historians love to think about the dramatic "what-ifs" of history. They have even given the name "counterfactual history" to this pursuit. How would history ~~had~~ *have* changed if some key event had been different? What would the consequences been if the weather has been different in a certain battle? What would had happened if a famous person had lived instead of died? These are the sorts of questions that are asked in two recent books that imagine how history might been under different circumstances: *What If?*, edited by R. Cowley and S. Ambrose; and *Virtual History*, edited by N. Ferguson.

Don't just wish you've been alive in a different era. Go back and explore what could have, should have, or might have happened at various times in history. You won't be sorry. You'll wish you'll gone back sooner!

Write

Imagine you are doing a project for a history class. The deadline is in two weeks, but your research isn't going well. Write an email to your instructor expressing regret for the delay and explaining the problems you've had and what you might have done differently. Use past unreal conditionals and at least one past wish or *if only* sentence.

1. **BRAINSTORM** Think about all the problems you've had and what you could have or should have done differently. Then use these categories to help you organize your email into paragraphs:

   - **Opening:** Say why you're writing. Express regret that you will miss the deadline.
   - **Body:** Explain the problems you've encountered. Talk about what you did and how things would have turned out differently if you had done things differently.
   - **Closing:** Make a polite request for an extension. Apologize again, and, if desired, say what you've learned from the experience.

2. **WRITE A FIRST DRAFT** Before you write your first draft, read the checklist below and look at the examples in D2 and D4 on pages 364–365. Write your draft using past unreal conditionals.

3. **EDIT** Read your work and check it against the checklist below. Circle grammar, spelling, and punctuation errors.

DO I ...	YES
organize my ideas into paragraphs?	☐
express regret using a past wish or an *if only* sentence?	☐
use one or more past unreal conditionals to talk about the results you might have had if you had done things differently?	☐
use an unreal future conditional to make a polite request in the closing?	☐

4. **PEER REVIEW** Work with a partner to help you decide how to fix your errors and improve the content. Use the checklist above.

5. **REWRITE YOUR DRAFT** Using the comments from your partner, write a final draft.

From:	Carlos Rivera
To:	Professor Walters
Subject:	Research Project Due March 24th

Dear Professor Walters,

I'm writing to let you know about the problems I'm having with my research project on the mysteries about the Mayans. I wish I had spoken to you earlier, but I'm afraid that I'm not going to be able to meet the deadline…

PART 6
TEST | Conditionals

Choose the correct word or words to complete each sentence.

1. If they had taken better precautions, _____ they have avoided the problems that they later encountered?

   a. could   **b.** will   **c.** may   **d.** must

2. The candidate said very clearly that he _____ cut funding for education under any circumstances if he were governor.

   a. didn't   **b.** wouldn't   **c.** can't   **d.** won't

3. If alternative sources of energy became widely available, how much more money _____ willing to pay for them?

   a. people are   **b.** people would be   **c.** will people be   **d.** would people be

4. I wish _____ start taking better care of yourself.

   a. he'll   **b.** you'll   **c.** you'd   **d.** you'll be able to

Choose the correct response to complete each conversation.

5. **A:** Did you argue with your brother?
   B: Yes, but _____

   a. I wish I hadn't.   **c.** I wish I did.
   b. I wish I had.   **d.** I wish I wouldn't.

6. **A:** What would you have done if you had missed the flight?
   B: _____

   a. I'd canceled the meeting.   **c.** I must have canceled the meeting.
   b. I'd cancel the meeting.   **d.** I'd have canceled the meeting.

7. **A:** I hope the plane lands early.
   B: _____

   a. When did it land?   **c.** I knew it would.
   b. That'd be nice.   **d.** I'm glad it will.

8. **A:** If only I didn't have to work tomorrow.
   B: _____

   a. Why don't you have to work?   **c.** Why do you have to work?
   b. Why did you have to work?   **d.** Why didn't you have to work?

Complete each conversation using the correct form of the word or words in parentheses. Do not use contractions.

9. **A:** She wanted to be an artist, but her father insisted on her studying medicine.

   B: If I'd been in her position, I _____ (refuse).

10. **A:** Kim's neighbors had another loud party last night. She didn't sleep at all.

    B: If it had been me, _____ (call) the police.

11. **A:** I washed my new sweater, and now it's too small.

    B: If it had been my sweater, _____ (take) it to the dry cleaner's.

Complete the question in each conversation using the correct form of the word or words in parentheses.

12. **A:** If your boss had given you the day off, _____ (you/take) it?

    B: Of course, I would have! But, unfortunately, she'd never do that!

13. **A:** _____ (you/bring) that laptop with you if you had had room in your suitcase?

    B: Definitely not. It's Mike's, and I would have worried about losing it.

14. **A:** Would you have bought the house if _____ (you/know) the economy was going to slow down?

    B: Probably not. We like the house, but it's a real struggle to afford it in this economy.

Match the response to the correct statement below.

_____ 15. I forgot to pay the electric bill.

_____ 16. We won the championship!

_____ 17. You should have apologized.

a. If only he'd seen the sign.

b. I wish I had seen the game.

c. You're right. I wish I had.

d. I wish you had waited.

e. If only I'd reminded you.

f. I wish I'd known her better.

What does each sentence express? Choose the correct answer from the box below.

promise	fact	warning	instruction	prediction	advice

18. If the printer runs out of paper, refill it immediately. _____

19. If you come over tomorrow, I'll help you. _____

20. If two hydrogen atoms combine with one oxygen atom, they form a water molecule.

_____

CHAPTER

17

Noun Clauses

A. **GRAMMAR IN DISCOURSE: Career Currents** 372

B. **FORM: Noun Clauses** 374

   Wh- **Clauses**
      He wondered **who I was.**
      Can you tell me **where he is?**

   If/Whether **Clauses**
      I wonder **if he left (or not).**
      Can you tell me **whether he arrived (or not)?**

   That **Clauses**
      I think **(that) he called.**

C. **MEANING AND USE 1:** *Wh-* **and** *If/Whether* **Clauses** ... 379

   Wh- **and** *If/Whether* **Clauses After Mental Activity Verbs**

   Wh- **and** *If/Whether* **Clauses After Other Verbs**

   Indirect Questions

   Vocabulary Notes: *If* **and** *Whether*

D. **MEANING AND USE 2:** *That* **Clauses** 384

   That **Clauses After Mental Activity Verbs**

   Tense Agreement After Mental Activity Verbs

   Exceptions to Tense Agreement Rules

   **WRITING: Write a Frequently Asked Questions
   Page for a Travel Website** 388

Career Currents

A1 Before You Read

Discuss these questions.

What is the best way to find a new job? Would you quit your job before you found a better one? Why or why not?

A2 Read

CD2 T44 Read this article from a website to find out some of the benefits of looking for a new job.

InfoWorld

Career Currents

Even if you're not sure whether you want a new job, it doesn't hurt to look.

Have you ever considered how bad your job has to be before you start looking for a new one?
5 Just how miserable do you have to be? Should you wait until you dread going to work each morning? I recently heard from a reader who was increasingly unhappy with his job and was asking himself these questions.

10 The reader didn't think that his managers treated him with respect. He was beginning to lose his enthusiasm for work. Although he was working toward a master's degree in information systems, he didn't feel that his managers recognized his efforts or his new skills. He wondered whether he should continue at his present job or start to look for a new one.

15 Unlike a lot of questions I receive from readers, this one has an easy answer: He should do both. He should also stop thinking that job hunting and working to improve his current job are opposites. In fact, they're closely related. A traditional job hunt can lead to a new job with a new company. But the steps that you go through to look for a new job can also help you improve your current job.

20   The first step in a job hunt is to find out what opportunities are out there. You learn what kinds of skills and experience are required to get those jobs. You also learn how much these positions pay. Then you update your résumé and begin selling yourself to potential employers in cover letters and interviews.

You may not know if you would actually end up switching jobs. Nevertheless, having an
25   updated résumé is still a good idea because you now have one if you need it, and creating a résumé forces you to think of all that you have accomplished in your current job. When you try to match your résumé to the jobs that are available, you will discover which areas you need more experience in and which skills you need to improve. You will also learn what opportunities are available and what the salaries are. This
30   information could put you in a good position to get a better deal from your current employer if you realize that you are not making enough money.

Try to use what you learn during your job hunt to improve your current position. This may mean that you should present your boss with the results of your salary research and a list of your accomplishments, and then ask for a raise. Or perhaps you should
35   take some classes or find out if you can work on different types of projects to expand your opportunities.

▼

Adapted from *InfoWorld.com*

---

dread: to have feelings of anxiety about something
miserable: extremely unhappy

potential: possible, though not yet actual or real
update: to make something current

A3 After You Read

Check (✓) the advice that is true according to the article.

✓ **1.** It's a good idea to find out about other available jobs even if you're not really thinking about quitting.

_____ **2.** Don't update your résumé.

_____ **3.** Quit your job before you look for a new one.

_____ **4.** Find out the salaries of jobs that are similar to yours before you ask for a raise.

_____ **5.** You can sometimes improve your current job by looking for a new job.

FORM

Noun Clauses

Think Critically About Form

A. Look back at the article on page 372 and complete the tasks below.

1. **IDENTIFY** There are many noun clauses underlined in the article. Find at least three examples of each of these types:
   a. noun clauses beginning with *wh-* words (e.g., *what, how, which*)
   b. noun clauses beginning with *if/whether*
   c. noun clauses beginning with *that*

2. **ANALYZE** Circle the subject and verb in one noun clause of each type. Are they in statement word order or question word order?

B. Discuss your answers with the class and read the Form charts to check them.

▶ Noun Clauses

ONLINE PRACTICE

WH- CLAUSES	
MAIN CLAUSE	**WH- CLAUSE**
He wondered	**who I was.** **what she was wearing.** **why I called.**
Can you tell me	**where he is**? **when the train arrives**? **how they do it**?

IF/WHETHER CLAUSES	
MAIN CLAUSE	**IF/WHETHER CLAUSE**
I wonder	**if he left (or not).**
I don't know	**if he's still here (or not).**
Can you tell me	**whether he arrived (or not)**? **whether (or not) he arrived**? **if he arrived (or not)**?

THAT CLAUSES	
MAIN CLAUSE	**THAT CLAUSE**
I think	**(that) he called.**
Did they doubt	**(that) he would call**?

Noun Clauses

• There are three different types of noun clauses: *wh-* clauses, *if/whether* clauses, and *that* clauses.

- Noun clauses are dependent clauses that can occur in the same place as a noun or noun phrase in a sentence. All noun clauses have a subject and a verb.

Wh- Clauses

- *Wh-* clauses are sometimes called indirect questions or embedded questions. Although *wh-* clauses begin with *wh-* words, they use statement word order.

   I wonder **where he is**.   x I wonder where is he. (INCORRECT)

- Use a question mark only if the main clause is a question.

   <u>Can you tell me</u> **what happened**?

If/Whether Clauses

- *If/whether* clauses are also sometimes called indirect questions or embedded questions. They also use statement word order.

   Do you know **if you're coming with us**?

   x Do you know if are you coming with us? (INCORRECT)

- *Or not* can be added to the end of *if/whether* clauses if the clauses are not very long.

   I wonder **whether she left <u>or not</u>**.   I wonder **if she left <u>or not</u>**.

- *Or not* can also immediately follow *whether*, but it can't follow *if*.

   I wonder **whether <u>or not</u> she left**.   x I wonder if or not she left. (INCORRECT)

That Clauses

- *That* can usually be omitted.

B1 Listening for Form

CD2 T45   Listen to the sentences. Do you hear a *wh-* clause, an *if/whether* clause, or a *that* clause? Check (✓) the correct column.

	WH- CLAUSE	IF/WHETHER CLAUSE	THAT CLAUSE
1.	✓		
2.			
3.			
4.			
5.			
6.			
7.			
8.			

B2 Identifying Noun Clauses

Read this information about résumés. Find the *wh-*, *if/whether*, and *that* noun clauses and underline them. Then circle the verb in the main clause related to each noun clause.

Many employment counselors (believe) that your résumé is a kind of personal advertisement. It summarizes what you have accomplished and describes what kind of work you want. Hopefully, it tells why *you* should be hired. A good résumé doesn't always determine whether you will get an interview, but a bad one will certainly eliminate your chances.

Résumés are only one tool that you need to use in your employment search. Many employers don't even use them; employers often decide whether they should hire you based on other information. Nevertheless, most employment counselors believe that it is worthwhile to write a good résumé. It helps you get organized. Most importantly, it helps you figure out what kind of job you really want and whether or not you have the qualifications.

B3 Working on *Wh-* Clauses

Work with a partner. Complete the noun clauses with the subjects and verbs in parentheses and the correct tense. Then practice the conversations.

1. Person A is looking for Yuki.

   A: Do you know where _____Yuki went_____ (Yuki/go) after lunch?
   1

   B: No, and I don't know what time _____she came back_____ (she/come back).
   2

2. Person A didn't receive any mail.

   A: I wonder why _____ (the mail/not/come) today.
   1

   B: Maybe I'll call the post office and ask what _____ (happen).
   2

   Do you know what time _____ (the post office/close)?
   3

3. Person A needs information about the chemistry exam.

   A: Do you know when _____ (the chemistry exam/be)?
   1

   B: Yes, it's on Thursday, but I'm not sure when _____
   2

   (it/start) or how long _____ (it/last).
   3

4. Person A is in a department store.

   A: I'd like to find out how much _____ (this/cost).
   ₁

   B: I'm not sure, but I'll ask the manager as soon as I find out where

   _____ (he/be).
   ₂

B4 Working on *If/Whether* Clauses

Work with a partner. Use your own words to complete the *if/whether* clauses. Use appropriate tenses depending on the context. Then practice the conversations.

1. Two friends are on the way home from work.

   A: Do you know if the bank _is open now?_ _____
   ₁

   B: I'm not sure if _it is or not._ _____ They've recently changed their hours.
   ₂

2. Person A is getting ready to leave for work.

   A: I wonder whether _____
   ₁

   B: Take your umbrella if you're not sure.

3. Person A is buying groceries.

   A: Can you tell me if _____
   ₁

   B: I'm not sure if _____ or not. I'll ask the manager.
   ₂

4. Person A is buying tickets for a concert.

   A: I was wondering if you could tell me whether _____
   ₁

   B: There aren't any seats left on that date. Should I check whether

   _____
   ₂

5. Person A needs to put gas in his car.

   A: Do you know if _____ near here?
   ₁

   B: I'm not certain if _____. Maybe you should ask
   ₂

   someone else.

6. Person A is planning a weekend trip.

   A: I wonder if _____ this weekend.
   ₁

   B: I didn't see the weather forecast, so I don't know whether

   _____ or not.
   ₂

B5 Unscrambling Sentences with *That* Clauses

Work with a partner. Unscramble the words to make a statement or a question with a *that* clause. Use every word. The first word of each sentence is underlined for you. *That* has been omitted from some of the sentences.

1. was/that/you/he/angry/notice/<u>did</u>

   Did you notice that he was angry?

2. predict/it/soon/happen/<u>they</u>/will

   _____

3. help/<u>I</u>/some/need/I/that/guess

   _____

4. that/due/remembered/my/is/rent/<u>I</u>/tomorrow

   _____

5. proved/could/<u>he</u>/do/it/he

   _____

B6 Completing Noun Clauses

A. Use the questions in parentheses to complete each main clause. You may have to add *if* or *whether* at the beginning of some noun clauses.

1. I was wondering _what experience you have._

   (What experience do you have?)

2. Could you tell me _____

   (How long did you work there?)

3. I was wondering _____

   (Did you like your job?)

4. Can you tell me _____

   (What is your greatest strength?)

5. Could you explain _____

   (Why are you changing jobs?)

B. Work with a partner. Pretend you are at a job interview. Take turns asking and answering the questions in part A.

Wh- and *If/Whether* Clauses

Think Critically About Meaning and Use

A. Read the sentences and complete the tasks below.

1a. Sally: I can't decide what I need for the trip. Did you get everything on your list?
1b. Pam: I don't know whether I did or not. I lost my list. I wonder if it's in the car.
2a. Excuse me. Is the bus late?
2b. Excuse me. Can you tell me if the bus is late?

1. **IDENTIFY** Underline the noun clauses in sentences 1a and 1b. Circle the verb that comes before each clause. Which verbs express mental activities?

2. **EVALUATE** Which question sounds more polite, 2a or 2b?

B. Discuss your answers with the class and read the Meaning and Use Notes to check them.

Meaning and Use Notes

ONLINE PRACTICE

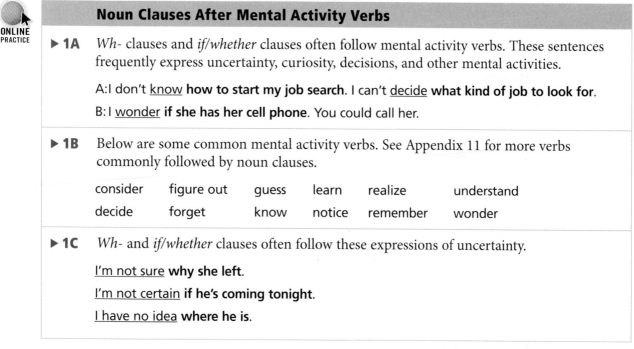

Noun Clauses After Mental Activity Verbs

▶ 1A *Wh-* clauses and *if/whether* clauses often follow mental activity verbs. These sentences frequently express uncertainty, curiosity, decisions, and other mental activities.

A: I don't <u>know</u> **how to start my job search**. I can't <u>decide</u> **what kind of job to look for**.

B: I <u>wonder</u> **if she has her cell phone**. You could call her.

▶ 1B Below are some common mental activity verbs. See Appendix 11 for more verbs commonly followed by noun clauses.

consider	figure out	guess	learn	realize	understand
decide	forget	know	notice	remember	wonder

▶ 1C *Wh-* and *if/whether* clauses often follow these expressions of uncertainty.

<u>I'm not sure</u> **why she left**.

<u>I'm not certain</u> **if he's coming tonight**.

<u>I have no idea</u> **where he is**.

(Continued on page 380)

Wh- and If/Whether Clauses After Other Verbs

▶ 2 Many other verbs and phrases are commonly followed by *wh-* and *if/whether* clauses.

ask	depend on	hear	rely on	see	tell (someone)
demonstrate	explain	notice	say	show	write

Indirect Questions

▶ 3A *Wh-* or *if/whether* clauses often follow certain phrases to express indirect questions. Indirect questions sound more polite than *Wh-* questions or *Yes/No* questions.

Direct Questions	**Indirect Questions**
When does the train arrive?	Can you (please) tell me **when the train arrives**?
	I was wondering **when the train arrives**.
Has the train arrived yet?	Do you know **if the train has arrived yet**?
	I'd like to find out **if the train has arrived ye**t.

▶ 3B Below are some common expressions used to introduce indirect questions.

Do you know…?	Do you remember…?
Can/Could you tell me…?	Do you have any idea…?
Can you remember…?	I'd like to know/find out…
Could you explain…?	I wonder/was wondering…

C1 Listening for Meaning and Use

▶ Notes 1A, 3A, 3B

CD2 T46 Listen to these situations. Choose the sentence that most appropriately follows what you hear.

1. **a.** Yes, it is.
   b. Yes, around eight.

2. **a.** So was I. Let's ask him.
   b. No, I don't.

3. **a.** Yes, she works.
   b. No, I don't.

4. **a.** I wonder who.
   b. I wonder why.

5. **a.** It did.
   b. I did.

6. **a.** Yes. It's over there.
   b. Yes. I know it.

7. **a.** In room 2.
   b. Sure. Let me look it up.

8. **a.** Yes. Be patient.
   b. It certainly is.

Work with a partner. Imagine you are witnesses at the scene of a traffic accident. Take turns asking and answering the police officer's questions. Use a *wh-* clause and a statement of uncertainty: *I can't remember, I'm not sure, I don't know, I'm not certain, I have no idea.*

1. Who was driving the truck?

   I'm not sure who was driving it.

2. What time did the accident occur?

3. What did the truck look like?

4. How many people were in the truck?

5. What was the license plate number on the truck?

6. How fast was the truck going?

7. What color was the truck?

8. What did the driver look like?

Vocabulary Notes

If and *Whether*

If and *whether* have the same meaning when they begin noun clauses. They are both found in informal situations, but *whether* is probably more common in formal situations.

I don't know **if she's at home**.   I don't know **whether she's at home**.

We often add *or not* to *if/whether* clauses if the clauses are not very long. In *if clauses*, *or not* goes at the end of the clause. In *whether* clauses, *or not* can appear in two positions.

I don't know **if she's at home or not**.   I don't know **whether or not she's at home**.
     I don't know **whether she's at home or not**.

C3 Adding *If/Whether* Clauses to Expressions of Uncertainty

A. Work with a partner. Read each situation and complete the sentences with an *if/whether* clause in the correct tense. Add *or not* to some of your noun clauses.

1. This is the first day of Sheila's new job. She's nervous on her way to work.

   a. She wonders *if she'll like her new job.*

   b. She's not sure _____

   c. She has no idea _____

2. Min-woo has seen the house of his dreams. He's going to make an offer to buy it tonight. He's been worrying about it all day.

   a. He wonders _____

   b. He doesn't know _____

   c. He's not sure _____

B. Work on your own. Think of a situation in which you did something for the first time and you were uncertain about it. Make a list of some of the problems you had. Then write a paragraph explaining your uncertainty in detail. Use some statements of uncertainty followed by *if/whether* clauses.

Before I moved to France, I had a lot of decisions to make. I wasn't sure whether I should sell my furniture or not. I wondered if it would be cheaper to buy new furniture after I arrived in France. However, I was surprised when I found out how much new furniture costs.

C4 Asking Indirect Questions with *If/Whether* Clauses

▶ Notes 3A, 3B

Work with a partner. Make each question less direct by using *I was wondering, Can/Could you (please) tell me, Do you know,* or *Do you have any idea* + an *if/whether* clause.

1. Did you have any trouble with the last assignment?

   I was wondering if you had any trouble with the last assignment.

2. Is the library closed during vacation?

3. Is the teacher going to show a film today?

4. Is the assignment due tomorrow?

5. Is the new language lab open yet?

6. Did I miss anything important yesterday?

C5 Asking Indirect Questions with *Wh-* Clauses

▶ Notes 3A, 3B

Work with a partner. Make up a polite question for each situation, using a *wh-* clause. Take turns asking and answering each question.

1. *At the airport*

   a. You're looking for a restroom.

      A: *Excuse me. Can you please tell me where the restroom is?*

      B: *It's downstairs on the left.*

   b. You're looking for the baggage claim.

2. *At a bus stop*

   a. You're asking someone for the time.

   b. You're looking for the bus schedule.

3. *In a department store*

   a. You're asking a salesperson the price of a shirt.

   b. You're asking a salesperson the size of a pair of pants.

4. *In the supermarket*

   a. You're looking for the manager.

   b. You're asking the clerk for the price of broccoli.

5. *On campus*

   a. You're looking for the history department.

   b. You want to pay your tuition bill.

D1 Listening for Meaning and Use

▶ Notes 2A–2D

 CD2 T47 Listen to these situations. Choose the sentence that most appropriately follows.

1. **a.** I hope she's on time.

   b. I hope she was on time.

2. **a.** I think it's Joan. I'll go find out.

   b. I thought it was Joan. I'll go find out.

3. **a.** Why did he leave?

   b. Why doesn't he leave?

4. **a.** How much did you buy?

   b. How much will you buy?

5. **a.** Yes, he was right.

   b. Good for him.

6. **a.** She was.

   b. She is.

D2 Thinking About Tense Agreement with *That* Clauses

▶ Notes 2A–2D

A. Complete the sentences by circling all of the phrases that can form grammatical sentences.

1. I thought it (is snowing/ was going to snow / snowed) in the mountains last night.

2. He doubts that (they'll accept / they accept / they accepted) credit cards.

3. I hoped my plane (won't be / wouldn't be / isn't) late.

4. I left the game early because I assumed our team (will win / had won / wins) the championship.

5. She decided that she (needs / needed / will need) help.

6. He's certain that the show (will start / starts / started) at 8:00.

B. Choose two of the grammatical sentences from part A and write two short dialogues using the sentences in appropriate contexts.

A: We can't ski today.

B: You're kidding. I thought it was going to snow in the mountains last night. I'm so disappointed.

D3 Giving Opinions Using *That* Clauses

▶ Notes 1A, 1B, 2A

A. Work in small groups. Take turns expressing your own opinions about each statement. Use as many mental activity verbs as you can with that clauses.

1. Our community could be doing more to protect the environment.

   I agree that we're not doing enough for the environment. I think...

2. Most people are basically honest.

3. Hybrid cars are a good idea.

4. You can't really change someone.

5. All children should leave home at 18.

6. We learn from our mistakes.

B. On your own, make up two more statements. Read them aloud and ask your group to give opinions using mental activity verbs.

D4 Expressing Opinions About Work

▶ Notes 1A–1C

A. Read these survey results on job satisfaction in the United States. Do people in your country have the same concerns? Discuss your ideas with a partner.

U.S. Workers find some major problems in the workplace.
In a survey of 1,000 adults it was found that:

95%	are concerned about spending more time with their family.
92%	don't have enough flexibility in their schedules to take care of family needs.
88%	are concerned about work-related stress.
87%	say they don't get enough sleep.
60%	would take training courses if they were paid for by the employer.
49%	believe on-site child care is important, but only 12% of employers offer this benefit.
46%	work more than 40 hours per week: 18% work more than 50 hours per week.
45%	had to work overtime with little or no advance notice.
44%	think the opportunity to telecommute is important, but only 17% of employers offer telecommuting opportunities.

from U.S. Newswire

B. How do you feel about the workers' concerns in part A? Use the mental activity verbs below and that clauses to organize your ideas. Then discuss with a partner.

I think/believe/agree that…   I don't believe/think that…
I feel/imagine/suppose that…   I doubt that…
It appears/seems that…   I hope/expect that…

I agree that most workers want to spend more time with their families.

Think Critically About Meaning and Use

A. Read each sentence and the statement that follows. Write *T* if the statement is true, *F* if it is false, and *?* if you do not have enough information to decide.

1. I regret that Mary left.

___F___ Mary is going to leave.

2. I think she passed the test.

_____ She passed the test.

3. I'm not sure who rang the bell.

_____ Someone rang the bell.

4. She realized how late it was.

_____ She didn't know if it was late.

5. I wonder whether they left or not.

_____ They didn't leave.

6. She doubts that she will come tonight.

_____ She doesn't think she'll come.

7. He regretted that he left early.

_____ He wasn't sorry that he left early.

8. We assumed they had won.

_____ They won.

B. Discuss these questions in small groups.

1. **GENERATE** How would you change the statements that follow 1 and 7 to make them true?

2. **SYNTHESIZE** How would you complete the following sentence so that it means the same as 8:

We supposed _____ (win), but _____ (not/know) for sure.

Edit

Find the errors in these sentences and correct them.

1. I wonder where ~~is he~~ *he is*.

2. I asked her if could borrow her pen.

3. I thought that she is sleeping when I called.

4. I can't remember who called?

5. Do you know if are you coming with us?

6. I didn't realize, that she was absent.

7. She thought he will come later.

8. Do you know if or not he's staying?

9. I need John's phone number, but I don't know where the phone book.

10. Frederica didn't understand what was saying the teacher.

Write

Imagine you write for the website of your country's national tourist organization. Write a Frequently Asked Questions (FAQs) page addressing the concerns that a first-time visitor to your country might have. Use mental activity verbs and noun clauses of different types.

1. **BRAINSTORM** Think of all the things a first-time visitor to your country might want to know about. Use some or all of these categories to organize your FAQ page.

- travel documents and shots
- best season(s) to travel
- sights and activities
- local food to eat
- accommodation
- transportation

2. **WRITE A FIRST DRAFT** Before you write your first draft, read the checklist below and look at the way noun clauses and indirect questions are used on pages 374–375 and 380. Write your draft using noun clauses.

3. **EDIT** Read your work and check it against the checklist below. Circle grammar, spelling, and punctuation errors.

DO I ...	YES
add a paragraph at the beginning to introduce the FAQs?	☐
use a range of mental activity and other verbs that are usually followed by noun clauses?	☐
use at least one example of a *wh-* clause, an *if/whether* clause, and a *that* clause?	☐
take care to use statement word order in indirect questions?	☐

4. **PEER REVIEW** Work with a partner to help you decide how to fix your errors and improve the content. Use the checklist above.

5. **REWRITE YOUR DRAFT** Using the comments from your partner, write a final draft.

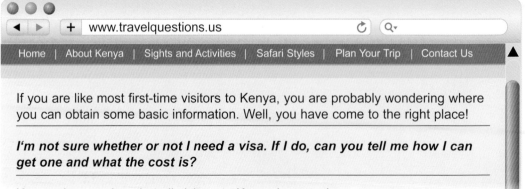

www.travelquestions.us

Home | About Kenya | Sights and Activities | Safari Styles | Plan Your Trip | Contact Us

If you are like most first-time visitors to Kenya, you are probably wondering where you can obtain some basic information. Well, you have come to the right place!

I'm not sure whether or not I need a visa. If I do, can you tell me how I can get one and what the cost is?

Kenyan law requires that all visitors to Kenya have a visa...

CHAPTER

18

Reported Speech

A. GRAMMAR IN DISCOURSE: Doctor-Patient Relationship in Critical Condition 392

B. FORM: Reported Speech 394

Statements
She says **(that) the report is on her desk.**

Yes/No **Questions**
He asked **if I was staying.**

Information Questions
I asked **where she had gone.**

Imperatives
He told me **to press the green button.**

Present Tense Reporting
Joe says (that) **it's raining.**

Past Tense Reporting
I said (that) **I needed a vacation.**

Vocabulary Notes: *Tell*, *Say*, and *Ask*

C. MEANING AND USE: Reported Speech 399

The Reporter's Point of View

Tense Changes

Keeping the Same Tense

Pronoun and Possessive Adjective Changes

Adverb Changes

Vocabulary Notes: More Reporting Verbs

WRITING: Write a Complaint 407

PART 7 TEST: Noun Clauses and Reported Speech 410

Doctor-Patient Relationship in Critical Condition

A1 Before You Read

Discuss these questions.

What are some qualities of a good doctor? Have you ever been to a doctor that you didn't like? What were the problems?

A2 Read

CD2 T48 Read this magazine article to find out what happens when doctors and patients don't communicate well.

Doctor-Patient Relationship
in Critical Condition

Have you ever walked out of the doctor's office feeling frustrated? Did you understand what the doctor said? Did your doctor understand what you said?

5   Concerns about doctor-patient communication are as important as health problems themselves. Like most other interpersonal relationships, success greatly depends on effective communication

10 between doctors and patients. But what if communication fails?

In a study at the Mayo Clinic, patients were asked to fill out a detailed questionnaire right after they had

15 completed a comprehensive medical examination. The survey asked patients to list their most serious health problems, according to their recent examination. At the same time, their physicians were

20 asked what health problems they had discussed with each patient. More than half of the patients did not know what their doctors considered to be their most important health problems. For example,

25 when physicians reported that cholesterol was a major concern, only 45 percent of those patients reported that they had such problems. Similarly, although doctors said their patients were suffering from obesity,

30 high blood pressure, or certain heart problems, 73 percent of the patients didn't report that they had an obesity problem, 62 percent didn't say they had high blood pressure, and 48 percent never

35 said that there was concern about their heart. The survey concludes that patients often misunderstand their doctors. It also proposes that doctors may be missing the most important concerns of

40 their patients.

The results suggest very clearly that doctors and patients both need to make improvements. First of all, during a discussion, doctors need to make sure to

45 establish eye contact with their patients and frequently ask them <u>if they understand</u>. Doctors should also stop and periodically ask whether there are any questions, and at the end of the visit, they

50 should summarize the discussion in simple terms. Experts suggest that doctors limit their use of medical jargon as much as possible.

Patients also have a lot of work to do.

55 Experts tell patients to plan their visits to the doctor very carefully. They urge making a list of questions, symptoms, and any other concerns, in order of importance, if possible. For example, if

60 there are several issues to discuss, they recommend that patients concentrate on the questions that are most important first. Many doctors complain that too often patients wait until the end of the

65 visit before bringing up important information. In other words, don't mention the wart on your finger before you tell your doctor that you have been experiencing chest pains. And don't be

70 embarrassed about certain issues. Research shows that no matter how embarrassing your problem may be, your doctor has probably dealt with it before.

Perhaps the research confirms

75 something that you have already noticed: the authoritarian doctor and passive patient relationship no longer seems to work. It needs to be replaced by a partnership based more on careful

80 planning, good communication, and shared decision making. In fact, your life may depend on it.

---

authoritarian: demanding that people do exactly what you tell them to do

cholesterol: a substance found in the cells of the body that helps to carry fats

concern: a worry or a matter of importance

critical: very serious or dangerous

jargon: the special language of a profession or trade

obesity: the condition of being very fat

passive: accepting what happens without questioning it

wart: a small, hard, dry growth on the skin caused by a virus

A3 After You Read

Check (✓) the suggestions that would be appropriate for either doctors or patients to follow.

___✓___ **1.** Make sure the discussion is summarized at the end of the visit.

_____ **2.** Learn more medical jargon.

_____ **3.** Plan visits carefully.

_____ **4.** Don't discuss embarrassing issues.

_____ **5.** Don't ask a lot of questions.

_____ **6.** Try to improve your communication skills.

B FORM

Reported Speech

Think Critically About Form

A. Look back at the article on page 392 and complete the tasks below.

1. **IDENTIFY** Examine the underlined examples of reported speech clauses. Each one follows a reporting verb in a main clause. Circle the reporting verb related to each example.

2. **CATEGORIZE** Which underlined reported speech clause is a *wh-* clause? a *that* clause? an *if/whether* clause? an infinitive?

3. **RECOGNIZE** Find other examples of reported speech in the third paragraph (lines 12–40). What reporting verbs are used?

B. Discuss your answers with the class and read the Form charts to check them.

▶ **Overview**

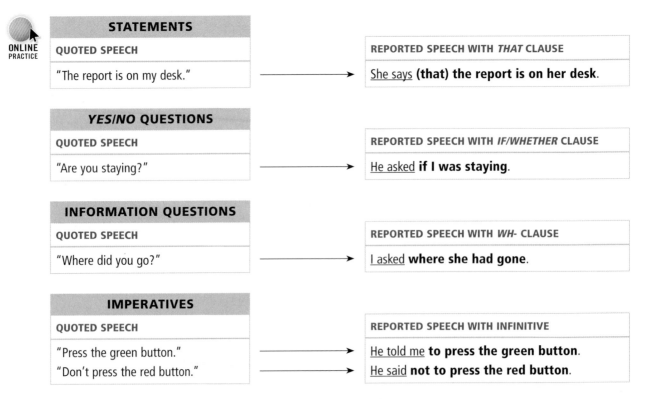

ONLINE PRACTICE

STATEMENTS	
QUOTED SPEECH	REPORTED SPEECH WITH *THAT* CLAUSE
"The report is on my desk."	She says **(that) the report is on her desk**.

YES/NO QUESTIONS	
QUOTED SPEECH	REPORTED SPEECH WITH *IF/WHETHER* CLAUSE
"Are you staying?"	He asked **if I was staying**.

INFORMATION QUESTIONS	
QUOTED SPEECH	REPORTED SPEECH WITH *WH-* CLAUSE
"Where did you go?"	I asked **where she had gone**.

IMPERATIVES	
QUOTED SPEECH	REPORTED SPEECH WITH INFINITIVE
"Press the green button."	He told me **to press the green button**.
"Don't press the red button."	He said **not to press the red button**.

▶ Present Tense Reporting

QUOTED SPEECH		REPORTED SPEECH WITH *THAT* CLAUSE	
"It**'s raining**."	⟶		it's raining.
"It**'s going to rain**."	⟶	Joe **says** (that)	it's going to rain.
"It **rained**."	⟶		it rained.

▶ Past Tense Reporting

QUOTED SPEECH		REPORTED SPEECH WITH *THAT* CLAUSE	
"I **need** a vacation."	⟶		I **needed** a vacation.
"I**'m working**."	⟶		I **was working**.
"I **left** early."	⟶		I**'d left** early.
"I**'ve finished**."	⟶		I**'d finished**.
"I**'ll see** you later."	⟶		I **would see** you later.
"I**'m going to win**."	⟶		I **was going to win**.
"I **can win**."	⟶	I **said** (that)	I **could win**.
"I **may leave**."	⟶		I **might leave**.
"I **have to try**."	⟶		I **had to try**.
"I **must take** a vacation."	⟶		I **had to take** a vacation.
"I **should stay**."	⟶		I **should stay**.
"I **ought to stay**."	⟶		I **ought to stay**.
"I **could stay**."	⟶		I **could stay**.

Reported Speech

- Reported speech (also called indirect speech) has a reporting verb in the main clause (for example, *say* or *ask*) followed by a noun clause or an infinitive.
- See the Vocabulary Notes on page 402 and Appendix 12 for a list of more reporting verbs.
- Reported speech often differs from quoted speech (also called direct speech) in tense, pronouns, and adverbs.
- Reported speech has no quotation marks or question marks.
- See Appendix 13 for punctuation rules for quoted speech.

(Continued on page 396)

Present Tense Reporting

- If the reporting verb (for example, *say*) is in the present tense, the tense in the *that* clause does not change from the tense of the original quotation.

Past Tense Reporting

- If the reporting verb is in the past tense (for example, *said*), the tense in the *that* clause often changes to a past form.
- The modals *should*, *ought to*, and *could* do not change forms in reported speech.

B1 Listening for Form

CD2 T49   Listen to these sentences and choose the clause that you hear.

1. **a.** that he didn't know

   b. if he didn't know

2. **a.** if he wanted some books

   b. if he wants some books

3. **a.** that I'd call him back on Monday

   b. I'd call him back on Monday

4. **a.** could I call on Tuesday instead

   b. if I could call on Tuesday instead

5. **a.** what he was doing on Monday night

   b. what was he doing on Monday night

6. **a.** he can't tell me yet

   b. that he couldn't tell me yet

7. **a.** if everything was OK

   b. is everything OK

8. **a.** I shouldn't worry

   b. not to worry

B2 Identifying Reported Speech

Underline all the examples of reported speech in these conversations. Circle the reporting verb in each sentence. What other reporting verbs besides *tell*, *ask*, and *say* did you find?

1. **A:** I don't think that the new manager is doing a good job.

   B: Me neither. He told me to come in early yesterday, and he forgot to show up.

   A: You're kidding. Julia said the same thing happened to her on Tuesday. I wonder whether we should complain to Allison. She hired him.

   B: I'm not sure if we should say anything yet. I asked Tom what he thought. He said that we should wait one more week.

2. **A:** Did you hear the news? Channel 7 reported that the superintendent just resigned.

B: I know. I wonder if something happened. Everyone says he was pleased with the way things were going.

A: Yesterday's news mentioned that he hadn't been feeling well lately. Maybe it's something serious and his doctor told him to resign.

3. **A:** Did you speak to the travel agent?

B: Yes. I asked whether I needed to change the flight. He admitted that he'd made a mistake, but he said that he would take care of it. He assured me that everything would work out.

A: Let's hope so. I told you to be careful during the holiday season. They're so busy that they often make mistakes.

Vocabulary Notes

Tell, *Say*, and *Ask*

Tell is used to report statements. It is followed by a noun or pronoun and a *that* clause. This noun or pronoun refers to the original listener.

> He **told me** that he was late.   I **told Julia** I'd be there soon.

Say is also used to report statements. Unlike *tell*, it is not followed by a noun or pronoun.

> He **said** that he was late.   x He said me that he was late. (INCORRECT)

Ask is used to report questions. It can be followed by a noun or pronoun. *Say* and *tell* are not used to report questions.

> She **asked** if it was time to leave.   She **asked him** if it was time to leave.
>
> x She said if it was time to leave. (INCORRECT)

Tell, *say*, and *ask* are used to report imperatives.

> He **told me** to go.   He **said** to go.   He **asked me** to go.

B3 Building Sentences with *Tell*, *Say*, and *Ask*

Build as many meaningful sentences as possible. You may omit the second or third column in some of your sentences. Punctuate your sentences correctly.

He asked them if it was raining.

he asked		if	leave early
I said	them	that	it was raining
she told		to	I had called earlier

B4 Restating Questions with Reported Speech

A. List questions people might ask when they first meet you.

1. *What's your name?*   4. _____

2. _____   5. _____

3. _____   6. _____

B. Use your questions to complete these sentences.

1. People often ask me *what my name is.* _____

2. They also ask me _____

3. They usually want to know _____

4. They sometimes want to know _____

5. Someone typically asks _____

6. Some people even ask _____

B5 Reporting Statements, Questions, and Imperatives

Work with a partner. Read this conversation between a doctor and his patient. Report what each person said, using the verbs *asked*, *said*, and *told*. Change tenses and pronouns where appropriate.

1. **Patient:** How long do I have to stay home from work?

   Doctor: Stay home for a couple of days.

   The patient asked how long she had to stay home from work.

   The doctor said to stay home for a couple of days. OR

   The doctor told her to stay home for a couple of days.

2. **Patient:** Can I have a copy of the test results?

   Doctor: The lab is sending one.

3. **Patient:** How often should I take the medicine?

   Doctor: Don't take it more than three times a day.

4. **Patient:** Do I need to come back?

   Doctor: That won't be necessary unless there's a problem.

5. **Patient:** I need to be better by the weekend.

   Doctor: Why?

6. **Patient:** I'm going out of town for a few days.

   Doctor: You'll be fine. Get lots of sleep.

Reported Speech

Think Critically About Meaning and Use

A. Read the sentences and answer the questions below.

    a. Emily said she has a headache. She needs to rest.
    b. Emily said she'd had a headache. It was very painful.
    c. Emily said she had a headache. Don't disturb her.

    1. ANALYZE In which two sentences does Emily still have a headache?

    2. ANALYZE In which sentence is Emily's headache gone?

B. Discuss your answers with the class and read the Meaning and Use Notes to check them.

Meaning and Use Notes

ONLINE PRACTICE

The Reporter's Point of View

▶ **1** Reported speech is used to tell what someone has said or written. It expresses the same meaning as quoted speech, but it expresses the speech from the reporter's point of view rather than from the original speaker's point of view.

Quoted Speech **(Speaker's Point of View)**	**Reported Speech** **(Reporter's Point of View)**
"**I'm having** a great time." ⟶	He said he **was having** a great time.

Tense Changes

▶ **2** The tense in the noun clause may change to a past form if the reporting verb is in the past tense. This tense change usually depends on whether the reporter thinks of the quoted sentences as part of the past.

Quoted Speech	**Past Tense Report**
Alice: **How are** you? ⟶	Alice asked Barbara how she **was**.
Barbara: **I'm** fine. ⟶	Barbara said she **was** fine.

(Continued on page 400)

Keeping the Same Tense

▶ **3A** There are several reasons why the reporter may *not* change the reported speech to a past tense. If the quoted speech just happened, the reporter often keeps the same tense because the time has not changed very much.

Quoted Speech	Immediate Reports (with Tense Unchanged)
"**I'm going out** for a while." A: What did she say? ⟶	She said she**'s going** out for a while. (This sentence was spoken only a few seconds after the first speaker's sentence.)
"Flight 403 **has arrived** at gate 9." A: What did the announcement say? ⟶	It said that flight 403 **has arrived** at gate 9. (This sentence was spoken only a few seconds after the announcement.)

▶ **3B** If the reporter wants to show that the quoted speech is a generalization that is always true, the present tense is used.

Quoted Speech	Generalizations (with Tense Unchanged)
"We **don't accept** checks." ⟶	The manager told me that the store **doesn't accept** checks. (The statement is true all the time, not just when the manager spoke.)

▶ **3C** If the event in the quoted speech hasn't happened yet, the future is often used.

Quoted Speech	Future Events (with Tense Unchanged)
"I **am going to appoint** a new judge next week." ⟶	The president announced that she **is going to appoint** a new judge next week. (The event hasn't happened yet.)

Pronoun and Possessive Adjective Changes

▶ **4A** Personal pronouns and possessive adjectives often change to represent the reporter's point of view, instead of the original speaker's point of view.

Quoted Speech	Reported Speech
"**I** need a vacation." ⟶	He said **he** needed a vacation.
"Please take **your** book." ⟶	She told me to take **my** book.
"I like **your** hat." ⟶	I said I liked **his** hat.

► **4B** The words can stay the same when the reporter is repeating his or her own words.

Quoted Speech	Reported Speech
"I can't find **my** keys." ⟶	<u>I said</u> I can't find **my** keys.

Adverb Changes

► **5** Adverbs of time (e.g., *today*, *yesterday*) and place (e.g., *here*, *there*) may change depending on the time of the reported speech and the location of the reporter. They change when the reporter's point of view is different from the speaker's.

Quoted Speech	Reported Speech
"I'll call you **tomorrow**." ⟶	He said he would call me **the next day**.
⟶	He said he'd call me **on Monday**.
⟶	He said he'll call me **tomorrow**.
"I'll be **here** until 6:00 P.M." ⟶	He said he'd be **there** until 6:00 P.M.
⟶	He said he'll be **here** until 6:00 P.M.

C1 Listening for Meaning and Use ▶ Notes 1–5

CD2 T50 Listen to the reported speech. Then choose the quoted speech that most closely expresses the meaning of the reported speech.

1. **a.** "Do you need a prescription?"
   b. "Do I need a prescription? ⟲

2. **a.** "She has a headache."
   b. "She had a headache."

3. **a.** "I called when I got the results."
   b. "I'll call when I get the results."

4. **a.** "When did the results come?"
   b. "When will the results come?"

5. **a.** "They had come the next day."
   b. "They'll come tomorrow."

6. **a.** "You missed your last appointment."
   b. "You'd miss your last appointment."

7. **a.** "Your ankle is sprained."
   b. "My ankle is sprained."

8. **a.** "We'd call back that day."
   b. "We'll call back today."

Vocabulary Notes

More Reporting Verbs

Although *say*, *tell*, and *ask* are the most common reporting verbs, there are many others.

Verbs Like *Tell* These verbs are followed by a noun or pronoun and a *that* clause. The noun or pronoun refers to the original listener.

assure	convince	inform	notify	persuade	remind

He **assured me** (that) he had an appointment at three o'clock.

The president **informed the Congress** (that) he was going to form a special committee.

Verbs Like *Say* The following verbs may be used without mentioning the original listener.

admit	complain	indicate	remark	shout
announce	confess	mention	reply	state
comment	explain	point out	report	swear

He **complained** it was too late.   I **explained** that I'd be there soon.

I **admitted** that I'd made a mistake.   She **replied** that she was pleased.

Note that if the original listener is mentioned, *to* is needed.

He **admitted** <u>to me</u> that he was sorry.

See Appendix 12 for a list of more reporting verbs.

C2 Understanding Reported Verbs

Circle the word that best completes the meaning of each sentence.

Kenji left school yesterday. He (**said** / told) that he couldn't complete the semester.
1
He (informed / explained) me that he had fallen behind in all of his courses. He
2
(assured / confessed) that he hadn't attended two of his courses for over a month. I
3
was shocked. He (reminded / explained) that he'd been looking for a job instead of
4
going to classes. I (told / asked) him if he could go to school part-time instead of
5
quitting. He (replied / persuaded) that it was too late. I (said / advised) him to speak
6   7
to his advisor. He (convinced / promised) that he would, but then he just left town.
8

When I spoke to one of his friends the next day, she (told / asked) me that Kenji
9
had (admitted / told) to her that he had found the work very difficult.
10

C3 Reporting Messages

▶ Notes 1, 2, 4A, 5

Today is Thursday, March 23. Your friend in the hospital has asked you to listen to and report back the messages on his answering machine at home. The messages are from March 20 to 23. Change each message to reported speech using appropriate verb tenses, pronouns, and adverbs.

1. *Monday, March 20*

    a. "This is Nora Green. Please call me back."

    Nora Green called on Monday. She said to call her back. OR
    She asked you to call her back.

    b. "This is Joe's Repair Shop. Call us back. We will be here until 6:00 P.M."

2. *Tuesday, March 21*

    a. "This is Bob. I'll call back later."

    b. "My name is Richard Smith. I'd like to speak to you about an insurance policy. My number is 555-1221."

3. *Wednesday, March 22*

    a. "This is Rosa. I'm just calling to say hello."

    b. "This is Stuart Lee. I've been calling for several days. Is anything wrong? Please call me back soon."

4. *Thursday, March 23*

    a. "This is Eric Martin. Where are you? I have some questions."

    b. "This is Gibson's. We'll be able to deliver the desk you ordered on Monday, March 27."

    c. "This is Tanya. I'm sorry I haven't called. I should have called sooner."

C4 Reporting a News Item

▶ Notes 2, 3A–3C, 4

A. Read this recent news item. Write three or four sentences explaining it, using reported speech. Think about the meaning of the article. Is the situation part of the present or past? How does that affect the tenses used in your report?

A recent news article reported that schools have begun...

News

Medical Schools Stress Communication

Medical schools have begun to put communication skills into the curriculum. "The time has come," says a spokesman for the Medical Association, "to focus more on doctor-patient communication."

The public seems to agree. According to the latest Smith Public Opinion Poll, "the best doctors talk with their patients. They encourage questions, they explain procedures, and they discuss alternatives. They also know how to listen. Sometimes they even use humor."

As a result, first-year medical students are spending more time speaking and listening in retirement homes, homeless shelters, soup kitchens, and other community agencies. Back in the classroom, they're discussing what kinds of communication skills they need to treat these patients. They're learning how to interact with patients in a variety of situations, instead of just studying diseases.

B. Compare your sentences with a partner's and discuss any differences you find.

Vocabulary Notes

Reporting Verbs Used for Advising

Base Form in *That* Clauses When the verbs below are followed by a *that* clause, they are often used to tell someone to do something. To express this meaning, the verb in the *that* clause is always in the base form, even if the main clause is in the past.

advise	ask	demand	insist	propose	recommend	suggest

I recommend (that) he stay. **They suggest** (that) she take a vacation.

I recommended (that) he stay. **They suggested** (that) she take a vacation.

Should in *That* Clauses with *Say/Tell* With the verbs *say* and *tell*, *should* is often used in a *that* clause to tell someone to do something. Remember that *say* and *tell* can also occur with an infinitive to express the same meaning. However, *say* and *tell* do not occur in the base form pattern of the verbs like *advise* above.

Doctor: Don't eat any spicy foods for a few days.

Patient: The doctor **said/told me that I shouldn't eat** any spicy foods for a few days.

The doctor **said/told me not to eat** any spicy foods for a few days.

C5 Reporting Advice

A. Maria is a 30-year-old elementary school teacher. She is thinking about finding a new career. Her family and friends have given her a lot of different advice. Complete each sentence by reporting each person's advice with an infinitive, a clause with *should*, or a clause with the base form of the verb.

1. Maria's friend told her __not to quit__ __her job until she knows what she__ __wants to do.__

Don't quit your job until you know what you want to do.

Go to an employment agency.

She also recommended that _____

_____

_____

2. Her husband suggested _____

_____

_____

He also advised _____

_____

_____

Think about getting another degree.

If I were you, I'd find out about different types of graduate programs.

3. Her grandmother proposed _____

_____

_____

She also said _____

_____

_____

Quit your job and have a baby.

Try to teach part-time instead of full-time.

4. Her father insisted _____

_____

_____

He also advised _____

_____

_____

Don't quit. Just take a leave of absence for a year.

Ask for a raise before you do anything else.

5. Her aunt suggested _____

_____

_____

She also said _____

_____

_____

Ask to teach a different grade next year.

Do whatever makes you happy!

B. Work in small groups. First, discuss what parents and other family members used to tell you to do when you were growing up. Use reported speech and try to include different types of reporting verbs such as *suggest, insist, demand, advise*, and so on.

My father always insisted that I be on time.
He said that I shouldn't keep people waiting.

C. Write a paragraph describing one of your examples in more detail.

Punctuality was important to my father. He always insisted that I be on time. He said that I shouldn't keep people waiting. He even suggested that I wake up 15 minutes earlier than necessary in the morning in order to be prepared for anything that might cause delay. Unfortunately, one day...

Think Critically About Meaning and Use

A. Read each sentence and the statements that follow. Write *T* if the statement is true, *F* if it is false, or *?* if you do not have enough information to decide.

1. Charles told me that I got a raise.

    _F_   **a.** Charles got a raise.

    _____ **b.** I got a raise.

2. Sandra told me that Amy had been sick.

    _____ **a.** Amy is sick.

    _____ **b.** Sandra spoke to Amy.

3. Hector asked his sister to pick up his laptop.

    _____ **a.** The laptop belongs to Hector.

    _____ **b.** Hector spoke to his sister.

4. I said I'd see Marie.

    _____ **a.** I saw Marie.

    _____ **b.** When I said that, I hadn't seen Marie yet.

5. She suggested that I go home.

    _____ **a.** I went home.

    _____ **b.** She wanted me to go home.

6. Amelia asked if I was sick.

    _____ **a.** I was sick.

    _____ **b.** Amelia inquired whether I was sick.

7. We told him not to drive.

    _____ **a.** He didn't drive.

    _____ **b.** We said he shouldn't drive.

8. It is recommended that we make a reservation.

    _____ **a.** Reservations are suggested.

    _____ **b.** Reservations are required.

(Continued on page 408)

B. Discuss these questions in small groups.

1. **COMPARE AND CONTRAST** What's the difference in meaning between 4 and the sentence "I said I'd seen her." How would you change each back to quoted speech?

2. **COMPARE AND CONTRAST** What's the difference in meaning between 6 and the sentence "Amelia asked if I'd been sick?" How would you change each back to quoted speech?

Edit

Find the errors in these paragraphs and correct them.

Linguist Deborah Tannen claims×men and women have different conversational styles. She argues that the differences can cause miscommunication between the sexes. Here's a typical example of what Professor Tannen means.

A married couple met at the end of the day. They greeted each other, and he asked her how had her day been. She replied that she has a very busy day. She explained him that she had attended several different meetings, and she had seen four clients. She described how she had felt and what had she been thinking. After that, she eagerly turned to her husband and asked how your day had been. He replied that it had been the same as usual. She looked disappointed, but quickly forgot about it until later that evening when they met friends for dinner. During the meal, her husband told the group that something extraordinary had happened to him today. He went on to explain the amusing details. Everyone laughed except his wife. She felt quite frustrated and confused. She didn't understand why he hadn't told her the story earlier in the evening.

According to Tannen, the answer relates to the difference in conversational styles between men and women. She tells that women use conversation to establish closeness in a relationship, but men consider conversation to be more of a public activity. Men use it to establish their status in a group. Do you agree with this distinction? Do you know men or women like this?

Write

Imagine that you have a problem with a company's product or service. You call Customer Service and have a bad experience with a representative. Write an email to the person's supervisor complaining about the problem. Use reported speech, where possible, with a variety of reporting verbs.

1. **BRAINSTORM** Think about all the details of the incident you want to complain about to the supervisor. Use these categories to help you organize your email into paragraphs:
   - **Opening:** Say why you're writing.
   - **Body:** Sum up the problem was and the bad experience with the representative.
   - **Closing:** Restate your dissatisfaction. Suggest actions you think should be taken.

2. **WRITE A FIRST DRAFT** Before you write your first draft, read the checklist below and look at the examples on pages 399–402. Write your draft using reported speech.

3. **EDIT** Read your work and check it against the checklist below. Circle grammar, spelling, and punctuation errors.

DO I ...	YES
organize my ideas into paragraphs?	☐
use reported speech to relate what was said?	☐
make needed changes in tense, pronouns, and adverbs in reported speech?	☐
use a range of reporting verbs, each followed by the correct structure?	☐

4. **PEER REVIEW** Work with a partner to help you decide how to fix your errors and improve the content. Use the checklist above.

5. **REWRITE YOUR DRAFT** Using the comments from your partner, write a final draft.

From:	Edward Krieg
To:	Tanya Robeson, Customer Service Supervisor
Subject:	Continuing Problems with Unauthorized Charges on My Credit Card Account

Dear Ms. Robeson,

I'm writing to inform you of the continuing problems I've had in removing unauthorized charges from my credit card account.

On April 22nd, I spoke to Ava Brown (ID # 199AF) and reported that my statement contained charges for items I had not bought...

Choose the correct word or words to complete each sentence.

1. Instead of learning specific job skills in college, students learn _____ to solve problems, the greatest skill of all.

   a. what b. that c. how d. if

2. Do you know when _____ ?
   a. the gift being purchased
   b. the gift purchased
   c. the gift is being purchased
   d. is the gift being purchased

3. It was announced that the university _____ accepted more students into the program.

   a. would b. had c. were d. be

4. Safety experts _____ motorists to make frequent stops during a long trip, especially at night.

   a. advise b. demand c. insist d. recommend

5. They _____ if I wanted a ride home, but I had already made other plans.

   a. said b. told me c. told d. asked

Choose the correct response to complete each conversation.

6. **A:** Do you know what Diane forgot?
   B: _____
   a. She didn't forget them.
   b. Yes, the keys.
   c. Yes, she did.
   d. No, I didn't.

7. **A:** I'm certain that I didn't tell Mary.
   B: _____
   a. Why didn't you?
   b. Why did you?
   c. When did you?
   d. Yes, she's sure.

8. **A:** What did Jeff say when he called last week?
   B: _____
   a. That it's raining.
   b. That it must rain.
   c. That it has been raining.
   d. That it was raining.

9. **A:** Emily said she'd found a job.
   B: _____
   a. I hope she does.
   b. I wonder if she will.
   c. I'm glad she did.
   d. I know she would

10. **A:** Why did you leave the game before the end?

    B: I was sure _____

      a. we will win.   **c.** we would win.

      b. we win.   **d.** we won.

11. **A:** Mr. Burns is going to resign.

    B: _____

      a. I know why.   **c.** I know who.

      b. I know what.   **d.** I know how.

12. **A:** What did you tell the boss about the report?

    B: _____

      a. He told me it was fine.   **c.** Yes, I was still working on it.

      b. No, I didn't ask him.   **d.** I said it would be on his desk in the morning.

13. **A:** The professor suggested that we look at a few articles.

    B: Which ones did he _____

      a. recommend?   **c.** promise?

      b. demand?   **d.** inform?

Change each direct question to an indirect question.

14. Did you like your job?

    I was wondering if _____

15. Why are you cleaning the house again?

    Could you explain _____

16. How much is this coat?

    I'd like to know _____

17. What experience do you have?

    I was wondering _____

Rewrite the reported speech as quoted speech. Include quotation marks. Use contractions where possible.

18. She told me not to come back the next day.

    _____

19. The patient asked the doctor how often he should take the medication.

    _____

20. He asked if I was staying.

    _____

Appendices

1 **Spelling of Verbs and Nouns Ending in** *-s* **and** *-es* A-2

2 **Pronunciation of Verbs and Nouns Ending in** *-s* **and** *-es* A-3

3 **Spelling of Verbs Ending in** *-ing* A-3

4 **Spelling of Verbs Ending in** *-ed* A-4

5 **Pronunciation of Verbs Ending in** *-ed* A-4

6 **Irregular Verbs** A-5

7 **Common Intransitive Verbs** A-6

8 **Gerunds** A-7

9 **Infinitives** A-8

10 **Verb + Infinitive or Gerund** A-9

11 **Mental Activity Verbs** A-9

12 **Reporting Verbs** A-9

13 **Punctuation Rules for Quoted Speech** A-10

14 **Contractions with Verb and Modal Forms** A-11

15 **Phrasal Verbs** A-12

16 **Phonetic Symbols** A-15

1   Spelling of Verbs and Nouns Ending in *-s* and *-es*

1. For most third-person singular verbs and plural nouns, add *-s* to the base form.

   Verbs   **Nouns**

   swim — swims   lake — lakes

2. If the base form ends with the letters *s, z, sh, ch,* or *x,* add *-es.*

   Verbs   **Nouns**

   miss — misses   box — boxes

3. If the base form ends with a consonant + *y,* change *y* to *i* and add *-es.*
   (Compare vowel + *y*: obey — obeys; toy — toys.)

   Verbs   **Nouns**

   try — tries   baby — babies

4. If the base form ends with a consonant + *o,* add *-s* or *-es.* Some words take *-s, -es,* or
   both *-s* and *-es.* (Compare vowel + *o*: radio — radios; zoo — zoos.)

-s	**-es**	**Both -s and -es**
auto — autos	do — does	tornado — tornados/tornadoes
photo — photos	echo — echoes	volcano — volcanos/volcanoes
piano — pianos	go — goes	zero — zeros/zeroes
solo — solos	hero — heroes	
	potato — potatoes	
	tomato — tomatoes	

5. If the base form of certain nouns ends in a single *f* or in *fe,* change the *f* or *fe* to *v*
   and add *-es.*

   calf — calves
   shelf — shelves
   knife — knives

   Exceptions

   belief — beliefs
   chief — chiefs
   roof — roofs
   scarf — scarfs/scarves

2 Pronunciation of Verbs and Nouns Ending in -s and -es

1. If the base form of the verb or noun ends with the sounds /s/, /z/, /ʃ/, /ʒ/, /tʃ/, /dʒ/, or /ks/, then pronounce -es as an extra syllable /ɪz/.

Verbs		Nouns	
slice — slices	watch — watches	price — prices	inch — inches
lose — loses	judge — judges	size — sizes	language — languages
wash — washes	relax — relaxes	dish — dishes	tax — taxes
		garage — garages	

2. If the base form ends with the voiceless sounds /p/, /t/, /k/, /f/, or /θ/, then pronounce -s and -es as /s/.

Verbs		Nouns	
sleep — sleeps	work — works	grape — grapes	cuff — cuffs
hit — hits	laugh — laughs	cat — cats	fifth — fifths
		book — books	

3. If the base form ends with any other consonant or with a vowel sound, then pronounce -s and -es as /z/.

Verbs	Nouns
learn — learns	name — names
go — goes	boy — boys

3 Spelling of Verbs Ending in -ing

1. For most verbs, add -ing to the base form of the verb.

    sleep — sleeping   talk — talking

2. If the base form ends in a single e, drop the e and add -ing (exception: be – being).

    live — living   write — writing

3. If the base form ends in ie, change ie to y and add -ing.

    die — dying   lie — lying

4. If the base form of a one-syllable verb ends with a single vowel + consonant, double the final consonant and add -ing. (Compare two vowels + consonant: eat — eating.)

    hit — hitting   stop — stopping

5. If the base form of a verb with two or more syllables ends in a single vowel + consonant, double the final consonant only if the stress is on the final syllable. Do not double the final consonant if the stress is not on the final syllable.

    admít — admitting   begín — beginning   devélop — developing   lísten — listening

6. Do not double the final consonants x, w, and y.

    fix — fixing   plow — plowing   obey — obeying

4 Spelling of Verbs Ending in -ed

1. To form the simple past and past participle of most regular verbs, add -ed to the base form.

   brush — brushed   play — played

2. If the base form ends with e, just add -d.

   close — closed   live — lived

3. If the base form ends with a consonant + y, change the y to i and add -ed. (Compare vowel +y: play — played; enjoy — enjoyed.)

   study — studied   dry — dried

4. If the base form of a one-syllable verb ends with a single vowel + consonant, double the final consonant and add -ed.

   plan — planned   shop — shopped

5. If the base form of a verb with two or more syllables ends in a single vowel + consonant, double the final consonant and add -ed only when the stress is on the final syllable. Do not double the final consonant if the stress is not on the final syllable.

   prefér — preferred   énter — entered

6. Do not double the final consonants x, w, and y.

   coax — coaxed   snow — snowed   stay — stayed

5 Pronunciation of Verbs Ending in -ed

1. If the base form of the verb ends with the sounds /t/ or /d/, then pronounce -ed as an extra syllable /ɪd/.

/t/	/d/
start — started	need — needed
wait — waited	decide — decided

2. If the base form ends with the voiceless sounds /f/, /k/, /p/, /s/, /ʃ/, /tʃ/, or /ks/, then pronounce -ed as /t/.

laugh — laughed	jump — jumped	wish — wished	fax — faxed
look — looked	slice — sliced	watch — watched	

3. If the base form ends with the voiced sounds /b/, /g/, /dʒ/, /m/, /n/, /ŋ/, /l/, /r/, /ð/, /v/, /z/, or with a vowel, then pronounce -ed as /d/.

rob — robbed	hum — hummed	call — called	wave — waved
brag — bragged	rain — rained	order — ordered	close — closed
judge — judged	bang — banged	bathe — bathed	play — played

6 Irregular Verbs

Base Form	Simple Past	Past Participle	Base Form	Simple Past	Past Participle
arise	arose	arisen	forget	forgot	forgotten
be	was/were	been	forgive	forgave	forgiven
beat	beat	beaten	freeze	froze	frozen
become	became	become	get	got	gotten
begin	began	begun	give	gave	given
bend	bent	bent	go	went	gone
bet	bet	bet	grind	ground	ground
bind	bound	bound	grow	grew	grown
bite	bit	bitten	hang	hung	hung
bleed	bled	bled	have	had	had
blow	blew	blown	hear	heard	heard
break	broke	broken	hide	hid	hidden
bring	brought	brought	hit	hit	hit
build	built	built	hold	held	held
burst	burst	burst	hurt	hurt	hurt
buy	bought	bought	keep	kept	kept
catch	caught	caught	know	knew	known
choose	chose	chosen	lay (= put)	laid	laid
cling	clung	clung	lead	led	led
come	came	come	leave	left	left
cost	cost	cost	lend	lent	lent
creep	crept	crept	let	let	let
cut	cut	cut	lie (= recline)	lay	lain
deal	dealt	dealt	light	lit	lit
dig	dug	dug	lose	lost	lost
dive	dove/dived	dived	make	made	made
do	did	done	mean	meant	meant
draw	drew	drawn	meet	met	met
drink	drank	drunk	pay	paid	paid
drive	drove	driven	prove	proved	proven/proved
eat	ate	eaten	put	put	put
fall	fell	fallen	quit	quit	quit
feed	fed	fed	read	read	read
feel	felt	felt	ride	rode	ridden
fight	fought	fought	ring	rang	rung
find	found	found	rise	rose	risen
fit	fit	fit	run	ran	run
flee	fled	fled	say	said	said
fly	flew	flown	see	saw	seen
forbid	forbade	forbidden	seek	sought	sought

Base Form	Simple Past	Past Participle	Base Form	Simple Past	Past Participle
sell	sold	sold	sting	stung	stung
send	sent	sent	stink	stank	stunk
set	set	set	strike	struck	struck
sew	sewed	sewn	string	strung	strung
shake	shook	shaken	swear	swore	sworn
shine	shone	shone	sweep	swept	swept
shoot	shot	shot	swim	swam	swum
show	showed	shown	swing	swung	swung
shrink	shrank	shrunk	take	took	taken
shut	shut	shut	teach	taught	taught
sing	sang	sung	tear	tore	torn
sink	sank	sunk	tell	told	told
sit	sat	sat	think	thought	thought
sleep	slept	slept	throw	threw	thrown
slide	slid	slid	understand	understood	understood
speak	spoke	spoken	undertake	undertook	undertaken
speed	sped	sped	upset	upset	upset
spend	spent	spent	wake	woke	woken
spin	spun	spun	wear	wore	worn
split	split	split	weave	wove	woven
spread	spread	spread	weep	wept	wept
spring	sprang	sprung	wet	wet	wet
stand	stood	stood	win	won	won
steal	stole	stolen	wind	wound	wound
stick	stuck	stuck	write	wrote	written

7 Common Intransitive Verbs

These verbs can only be used intransitively. (They cannot be followed by an object.)

ache	emerge	itch	sit
appear	erupt	laugh	sleep
arrive	faint	live	smile
be	fall	look	snow
come	frown	matter	stand
cry	go	occur	stay
depart	grin	rain	talk
die	happen	remain	weep
disappear	hesitate	seem	

8 Gerunds

Verb + Gerund

These verbs may be followed by gerunds, but not by infinitives:

acknowledge	detest	keep (= continue)	recall
admit	discuss	loathe	recollect
anticipate	dislike	mean (= involve)	recommend
appreciate	endure	mention	regret
avoid	enjoy	mind (= object to)	report
can't help	escape	miss	resent
celebrate	excuse	omit	resist
consider	feel like	postpone	resume
defend	finish	practice	risk
defer	go	prevent	suggest
delay	imagine	prohibit	tolerate
deny	involve	quit	understand

Verb with Preposition + Gerund

These verbs or verb phrases with prepositions may be followed by gerunds, but not by infinitives:

adapt to	believe in	depend on
adjust to	blame for	disapprove of
agree (with someone) on	care about	discourage (someone) from
apologize (to someone) for	complain (to someone) about	engage in
approve of	concentrate on	forgive (someone) for
argue (with someone) about	consist of	help (someone) with
ask about	decide on	

Be + Adjective + Preposition + Gerund

Adjectives with prepositions typically occur in be + adjective phrases. These phrases may be followed by gerunds, but not by infinitives:

be accustomed to	be famous for	be proud of
be afraid of	be fond of	be responsible for
be angry (at someone) about	be glad about	be sad about
be ashamed of	be good at	be successful in
be capable of	be happy about	be suitable for
be certain of/about	be incapable of	be tired of
be concerned with	be interested in	be tolerant of
be critical of	be jealous of	be upset about
be discouraged from	be known for	be used to
be enthusiastic about	be nervous about	be useful for
be familiar with	be perfect for	be worried about

9 Infinitives

These verbs may be followed by infinitives, but not by gerunds:

Verb + Infinitive

agree	decide	manage	struggle
aim	decline	plan	swear
appear	demand	pledge	tend
arrange	fail	pretend	volunteer
care	guarantee	refuse	wait
claim	hope	resolve	
consent	intend	seem	

Verb + Object + Infinitive

advise	get	persuade	tell
command	hire	remind	trust
convince	invite	require	urge
force	order	teach	warn

Verb + (Object) + Infinitive

ask	desire	need	promise
beg	expect	offer	want
choose	help	pay	wish
dare	know	prepare	would like

Adjective + Infinitive

afraid	distressed	hesitant	reluctant
alarmed	disturbed	impossible	right
amazed	eager	interested	sad
anxious	easy	likely	scared
astonished	embarrassed	lucky	shocked
careful	excited	necessary	sorry
curious	fascinated	pleased	surprised
delighted	fortunate	possible	unlikely
depressed	frightened	prepared	unnecessary
determined	glad	proud	willing
difficult	happy	ready	wrong
disappointed	hard	relieved	

10 Verb + Infinitive or Gerund

These verbs may be followed by infinitives or gerunds:

attempt	cease	like	propose	stop
begin	continue	love	regret	try
can't bear	forget	neglect	remember	
can't stand	hate	prefer	start	

11 Mental Activity Verbs

These mental activity verbs are followed by noun clauses:

agree	decide	find (out)	learn	recognize
assume	discover	forget	mean	regret
believe	doubt	guess	notice	remember
bet	dream	hear	pretend	suppose
calculate	expect	hope	prove	think
conclude	feel	imagine	realize	understand
consider	figure out	know	recall	wonder

12 Reporting Verbs

Verb + Noun Clause

These reporting verbs are followed by noun clauses:

acknowledge	conclude	instruct (someone)	report
add	confess	maintain	respond
admit	confirm	mention	roar
advise (someone)	convince (someone)	murmur	say
affirm	cry	mutter	scream
agree	declare	note	shout
announce	demand	notify (someone)	shriek
answer	deny	observe	sneer
argue	emphasize	persuade (someone)	stammer
ask	estimate	point out	state
assert	exclaim	promise	suggest
assure (someone)	explain	propose	swear
boast	grumble	protest	tell (someone)
brag	guess	recommend	threaten
caution	imply	remark	
claim	indicate	remind (someone)	
comment	inform (someone)	repeat	
complain	insist	reply	

Verb + Infinitive

These reporting verbs are used with infinitives:

advise (someone) to
ask (someone) to
beg (someone) to
command (someone) to
direct (someone) to

forbid (someone) to
instruct (someone) to
oblige (someone) to
order (someone) to
request (someone) to

tell (someone) to
urge (someone) to
want (someone) to

13 Punctuation Rules for Quoted Speech

1. If quoted speech comes after the reporting verb:
    - Place a comma after the reporting verb.
    - Place quotation marks at the beginning and end of reported speech. Put them near the top of the letter.
    - Begin quoted speech with a capital letter.
    - Use the correct punctuation (a period, an exclamation mark, or a question mark) and place the punctuation inside the quotation marks.

    Examples
    He said, "We are staying."
    He shouted, "We are staying!"
    He asked me, "Are we staying?"

2. If quoted speech comes before the reporting verb:
    - Place quotation marks at the beginning and end of reported speech. Put them near the top of the letter.
    - Begin quoted speech with a capital letter.
    - Use a comma if the quoted speech is a statement. Use an exclamation if the quoted speech is an exclamation. Use a question mark if the quoted speech is a question. Place the punctuation inside the quotation marks.
    - Begin the phrase that follows the quoted speech with a lowercase letter.
    - Use a period at the end of the main sentence.

    Examples
    "We are staying," he said.
    "We are staying!" he shouted.
    "Are we staying?" he asked me.

14 Contractions with Verb and Modal Forms

Contractions with *Be*

I am	= I'm
you are	= you're
he is	= he's
she is	= she's
it is	= it's
we are	= we're
you are	= you're
they are	= they're

I am not	= I'm not
you are not	= you're not / you aren't
he is not	= he's not / he isn't
she is not	= she's not / she isn't
it is not	= it's not / it isn't
we are not	= we're not / we aren't
you are not	= you're not / you aren't
they are not	= they're not / they aren't

Contractions with *Be Going To*

I am going to	= I'm going to
you are going to	= you're going to
he is going to	= he's going to
she is going to	= she's going to
it is going to	= it's going to
we are going to	= we're going to
you are going to	= you're going to
they are going to	= they're going to
you are not going to	= you're not going to / you aren't going to

Contractions with *Will*

I will	= I'll
you will	= you'll
he will	= he'll
she will	= she'll
it will	= it'll
we will	= we'll
you will	= you'll
they will	= they'll
will not	= won't

Contractions with *Would*

I would	= I'd
you would	= you'd
he would	= he'd
she would	= she'd
we would	= we'd
you would	= you'd
they would	= they'd
would not	= wouldn't

Contractions with *Was* and *Were*

was not	= wasn't
were not	= weren't

Contractions with *Have*

I have	= I've
you have	= you've
he has	= he's
she has	= she's
it has	= it's
we have	= we've
you have	= you've
they have	= they've
have not	= haven't
has not	= hasn't

Contractions with *Had*

I had	= I'd
you had	= you'd
he had	= he'd
she had	= she'd
it had	= it'd
we had	= we'd
you had	= you'd
they had	= they'd
had not	= hadn't

Contractions with *Do* and *Did*

do not	= don't
does not	= doesn't
did not	= didn't

Contractions with Modals and Phrasal Modals

cannot/can not	= can't
could not	= couldn't
should not	= shouldn't
have got to	= 've got to
has got to	= 's got to

15 Phrasal Verbs

Separable Phrasal Verbs

Many two-word phrasal verbs are separable. This means that a noun object can separate the two words of the phrasal verb or follow the phrasal verb. If the object is a pronoun *(me, you, him, her, it, us, them)*, the pronoun must separate the two words.

Noun Object	Pronoun Object
She **turned** the offer **down**.	She **turned** it **down**.
She **turned down** the offer.	x She turned down it. (INCORRECT)

These are some common separable phrasal verbs and their meanings:

Phrasal Verb	Meaning
ask (someone) out	invite someone to go out
ask (someone) over	invite someone to come to your house
blow (something) up	inflate, cause something to explode
boot (something) up	start or get a computer ready for use
bring (someone) up	raise a child
bring (something) up	introduce or call attention to a topic
burn (something) down	destroy by fire
call (someone) back	return a phone call to someone
call (something) off	cancel something
call (someone) up	telephone
call (something) up	retrieve from the memory of a computer
check (something) out	borrow a book, tape, video from the library; verify
clean (something) out	clean the inside of something thoroughly
clean (something) up	clean thoroughly and remove anything unwanted
clear (something) up	explain a problem
cross (something) out	draw a line through
cut (something) up	cut into little pieces
do (something) over	do something again
figure (something) out	solve a problem
fill (something) in	write in a blank or a space
fill (something) out	write information on a form
fill (something) up	fill completely with something
find (something) out	discover information
give (something) back	return something
give (something) up	quit something; get rid of something
hand (something) in	submit homework, a test, an application
hand (something) out	distribute something
hang (something) up	put on a clothes hanger; end a telephone call
keep (someone) up	prevent someone from going to sleep
kick (someone) out	force someone to leave
leave (something) out	omit

Phrasal Verb	Meaning
look (something) over	examine carefully
look (something) up	look for information in a book
make (something) up	create or invent something; do work that was missed
make (something) up to (someone)	return a favor to someone
pay (someone) back	return money owned to someone
pick (something) out	choose
pick (something/someone) up	lift something or someone; stop to get something or someone
point (something) out	mention, draw attention to something
put (something) away	put something in its usual place
put (something) back	return something to its original place
put (something) down	stop holding something
put (something) in	install
put (something) off	postpone
put (something) on	get dressed
put (something) out	extinguish a fire, cigarette, or cigar
put (something) over on (someone)	deceive someone
set (something) up	make something ready for use
shut (something) off	turn off a machine
start (something) over	start again
take (something) away	remove
take (a time period) off	have a break from work or school
take (something) off	remove
take (someone) out	accompany to the theater, a restaurant, a movie
take (something) out	remove something from something else
tear (something) down	destroy completely
tear (something) off	detach something
tear (something) up	tear into pieces
think (something) over	reflect upon something before making a decision
think (something) up	invent
throw (something) away	put something in the trash
throw (something) out	put something in the trash
try (something) on	put on clothing to see how it looks
turn (something) down	lower the volume; refuse an offer or invitation
turn (something) in	return; submit homework, a test, an application
turn (something) off	stop a machine or light
turn (something) on	start a machine or light
turn (something) up	increase the volume
use (something) up	use something until no more is left
wake (someone) up	cause someone to stop sleeping
wear (someone) out	cause someone to become exhausted
work (something) out	solve something
write (something) down	write something on a piece of paper

Nonseparable Phrasal Verbs

Some two-word verbs and most three-word verbs are nonseparable. This means that a noun or pronoun object cannot separate the two parts of the phrasal verb.

Noun Object

The teacher **went over** the lesson.

x The teacher went the lesson over. (INCORRECT)

Pronoun Object

The teacher **went over** it.

x The teacher went it over. (INCORRECT)

These are some common nonseparable phrasal verbs and their meanings:

Phrasal Verb	Meaning
blow up	explode
break down	stop functioning properly
break up with (someone)	end a relationship with someone
burn down	be destroyed by fire
call on (someone)	ask someone to answer or speak in class
catch up with (someone/something)	travel fast enough to overtake someone who is ahead
check out of (a hotel)	leave a hotel after paying the bill
clear up	become fair weather
come back	return
come over	visit
come up with (something)	think of a plan or reply
cut down on (something)	reduce
eat out	have a meal in a restaurant
face up to (something)	be brave enough to accept or deal with
fall down	leave a standing position; perform in a disappointing way
get away with (doing something)	not be punished for doing something wrong
get down to (something)	begin to give serious attention to
get off (something)	leave a plane, bus, train
get on (something)	enter a plane, bus, train
get over (something)	recover from an illness or serious life event
get up	arise from a bed or chair
give up	stop trying, lose hope
go back	return
go down	(of computers) stop functioning; (of prices or temperature) become lower; (of ships) sink; (of the sun or moon) set
go off	stop functioning; (of alarms) start functioning; explode or make a loud noise
go on	take place, happen
go out	leave one's house to go to a social event
go out with (someone)	spend time regularly with someone
go over (something)	review
grow up	become an adult

Phrasal Verb	Meaning
hold on	wait on the telephone
keep on (doing something)	continue doing something
keep up with	stay at the same level or position
look out for (something/someone)	be careful of something or someone
move out	stop occupying a residence, especially by removing one's possessions
pack up	prepare all of one's belongings for moving
put up with (something/someone)	tolerate
run out	come to an end, be completely used up
run out of (something)	have no more of something
show up	appear, be seen, arrive at a place
sit down	get into a seated position
stay out	remain out of the house, especially at night
stay up	remain awake, not go to bed
take off	leave (usually by plane)
turn up	appear
wake up	stop sleeping
work out	exercise vigorously

16 Phonetic Symbols

Vowels

i	see /si/	u	too /tu/	oʊ	go /goʊ/
ɪ	sit /sɪt/	ʌ	cup /kʌp/	ər	bird /bərd/
ɛ	ten /tɛn/	ə	about /əˈbaʊt/	ɪr	near /nɪr/
æ	cat /kæt/	eɪ	say /seɪ/	ɛr	hair /hɛr/
ɑ	hot /hɑt/	aɪ	five /faɪv/	ɑr	car /kɑr/
ɔ	saw /sɔ/	ɔɪ	boy /bɔɪ/	ɔr	north /nɔrθ/
ʊ	put /pʊt/	aʊ	now /naʊ/	ʊr	tour /tʊr/

Consonants

p	pen /pɛn/	f	fall /fɔl/	m	man /mæn/
b	bad /bæd/	v	voice /vɔɪs/	n	no /noʊ/
t	tea /ti/	θ	thin /θɪn/	ŋ	sing /sɪŋ/
ţ	butter /ˈbʌţər/	ð	then /ðɛn/	l	leg /lɛg/
d	did /dɪd/	s	so /soʊ/	r	red /rɛd/
k	cat /kæt/	z	zoo /zu/	j	yes /jɛs/
g	got /gɑt/	ʃ	she /ʃi/	w	wet /wɛt/
tʃ	chin /tʃɪn/	ʒ	vision /ˈvɪʒn/		
dʒ	June /dʒun/	h	how /haʊ/		

Glossary of Grammar Terms

ability modal *See* **modal of ability.**

active sentence In active sentences, the agent (the noun that is performing the action) is in subject position and the receiver (the noun that receives or is a result of the action) is in object position. In the following sentence, the subject **Alex** performed the action, and the object **letter** received the action.

> Alex mailed the letter.

adjective A word that describes or modifies the meaning of a noun.

> the **orange** car   a **strange** noise

adjective clause *See* **relative clause.**

adjective phrase A phrase that functions as an adjective.

> These shoes are **too tight.**

adverb A word that describes or modifies the meaning of a verb, another adverb, an adjective, or a sentence. Adverbs answer such questions as *How? When? Where?* or *How often?* They often end in **-ly.**

> She ran **quickly.**   She ran **very** quickly.
> a **really** hot day   **Maybe** she'll leave.

adverb of frequency An adverb that tells how often a situation occurs. Adverbs of frequency range in meaning from *all of the time* to *none of the time.*

> She **always** eats breakfast.
> He **never** eats meat.

adverbial phrase A phrase that functions as an adverb.

> Amy spoke **very softly.**

affirmative statement A positive sentence that does not have a negative verb.

> Linda went to the movies.

agent The noun that is performing the action in a sentence. *See* **active sentence, passive sentence.**

> The letter was mailed by **Alex.**

agentless passive A passive sentence that doesn't mention an agent.

> The letter was mailed.

agreement The subject and verb of a clause must agree in number. If the subject is singular, the verb form is also singular. If the subject is plural, the verb form is also plural.

> **He comes** home early.
> **They come** home early.

article The words **a**, **an**, and **the** in English. Articles are used to introduce and identify nouns.

> **a** potato   **an** onion   **the** supermarket

auxiliary verb A verb that is used before main verbs (or other auxiliary verbs) in a sentence. Auxiliary verbs are usually used in questions and negative sentences. **Do, have,** and **be** can act as auxiliary verbs. Modals (**may, can, will,** and so on) are also auxiliary verbs.

> **Do** you have the time?
> I **have** never been to Italy.
> The suitcase **was** taken.   I **may** be late.

base form The form of a verb without any verb endings; the infinitive form without *to.* Also called *simple form.*

> sleep   be   stop

clause A group of words that has a subject and a verb. *See also* **dependent clause** and **main clause.**

> If I leave,...   The rain stopped.
> ...when he speaks.   ...that I saw.

common noun A noun that refers to any of a class of people, animals, places, things, or ideas. Common nouns are not capitalized.

> man   cat   city   pencil   grammar

communication verb *See* **reporting verb.**

comparative A form of an adjective, adverb, or noun that is used to express differences between two items or situations.

This book is **heavier than** that one.
He runs **more quickly than** his brother.
A CD costs **more money than** a cassette.

complex sentence A sentence that has a main clause and one or more dependent clauses.

When the bell rang, we were finishing dinner.

conditional sentence A sentence that expresses a real or unreal situation in the *if* clause, and the (real or unreal) expected result in the main clause.

If I have time, I will travel to Africa.
If I had time, I would travel to Africa.

contraction The combination of two words into one by omitting certain letters and replacing them with an apostrophe.

I will = **I'll**   we are = **we're**   are not = **aren't**

count noun A common noun that can be counted. It usually has both a singular and a plural form.

orange — oranges   woman — women

defining relative clause *See* **restrictive relative clause**.

definite article The word **the** in English. It is used to identify nouns based on assumptions about what information the speaker and listener share about the noun. The definite article is also used for making general statements about a whole class or group of nouns.

Please give me **the** key.
The scorpion is dangerous.

dependent clause A clause that cannot stand alone as a sentence because it depends on the main clause to complete the meaning of the sentence. Also called *subordinate clause*.

I'm going home **after he calls**.

determiner A word such as **a**, **an**, **the**, **this**, **that**, **these**, **those**, **my**, **some**, **a few**, and **three**, that is used before a noun to limit its meaning in some way.

those videos

direct speech *See* **quoted speech**.

embedded question *See* **wh- clause**.

future A time that is to come. The future is expressed in English with **will**, **be going to**, the simple present, or the present continuous. These different forms of the future often have different meanings and uses. *See also* **future continuous**.

I **will** help you later.
David **is going to** call later.
The train **leaves** at 6:05 this evening.
I'm driving to Toronto tomorrow.

future continuous A verb form that expresses an activity in progress at a specific time in the future. It is formed with **will** + **be** + main verb + **-ing**.

I'll **be leaving** for Hawaii at noon tomorrow.

general quantity expression A quantity expression that indicates whether a quantity or an amount is large or small. It does not give an exact amount.

a lot of cookies   **a little** flour

general statement A generalization about a whole class or group of nouns.

Whales are mammals.
A daffodil is a flower that grows from a bulb.

generic noun A noun that refers to a whole class or group of nouns.

I like **rice**.
A bird can fly.
The laser is an important tool.

gerund An **-ing** form of a verb that is used in place of a noun or pronoun to name an activity or a situation.

Skiing is fun.   He doesn't like **being sick**.

identifying relative clause *See* **restrictive relative clause**.

***if* clause** A dependent clause that begins with **if** and expresses a real or unreal situation.

If I have the time, I'll paint the kitchen.
If I had the time, I'd paint the kitchen.

***if/whether* clause** A noun clause that begins with either **if** or **whether**.

I don't know **if they're here**.
I don't know **whether or not they're here**.

imperative A type of sentence, usually without a subject, that tells someone to do something. The verb is in the base form.

> **Open** your books to page 36.
> **Be** ready at eight.

impersonal *you* The use of the pronoun **you** to refer to people in general rather than a particular person or group of people.

> Nowadays, **you** can buy anything on the Internet.

indefinite article The words **a** and **an** in English. Indefinite articles introduce a noun as a member of a class of nouns, or make generalizations about a whole class or group of nouns.

> Please hand me **a** pencil.
> **An** ocean is **a** large body of water.

independent clause *See* **main clause**.

indirect question *See* **wh- clause**.

indirect speech *See* **reported speech**.

infinitive A verb form that includes **to** + the base form of a verb. An infinitive is used in place of a noun or pronoun to name an activity or situation expressed by a verb.

> Do you like **to swim**?

information question A question that begins with a **wh-** word.

> Where does she live? Who lives here?

intransitive verb A verb that cannot be followed by an object.

> We finally **arrived**.

irregular verb A verb that forms the simple past in a different way than regular verbs.

> put — put — put   buy — bought — bought

main clause A clause that can be used by itself as a sentence. Also called *independent clause*.

> I'm going home.

main verb A verb that can be used alone in a sentence. A main verb can also occur with an auxiliary verb.

> I **ate** lunch at 11:30.
> Kate can't **eat** lunch today.

mental activity verb A verb such as **decide, know**, and **understand**, that expresses an opinion, thought, or feeling.

> I don't **know** why she left.

modal The auxiliary verbs **can, could, may, might, must, should, will**, and **would**. They modify the meaning of a main verb by expressing ability, authority, formality, politeness, or various degrees of certainty. Also called *modal auxiliary*.

> You **should** take something for your headache.
> Applicants **must** have a high school diploma.

modal of ability **Can** and **could** are called modals of ability when they express knowledge, skill, opportunity, and capability.

> He **can** speak Arabic and English.
> **Can** you play the piano?
> Yesterday we **couldn't** leave during the storm.
> Seat belts **can** save lives.

modal of possibility **Could, might, may, should, must**, and **will** are called modals of possibility when they express various degrees of certainty ranging from slight possibility to strong certainty.

> It **could / might / may / will** rain later.

modal auxiliary *See* **modal**.

modify To add to or change the meaning of a word.

> expensive cars (The adjective **expensive** modifies **cars**.)

noncount noun A common noun that cannot be counted. A noncount noun has no plural form and cannot occur with **a, an**, or a number.

> information   mathematics   weather

nondefining relative clause *See* **nonrestrictive relative clause**.

nonidentifying relative clause *See* **nonrestrictive relative clause**.

nonrestrictive relative clause A relative clause that adds extra information about the noun that it modifies. This information is not necessary to identify the noun, and it can be omitted. Also called *nondefining* or *nonidentifying relative clause*.

> Rick, **who is seven**, plays hockey.

nonseparable Refers to two- or three-word verbs that don't allow a noun or pronoun object to separate the two or three words in the verb phrase. Certain two-word verbs and almost all three-word verbs are nonseparable.

Amy **got off** the bus.
We **cut down on** fat in our diet.

noun A word that typically refers to a person, animal, place, thing, or idea.

Tom   rabbit   store   computer   mathematics

noun clause A dependent clause that can occur in the same place as a noun, pronoun, or noun phrase in a sentence. Noun clauses begin with **wh-** words, **if**, **whether**, or **that**.

I don't know **where he is**.
I wonder **if he's coming**.
I don't know **whether it's true**.
I think **that it's a lie**.

noun phrase A phrase formed by a noun and its modifiers. A noun phrase can substitute for a noun in a sentence.

She drank **milk**.
She drank **chocolate milk**.
She drank **the milk**.

object A noun, pronoun, or noun phrase that follows a transitive verb or a preposition.

Steve threw **the ball**.
She likes **him**.
Go with **her**.

object relative pronoun A relative pronoun that is the object of a relative clause. It comes before the subject noun or pronoun of the relative clause.

the letter **that / which** I wrote
the man **who / whom** I saw

passive sentence Passive sentences emphasize the receiver of an action by changing the usual order of the subject and object in a sentence. The subject (**The letter**) does not perform the action; it receives the action or is the result of an action. The passive is formed with a form of **be** + the past participle of a transitive verb.

The letter was mailed yesterday.

past continuous A verb form that expresses an action or situation in progress at a specific time in the past. The past continuous is formed with **was** or **were** + verb + -**ing**. Also called *past progressive*.

A: What **were** you **doing** last night at eight o'clock?
B: I **was studying**.

past modal A modal that is used to express past certainty, past obligations, and past abilities or opportunities. It is formed with a modal + **have** + past participle of the main verb. Also called *perfect modal*.

He **must have arrived** late.
I **should have called**, but I forgot.
We **could have come**, but no one told us.

past participle A past verb form that may differ from the simple past form of some irregular verbs. It is used to form the present perfect, present perfect continuous, past perfect, past perfect continuous, and the passive.

I have never **seen** that movie.
He's **been** working too much lately.
By noon, we had already **taken** the exam.
She had **been** working since 8:30.
The letter was **sent** on Monday.

past perfect A verb form that expresses a relationship between two past times. The past perfect indicates the earlier event or situation. It is formed with **had** + the past participle of the main verb.

I **had** already **left** when she called.

past perfect continuous A verb form that is like the past perfect, but it emphasizes the duration of the earlier event or situation. It is formed with **had** + **been** + main verb + -**ing**.

When I was offered the position, I **had been looking** for a new job for several months.

past perfect progressive *See* **past perfect continuous**.

past progressive *See* **past continuous**.

past phrasal modal Examples of past phrasal modals are **ought to have**, **have to have**, and **have got to have**.

past unreal conditional sentence A **conditional** sentence that expresses an unreal condition about the past and its imaginary result. It has an **if** clause in the past perfect and a main clause with **would have** + the past participle of the main verb.

> If I had been smarter, I would have complained to the manager.

past *wish* sentence A **wish** sentence that expresses a desire for something that didn't actually happen in the past. It is formed with a **wish** clause + a past perfect clause.

> I wish I had moved to Colorado.

perfect modal *See* **past modal**.

phrasal modal A verb that is not a true modal, but has the same meaning as a modal verb. Examples of phrasal modals are **ought to**, **have to**, and **have got to**.

phrasal verb A two- or three-word verb such as **turn down** or **run out of**. The meaning of a phrasal verb is usually different from the meanings of its individual words.

> She **turned down** the job offer.
> Don't **run out of** gas on the freeway.

phrase A group of words that can form a grammatical unit. A phrase can take the form of a noun phrase, verb phrase, adjective phrase, adverbial phrase, or prepositional phrase. This means it can act as a noun, verb, adjective, adverb, or preposition.

> The **tall man** left.
> Lee **hit the ball**.
> The child was **very quiet**.
> She spoke **too fast**.
> They ran **down the stairs**.

possibility modal *See* **modal of possibility**.

preposition A word such as **at**, **in**, **on**, or **to**, that links nouns, pronouns, and gerunds to other words.

prepositional phrase A phrase that consists of a preposition followed by a noun or noun phrase.

> on Sunday   under the table

present continuous A verb form that indicates that an action is in progress, temporary, or changing. It is formed with **be** + verb + **-ing**. Also called *present progressive*.

> I**'m watering** the garden.
> Ruth **is working** for her uncle.
> He**'s getting** better.

present perfect A verb form that expresses a connection between the past and the present. It indicates indefinite past time, recent past time, or continuing past time. The present perfect is formed with **have** + the past participle of the main verb.

> I**'ve seen** that movie.
> The manager **has** just **resigned**.
> We**'ve been** here for three hours.

present perfect continuous A verb form that focuses on the duration of actions that began in the past and continue into the present or have just ended. It is formed with **have** + **been** + verb + **-ing**.

> They**'ve been waiting** for an hour.
> I**'ve been watering** the garden.

present perfect progressive *See* **present perfect continuous**.

present progressive *See* **present continuous**.

pronoun A word that can replace a noun or noun phrase. **I**, **you**, **he**, **she**, **it**, **mine**, and **yours** are some examples of pronouns.

proper noun A noun that is the name of a particular person, animal, place, thing, or idea. Proper nouns begin with capital letters and are usually not preceded by *the*.

> Peter   Rover   India   Apollo 13   Buddhism

purpose infinitive An infinitive that expresses the reason or purpose for doing something.

> **In order to operate this machine**, press the green button.

quantity expression A word or words that occur before a noun to express a quantity or amount of that noun.

> **a lot of** rain   **few** books   **four** trucks

quoted speech The form of a sentence that uses the exact words of a speaker or writer. Written quoted speech uses quotation marks. Also called *direct speech*.

"**Where did you go?**" he asked.

real conditional sentence A sentence that expresses a real or possible situation in the **if** clause and the expected result in the main clause. It has an **if** clause in the simple present, and the **will** future in the main clause.

If I get a raise, I won't look for a new job.

receiver The noun that receives or is the result of an action in a sentence. See **active sentence**, **passive sentence**.

The letter was mailed by Alex.

regular verb A verb that forms the simple past by adding -**ed**, -**d**, or changing **y** to **i** and then adding -**ed** to the simple form.

hunt — hunted   love — loved   cry — cried

rejoinder A short response used in conversation.

A: I like sushi.
B: **Me too.**
C: **So do I.**

relative clause A clause that modifies a preceding noun. Relative clauses generally begin with **who**, **whom**, **that**, **which**, and **whose**.

The man **who called** is my cousin.
We saw the elephant **that was just born**.

relative pronoun A pronoun that begins a relative clause and refers to a noun in the main clause. The words **who**, **whom**, **that**, **which**, and **whose** are relative pronouns.

reported speech A form of a sentence that expresses the meaning of quoted speech or writing from the point of view of the reporter. **Wh-** clauses, **if/whether** clauses, and **that** clauses are used to express reported speech after a reporting verb.

He explained why he was late.
He said that he was tired.
We asked if they could come early.

reporting verb A verb such as **say**, **tell**, **ask**, **explain**, and **complain** that is used to express what has been said or written in both quoted speech and reported speech.

Tony **complained**, "I'm tired."
Tony **complained** that he was tired.

restrictive relative clause A relative clause that gives information that helps identify or define the noun that it modifies. In the following sentence, the speaker has more than one aunt. The relative clause **who speaks Russian** identifies which aunt the speaker is talking about. Also called *defining* or *identifying relative clause*.

My aunt **who speaks Russian** is an interpreter.

separable Refers to certain two-word verbs that allow a noun or pronoun object to separate the two words in the verb phrase.

She **gave** her job **up**.

short answer An answer to a *Yes/No* question that has *yes* or *no* plus the subject and an auxiliary verb.

A: Do you speak Chinese?
B: **Yes, I do. / No, I don't.**

simple past A verb form that expresses actions and situations that were completed at a definite time in the past.

Carol **ate** lunch.   She **was** hungry.

simple present A verb form that expresses general statements, especially about habitual or repeated activities and permanent situations.

Every morning I **catch** the 8:00 bus.
The earth **is** round.

social modals Modal auxiliaries that are used to express politeness, formality, and authority.

Would you please open the window?
May I help you?
Visitors **must** obey the rules.

stative verb A type of verb that is not usually used in the continuous form because it expresses a condition or state that is not changing. **Know**, **love**, **resemble**, **see**, and **smell** are some examples.

subject A noun, pronoun, or noun phrase that precedes the verb phrase in a sentence. The subject is closely related to the verb as the doer or experiencer of the action or state, or closely related to the noun that is being described in a sentence with *be*.

> **Erica** kicked the ball.
> **He** feels dizzy.
> **The park** is huge.

subject relative pronoun A relative pronoun that is the subject of a relative clause. It comes before the verb in the relative clause.

> the man **who** called

subordinate clause *See* **dependent clause**.

superlative A form of an adjective, adverb, or noun that is used to rank an item or situation first or last in a group of three or more.

> This perfume has **the strongest** scent.
> He speaks **the fastest** of all.
> That machine makes **the most noise** of the three.

***that* clause** A noun clause beginning with **that**.

> I think **that the bus is late**.

three-word verb A phrasal verb such as **break up with**, **cut down on**, and **look out for**. The meaning of a three-word verb is usually different from the individual meanings of the three words.

time clause A dependent clause that begins with a time word such as **while**, **when**, **before**, or **after**. It expresses the relationship in time between two different events in the same sentence.

> **Before Sandy left**, she fixed the copy machine.

transitive verb A verb that is followed by an object.

> I **read** the book.

two-word verb A phrasal verb such as **blow up**, **cross out**, and **hand in**. The meaning of a two-word verb is usually different from the individual meanings of the two words.

unreal conditional sentence A sentence that expresses an unreal situation that is not true at the present time, and its imaginary result. It has an **if** clause in the simple past and a main clause with **would** + main verb.

> If I had the time, I'd walk to work.

used to A special past tense verb. It expresses habitual past situations that no longer exist.

> We **used to** go skiing a lot. Now we go snowboarding.

verb A word that refers to an action or a state.

> Gina **closed** the window.
> Tim **loves** classical music.

verb phrase A phrase that has a main verb and any objects, adverbs, or dependent clauses that complete the meaning of the verb in the sentence.

> Who **called you**?
> He **walked slowly**.
> I **know what his name is**.

voiced Refers to speech sounds that are made by vibrating the vocal cords. Examples of voiced sounds are /b/, /d/, and /g/.

> **b**at   **d**ot   **g**et

voiceless Refers to speech sounds that are made without vibrating the vocal cords. Examples of voiceless sounds are /p/, /t/, and /f/.

> u**p**   i**t**   i**f**

***wh-* clause** A noun clause that begins with a **wh**-word: **who**, **whom**, **what**, **where**, **when**, **why**, **how**, and **which**. Also called *indirect question* or *embedded question*.

> I would like to know **where he is**.
> Could you tell me **how long it takes**?

***wh-* word** Who, whom, what, where, when, why, how, and which are **wh**- words. They are used to ask questions and to connect clauses.

***wish* sentence** A sentence that has a **wish** clause in the simple present, and a simple past clause. A **wish** sentence expresses a desire to change a real situation into an unreal or impossible one.

> I wish I had more time.

***Yes/No* question** A question that can be answered with the words **yes** or **no**.

> Can you drive a car? Does he live here?

Index

A

a/an, see Indefinite articles
Ability, and past modals, 180
Academic discourse, and passive
    sentences, 221
Actions, *see also* Conditions;
    Events; Repeated actions;
    Situations; States
  and cause and effect
    and real conditionals, 335
    and simple past, 41
  completed actions
    and past perfect, 136
    and present perfect continuous,
      114
    and simple present, 93
  continuing actions, and past
      perfect continuous, 135, 136
  and indefinite past time, 85
  interrupted actions, 42
  performer of actions, with
      gerunds and infinitives, 247–
      248
  and simple past vs. past
      continuous, 35–36
Active meaning, verbs with, 18
Active sentences, 198–201
  and focus on noun, 206
Activities, *see* Actions; Events;
    Situations
Activities in progress
  and extended present, 13
  and future continuous, 58
  and past continuous, 35–36
  and present continuous, 13
  and present perfect continuous,
    109
Adjective clauses, *see* Relative
    clauses
Adjectives
  with *be*
    for behavior, 18
    and preposition + gerund, 243,
      244, A-7
    with definite articles, 259

    with infinitives, 244, A-8
  after *it* + verb, with infinitives,
    233
  with *must be* and *must feel,* 154
  possessive adjectives
    with gerunds, 247
    and reported speech, 400
Adverbs
  for emotions, 22
  of frequency, and present
    continuous, 13
  and past perfect, 131
  of possibility, with *will,* 161
  and present continuous, 13, 22
  and present perfect, 85, 88, 91, 94
  and present perfect continuous,
    109
  and reported speech, 401
Advice
  and past modals, 181
  and past unreal conditionals, 360
  and real conditionals, 336
  and reported speech, 404
  and *should* and *ought to,* 154, 161
Affirmative short answers, *see* Short
    answers
Affirmative statements, *see*
    Statements
after
  with future, to order events, 67
  in past time clauses, 131
  with simple past, 41
Agent, and passive sentences,
    198–199, 202–203, 218–220
Agentless passives, 202–203, 218
all, and present perfect, 89
already
  and past perfect, 131
  and present perfect, 85, 94
although, and past perfect and past
    perfect continuous, 136
always, and simple present, 13
am, see *be*
and
  nouns combined with, 259

  present perfect verb phrases
    combined with, 81
announce, with *regret,* 239
another, vs. *the other,* 268
any, as indefinite article, 258, 259,
    263
Apologies, and present perfect
    continuous, 110
are/aren't, see also *be*
  in *Yes/No* questions in present
    continuous, 11
are not, 7
arrive, and instant events, 89
Articles, 255–278, *see also* Definite
    articles; Indefinite articles; No
    article
ask, in reported speech, 396, 402
as soon as, 67
at this moment, and present
    continuous, 13
Attitudes, and stative meaning, 17
Auxiliary verbs
  in future continuous, 52–53
  with modals
    modals of possibility, 148–149
    past modals, 170–171
  in passive sentences, 194–195,
    214–215
  in past continuous, 30–31
  in past perfect, 124–126
  in past perfect continuous,
    124–126
  in present continuous, 6–7, 11
  in present perfect, 80–81
  in present perfect continuous,
    104–105

B

Background information
  and past continuous, 36
  and past perfect and past perfect
    continuous, 136, 139
Base form of verb
  after *help/make/have/let* + object,
    248

Base form of verb (*continued*)
  in reported speech, 404
  and spelling and pronunciation,
    A-2 to A-4
be, see also *are/aren't; been; is/isn't;
    was/wasn't; were/weren't*
  with adjectives
    for behavior, 18
    and preposition + gerund, 243,
      244, A-7
  and classifying or describing nouns,
    263
  in continuous tenses
    future continuous, 52, 53
    future with present continuous, 53
    present continuous, 6, 7
  contractions with, A-11
  after *it* as subject, 233
  with modals
    modals of possibility, 148–149
    past modals, 170
  omission of
    in newspaper headlines, 222
    in relative clauses, 289, 295
    in passive sentences, 194–195,
      214–215, 224
  in unreal conditionals, 331
be able to, in unreal conditionals, 341
because, and past perfect and past
    perfect continuous, 136
been
  in past perfect continuous,
    124–126
  in present perfect continuous, 104,
    105
before
  with future, 67
  in past time clauses, 131
  with simple past, 41
begin, with gerunds and infinitives,
    238
be going to
  forms of, 53
    contractions with, A-11
    in future passive, 214, 215
  meaning and use of, 61–62, 65–67
    in discourse, 71
    in noun clauses, 385
    for plans and intentions, 61, 66
    for predictions and expectations,
      62, 65–66
    for scheduled events, 62

Behavior, and *be* + adjective, 18
being, in passive sentences, 195
Beliefs, and stative meaning, 17
but
  and past unreal conditionals, 360
  and wishes about past, 355
by
  later time expressed with, 131
  in passive sentences, 194–195,
    214–215
by the time
  with future time clauses, 67
  in past time clauses, 131

C

can't, see also *can't have*
  and certainty, 155, 160
  as modal of possibility, 148–149
  and surprise or disbelief, 155
can't have, as modal of past possibility,
    176, 177
Cause and effect
  and real conditionals, 336
  and simple past, 41
Certainty, see also Uncertainty
  and modals of future possibility,
    160–161
  and modals of present possibility,
    153–155
  and real conditionals, 335–336
Changing situations, 13
Classification, with generic nouns,
    272
Clauses, see Dependent clauses;
    if clauses; *if/whether* clauses; Main
    clauses; Noun clauses; Relative
    clauses; Result clauses; *that*
    clauses; Time clauses;
    wh- clauses
Combining sentences
  with *and,* and present continuous, 8
  with relative clauses
    with object relative pronouns, 305
    with subject relative pronouns,
      284, 293
Comma
  with *if* clauses, 330, 331, 354
  with nonrestrictive relative clauses,
    283, 305
  with quoted speech, A-10
  with time clauses, 32
Complaints
  and present continuous, 13

and wishes, 344
Completed actions
  and past perfect, 136
  and present perfect continuous, 114
  and simple present, 93
Conclusions
  and modals
    modals of past possibility, 177
    modals of present possibility,
      153–154
  and past perfect and past perfect
    continuous, 136
  and present perfect continuous, 110
Conditionals, 325–368, see also Past
    unreal conditionals; Past wishes;
    Real conditionals; Unreal
    conditionals; Wishes
Conditions, see also States
  and simple present, 17
constantly, 13
continue, with gerunds and infinitives,
    238
Continuing actions, and past perfect
    continuous, 135, 136
Continuing time up to now
  and present perfect, 89, 113–114
  and present perfect continuous, 109,
    113–114
continuously, and simple present vs.
    present continuous, 13
Continuous tenses, see also Past
    continuous; Past perfect
    continuous; Present continuous;
    Present perfect continuous
  infinitives with, 238
Contractions, A-11
  with *be,* A-11
  with *be going to,* A-11
  with *did,* A-11
  with *do,* A-11
  in future forms, 52, 53
  with *had,* A-11
  with *have,* A-11
  with modals, A-11
    modals of possibility, 148–149
    past modals, 170–171
    phrasal modals, A-11
  in passive sentences, 194–195, 214–
    215
  in past continuous, 30–31
  in past perfect, 124–126
  in past perfect continuous, 124–126
  in past unreal conditionals, 354

in present continuous, 6–7
in present perfect, 80–81
in present perfect continuous, 104,
105
in simple past, 30–31
in simple present, 6–7
with *was* and *were,* A-11
with *will,* A-11
with *would,* A-11
Contrasts, and past perfect and past
perfect continuous, 136
could/couldn't, see also *could have;*
couldn't have
and certainty, 155, 157, 160
and guesses, 154, 161, 176
as modal of possibility, 148–149
and past ability and opportunity,
180
in reported speech, 396
and surprise or disbelief, 155
in unreal conditionals, 330, 331,
340, 341
in wishes, 331, 344, 345, 355
could have
as modal of past possibility, 176
as past modal, 170, 180
in past unreal conditionals, 354, 359
in past wishes, 355
couldn't have
as modal of past possibility, 176,
177
in past unreal conditionals, 359
Count nouns
forms of, 258–259
as generic nouns, 272

D

-d/-ed (for simple past and past
participle), 30, 31
pronunciation of verbs ending in,
A-4
spelling of verbs ending in, A-4
Definite articles
forms of, 258–260
meaning and use of
to connect information, 269
with generic nouns, 271–275
and identifying nouns, 265–266
the other as, 268
Definite nouns, 259
Definitions
with generic nouns, 272

with restrictive relative clauses,
288–289
and simple present, 12
Dependent clauses, *see also* Noun
clauses; Relative clauses
if clauses, 330
that clauses, 331
time clauses, 32
Descriptions, and stative meaning, 17
did/didn't, see also *do*
contractions with, A-11
and simple past, 30–31
Disbelief, and *couldn't* and *can't,* 155,
177
Discourse, *see also* Background
information; Narrative
and connecting past and present,
116
future in, 71
indefinite generic nouns in, 275
and introducing topics, 16, 97
and passive sentences, 221, 222
simple past in, 40
simple present in, 16, 40
Dissatisfaction, and past wishes, 363
do, see also *did/didn't; does/doesn't*
contractions with, A-11
and phrasal modal passives, 215
in simple past, 30, 31
in simple present, 6, 7, 11
does/doesn't, see also *do*
and simple present, 6–7
as future, 31

E

-ed (for simple past and past
participle), see *-d/-ed*
Embedded questions, *see if/whether*
clauses; *wh-* clauses
Emotions
and present continuous, 22
and stative meaning, 17
Emphasis
and *if only,* 345
in negative short answers, 7
in simple present, 7
-es (for simple present), see *-s/-es*
even though, and past perfect and past
perfect continuous, 136
Events, *see also* Actions; Situations
instant events, 89
order of events

in future, 67
and past perfect and simple past,
130–131
and past perfect continuous, 135
and simple past, 41, 130–131
scheduled events, 62
simultaneous events, 42
ever
and indefinite past time, 85
and past perfect, 131
every hour, and simple present, 12
Excuses and apologies, and present
perfect continuous, 110
Expectations
and agent in passive sentences, 218
and future, 58, 65–66
and modals of future possibility, 161
and modals of present possibility,
153–154
Extended present, 13

F

Facts, *see also* Definitions;
Descriptions
and real conditionals, 336
and simple present, 12, 13
Factual conditionals, 335
for
and continuing activities up to now,
109
and continuing past time, 89
and order of events, 135
and past perfect, 131
forever, and simple present vs. present
continuous, 13
forget, with gerunds and infinitives,
239
Formality/informality
and generic nouns, 272
and *had,* 129
and *if/whether* clauses, 382
and indirect questions, 380
and object pronouns vs. possessive
adjectives with gerunds, 247
and object relative pronouns, 307
in relative clauses ending or
beginning with prepositions,
314, 317
and passive sentences with *get,* 224
and past modals, 175
and past unreal conditionals, 357
and present continuous, 11, 22

Formality/informality *(continued)*
  and present perfect, 84
  and present perfect continuous, 108
  and simple present, 11
  and *was* in unreal conditionals and
    wishes, 334
Future, 49–74, *see also be going to;*
    Future continuous; Future passive;
    Modals of future possibility; *will*
    (for future)
  forms of, 52–57
    present continuous, 53
    simple present, 53
    in time clauses, 54
  meaning and use of, 58–74
    and real conditionals, 330–331,
      336
    and reported speech, 400
    and time clauses, 67
    and unreal conditionals, 330–331
Future continuous
  forms of, 52–53
  meaning and use of, 58–59, 65–67
    in discourse, 71
Future modals, *see* Modals of future
    possibility
Future passive, forms of, 214–215

G

Generalizations, and reported speech,
    400
General truths
  and real conditionals, 336
  and simple present, 12
Generic nouns
  articles with, 271–275
  in discourse, 274
Gerunds, 232–252
  forms of, 232–237, 243–246
    be + adjective + preposition with,
      A-7
    verbs with, 232–234, 238–242,
      A-7, A-9
  meaning and use of
    performer of gerund actions, 247
    as subject, 233
    with verbs, 238–242
get, in passive sentences, 224
got to, as past modal, 171
Guesses
  and modals of future possibility, 161
  and modals of past possibility, 176

and modals of present possibility,
    153–154

H

h, and indefinite articles, 259
Habits
  and real conditionals, 336
  and simple present, 12, 13
had/hadn't, see also had to have; have
  contractions with, A-11
  in informal speech, 129
  in past perfect, 124–126
  in past perfect continuous, 124–126
  in past unreal conditionals, 354, 355
had to have, 171
has got to
  as modal of possibility, 149
  as past modal, 171
has/hasn't, 81, 214, see also *has got to;*
    has to; have
has to
  as modal of possibility, 149
  as past modal, 171
hate
  with gerunds and infinitives, 238
have, see also can't have; could have;
    couldn't have; had/hadn't; had to
    have; has/hasn't; have got to; have
    got to have; have to; have to have;
    may have; may not have; might
    have; might not have; must have;
    must not have; ought not to have;
    ought to have; should have;
    shouldn't have; would have;
    wouldn't have
  with base form of verb, 248
  contractions with, A-11
  in passive sentences, 214, 215
  with past modals, 170–171, 175
  in past unreal conditionals, 354,
    357, 359, 360
  in present perfect, 80–81, 84
  in present perfect continuous, 104,
    105, 108
  stative vs. active meaning of, 18
  in wishes about past, 355
have got to
  and certainty about present, 160
  as modal of possibility, 149
  as past modal, 171
  as phrasal modal passive, 215
  and strong certainty, 154, 177

have got to have, 171, 176, 177
have to
  and certainty, 154, 160, 177
  as modal of possibility, 149
  as past modal, 171
  as phrasal modal passive, 215
have to have, 171, 176, 177
help, with base form of verb or
    infinitive, 248
hit, and instant events, 89

I

Identifying nouns
  with articles, 265–266
  with restrictive relative clauses,
    288–293, 309
if clauses
  omission of, 343
  in real conditionals, 330–331, 335–
    336, 339
  in unreal conditionals, 330–331,
    340–341, 343
    past unreal conditionals, 354,
      359–360
  and wishes, 345
if I had been you, in past unreal
    conditionals, 360
if I were you, in unreal conditionals,
    341
if only, 345, 363
if/whether clauses
  forms of, 374, 375
  meaning and use of, 379–383
    if vs. *whether,* 382
    in reported speech, 394
I had no idea, 384
I'm afraid, with *that* clauses, 384
Imaginary situations, *see* Past unreal
    conditionals; Unreal conditionals;
    Wishes
I'm not certain, with *that* clauses, 384
I'm not sure, with *that* clauses, 384
Imperatives
  in real conditionals, 330, 336
  in reported speech, 394
    with *should,* 404
    with *tell,* 396
Indefinite articles, *see also* No article
  another as, 268
  forms of, 258–259
  meaning and use of, 262–263

and classifying and describing nouns, 263
to connect information, 269
with generic nouns, 271–275
and introducing nouns, 262–263
some and *any* as, 258, 259
Indefinite nouns, 259
Indefinite past time, and present perfect, 85, 93
Indirect questions, 380, *see also if/whether* clauses; *wh-* clauses
Indirect speech, *see* Reported speech
Inferences, *see* Conclusions
Infinitives, 232–252
forms of, 232–237, 244–246
with adjectives, 244, A-8
and short answers, 236
with verbs, 232–234, A-8, A-9, A-10
meaning and use of
performer of infinitive actions, 248
in reported speech, 394
as subject, 233
with verbs, 238–242
inform, with *regret,* 239
Informality, *see* Formality/informality
Information, *see also* Certainty; Classification; Conclusions; Expectations; Generalizations; Guesses; Plans; Predictions; Reasons
background information
and past continuous, 36
and past perfect and past perfect continuous, 136, 139
definitions
with generic nouns, 272
with restrictive relative clauses, 288
and simple present, 12
facts
and real conditionals, 336
and simple present, 12, 13
general truths
and real conditionals, 336
and simple present, 12
and generic nouns, 272
and identifying nouns
with articles, 265–266
with restrictive relative clauses, 288–293, 309

instructions, and real conditionals, 336
new information
and agent in passive sentences, 218
and restrictive relative clauses, 289
in nonrestrictive relative clauses, 294–297
in restrictive relative clauses, 288–289, 309
schedules, and simple present, 12
and stative meaning, 17
Information questions
in future continuous, 53
with passive sentences, 194–195
with future passive with *be going to,* 214
with future passive with *will,* 214
with modal passive, 215
with phrasal modal passive, 215
with present perfect passive, 214
in past continuous, 31
in past perfect, 125
in past perfect continuous, 125
and phrasal modal passive, 215
in present continuous, 7
in present perfect, 81
in present perfect continuous, 105
in reported speech, 394
in simple past, 31
in simple present, 7
-ing, see also Continuous tenses; Gerunds
with *be* + verb, after modals of possibility, 148–149
spelling of verbs ending in, A-3
in order, with infinitives, 244
Instant events, 89
Instructions, and real conditionals, 336
Intentions, 61
Interrupted actions, and simple past and past continuous, 42
Intransitive verbs, A-6
and passive sentences, 201
Introducing topics
and present perfect, 97
and simple present, 16
Irregular verbs, 81, A-5 to A-6
is/isn't, 81, see also *be*
is not, 7

it, as subject, with infinitives, 233
it appears, with *that* clauses, 384
it seems, with *that* clauses, 384

J

just
in informal speech, 22
and past perfect, 131
and present perfect continuous, 109
and recent past time, 88, 91, 94
and simple past and present perfect, 94

K

Knowledge, and stative meaning, 17

L

lately
and present perfect continuous, 109
and recent past time, 88, 91
let, with base form of verb, 248
like, with gerunds and infinitives, 238
love, with gerunds and infinitives, 238

M

Main clauses
in conditionals, 330–331
in past unreal conditionals, 354
and noun clauses, 374
and relative clauses
with object relative pronouns, 304–305, 313–314
with subject relative pronouns, 282–284
and time clauses, 32
make, with base form of verb, 248
may
and guesses, 154, 161, 176
as modal of possibility, 148–149
as past modal, 170
and permission, 181
maybe, 149, 161
may have, as modal of possibility, 176
may not
as modal of possibility, 148–149
and permission, 181
may not have, as modal of possibility, 170, 176
Measurements, and stative meaning, 17

Mental activity verbs, 379, 384–385, A-9

might
   and guesses, 154, 161, 176
   as modal
      modal of possibility, 148–149
      past modal, 170
   in unreal conditionals, 330, 331, 340, 341
      past unreal conditionals, 354, 359
might have
   as modal of possibility, 176
   in past unreal conditionals, 354, 359
might not, as modal of possibility, 148–149
might not have
   as modal of possibility, 170, 176
   in past unreal conditionals, 359
Modal passive, 215
Modals, 143–187, *see also* Modals of possibility; Past modals
   and advice, 341, 360
   and asking permission, 341
   in conditionals, 330, 336, 354
   contractions with, A-11
   modal passive, 215
   in past wishes, 355
Modals of future possibility, *see also* Phrasal modals of future possibility
   forms of, 148–152
   meaning and use of, 160–166
Modals of past possibility, 176–178
Modals of possibility, 145–166, *see also* Modals of future possibility; Modals of present possibility
   modals of past possibility, 176–178
Modals of present possibility, 148–159, 165–166, *see also* Phrasal modals of present possibility
   forms of, 148–152
   meaning and use of, 153–159
      to express degrees of certainty about guesses, expectations, and inferences, 153–155
Modification of nouns, 253–324, *see also* Adjectives; Articles; Relative clauses
Musical instruments, 272
must
   and certainty about present, 160
   as modal of possibility, 148–149

and necessity, 181
   as past modal, 170
   and strong certainty, 154, 177
must be, and understanding, 154
must feel, and understanding, 154
must have, as modal of possibility, 176, 177
must not, as modal of possibility, 148–149
must not have, as modal, 170, 176, 177

N

Narrative, *see also* Background information
   and past continuous vs. simple past, 36
Necessity
   and past modals, 181
   and *should* and *ought to,* 154, 161
need to, as phrasal modal passive, 215
Negative gerunds, 232
Negative infinitives, 232
Negatives, *see also* Negative short answers; Negative statements
   in conditionals, 331, 339, 354
   gerunds and infinitives, 232
Negative short answers
   emphasis in, 7
   in future continuous, 52
   with passive sentences, 194–195
      with future passive with *be going to,* 214
      with future passive with *will,* 214
      with modal passive, 215
      with phrasal modal passive, 215
      with present perfect passive, 214
   in past continuous, 31
   in past perfect, 125
   in past perfect continuous, 125
   in present continuous, 7
   in present perfect, 80
   in present perfect continuous, 104
   in simple past, 31
   in simple present, 7
Negative statements
   with *any,* 259
   in future continuous, 52
   with modals
      modals of future possibility, 148
      modals of present possibility, 148
      past modals, 170
      past phrasal modals, 171

phrasal modal passive, 215
   with passive sentences, 194–195
      with future passive with *be going to,* 214
      with future passive with *will,* 214
      with modal passive, 215
      with phrasal modal passive, 215
      with present perfect passive, 214
   in past continuous, 30
   in past perfect, 125
   in past perfect continuous, 125
   in present continuous, 6
   in present perfect, 80
   in present perfect continuous, 104
   in simple past, 30
   in simple present, 6
never
   and indefinite past time, 85
   and past perfect, 131
   in statements, 85
New information
   and agent in passive sentences, 218
   and restrictive relative clauses, 289
New situations, and present continuous, 13
No article (Ø), 258, 259, 262, 263, 272
Noncount nouns
   forms of, 258–259
   as generic nouns, 272
Nonrestrictive relative clauses
   forms of
      relative clauses with object relative pronouns, 305, 307, 313–316
      relative clauses with subject relative pronouns, 283
   meaning and use of, 294–297
      and adding extra information, 294
      reduction of, 295, 317
      vs. restrictive relative clauses, 295
No object relative pronoun (Ø), 304–305, 307, 313–314, 317–318
not, see also Negatives; Negative short answers; Negative statements
   in *if/whether* clauses, 374, 375, 382
not ever, in statements, 85
Noun clauses, 371–390, *see also* *if/whether* clauses; *that* clauses; *wh-* clauses
   forms of, 374–378
   with mental activity verbs and reporting verbs, A-9
Nouns, *see also* Articles; Relative clauses

classification and description of, 263

count nouns, 258–259, 272

definite nouns, 259

focus on, with passive and active sentences, 206

forms of, 258–261

generic nouns
  articles with, 271–275
  in discourse, 275

indefinite nouns, 259

introduction of, 262–263

modification of, 253–324

noncount nouns, 258–259, 272

pronunciation of plural nouns with -s/-es, A-3

proper nouns, and nonrestrictive relative clauses, 294

spelling of plural nouns with -s/-es, A-2

now, 13

Numbers, with nouns, 259

O

Ø (no article), 258, 259, 262, 263, 272

Ø (no object relative pronoun), 304–305, 307, 313–314, 317–318

Object
  with infinitives, 234, A-8
  in passive vs. active sentences, 198
  and performer of actions, with gerunds and infinitives, 247–248

Object pronouns, with gerunds, 247

Object relative pronouns, 304–305, 307, 313–314, *see also* No object relative pronoun; Relative clauses with object relative pronouns
  omission of, from relative clauses, 305, 307, 314, 317–318
  with prepositions, 313–316
  when and *where* as replacements for, 320

Obligations, and past modals, 181

Opportunity, and past modals, 180

or, and present perfect verb phrases, 81

Order of events
  in future, 67
  and past perfect and simple past, 130–131

and past perfect continuous, 135

and simple past, 41, 130–131

or not, in *if/whether* clauses, 374, 375, 382

ought not to have, as past modal, 171, 181

ought to
  and expectations, 154, 161
  as modal of possibility, 149
  and obligations about the past, 181
  as past modal, 171
  in reported speech, 396

ought to have, as past modal, 171, 181

P

Passive sentences, 191–228
  forms of, 194–197, 214–217
    and verbs, 201
  future passive, 214–215
  meaning and use of, 198–210, 218–228
    in academic and public discourse, 221–222
    and agent, 202–203, 218
    to focus on noun, 206
    to focus on results or processes, 202
    reasons for using passive sentences, 202–210
  modal passive, 215
  past continuous passive, 195
  past passive, 194–200
  present continuous passive, 195
  present passive, 194–197
  present perfect passive, 214–215

Past, 27–48, *see also* Continuing time up to now; Indefinite past time; Past continuous; Past modals; Past participles; Past passive; Past perfect; Past perfect continuous; Past time clauses; Past unreal conditionals; Past wishes; Present perfect; Present perfect continuous; Recent past time; Simple past
  and reported speech, 395, 396

Past continuous
  forms of, 30–34
  meaning and use of, 35–48
    and actions in progress, 35–36
    and interrupted events, 42
    and simultaneous events, 42

and time clauses, 32, 41–42

with unreal conditionals, 331

and wishes, 344

Past continuous passive, 195

Past modals, 167–188
  forms of, 170–175
    in informal speech, 175
    past phrasal modals, 171–175
  meaning and use of, 176–188
    and advice, obligations, and regrets about the past, 181
    and past ability and opportunity, 180
    and past permission and necessity, 181

Past participles
  of irregular verbs, 81, A-5 to A-6
  in passive sentences, 194–195, 214–215
  with past modals, 170–171
  in past unreal conditionals, 354
  in past wishes, 355
  in present perfect, 80–81

Past passive
  forms of, 194–197
  meaning and use of, 198–199, 202–203, 206

Past perfect, 121–142
  forms of, 124–129
    in informal speech, 129
  meaning and use of, 130–142
    and background information, 136, 139
    and noun clauses, 385
    and order of events, 130–131
    vs. past perfect continuous, 136
    and past time clauses, 131
    in past unreal conditionals, 354, 357, 359–360
    and stative meaning, verbs with, 126
    in wishes about past, 355

Past perfect continuous, 121–142
  forms of, 124–129
    in informal speech, 129
  meaning and use of, 134–142
    and background information, 136, 139
    and order of events, 135–136
    vs. past perfect, 136

Past phrasal modals, 171–175

Past time clauses
  and past perfect and simple past,
    131
  and past perfect continuous, 135
Past unreal conditionals
  forms of, 354–358
  meaning and use of, 359–362
    and advice, 360
    and *but* in restatement of, 360
Past wishes
  forms of, 354–358
  meaning and use of, 363–365
    and *if only*, 363
    and regret or dissatisfaction, 363
Perfect modals, *see* Past modals
Performer of actions, with gerunds
    and infinitives, 247–248
perhaps, 161
Permanent situations, and simple
    present, 13
Permission, and past modals, 181
Phonetic symbols, A-15
Phrasal modal passive, 215
Phrasal modals of future possibility
  contractions with, A-11
  forms of, 149–152
  meaning and use of, 160–166
    to express degrees of certainty
      about predictions, 160–161
Phrasal modals of present possibility
  contractions with, A-11
  forms of, 149–152
  meaning and use of, 153–159
    to express degrees of certainty
      about guesses, expectations,
      and inferences, 153–155
Phrasal verbs, A-12 to A-15
  and gerunds, 244
Phrases, with gerunds and infinitives,
    232
Physical sensations, and stative
    meaning, 17, 18
Plans, 58, 61, 66
Plural nouns, 258–259
  generic nouns, 272
  pronunciation of, with *-s/-es,* A-3
  spelling of, with *-s/-es,* A-2
Point of view, and reported speech,
    399, 400, 401
Politeness, *see* Formality/informality
Possession, and stative meaning, 17

Possessive adjectives
  with gerunds, 247
  and reported speech, 400
Predictions
  and future, 62, 65–66
  and modals of future possibility,
    160–161
  and real conditionals, 336
prefer, with gerunds and infinitives,
    238
Prepositions
  with gerunds, 243, 244, A-7
  with object relative pronouns,
    313–314
  and past perfect, 131
Present, 3–26, *see also* Modals of
    present possibility; Present
    continuous; Simple present
  and real conditionals, 330–331
  and reported speech, 395, 396
  simple present passive, 194
  and unreal conditionals, 330–331
Present continuous, 6–26
  forms of, 6–11
    informal *Yes/No* questions, 11
  meaning and use of, 12–23
    and actions in progress, 13
    and active meaning, 18
    and *be* + adjective for behavior, 18
    and complaints, 13
    and emotions, 22
    and extended present, 13
    and future, 53, 61–62
    and *have,* 18
    and modals of future possibility,
      149
    with real conditionals, 331
    and sensation verbs, 18
    and sense verbs, 18
    and temporary or new
      situations, 13
Present continuous passive, 195
Present modals, *see* Modals of present
    possibility
Present passive, 194–197
Present perfect, 77–100
  forms of, 80–84
    in informal speech, 84
  meaning and use of
    and completed activities, 114
    in connecting past and present,
      116

  and continuing time up to now,
    89, 93, 113–114
  and indefinite past time, 85, 93
  and introducing topics, 97
  with *just, already,* and *yet,* 94
  vs. present perfect continuous,
    113–114
  and recent past time, 88
  and repeated activities, 114
  vs. simple past, 93–94
Present perfect continuous, 101–120
  forms of, 104–108
  meaning and use of, 109–120
    in connecting past and present,
      116
    and continuing time up to now,
      109, 113–114
    and excuses and apologies and
      conclusions, 110
    vs. present perfect, 113–114
    and recent past time, 109, 114
Present perfect passive, 214–215
probably, 161
Processes, and passive sentences, 202
Promises
  and real conditionals, 336
  and *will* (for future), 58
Pronouns, *see also* Object relative
    pronouns; Subject relative
    pronouns
  object pronouns, with gerunds, 247
  and reported speech, 400
Pronunciation
  of nouns ending in *-s/-es,* A-3
  of verbs ending in *-ed,* A-4
  of verbs ending in *-s/-es,* A-3
Proper nouns, and nonrestrictive
    relative clauses, 294
Public discourse, and passive
    sentences, 222
Punctuation, with quoted speech,
    A-10
Purpose infinitives, 244

Q

Questions, *see also* Indirect questions;
    Information questions;
    Yes/No questions
  with *some* and *any,* 259
Quoted speech
  punctuation with, A-10

vs. reported speech, 394–395, 399–401

R

Real conditionals
  forms of, 330–334
  meaning and use of, 335–339
    and advice, warnings, and
      instructions, 336
    and certainty, 335–336
    and predictions and promises, 336
    with *unless* vs. *if,* 339
realize, and instant events, 89
really, in informal speech, 22
Reasons, and past perfect and past
  perfect continuous, 136
Receiver, in passive vs. active
  sentences, 198–199
recently
  and present perfect continuous, 109
  and recent past time, 88, 91
Recent past time
  and adverbs, 91
  and past perfect, 130
  and present perfect, 88, 89
  and present perfect continuous, 109,
    114
regret, with gerunds and infinitives,
  239
Regrets
  and past modals, 181
  and wishes, 345
  past wishes, 363
Relationships, and stative meaning, 17
Relative clauses, 279–324, *see also*
    Nonrestrictive relative clauses;
    Relative clauses with object
    relative pronouns; Relative clauses
    with subject relative pronouns;
    Restrictive relative clauses
Relative clauses with object relative
    pronouns, 301–324
  forms of, 304–308
    nonrestrictive relative clauses,
      305–308, 313–314
    relative clauses ending or
      beginning with prepositions,
      313–316
    restrictive relative clauses, 304,
      305–308, 313–314
  meaning and use of, 309–312,
    317–324

nonrestrictive relative clauses,
    310, 317
  restrictive relative clauses, 309,
    317–318
  when and *where* in, 320
Relative clauses with subject relative
    pronouns, 279–300
  forms of, 282–287
    nonrestrictive relative clauses, 283
    restrictive relative clauses, 282,
      283
  meaning and use of
    nonrestrictive relative clauses,
      294–300
    restrictive relative clauses, 288–
      293
Relative pronouns, *see* Object relative
    pronouns; Subject relative
    pronouns
remember, with gerunds and
    infinitives, 239
Repeated actions, 12
  habits, 12, 13, 336
  and indefinite past time, 85
  and past perfect, 136
  and present perfect, 114
  routines, 12, 336
  schedules, 12
Reported speech, 391–409
  forms of, 394–398
  meaning and use of, 399–409
    and adverbs, 401
    and point of view, 399, 400, 401
    and pronouns and possessive
      adjectives, 400–401
    and reporting verbs, 395, 396,
      402, 404
    and tense, 399, 400
Reporting verbs, 395, 396, 402, 404,
    A-9
Requests, 58
Restrictive relative clauses
  forms of
    relative clauses with object relative
      pronouns, 304, 305, 307, 313–
      316
    relative clauses with subject
      relative pronouns, 282, 283
  meaning and use of, 288–293
    and identifying nouns, 288–289,
      305

vs. nonrestrictive relative clauses,
    295
  reduction of, 289, 317–318
Result clauses, 335–336, 340–341,
    343, 359–360
Results, and passive sentences, 202
right now, and present continuous, 13
Routines
  and real conditionals, 336
  and simple present, 12

S

say
  with *regret,* 239
  as reporting verb, 396, 402
Scheduled events, 62
Schedules, and simple present, 12
Sensations, and stative meaning, 17,
    18
Senses, and stative meaning, 17, 18
Sentences, *see* Active sentences;
    Combining sentences; Passive
    sentences
Sequence of events, *see* Order of
    events
-*s*/-*es* (for plural)
  pronunciation of nouns with, A-3
  spelling of nouns with, A-2
-*s*/-*es* (for simple present), 6, 7
  pronunciation of verbs with, A-3
  spelling of verbs with, A-2
Short answers
  with *be* and modals of present
    possibility, 149
  and *could* as modal of future
    possibility, 149
  and *could have* and *should have* as
    past modals, 170
  in future continuous, 52
  with infinitives, 236
  with passive sentences, 194–195
    with future passive with *be going
      to,* 214
    with future passive with *will,* 214
    with modal passive, 215
    with phrasal modal passive, 215
    with present perfect passive, 214
  in past continuous, 31
  in past perfect, 125
  in past perfect continuous, 125
  in present continuous, 7
  in present perfect, 80

as subject relative pronoun,
282–283

while
with past continuous, 42
with simple past, 42

who
as object relative pronoun,
304–305, 307, 313–314
as subject relative pronoun,
282–283

whom, as object relative pronoun,
304–305, 307, 313–314

Wh- questions, *see* Information
questions

wh- words, *see* Information
questions; *wh-* clauses

will, see also *will* (for future); *won't*
contractions with, A-11
as modal of possibility, 148–149
and strong certainty, 161

will (for future), *see also* Future
continuous
forms of, 53
contractions with, A-11
in future passive, 214, 215
meaning and use of, 58–59, 65–67
in discourse, 71
and predictions and expectations,
65–66
and promises and requests,
58–59
and quick decisions, 66
and real conditionals, 336

will never, with *forget*, 239

wish, see also *wish* clauses; Wishes
short answers with, 331

wish clauses
in wishes about past, 355
in wishes about present and future,
331, 344–345

Wishes, *see also* Past wishes
forms of, 331–334
meaning and use of, 344–347
and complaints and regrets, 345
and *if only,* 345

won't
and future continuous, 52, 53
and strong certainty, 161

would have, in past unreal
conditionals, 354, 357, 359, 360

would it be OK, 341

would it bother you, 341

wouldn't have, in past unreal
conditionals, 354, 357, 359, 360

would/wouldn't, see also *would have*;
wouldn't have
contractions with, A-11
in noun clauses, 385
in unreal conditionals, 330, 331,
340–341, 343
vs. *used to*, 39
in wishes, 331, 344, 345

would you mind, 341

Y

Yes/No questions
with conditionals, 331, 354
with *could* and *can*, 149
with *could have* and *should have*,
170
in future continuous, 52, 59
with passive sentences, 194–195
with future passive with *be going
to*, 214
with future passive with *will*, 214
with modal passive, 215
with phrasal modal passive, 215
with present perfect passive, 214
in past continuous, 31
in past perfect, 125
in past perfect continuous, 125
and phrasal modal passive, 215
in present continuous, 7, 11
in present perfect, 80
in present perfect continuous, 104
in reported speech, 394
and *ask,* 396
in simple past, 31
in simple present, 7, 11
with *wh-* clauses, 375
with *will* vs. future continuous, 59

yet
and indefinite past time, 85
and past perfect, 131
and simple past and past
continuous, 94

you
in present continuous, 11
in present perfect, 84

Z

Zero article (Ø), 258, 259, 262, 263,
272
Zero object relative pronoun (Ø),
304–305, 307, 313–314, 317–31

Grammar Sense

ONLINE PRACTICE

Follow the steps to register for *Grammar Sense Online Practice*.

1. Go to www.grammarsensepractice.com and click on **Register**

2. Read and agree to the terms of use.  **I Agree.**

3. Enter the Access Code that came with your Student Book. Your code is written on the inside back cover of your book.

   ☐ ☐ ☐ ☐ **Enter**

4. Enter your personal information (first and last name, email address, and password).

5. Click on the Student Book that you are using for your class.

> It is very important to select your book. You are using Grammar Sense 3. Please click the **RED** Grammar Sense 3 cover.

If you don't know which book to select, **STOP**. Continue when you know your book.

6. Enter your class ID to join your class, and click NEXT. Your class ID is on the line below, or your teacher will give it to you on a different piece of paper.

   _____ **Next**

   You don't need a class ID code. If you do not have a class ID code, click Skip. To enter this code later, choose Join a Class from your Home page.

7. Once you're done, click on Enter Online Practice to begin using *Grammar Sense Online Practice*.

   Enter Online Practice

Next time you want to use *Grammar Sense Online Practice*, just go to www.grammarsensepractice.com and log in with your email address and password.